ELIZABETH FOX-GENOVESE

ELIZABETH FOX-GENOVESE

Paternalism's Daughter

Deborah A. Symonds

University of Virginia Press • *Charlottesville and London*

University of Virginia Press

Printed in the United States of America on acid-free paper

First published 2021

9 8 7 6 5 4 3 2 1

Library of Congress Cataloging-in-Publication Data

Names: Symonds, Deborah A., author.
Title: Elizabeth Fox-Genovese : paternalism's daughter / Deborah A. Symonds.
Description: Charlottesville : University of Virginia Press, 2020. | Includes bibliographical references and index.
Identifiers: LCCN 2021010959 (print) | LCCN 2021010960 (ebook) | ISBN 9780813945132 (cloth) | ISBN 9780813945149 (ebook)
Subjects: LCSH: Fox-Genovese, Elizabeth, 1941–2007. | Historians—United States—Biography. | Feminists—United States—Biography.
Classification: LCC E175.5.F698 S96 2020 (print) | LCC E175.5.F698 (ebook) | DDC 907.2/02 [B]—dc23
LC record available at https://lccn.loc.gov/2021010959
LC ebook record available at https://lccn.loc.gov/2021010960

Cover photograph/frontispiece: Dr. Elizabeth Fox-Genovese (Stuart A. Rose Manuscript, Archives & Rare Book Library, Emory University)

For my wife, Melissa, and our children, Sarah and Samuel

CONTENTS

PREFACE

THE MANY BETSEYS

Elizabeth Fox-Genovese was my mentor and friend. I first met her in 1980, when I was a graduate student at what was then the State University of New York at Binghamton. The next year I asked her to chair my dissertation committee. I had no idea who she was nor who Eugene D. Genovese, her husband, was either. She was obviously smart, interested in women's history, and moving from French economic to U.S. women's history. She, for the most part, happily lived a life driven by work: writing, teaching, editing, speaking, dining with colleagues and students, and, with her husband and many others, coauthoring books and essays, watching baseball, walking dogs. She also drove fast cars, constantly. Visiting her could be exhausting.

Until the end of the 1990s, I saw her less often once I'd finished my graduate work. Then, yet again, as about every decade, Betsey and Gene decided to lead in forming another scholarly group, this time The Historical Society. I joined, and I saw them more often, saw them proofreading the first volume of *The Mind of the Master Class* and editing material for the *Journal of the Historical Society.* Betsey's health constantly declined, not only from various illnesses but from the cocktail of drugs required to control them. One day she called, wanting to discuss moving to a condominium. Late in 2006, Gene called, demanding that I speak to his wife, because, he claimed, she was killing herself. Betsey promptly took the phone from him and insisted that all was well and that he was overreacting. I suspected that he wasn't. There was little I could do.

I knew Betsey for twenty-six years, but the impressions she made on me will only be the memories of one person. I have tried to judge my own recollections as critically as I would others'. What makes this biography meaningful is the impact Betsey had. What makes the telling possible are the voluminous personal and less personal papers she left, including her published work, coupled with the recollections, letters, emails, and interviews of many others. The interviews were often ongoing phone and email conversations lasting for several years, not the interviews journalists and oral historians conduct. Many people were more than willing to search for old letters, examine their memories, ponder dates, and recommend other resources. A few others were willing to answer brief questions, often requesting anonymity. And significantly, there are also silences—many people who refused to recall or remember her, and interactions Betsey chose not to keep a record of. Lest that imply embarrassments hidden by Betsey, some of what she preserved in her open archive are very unflattering depositions by old students, collected for and in the course of Dr. Virginia Gould's lawsuit against her. Letters, digital records, and files, all placed in my hands by Eugene D. Genovese, and other materials from colleagues and friends will, with permission, go to the Fox-Genovese Papers in the Southern Historical Collection, as will, again with permission, email correspondence and significant notes. Much of the material left by Betsey is what it is, produced in real time, including letters from her parents' and grandparents' lives. Much of the commentary I solicited from colleagues, students, and friends, much of it looking back over decades, is better described by a line from Florence Reece's old union song from the Harlan County coal wars: "There is no neutral there."

BECAUSE BETSEY became a public intellectual, as well as an organizer of dinners and scholarly societies, her interactions ranged beyond the networks reflecting her academic foci. In recognition, centers and foundations importantly supported this project. Betsey's sister and brother provided critical information and insights. Many of her colleagues, former students, and friends, in addition to numerous archivists, librarians, and book dealers, have also helped me reconstruct her life and understand her work. Here, let me acknowledge them by name.

The institutional apparatus and the money to support research matters, and in the spirit of Betsey's early Marxism, I thank my two department chairs at Drake University, Glenn McKnight and Karen Leroux; my dean, Joseph Lenz; and Drake University's Center for the Humanities and its chairs, Craig Owens and Jennifer Harvey. Beyond this institution, first, the Watson-Brown Foundation supported publication of Fox-Genovese's fugitive writings, referred to as *Selected Writings,* and brought me into the company of some of her colleagues in southern and American studies. I am especially indebted to Ehren Foley, who compiled a thorough bibliography of Fox-Genovese's work, and to all of the other editors, because it was a collaborative project. Most especially, I thank Peter N. Stearns for his introduction to the volume I edited, Robert L. Paquette for conversations and questions answered, and the editors of the second volume of *Selected Writings, Ghosts and Memories,* Kibibi Mack-Shelton and Christina Bieber Lake, and also the author of the foreword, Mark Bauerlein, for a volume I used frequently. Second, the Earhart Foundation was very generous in its support over several years, even inviting me to a conference and making time away from teaching possible.

Many people, some of whom I knew and many I did not, offered help. Those closest to Elizabeth Fox-Genovese have been particularly generous and informative: Eugene D. Genovese, who called me "Miss-No-Socially-Redeeming-Value" for years, shared papers and photographs still in his house (in many cases, at the backs of closets), loaned me journals, and gave me access to Betsey's last computer. Rebecca MacMillan Fox, Betsey's sister, called and emailed more than her busy schedule allowed. Edward W. Fox Jr., Betsey's brother, sent detailed reports on family matters, travel, and recollections. Robert Edward Simon Jr., Fox-Genovese's uncle, spoke with me several times, offering insight into the Manhattan life of the Simons in the 1920s and 1930s. Nancy Wilson, Betsey's best friend since their years at Bryn Mawr, sent copies of letters Betsey had written her years ago, spending hours on the phone with me, while her husband, Peter Wilson, also answered questions. William Hungeling, the executor of the Genovese estate, facilitated many things, for instance sending numerous computer disks left in the house and a copy of *The Sweetness of Life.*

I am also grateful to those who knew Betsey over the decades and shared insights, memories, anecdotes, and occasionally correspondence: Lewis Bateman, D'Ann Campbell, Stanley Engerman, William W. Freehling, Tracy Mitrano, Michael O'Brien, Robert Paquette, and Stephen A. Schuker. Stephen and I spent one or two afternoons using email and street-view mapping to find Betsey's apartments in Cambridge, he from memory and I from addresses on letters in the Fox-Genovese Papers. Louis A. Ferleger talked, read, and sent various papers and letters. D'Ann Campbell and David Moltke-Hansen contributed to creating the title with insight, tinkering, and patience far beyond mine.

Laura Crawley and Maggi Shade, students of Fox-Genovese at different times and, in Laura's case, personal assistant and then managing editor of the *Journal of the Historical Society,* both offered constant and often detailed answers to my questions—for years. David Moltke-Hansen, there is no thanks that could be sufficient. He has read every chapter more than once—and more than thrice. He offered advice and insights and time, all of which make this a better book. Many others responded to questions, read sections, offered advice, wracked their brains, shared memories of both Genovese and Fox-Genovese at a memorial panel, and reaffirmed my belief in the collegial nature of academia and beyond: Thomas Africa, Paula R. Backscheider, Mary Lynn Broe, Martine W. Brownley, Joan E. Cashin, Ann Short Chirhart, Peter Coclanis, Christopher M. Curtis, Mario A. DiCesare, Andrew Doyle, Renee E. Dye, Sarah Elbert, William W. Freehling, Sarah E. Gardner, Deborah Hertz, Evelyn Brooks Higginbotham, Gerald E. Kadish, Richard Kaeuper, Robert Kreiser, Walter F. LaFeber, Carol Leonard, Karen Leroux, Monsignor Richard Lopez, Stephanie McCurry, Lawrence McDonnell, Amy Mittelman, Sheila O'Connor-Ambrose and Douglas Ambrose, Carl Prince, Mark M. Smith, Tina Trent, and Mary Young. David Veeder, a Drake colleague, translated a letter from the German. And I owe a real debt to the two anonymous readers at the University of Virginia Press who have gone beyond duty in addressing weaknesses and infelicities. And the editors at the University of Virginia Press, Richard K. Holway, Nadine Zimmerli, and Mark Mones, and their excellent copyeditor Margaret A. Hogan are also due thanks for patience and good humor. For all the errors and wrongheadedness that remain, I am to blame.

Archivists for the Southern Historical Collection at the Wilson Library, notably Matthew Turi, Laura Clark Brown, Tim Hodgdon, and Rebecca Williams, were the backbone of my research. At Atlanta

Vintage Books, which handled the sale of the bulk of the Genovese and Fox-Genovese library, Jan Bolgla, Mallory Herrman, and Bob Roarty answered questions about the size and nature of the collection. At Binghamton University Libraries' Special Collections, Yvonne J. Deligato fielded questions about Fox-Genovese in their records. At Wesleyan University Press Suzanna Tamminen provided information on Betsey's never-completed book project with Jeannette Hopkins. At the Office of the Registrar, Cornell University, Lisa, who never used her last name, provided information on courses Fox-Genovese took there in 1958 with her father, and at the Institute of Psychoanalysis in London, Joanne Halford and Amanda Menezes searched records for me, as did Angela Haselton at the Tavistock and Portman NHS Foundation Trust. For information on Agnes and Philip Fox in Springfield, Massachusetts, Margaret Humbertson at the Lyman and Merrie Wood Museum of Springfield History checked transit maps and provided assistance on state records. Kimberly Corwin Gray, director of alumni relations at North Country School, provided school reports for the young Betsey Fox. At Eleutherian Mills, now the Hagley Museum and Library, Marsha Mills provided assistance. At Vassar College Libraries, Special Collections, Dean M. Rogers searched, and at Houghton Mifflin Harcourt, Susan Steinway looked for records of Betsey Fox's early employment there. At the University of Rochester, University Archivist Melissa S. Mead provided useful information. At Rutgers Special Collections, Erika Gorder plowed through twenty boxes of the Warren I. Susman Papers to find a handful of letters from Eugene D. Genovese. Finally, at Brandeis University, Chloe Morse-Harding at the Robert D. Farber University Archives and Special Collections sent Frank E. Manuel's notes on Thomas Hobbes and Sigmund Freud, suggesting Fox-Genovese's connection to the Manuels' intellectual tastes and generation.

Elizabeth Fox-Genovese was noted and notorious, kind and cutting. To those whom I contacted who refused to speak or write: I understand. Some others agreed to discuss certain matters but not any and all I raised. Fair enough. That many decided on frankness without apparent reserve means I have been able to develop understandings and share revealing details that otherwise I would not have had access to. That most of those to whom I reached out received my inquiries courteously made this aspect of my research more rewarding than daunting.

While somewhat shaped by the creator, as archivists call the generator, collector, and compiler of an archive, the documentation Betsey left reveals far more than most of us would choose to share. Some parts—for instance, many receipts and bills, as well as depositions and related correspondence from a court case—I concluded do not really, or only very selectively, advance the telling and understanding of Betsey's life, whatever other purposes such items may serve in the future. Many parts of the collections provide context. In the end, however, it would have unbalanced the life telling had I drawn on them for more than background.

The same is true also of Betsey's voluminous printed oeuvre: 2 million–plus words over three-plus decades. Thanks to the five selected, collected volumes of Fox-Genovese's fugitive writings, in addition to the books she wrote, cowrote, and edited, much of this material was readily available to inform my search for meaningful patterns, changes, and influences in Fox-Genovese's intellectual preoccupations and developments. Yet, not all of her published work advanced equally understanding of those continuing and changing engagements. Of course, some texts proved central; others useful; still others at most incidentally worthwhile. After all, people called on Fox-Genovese to speak and write often on subjects she had previously treated. From time to time, too, she responded to requests to package abiding concerns and original research for nonspecialist or secondary audiences. She also tested out ideas and floated preliminary conclusions in iterative fashion, contributing dozens of essays and articles and making multiple addresses in the course of most of her years as a scholar, woman of letters, and public intellectual.

Every writer on a richly documented subject must confront and make such choices. Another biographer of Fox-Genovese would make different ones than I have. The richness of the record invites other studies as well. The time is passing, however, to share and debate findings with those whom Betsey knew. Even the youngest of her many former students now are in their forties; others are reaching retirement age. Furthermore, in the last years of her life, Betsey found herself, in the face of her multiple sclerosis, increasingly severe stenosis, and the associated drug regimens, progressively less able to attend meetings and address publics. As a result, younger people know her only as a name in the culture wars or in bibliographies and assessments of the scholarly studies she at one time influenced.

In short, the historian is becoming history. She understood the inevitability. Indeed, her archive reflected her commitment to the process. Having found lives telling in her psychoanalysis, then in her scholarship, and later in her career as a contemporary controversialist, she felt compelled to accept that her life, like any other, only gains meaning when the personal becomes public. She therefore committed to lose control of her self-narrative rather than craft it in autobiography. The archive she gave as a result makes her available to multiple, conflicting readings. This is mine in part, but it bears the shaping influences of the many informants and readers who critiqued earlier versions. Nonetheless, errors and infelicities that remain are entirely my responsibility.

One last point about her willingness to lose control of her written life is worth making: she included journals in her archive that contain, among reflections, dreams she recorded for her psychoanalysts. I have occasionally used those dreams as a means to understand her inner life, knowing that I am not an analyst—but she very nearly was. My own assumption has been that her Freudian belief informed her dreaming, that on waking she understood those dreams through Freud, and that that would be the way to unpack them. The only historical use of dreams I can think of is in Carlo Ginzburg's *The Night Battles,* Christina Larner's *Enemies of God,* and other works on witchcraft. These aren't altogether relevant to twentieth-century women who have read Freud. Freud, and Fox-Genovese's understanding of Freud, have been my guide, together with my appreciation of how important the dreams were to this dreamer, who was after all describing them in the morning with all the filters and editing of a conscious mind in play.

ELIZABETH FOX-GENOVESE

Prologue

A LIFE WRITER'S UNWRITTEN LIFE

> [She] not busy being born is busy dying.
>
> —Bob Dylan, 1964

Let me explain why I wrote this book and why I think it matters, at least for some. Elizabeth Fox-Genovese was my mentor and friend. She also terrified me. Amid her considerable *joie de vivre* I always sensed an edginess, a steely will to defend herself. I never knew from what. There were always things I sensed I could not say, topics I could not broach. Her determination to work, coupled with her anorexia early and the multiple sclerosis and spinal stenosis of her later life, wore her out, but she would not—could not—stop. Work was, and I will emphasize this—her drug of choice.

That Fox-Genovese should have worked hard and, for all her years of psychoanalysis, failed to shake some profound discomfort is not remarkable. Two things about her invite attention. One is her influential and controversy-driven intellectual career, beginning with Marx, Freud, and feminism, and later continuing into an extremely conservative Catholicism. The other was her complex, waning and waxing acceptance of herself as a woman. That she turned from left to right only makes her one of many. She did so, however, while not only clinging to the canonical—old school—education her parents gave her but—and this may surprise—using that education to support her rejection of their liberalism, first from the left and then from the right. Perhaps what best explains her transitions is simple: she perceived herself as playing for the underdog, and underdogs do rise. As women and leftists rose into the liberal pantheon, she abandoned them for the new outcasts, the unborn and traditional conservatives. Her hatred of liberalism, having read C. B. Macpherson on possessive individualism with great attention, drove all. Third on the list is her love of systematic thought, in the shape of Marx, Freud, and Catholic theology, among other forms, and her canonical old-school education. That old-school education, overseen by her father, dictated much. If she kicked against her father's control in graduate school, the education he insisted on made her instantly recognizable as a scholar to the men who would hire her again and again, until its limits reined her in during the 1980s.

During her thirty-three-year professional career, Betsey Fox-Genovese wrote, on average, over six thousand publishable words a month.[1] The quantity tells us how much she needed to work, as does something she wrote in 1972: "I realize I'm very uneasy about myself as a woman. The thing which gives me real satisfaction is my work. I don't feel I'm getting enough done, but my mind at least is working well. And that is where I feel surest and most myself."[2] At the time, she was thirty-one, a graduate student, about to pound out a dissertation on an IBM Selectric, and the wife of one of the most noted and notorious Marxist historians in the country.

Absorbing the feminisms of her paternal grandmother, a committed Republican ward boss in Massachusetts in the 1920s, and her mother, a graduate student and social activist in the 1930s, Fox-Genovese found her voice. Once through the crisis of writing her dissertation—both intellectual and anorexic—she starred in critical academic and public debates, literary, political, and social, until her death at the beginning of 2007. In this whirlwind of writing and speaking, she examined French economic history, U.S. southern history, women's history, especially southern and French; literary criticism, especially of women's fiction and of mystery writer Dick Francis; Freudian psychohistory; autobiography and biography; and feminism. She also wrote essays of all sorts, including on baseball, religion and feminism, and women and law. She spoke on these subjects as well, and by 1991 on abortion, which she disliked but did not reject outright until shortly before her conversion to Catholicism four years later. She refused to claim a single specialty as she moved from field to field, presenting herself precisely groomed, dressed for roles that she played hard but just for limited engagements. In contrast to Genovese's mastery of New World slavery and the southern planter class, Fox-Genovese became mistress of an Atlantic world filled with people, stretching from the early modern period to her present.

Despite her continuing to add to the range of her engagements, Fox-Genovese continued to center her work in the fields of her early historical studies: the prerevolutionary world of the Enlightenment, of nascent individualism still embedded in community and hierarchy, the world of Pierre Samuel du Pont de Nemours and Benjamin Franklin struggling with the autobiographical form, of Adam Smith's belief in sympathetic ties that bound, and the later Scot, Henry Cockburn, balancing Whig ideals with the paternalism of his father. Like Cockburn, she batted left and right in the culture wars of their different eras.[3] Dualisms abounded, as did conflict, and she remained a dialectical thinker throughout most of her life. For her, the great revolution was in the minds of eighteenth-century thinkers, not the Boston Massacre, the fall of the Bastille, or the raw communalism of St. Petersburg in 1917. Unlike her husband, she had few ties, except through marriage, to the leftists of the 1960s.

Her critique of systematic individualism became complicated by her interest in the individual mind and the construction of self, much abetted by her extensive reading in Freud as a graduate student, coupled with her years of psychoanalysis.[4] She remained interested, as she remarked in the 1980s, in how women become women—in the becoming, not the final result. That interest did not emerge in a vacuum. She came of age in the Cold War, during the McCarthy hearings on communists in American life, and perhaps most importantly, in the last days of the absolute dominance of white Anglo-Saxon men in political and academic life. In that world, Gene Genovese stood out as an Italian and an ex-communist, not a WASP by a long shot. Although outwardly old New England WASP, Betsey in her turn felt herself alloyed: she had a Jewish mother and also southern antecedents. The accomplished individualism she first knew was that of men like her father, Edward Whiting Fox, descendant of Puritan New England.

Ed, whom Betsey once described as an iron fist in a velvet glove, did not begin as an indomitable example of the WASP individual. He, like Betsey in this one way, had been seriously ill and had struggled. In his case, the challenge was rheumatoid arthritis when he should have been in high school. He fought back and survived, but with limits and an enduring thirst for control. Betsey grew up to battle severe anorexia in graduate school and, to a lesser extent, for the rest of her life, as a September 1986 journal entry shows:

> Last night, I made us a paella—rice, olive oil, and all. Who (but Becky?) would know what a victory that was—and it didn't even feel dangerous. Even so, when I got out plates and told Gene to serve himself (no need to control) he took the plate I had intended for myself (thinner rim) and I said "no" and handed him the other. He said "you're crazy." I said "yes." And took the plate I wanted. Little did he know how much I was not being crazy about.[5]

Fox-Genovese struggled not only with herself, but with the last of the East Coast male academic elite in view as she developed her antipathy to individualism in the 1960s. Settling in at the University of Rochester in 1969, Fox-Genovese joined a consciousness-raising group. Her communal opposition to individualism emerged as both socialist, from her reading, and more importantly feminist, from her immediate experience.

By the later 1980s she saw feminism, from her limited perspective, rise into a branch of liberal individualism. Soon thereafter she favored the corporatist opposition of the Catholic far right. Her enemy, no longer the WASP men of her youth, had morphed into the successful and self-possessed television character Murphy Brown—and, I suspect, neoconservatism. Earlier, her sights were fixed on male individuals. In 1972 she had nightmares about her father and bouts of anger at her husband:

> I was dozing off. I did not want to see him [Gene]. I am harboring a goodly store of cold anger against him at the moment. I don't want him to touch me. This only arises when we go to bed at night or in the morning, and then only rarely, but it is there. It is strange in that in most ways our relations are very warm, and when we make love it is very good. But the anger is there, and with it a certain contempt—my mother's contempt for my father?[6]

In the same year Betsey wrote, "There are problems with Gene and me working at the same place. I don't want to be second. No more do I want to be second around the house. And that is where Gene felt threatened—that I should want my work to come first."[7] There was no easy resolution. Genovese spent the 1973–74 academic year in California writing *Roll, Jordan, Roll.* Fox-Genovese moved with him, could not bear either the intellectual and social isolation or the condescension of being treated as merely a spouse, and took a fellowship at the Hagley Museum and Library in Delaware, finishing her dissertation quickly. The writing that had been difficult, almost impossible, for many years had eased, opening the way to her prodigious later writing.

Given Betsey's interest in individualism, her archive at the University of North Carolina at Chapel Hill's Wilson Library is no accident. While not the creation of a tangible self, as through autobiography, the compilation of autobiographical sources gave her the sense of projecting herself into the future. She preserved thousands of pages but did so by getting rid of them, sending them away and making space for new work after 1995, as she finished writing *Feminism Is Not the Story of My Life.*

Difficulties with reshaping Emory University's women's studies program into a more canonical, conservative program, her emerging opposition to abortion, and her rebirth as a traditional conservative and a Catholic coincided with the manifestation of physical ills that would eventually lead to a diagnosis of multiple sclerosis. Illness tied her more closely to her parents' generation: her father and paternal grandfather had died from Parkinson's disease, bound in braces and wheelchairs and pain, exactly as she would be. However, Catholicism was anathema to her father's family of stoic New England Congregationalists.

Fox-Genovese's turn to conservative Catholicism in 1995 gave her conservatism a richer, more public, and more ritualized form than her 1991 claim to be a Red Tory. The turn was framed by the culture wars, but Fox-Genovese's conversion was never to the neoconservatism of journalist Irving Kristol and other former leftists; she was moving tactically to oppose the neoconservative, libertarian right more than the enfeebled left.

Catholic theology came to her as a revelation, and she refilled her shelves with writings mostly new to her, especially those of Saint Teresa of Avila, Edith Stein (Saint Teresa Benedicta of the Cross), and Joseph Ratzinger, later Pope Benedict XVI. As Genovese remarked after her death, she was a convert, and consequently more Catholic than the pope. Gene had imagined that she would have a late career as a theologian.

Betsey did not live to do so, nor did the crippling pain of spinal stenosis, or the unpredictable damages of multiple sclerosis, allow it. Her late work was work-in-progress, work unfinished, with one exception. Much time went to work with Genovese on their last and biggest collaboration, the three volumes of *The Mind of the Master Class* series, and her spiritual life. Much time went as well to short essays and speaking engagements about family, traditional marriage, the pro-life movement, and conservative feminism. It was not the life she had lived earlier but the consequence of intellectual shifts that reflected defensive positions she had taken.

When Elizabeth Fox-Genovese died at the age of sixty-five, the array of work she left belies its centripetal aims, always returning to her linked curiosities about individualism, the meaning of I, of autobiography, of silences. These foci complemented her lifelong commitment to the critique of liberal individualism, in her view the most haunting and selfish error embedded in modernity.

That preoccupation grew out of the great difficulty she faced in graduate school in the 1960s, finding a voice independent of and equal to the professorial and paternal voices on whose guidance she relied. She became anorexic, worked with psychoanalysts, and in 1973 wrote her dissertation in a year, masterfully reinterpreting a group of French economic writers working on the eve of the French Revolution, exposing their temerity in proposing radical economic innovation to a conservative monarchy. Given Betsey's own tenuous position as a woman in the overwhelmingly male academic world of the early 1970s, she grasped the subordinate and liminal position in which the Physiocrats found themselves, and in turn the Physiocrats' temerity helped her find her voice.

Fox-Genovese's reading in eighteenth-century French history drew her into that early modern political discourse of individual rights, and there Betsey discovered a second framework for the study of individualism, beyond what Freud offered. Informed by Freud and Marx, Fox-Genovese created a powerful, dynamic double vision, dialectical but enriched and reshaped by vocabularies Marx had never known. Using the old 1960s mantra of Marx and Freud, she applied them as she read biographical material and fiction as a way of making political economy palpable and as she turned political and economic material into a stage on which personality played. Her introduction to *The Autobiography of Du Pont de Nemours* set Du Pont's autobiography properly in the midst of the French Revolution and examined his attempt, while facing threatened execution, to preserve aspects of his life for his sons in a new and very bourgeois form. It is an extraordinary essay, differentiating a newly emerging, liberal, bourgeois self-consciousness from the ahistorical consciousness of sentient beings that figured in earlier self-writings.

Betsey did this repeatedly: in *Within the Plantation Household* she used a complex essay on the household economy of the South as the opening chapter, preceded by an intimate reading of one southern woman's journal, followed by several hundred pages of personal musings, or as close to personal writing as she could get, from Black and white women. She wanted to understand lives in their specificity: Zora Neale Hurston's in her *Dust Tracks on the Road,* the fictional lives in Kate Chopin's *The Awakening* and Toni Morrison's *Beloved.* She planned but never completed a book on African American women's writings about their lives, *Ghosts and Memories: History in the Fictions of African-American Women Writers.*[8] As seriously as she initially took the possibility of psychohistory, however, she was acutely wary of the simplifications it might engender and vigorously criticized these too easy analyses in her review of Michael Paul Rogin's biography of Andrew Jackson.[9]

She developed her method of putting personal and political into conversation through her experience and reading, recommending Karl Polanyi's *The Great Transformation: The Political and Economic Origins of Our Time* at one moment and Tillie Olsen's *Silences* the next. Her core texts, however, were those of tentative, emergent individualisms: Adam Smith's *The Theory of Moral Sentiments,* Virginia Woolf's

A Room of One's Own, Zora Neale Hurston's *Dust Tracks on the Road.* Fox-Genovese knew that for eighteenth-century Scots the individual existed within a community, within a synergy, a collaboration typical of Enlightenment sociability in Scotland. For Adam Smith, sympathy drove individual consciousness and created community ties.[10]

This resonated for her in the 1970s, in the heady early days of the second-wave women's movement, when Betsey (among many other women) joined consciousness-raising groups to find themselves, within the company of other women. We know that groups mattered to her; there was rarely a time in her life when she and her husband, Gene, did not seek to build communities—many of which came to grief because of the strength of the personalities they gathered. She had a keen eye for weighing the historical self within the expectations, laws, and possibilities of his or her society.

This book is a direct result of Betsey's fascination with biography and autobiography, forms critical to her investigation and criticism of liberal individualism. She spent the last decade of her life archiving her own and her extended family's papers, to enable others to examine her life as she had not done. Liberal individualism, which Fox-Genovese could easily trace from its early proponents in the seventeenth century, became her bête noire; the conflict-ridden road to maturity in Freud and the opposing forces of Marx appealed to her. Individualism, however, emerged her enemy only in its mature form as it became the new orthodoxy for some men after the great revolutions that ended the eighteenth century. Nascent individualism, the process of becoming, attracted her; achieved individualism, static, self-satisfied, and classist repelled her.

Betsey's life was marked by new projects in new fields, travel, starting over, becoming. The most dramatic change, the most remarked upon, was from a communal left to an authoritarian, corporatist right, but this was completely in keeping with her long record of engaging major intellectual currents—feminism, the literary turn—while remaining constant in critiquing liberal individualism. Fox-Genovese was not following the parade of earlier leftists moving to neoconservatism well before the Soviet Union collapsed, although that collapse mattered to her. She did make ample use in the 1990s of the slogans the right threw up for public use, of the horrors of political correctness and intolerant "feminazis." In the wake of the Soviet Union's dissolution, much of the left that she recognized, but had always distrusted, was in disarray. While she had friends on the left, she had seen many as members of a club to which she did not belong.

Betsey's life deserves attention from those outside her circle for multiple reasons. The documentation that she left, and colleagues and family provided, enriches markedly the telling of a significant academic and public intellectual life. She became a lightning rod in the culture wars after having already gained outsized influence as a scholar of the American South and women. Together, she and her husband did more than any to implement the Gramscian-inflected Marxist analysis of the hegemonic culture of southern elites in the United States that they asserted. They continued in this commitment even after leaving the political left and (re)joining the Catholic Church. Betsey's story resonates as well, however, because she, like so many other women, perhaps especially talented women, was uncomfortable, and she kept coming and going, fleeing from any fixed specialization, surviving by her wits, never holding for long to any one identity. Her one comfort was to settle into the criticism of individualism, and to do so from the margins of left and right, as someone who could not imagine herself at the center of her world. This stand against what she judged the ruling ethos of her culture may have made her a voice crying in the wilderness, but she nonetheless was heard by many. Some applauded, some snorted, many felt bemused. That fact in her mind justified her tilting against windmills and gave her life, like Don Quixote's, meaning and value beyond the self.

The documentation that she left is more than extensive, bordering on exhausting and exhaustive, reaching back beyond her grandparents' lives. She thus connected herself to a lineage and to parents who in turn were shaped by their world and their parents. She never abandoned Freud completely, because he took childhood seriously, and she was quick to connect childhood and adolescence with both cultural continuity and revolution, as she had with her work on Du Pont de Nemours's autobiographical writings.

Her concerns shaped her archive and therefore this book, which begins with her parents' childhoods in the 1920s, and courtship in the 1930s. Betsey Fox was born in 1941, and her education in public and private schools, including a year in her father's courses at Cornell University, are richly documented. Her years at Harvard, her graduate program—as it had been her father's and her mother's, through Radcliffe—emerge not only through correspondence but through the lens of the 162-page journal she kept for her psychoanalyst as she struggled with anorexia. After she married and began teaching, her journals shrunk to fewer pages as her professional writing grew. By the 1990s, email accounted for much of her correspondence, and she archived the contents of her hard drives. All together, the Fox-Genovese Papers amount to 18,400 items, some of which run to many pages. Betsey's parents' papers total another 3,000 items.

Betsey wanted someone to read these collections, to explore her life as seriously as she had that of Du Pont de Nemours. I have tried to do that, with attention to three questions. The first is the price paid by bright little girls who wished to become intellectuals in her day. As Betsey wrote in 1972, on the verge of finally finishing her dissertation: "This whole 'exceptional' question is hard for me. Scared to death not to be best for fear of not being loved, scared of being best for fear of being hated."[11] The second goal is to trace Betsey's lifelong critique of systematic individualism through her writings and public commitments. The third is to understand why and how she became—and stayed—more a product of her parents' generation than her own. The last seems to me a function of her traditional education, virtually unchanged from her parents'. Of course, she did not only embrace the canon with which her parents were reared. She also sought its enlargement. She did so as she used the expanded canon to defy her parents' liberal values. Nevertheless, having allied herself with her parents' generation, she doomed herself, like a latter-day Miss Jean Brodie, to a very short prime. Easily a leader in progressive circles in the 1970s, she could no longer lead or tolerate those enlarged circles by 1990.

These three goals, and the documentation that enables and shapes their address, have resulted in a three-part book, each of three chapters. The first part presents Betsey's family, childhood, and education, as well as her early years of marriage and the anorexia and psychotherapy that accompanied her graduate work. The second part follows the trajectory of her professional rise and intellectual acclaim as a scholar, woman of letters, and feminist. The last part carries her through the years that saw her break with second-wave feminism, turn from leftist communitarianism to Catholic corporatism, and, in the midst of debilitating illness, work on the projects that occupied her last decade—the volumes of *The Mind of the Master Class* series treating the worldview of southern planters before the American Civil War, the founding of The Historical Society and editing of its journal, and speaking and writing on women's issues and family from the perspective of conservative Catholicism.

PART I

FAMILY AND UPBRINGING

1

The Family as Matrix

WHEN ELIZABETH ANN WAS A CAR, 1922-1941

> Since Freudian thought emphasizes the individual as an organic member of the species and emphasizes the centrality of early-childhood experience in shaping adults, it offers historians an important insight into the mysterious dynamics of culture—the ability of one generation forcefully to transmit its values to the next.
>
> —ELIZABETH FOX-GENOVESE, "Poor Richard at Work in the Cotton Fields" (1983), 106–7

ELIZABETH FOX-GENOVESE became a powerful, mobile, unpredictable, and firmly dialectical intellectual, persistently scraping flint against steel, setting fire to whatever she had been, becoming something else. Her roots in dialectical thought grew well before her familiarity with Marx, from the family, era, and place into which she was born: Massachusetts, May 1941. She was six months old as World War II started, and she would be at war, intellectually, for the rest of her life.

Springfield

Edward Whiting Fox, Betsey's father, spent more of his youth in Springfield, Massachusetts, than anywhere else, and that is where this story begins, because he dominated her childhood. Carved out of native fields and trails in 1636, by 1929 Springfield had become an industrial hub, filling with immigrants, shoulder to shoulder with white Anglo-Saxon Protestants. With manufacturing on the banks of three rivers, it became the fourth largest city in New England, and in the decade before the Great Depression it hummed with life. Union Station, central to Boston, Albany, and Hartford, was enlarged in 1926; trolleys ran constantly.

Crippled by arthritis and rheumatism in his teens and, for a while, near death, Edward Fox became obsessed with rivers and rowing, like his father, Philip. Edward endured pain and immobility. When he should have been in high school, he kept to bed and ate raw liver. Meanwhile, his father walked to work at the old Trade High School, coached rowing, and walked to church with his wife, Agnes. They had a car, perhaps a necessity with Edward's arthritis, and lived a stone's throw from a trolley route. It was in Springfield, as his father drove past Catholic churches, that Edward was repeatedly told that Catholicism was the root of all evil. Philip, Agnes, and Edward were very much part of the old Anglo-Saxon elite—not of money but birth—in what were the last days of its ascendancy.

1935

In June 1935, Agnes Fox wrote to her old friend Clara McRae, seeking Clara's opinion about the impending marriage of Edward to Elizabeth Simon, and McRae responded honestly:

> You ask how I would feel about a situation like Edward's in becoming engaged to a Jewess.
>
> I think I would be sorry it turned out that way to be frank, but would feel much as you do. That after all, it *is* his life that is being planned and being of an age of discretion and a good sensible fellow too. I should accept it and her, and make them as happy as possible. . . .
>
> Personally I would rather my son married a Jewess than a Catholic.
>
> I find much to like and admire in the Jews, and I know I don't have the prejudice of some.[1]

Agnes Fox, Elizabeth Fox-Genovese's paternal grandmother, would care for Betsey often, from her birth and for weeks at a time during summer school vacations. Agnes was a tough woman, a deft, politic, opinionated vice-chairman for the Republican City Committee in Springfield; active in church, civic, and women's organizations; and deeply concerned by the Great Depression. Born in Iowa, by 1935 she had been an elementary school teacher in Tacoma, Washington; taught

Americanization classes for Polish immigrants in Springfield; and had seen her son through crippling, potentially deadly rheumatism and arthritis. She welcomed Elizabeth Simon, known as Betty, warmly.[2] But the message of McRae's letter lingered: Massachusetts was white Anglo-Saxon Protestant territory.

Fox-Genovese—born Elizabeth Ann Fox—was shaped by the turbulent world in which her parents, Elizabeth Mary Simon and Edward Whiting Fox, lived, and Clara McRae's pronouncement, better "a Jewess than a Catholic," reminds us of the social and political realities of the Depression era in New England. Much of the cultural as well as physical and medical frameworks within which the mature Betsey Fox-Genovese lived were set in place in the 1930s by her grandparents' and her parents' generations. The debilitating illnesses of her father and his parents prefigured her own, and incongruities of religion and class within her family contributed to her intellectual preoccupations.

The Massachusetts of her father's and her childhood divided sharply on religious and ethnic lines, which some supposed were markers of class divisions. Protestants were Republicans and, almost by default, middle class or better; Catholics were Democrats, immigrants, and workers—but not always. Jews were confusing, but Agnes Fox's question displays her discomfort. The Simons, who were exorbitantly wealthy by the Foxes' standards, Democrats, and prominent people in Manhattan business and government, were wary of how their daughter would be treated by Edward's parents. In 1934, as Betty and Edward first met each other's parents, Robert E. Simon Sr. quietly inquired of his daughter, "We are also very very much interested to know about your meeting with his parents—how they happened to be in Cambridge, & what you think of them & how they received you?" Simon was protective of his daughter and probably right to wonder "how they happened to be in Cambridge." Agnes and Philip had spent a good many years watching and worrying over their own child Edward.[3]

Betsey grew up at the confluence of these two very different families. The Foxes embodied the spare, hardworking, New England middle class; the Simons the patrician yet careful German Jewish *grande bourgeoisie* of Manhattan. Hegemony, bourgeois individualism, and women in politics all had backstories in Betsey's family.

When Fox-Genovese read selections from Antonio Gramsci's *Prison Notebooks,* edited by Quentin Hoare and Geoffrey Nowell Smith and published in 1971, and the "Prison Letters," selected and translated by Scottish socialist poet and folklorist Hamish Henderson and published in the *New Edinburgh Review* in 1974, hegemony made perfect sense to her; Gramsci's work was rooted in her parents' world.

Florida in 1929

The first insight we have into Betsey's complex family life comes from a car trip by her then eighteen-year-old father, Edward, from Baltimore, Maryland, to Melbourne, Florida, in 1929.[4] Because Edward's father, Philip, went only as far as Baltimore and Ed's mother was just learning to drive, Edward did all the driving on this months-long excursion designed to help his recovery from rheumatoid arthritis. Correspondence from this trip reveals much about Betsey's father and his intense connection to his parents. As with many boys especially, his relationship with his father was mediated through reports about the family car, which Edward called "Elizabeth Ann," thus naming his first child thirteen years before her birth.

For weeks in 1929, cards, letters, and telegrams went back and forth between Springfield and various southern cities. On their first day on the road, Agnes and Edward—his father called him Teddie, his mother did not—reached Petersburg, Virginia, and Agnes sent a card to her husband:

> Went directly thru Wash[ington] as traffic down Penn. Ave was rather hectic tho not frightening got a two inch fender tick but came out on top. Lunch in a grove and straight thru to Richmond. . . .
>
> Love, Agnes & Ed[5]

That night, "at a lovely old southern home [they] spent the evening in front of the living room fire with the family." The father, "Preston Huntly[,] a handsome white haired man of fifty odd, raise[d] cotton, use[d] darkeys, and dislike[d] working with whites. He ha[d] attended all the Dem. Inaugurations and did not like Coolidge, but [thought]

Hoover [might] do." One imagines a woman not shy about asking questions, politically astute, pleased but not blinded by her surroundings: "Fire places in every room including our bedroom," she noted, adding, "wonderful food in great abundance and fresh flowers every where. Treated us like old friends, southern hospitality—not too high priced either."[6] She used her last clause to reduce Huntly to an innkeeper whose house fell within the budget of a careful economizer. She was acutely attentive to the condition of rich and poor as they drove and the prices of vegetables, but not the car, which was Edward's business.

Reaching Florida, she wrote her husband that "Edward seems pretty well, but I am anxious to feed him."[7] The two headed south for the boy's poor health. He would not finish high school until he was twenty, in 1931, but he was well enough to drive, and he loved Elizabeth Ann.[8] After leaving Petersburg, he proudly wrote, "Dear Papa—Arrived here at 10 after a 6 o'clock start (140 mi). Got a scare when my am[m]eter registered low but found my winshield wipper [*sic*] was the cause—it's a hard rain ever since we struck N.C. at 8." At the end of a postcard from Raleigh, he told his father, "Elizabeth is going like a bird and I feel fine and get around well everything OK Love Teddie."[9] He adhered to his invalid's regimen assiduously—just as assiduously as he cared for the car. Most of his letters to his father were about servicing the car, garagemen's comments about Fords like theirs, and his usually improving health. His letters exposed his correlation of his health with that of the car.[10]

His mother, as a good New Englander, although born in Iowa, was skeptical about Florida, writing from St. Petersburg in March: "It seems to us Florida is greatly over rated." Then again, the good vegetables in March pleased her—"lovely fresh green beans and spinach and steak and .75 worth of dishes for cooking and eating and we have had two sumptuous meals."[11] She was unhappy about how slowly her son improved, although he did seem to do so. By early April, she could write, "Edward begins to look fine[,] good color. He has not gained lately in spite of a quart and a half of milk [per day]. However he walks almost two miles a day—good for him." What interested him was driving, and by March 27 he had mapped their return route, writing to his father about "my way home—via Norfolk," and then crossing out the "my" for "our."[12]

Agnes was counting her pennies. At the end of March, she wrote to her husband, "My dear Boy, The money came and many thanks, I still had a little. Living is really high here mostly higher than Springfield. Tho a few things are lower. . . . I finally did up my sweeping and beds and sat down again."[13] Slowly she acclimated and came to appreciate the sky and the water. By the first week of April, she wrote, "This is a heavenly June day, sky and ocean as blue as blue, and a soft cool breeze, not a wind. We had a very pleasant surf bath this morning and after we were first wet the water felt warm when it struck us."[14]

Agnes and Edward had left behind an unusually cold March, and Agnes's complaints about the enervating heat must be balanced against her joy: Edward's "clothes are getting too small. And he is *so* much better than last year! Thank God!"[15] Edward developed his own voice, writing to his father with confidence and frankness, sometimes assuming a bit of superiority over his mother, especially when it came to managing the car:

> Elizabeth seems to be OK now except that I have a hard time keeping her tires up to pressure. They go down pretty fast, but not fast enough for a leak. Mother's learning to navigate; I think she's doing quite well but she gets pretty excited about it and rattles easily. She can shift and get the car going all right but sometimes she'll stall it or get it backing when she's getting it going in low and then she sort of gets lost. She thinks she wants to help me drive home but of course that's not probable.[16]

He determined to get well. His mother recorded that he was "dog trotting around, walks well, chinned himself at the beach today, has a good appetite besides a qt & half of milk a day. His weight is up again."[17] This activity came even in what they both reported as enervating heat.

His devotion to the car showed repeatedly: "The garage man in Raleigh wouldn't drain my alcohol—said I might need it yet but we heated up some yesterday and went pretty dry so I did it just now. Everything is OK and I'm liking it better than I expected."[18] He explored his competence: driving, sleeping in the sun, thinking about rowing again, getting better. His mother slowly admitted as much in April: "Edward is beginning to talk river. His body looks great to me. It may have been worth it." She had been reluctant to incur the expense of the trip and frequently complained. In one letter, returning papers to her husband that she had cosigned for a loan, she indulged in over three closely written pages of worry. They had had roughly eight weeks south of Baltimore, and it seems to have been all they could afford.[19]

Edward enjoyed something of a coming of age. He bought a Kodak in Jacksonville, swam with porpoises, and kept up a correspondence with several friends, but his chief joy was the car, which gave him mobility, control, and something of the position of an adult, all things that his crippling arthritis had denied him. He complained that Georgia cars "crowded me to the last inch!" And "once or twice big cars came at me so far over on my side that I just slammed on my brakes and stopped in the middle and made them drive around me." Edward closed his letter to his father by insisting that he drove carefully and took no chances, but as he made clear, he also was a force to be reckoned with as a man behind the wheel.[20]

Edward was well enough to enter Harvard in 1931, and as he walked on beaches and by rivers in 1929, rode a ferry, watched cars, studied roads, and followed his father's interest in rowing, one can see the roots of his later interest in geography and riverine systems.[21] More immediately important, taking control of the car allowed him also to take control of his relationship with his father and to make himself a parent—an equal with Philip—in shouldering responsibility. Hence, his later reuse of the car's name for his first child and his constant attention to that daughter. She would become a French historian, like her father. Control would shape his care and direction of her, as it had earlier freed him from an adolescent life in which he was his mother's patient more often than her son.

The world, in the shape of the Great Depression, loomed, and Agnes received a letter from her father in which the old man claimed, "if business did not pick up pretty soon he would be a burden to his children." Agnes and Philip had borrowed money for this trip, and perhaps to pay the bills of the Boston specialist they had engaged for Edward. This would explain Agnes's anxious comment: "Do I take the joy out of life? And yet I am very conscious that it is a great privilege to be here and if it boosts Ed along the way it will be more than worth while."[22]

Edward Fox and His Family

Edward Whiting Fox was born in Seattle, Washington, in 1911. There Agnes taught school and Philip worked as a civil engineer.[23] They moved often, following Philip's construction projects, until settling in Springfield at 67 Dunmoreland Street. Philip coached rowing and taught mathematics and surveying at Trade High School. Edward's mother no longer taught, becoming deeply engaged in precinct- and state-level Republican Party politics, the League of Women Voters, the Salvation Army, and countless charitable efforts during the Great Depression. And on Sundays they attended Reverend James Gordon Gilkey's historic South Congregational Church on Maple Street.

Edward's physician, Dr. Loring T. Swaim, an internationally recognized specialist, practiced and taught at the Robert B. Brigham Hospital in Boston. Swaim was a curiously broadminded man whose work explored the effects of posture on chronic arthritis, the possibility of emotional and psychosomatic causes of arthritis, and the importance of treating the whole person. His care helped.[24] After returning from Florida, Edward spent two more years at Central High School in Springfield. Dr. Swaim was "delighted" with the plan to then send Edward to Harvard and "sure that it w[ould] be good for Edward to have this stimulus to work for."[25] As Edward finished his first degree in 1935, Clara McRae remarked in a letter to Agnes Fox, "Will and I think it little less than a miracle the way Edward has gotten along and overcome that early handicap."[26]

Teddie matured into Edward, and glimpses of his growing maturity matter, for his relations with his parents shaped his own child-rearing habits. He exorcised his invalid past with glee. By the summer of 1932, after a year at Harvard, he was sailing the New England coast with Skip, a friend, and writing to his mother in a curiously teasing way about new injuries that were specific to an athletic life: "We had a little delay this morning while I got my back strapped. Breaking out heavy anchors etc lamed it up a bit & one of Skip's doctor friends here sent me up to the hospital to get it strapped." Roughly a day later he wrote to advise Agnes, "The back feels fine now however. I stubbed my left foot badly last night but it is getting better. I tried to kick over a part of a concrete wall—Much love Edward."[27] Illness had colored his relations with his parents, making him too often a patient, but he was now taking joy from injuries that were evidence of physical exuberance.

Edward, Harvard, and Betty

Before graduating in 1935, Edward abandoned his intention to become a high school English teacher and rowing coach, turning instead to graduate work in modern European history. That he "did poorly" on his oral examination in Renaissance literature and history tells us that he had already lost interest, and he graduated without honors. Perhaps the political climate had encouraged him to take up modern history, but more compelling was his meeting with Elizabeth (Betty) Simon in 1934. They married in 1935, on June 14. Both were pursuing graduate degrees, but Betty, having graduated from high school on time, was several years ahead of him. She was the student and research assistant of Harvard's most eminent modern European historian William Langer. Edward was not merely smitten with Betty but with her world. When he announced his failed oral exam to his mother, his brief letter suggested that she already knew where his new interest lay.[28]

By 1961 Edward would claim that his choice of modern France was "determined to a large extent by the events of 1935," but it must have been Betty who shook him out of the Renaissance.[29] Betty's expertise in modern Europe—she had earned her A.M. from Harvard through Radcliffe in 1932—was matched by later political research, possibly connected to the Model League of Nations movement, and work at the *New York Times*. She was fiercely independent then and very smart. Nonetheless, the events of 1935 would have given Edward a good push toward France. Europe was rearming. The short-lived Flandin government in France fell on May 31, the franc was collapsing, and the French Popular Front, uniting with difficulty, paraded on Bastille Day, July 14, the French national holiday. Edward Fox and Betty Simon were caught up in the grim early tremors of World War II.

Their marriage was a simple, if elegant, gathering of the two families at the Simons' home on Riverside Drive in Manhattan. A single paragraph in the *New York Times* mentioned a short wedding trip and identified the minister who officiated, Reverend C. Leslie Glenn, the Episcopalian rector of Christ Church in Cambridge, Edward and Betty's territory. For a student who had been held back by illness for years, Edward worked hard. After six weeks of marriage, Betty wrote to Agnes and Philip: "Ed is working like a fiend." Dr. Swaim had told him earlier that summer that he might "go forth and live a normal, if moderate, life," but Edward, like Agnes, was not moderate, and he had a thesis on Renaissance literature to finish before he could move forward.[30]

Young Historians

Between 1935 and 1941 Edward and Betty studied with William Langer; Betty continued as his research assistant. In February 1936, Edward wrote to his mother detailing his decision-making about his studies: "I'm taking innumerable courses in an attempt to try to decide which ones I want to continue with. I'm taking Langer's European History from 1871–1914 which is excellent, & I'm listening to a course of his on the Near East. Also I'm doing individual reading courses with two different men in French History, & listening to some others. I shall settle down very soon & concentrate on a few." Edward, more comfortable in modern history, reported his fall grades to his mother, two As and one B, concluding, "at least it's no discredit."[31]

Edward and Betty were not wealthy nor were they poor. They drove to the Southwest that summer for Betty's sinus troubles, and they made do, often with help from Agnes and Philip, sometimes with a check from Betty's mother, Elsa Weil Simon.[32] The autumn before, in October 1935, Betty was discussing curtains with Agnes: "Have you gotten the India print? Those we'd really love."[33] The young couple had moved into a block of Harvard-owned apartments at 1306 Massachusetts Avenue; Philip and Agnes helped them in their first years of marriage, shopping for curtains, altering Edward's jacket, building an end table, sending cookies, and making doors for a wardrobe. Ten days before Christmas 1936 Edward was checking radio prices for his mother, which suggests political news—or escape from the news—was important.[34] He thanked his father for the end table and sent sketches for the wardrobe doors. He then begged his father's help for a teachers' union representative, a Miss Petersen, with organizing in Springfield and Northampton. He explained that "she is aware of the added complication of the Faith hereabouts," indicating his problematizing of Catholicism.[35]

By 1937 Agnes wrote to Philip, "Betty [is] anxious to get back to work."[36] She had been helping Edward with his master's thesis, as Edward wrote to his mother that winter: "My thesis is due to day & Betty just finished typing it last night. It is some eighty pages, & every bit of it had to be edited as well as typed, which is no small job. Betty says to tell you she'll write as soon as she catches her breath."[37] That Betty could type was unusual, possibly something she had learned in extramural classes added by Radcliffe in the early years of the Great Depression to help graduates find any possible job. That Edward could not type was usual.[38]

And then a new car with a new name appeared: "Would you ask Papa how Pocahontas fares? I'm afraid I'm getting a pretty bad itch to have a wheel in my hands again." He was impatient about repairs but turned to discussing furniture and a design for a dressing table for his mother. It seems likely that this table and other pieces, and the car repairs, were projects to be completed at the Smith School, the trade school in Northampton where Philip was making his mark as an innovative supervisor.[39]

Betty was also working in 1937, as Edward reported: "Langer isn't doing all his lecturing this week so she has to work extra." He continued, "You and Papa certainly are past masters at graceful presents . . . & you've helped make one little girl very happy on several occasions."[40] For all Betty's worldliness, Edward easily called her a little girl. Yet, when they had met, she was not only much farther along in her studies but also much more sophisticated and worldlier than he. His French was never good; she spoke French, German, and Italian, and, besides, Henry Morgenthau Jr., then secretary of the treasury, was her mother's cousin. By 1937 Edward no longer felt awe.

Agnes and Philip Fox in the Depression

While he happily sailed up and down the East Coast in 1932, Agnes and Philip were left to cope with the Great Depression. They received a letter that year from friends who had moved to a cottage or summer home in northern Massachusetts: "Well the Reaveys are up in the wilds—leading the simple life—very, very simply. Well and healthy but financially desperate."[41] The writer went on to ask Philip to take out a loan for two hundred dollars for him; he could not borrow again, as he was paying off one loan already. This scraping and pinching—for the Foxes too—was hidden from Edward. A notebook draft of Philip's painstaking reply to Mr. Reavey survives. Philip chose his words carefully, scratching out some:

> I have been quite a time answering your letter, but at least I have been trying to do things.
>
> In the first place it is out of the question for me to take out a loan for you. My income this coming year will be over $1000 less than it was last year. To pay Teddie's bills last year we borrowed $250, which is not all paid back. In addition we are carrying much more than that in notes to the bank, and the bank has been requesting heavier payments. Just how we are going to finance Teddie is not quite clear now, but we must keep any remaining borrowing capacity clear for emergency, for because of Teddie's condition we feel that we must not jeopardize the possibility of keeping him at college.[42]

So the Reaveys were turned away, but with advice. Philip looked into other sources of loans to schoolteachers and offered them a prospect. Letters from others indicate that the Reaveys were far from unusual, as friends wrote from newly acquired, obscure—and implicitly embarrassing—addresses during the 1930s.[43] Agnes and Philip also struggled, raising and canning vegetables, spending little. Their car, Elizabeth Ann, disappeared from letters in the 1930s, possibly destroyed in an accident in 1935 that made Philip's hair turn white.[44] That same summer, however, good fortune returned; they would no longer need to take in boarders.[45]

Philip was appointed director of the Smith School for trades in Northampton, Massachusetts. On Tuesday morning, 16 July 1935, Agnes wrote to Philip:

> Last night I guess I was a bit excited, and you may have wondered how pleased I was. I guess I hadn't come to that part yet. But, I lay a long time, after Vella brought us back from seeing the eclipse out on the long view out of Wilbraham, and I know how important this is for both of us.
>
> I think it is the grandest thing ever in the way of a job. I believe you will, at last, be where you belong in school work, the directing end.
>
> It is going to be thrilling for you to work it out up there, hard work but exciting and I am going to stand by and try to be the perfect wife in the background.[46]

Agnes Fox was never meant to be the perfect wife in the background. Springfield politicians, at least one of whom complained about the Republican ward organizations being overrun by women, courted her. Republican committeewomen in Northampton were thrilled to hear that Agnes was coming. She had directed canvassing, overseen the polling station for ward 5 in Springfield, and been privy to political squabbles. She was intensely sociable, worldlier than Philip, often at party meetings and conferences.[47]

The troubles of the 1930s survive in her letters. In 1936, Carl Thomas ranted to Agnes about changes in the Republican Party:

> I think you'll find there'll be no more Elephant as we have known it—The old dried prunes—billionaires busting with bullion—& quite a lot of the young Lemons, not only locally but nationally, must be gotten rid of—nay must be exterminated politically.
>
> Women too!—Now now—Yes & I'm sure you'll realize it too! No matter where you go—what meeting you read of—what picture in the paper—what meeting you attend—Emma Brigham!—Hazel Oliver!! Eleanor Johnson!!! . . . AD DAMNUM
>
> And, what the women haven't done to the Party statewide the Jews have! There's no question Tham Thimous with the help of Josiah Brooks killed the Nazis in *this* City.[48]

Thomas had no idea that Fox's daughter-in-law was Jewish, and no clue that Agnes belonged to the League of Women Voters and had organized a roundtable discussion of peace and disarmament with the Unitarian Margaret B. Barnard earlier that year. Whatever Carl Thomas's sort of Republican was, she wasn't it. Another letter, from her good friend and political colleague Grace Tyler in 1939, made that clear: "Well, it's just a man's world after all. Just to turn it upside down!"[49]

Philip—humorous, patient, earnest, and hardworking—remains the shadow figure in the letters. What he wrote was dictated by his work or consisted of lengthy descriptions of rowing—crew—with newspaper clippings. Rowing was his great love, and he coached the Trade High School team on the Connecticut River for many years.

Betty's Family

Elizabeth, or Betty, Simon connected Betsey to a different family, not Congregationalists but non-practicing Jews; not wage-earning but property-owning. Betty sailed through Vassar and took Harvard courses through Radcliffe, with her eye on a doctorate in modern history.[50] The Simons owned a controlling interest in Carnegie Hall and other real estate in New York City in the 1930s.[51] Betty's brother, Robert Simon Jr., graduated from Harvard in 1935, when his father's sudden death forced him into the family's real estate firm. He rescued family property from foreclosure, as tenants were unable to pay rent, and went on to preserve and protect Carnegie Hall. Betty never forgave him for eventually selling it, and Betsey would grow up well aware of her mother's enmity.

Betsey grew up between her father's Massachusetts family and her mother's New York kin, including the Simons, Weils, and Morgenthaus. Betty and Edward persisted in creating a family beyond and apart from the Foxes and the Simons. Religion was, in practice, not the greatest difference between the families. The Foxes went to South Congregational Church in Springfield. Robert Simon Sr. attended the nondenominational, resolutely liberal Riverside Church in Manhattan. Elsa Simon took Betty and Robert to Christian Science services. However, the Simons were certainly seen as Jewish, rich, and urban by others, and the 1930s magnified those differences—all of them disconcerting to New Englanders.

Those other differences: social class, the urbanity of New York, and politics. Robert Simon Sr. wanted Tammany out but was happy to see Henry Morgenthau work with Franklin D. Roosevelt and to form connections of his own with the Roosevelts. However promising their social connections were, glamorous nights out were not often to their taste. In late February 1935, Betty's father wrote, "Friday night Mother and I were very gay— . . . Then to the Rainbow Room, if you please & ate and danced until one thirty—Beatrice Lilly was as good as usual."[52] While this night out was rare for the Simons, who preferred small dinners at their home with one or two interesting companions, it illustrates one kind of distance between the two families. Another is unexpected. Robert Simon Sr., the son of Pauline Morgenthau and Edward S. Simon, left school at fourteen to work in a ribbon factory and was fired after two weeks because he was colorblind and couldn't tell the ribbons apart. His wife's uncle Henry Morgenthau Sr. found work for him as an office boy with L. J. Phillips, a real estate investor.

Simon became a partner there at twenty-one, working with Morgenthau and emerging as an adept investor, and went on to become a firm supporter of the education he had missed.[53] Robert and Elsa Simon worked to improve public schools in New York, founding the United Parents' Association, a union of public school parents' associations in New York City, to bring parents into political debates affecting schools.[54] The Simons were solidly among the upper middle class, the *grande bourgeoisie*—albeit struggling to meet mortgage payments on their holdings by then. Robert Sr., however, had not been to Harvard. Philip Fox had, plus the Foxes' deep New England roots were priceless. Betsey's family was a dialectical conundrum, a not unusual fact in the United States at the time.

While Philip's and Agnes's mail was full of letters from friends announcing financial sorrows, Robert Simon Jr. recalled that after his father's death, his mother gave him the job of firing one of their two servants and of explaining to his siblings that there would be no inheritances at this time.[55] The Simon fortune—Robert Simon Sr. estimated mortgages held by himself and possibly a consortium of his friends at a gross value of $700 million in 1933—was in danger. Betty's father had more than a few awful nights between 1933 and his death late in 1935. Earlier in 1935 he had sent Betty a letter "which is for you & Bob in accordance with the plan we discussed." Whether he sensed his own imminent death or feared bankruptcy, we cannot know. But a few lines further down, he continued, "What care I what the future may have in store for us financially as long as we have such riches in love and affection."[56]

Robert Simon Sr. died, exhausted, in 1935. Tired enough to seek medical advice, his doctor had told him he was in "good shape" the afternoon before. Constantly busy, he admitted to Betty that he fell asleep often, having "dozed" at a concert the night before after dozing that afternoon. Then he had a meeting of the executive committee of a museum that lasted until midnight, and later in the week a photograph taken with Gladys Irene Roosevelt, wife of the president's eldest son James, at a luncheon to raise funds for the UPA. At the end of the week, he and Elsa took relatives out to dinner "at a cute little French place on E. 61st St.," after which they went on alone to see a play.[57]

The play they chose, *Rain from Heaven*, gives us a brief glimpse of how difficult it was for the elder Simons to be and not be Jewish in 1935:

> Left them to see Rain from Heaven—Jane Cowl & John Halliday. I enjoyed much of it, but the second act was "not so good." It has to do with refugees from Russia and Germany in England. There were some hard cracks by the 1/8th Jewish refugee & Mary Hemingway & her husband were a few rows back of us—You get the point n'ce pas? Lillian Wald [the activist] was there too—& of course many other people—Mother has a special fascination for picking out the mink coats worn by women who do not have the faces or the bearing to go with mink and there are many such at the (Theatre) Guild. They all have ancestors of course but not among the pilgrims or the D.A.R.[58]

The play put refugees from fascist Germany and communist Russia in an English country house, and a 1987 reviewer of a later production argued that the playwright, S. N. Behrman, had identified "the possibility of a Jewish holocaust" by 1934, when the play first opened.[59]

Robert and Elsa must have known what they would see, yet the German Jewish refugee's voice, the "hard cracks," clearly put them on edge. And Elsa had a sharp eye for women in mink who struck her as impostors. Robert echoed her. Did the Simons' respect for those with relatives "among the pilgrims" drive Betty to Edward?

Edward was precisely the sort of Protestant knight, quiet and utterly self-possessed, that Betty's parents had led her to seek. Yet his self-possession cracked a bit; he was head-over-heels in love with Betty, obsessed, writing letters morning and night, filled with poems and declarations:

> I'm affraid [*sic*] that I've been guilty of two great sins—pride & fear—& like great sins they were deep and unconscious. . . . Darling—I don't know whether it was "original sin," or "historical determinism" that made me as I was. Perhaps I was just young. Dear I think you've lost your baby—and it's about time. . . . I suddenly found that I could let you inside me—completely—where you belong.[60]

Shortly after her marriage, Betty thanked her father for a wonderful letter: "Somehow you always know how to say the thing one never dreamed anyone could say but you do." She was explaining that "the reason I'm so happy is that Ed comes so close in so many ways to the ideal which you've always been frightened of my setting up—but which seems so right now that it's come true—& so like you—in all the important ways." Robert Simon's letter about love survives, and he warned his daughter against waiting to fall in love and instead seek "character, disposition, health, then—education, a reasonable open-minded attitude toward life & one's environment, & tolerance."[61]

Betty in the 1920s

There were many boyfriends, crushes, and attractions in Betty's early days. In 1928, sailing to Europe, she gushed to her parents about her new friends: "It's been simply marvelous—awfully nice girls and boys—Princeton and Harvard—we've been going with the Princeton ones they're darling! All Colonial except one Cap and Gown."[62] The

Colonial Club and Cap and Gown were Princeton eating clubs, and she, her friends, and her parents valued those clubs and their traditions.

Bound for London in the summer of 1928, she was careful to flirt only with appropriate young Americans. At the end of one letter to her parents she added a parenthesis: "(Have you ever heard the song 'I'm in Love Again'—well I am—heaven help your poor weak daughter—the moon & the sea are a fierce combination.)"[63] But her flirting was extensive. By the time they landed in London, she had disposed of the attentions of a fellow called Larry and was telling her mother about Reese, "Princeton '30," who "said he was coming up to Vassar to see me—he's darling and *Colonial Club* which makes it marvelous." But "the one" who really interested her was "Harvard '28 and goes to Business School next yr—very good-looking."[64]

Once ashore, she described a thoughtful interlude: "Saturday morning we went to the Bodleian & had a heavenly time—It was thrilling seeing the old mss. after medieval history—everything means more now—particularly Oxford and the Cathedrals 'cause we studied them so much—We saw the first folio again." If she sounded sophomoric, that was what she was in 1928, on her way into her sophomore year at Vassar. She was earnest, and in a marginal note in the same letter told her father, "I can't get to see a factory here—I'll read about them."[65] She went to the British Museum and read some of Lord Byron's letters. She wrote to her parents, demanding their opinions on a long list of questions, including:

1. Is the U.S.A. the best country in the world—or one of the best[?]
2. Isn't the "melting-pot theory" not so bad[?]
3. Aren't politics essentially based on rottenness[?][66]

Betty concluded the letter with an eye on the 1928 election, asking for information about Al Smith and Herbert Hoover. Her father responded with dry wit: "Hoover and Smith are both preparing their acceptance speeches."[67] Meanwhile, the young women and their chaperone, a Miss Baker, visited cathedrals, castles, and museums and bought trinkets. It is worth remembering that in 1928, an equally young

Edward Fox was battling severe arthritis in Springfield, near death for several months.

Betty's mother fussed when Betty was not chosen for the daisy chain, a Vassar ritual in which a group of sophomores carried the seniors' daisy chain the day before graduation. Popularity and beauty were the criteria, being noticed by older students the point, and her mother had "made the daisy chain" years before. Betty's failure to acquiesce and be "amiable" had irked her mother since her childhood. Early letters show Betty as fierce and intelligent yet intermittently fawning toward her parents. In an extraordinary note titled "Elizabeth's Lesson," Elsa imposed her reality and her demands on Betty: "Elizabeth must learn to be kind and considered [*sic*] of people and must not say things which are not so. . . . [She] must learn to be grateful and thankful for the many things the people who love her do for her." One can almost feel the fountain pen digging into the paper as her mother continued: "Elizabeth must learn that her mother's love for her is so great that Elizabeth must feel no matter what happens, she must think lovingly and gratefully of her mother." Elsa, exasperated that Betty had said "You always want the best things" and "You kicked me," and far more concerned with her own feelings than those of her child, retaliated. Betty was to lose her "May party" and to learn "that kind thoughts must be had in one's heart and mind if one hopes to deserve love and kindness in return," words her mother might have taken to heart. The note was remorseless, and Betty carefully preserved it.[68]

Betty was something of a firecracker, with lines scribbled on her calling card in youthful handwriting: "With loads of love from your grateful daughter for all you've done to make my awful character better! I really don't mean what I say when I'm bad."[69] That was not atonement, it was revenge.[70] Schooled in Paris for a year while her parents traveled, her grades were good, especially in mathematics and ancient civilizations. She was clearly pleased with her work, enough so that she dared to decorate her letters with red, blue, and green hypotrochoid designs, even while apologizing for them. In another letter, probably written from Paris to her father—"Dearest Popsie"—she wrote, "I am trying hard to be more amiable and Aunt B. [Bianca Simon] says that I am improving."[71]

Betty in the 1930s

Long after those lessons in Paris and preparatory work at the Horace Mann School, her grades from the fall semester of her last year at Vassar were exceptional: four As and one B, in religion, history, Italian, political science, and comparative literature, respectively.[72] She was elected to Phi Beta Kappa that February, something far more significant than the daisy chain. Her father, just returning from a social engagement, replied to her letter at midnight: "Your special delivery letter had been slipped under the door. In the auto on the way down Mother told me the glorious news. I shall not attempt to express my feelings dear—it just cannot be done." It was, her father mentioned, twenty-four years to the day after he and her mother had first met, and he went on to call Betty a "fine, splendid worth while daughter." Perhaps these words eased the memory of not being amiable enough or of failing election to the daisy chain. Yet her father's four pages, carefully framing her success in his terms, reiterated the importance of sociability: "At no time did you grind for a goal to the exclusion of recreation or other college activities."[73] Betty responded by reproaching herself. After reading her parents' congratulations, she described her anxiety and shock at her election to Phi Beta Kappa, concluding, "There's one thing I'm sure of—the real reason I'm glad is because of you both—& because parents like you deserve to have worthless daughters like me do something the world thinks is good." About to graduate, she still framed herself as the bad daughter, denying herself credit for work done.[74]

Two months later, in April 1931, her father wrote with almost equal pride to tell her that one of the young men who worked for him had heard that Miss Simon had been not only quite capable but the best "looker" at a student conference at Princeton.[75] Yet, his pride in her did not extend to seeing her at the helm. When Robert Sr. died three years later, Robert Jr., barely out of college and untrained in real estate, took over the family's business. Betty would criticize her brother's handling of the family's affairs for the rest of her life.

Just before graduating from Vassar in 1931, Betty, using her father's connections, contacted Vera Micheles Dean, a foreign policy expert who had impressed Robert Simon with a speech she gave at the Economic Club of New York. Dean was a Russian émigré with a recent

Radcliffe/Harvard Ph.D., and Betty asked for help representing Italy at a Model League of Nations conference at Brown University and registering for graduate work at Radcliffe.[76] As Betty finished at Vassar, her life became a blur of classes, job interviews, plans, and life as an independent woman. Writing on Vassar stationery to her parents, she mentioned, "Dave & I slept together." She noted too that she thought she had "a chance at" a research job at American University but insisted that "I'd rather be in Moscow (I'm *quite* serious or with the Carnegie Foundation)." Mixed in were news of other dates, parties, leaving to attend a "Model League," and "tomorrow work at the World Peace Foundation." Sounding much like her father in her constant commitments, she was living to the full.[77] Then, in the summer of 1931, she chose Harvard, via the Radcliffe registration that Dean helped her arrange.

Committing to Langer

"I've been working like blazes without a break until Friday but seminar was marvelous—& afterwards Mrs Langer came and asked me to come and see her cello—then we played a perfectly lovely and very simple Corelli thing (I at the piano—) and talked for hours," Betty wrote in 1932. She took William Langer's seminar; became friends with both William and his wife, the philosopher Susanne Knauth Langer; and set her course for the next ten years. But not simply.[78]

Approaching the date of her general exams at Radcliffe, perhaps in early 1932, she applied for and got "the Parsons job," working for a young faculty member at the new Harvard sociology department, Talcott Parsons. She was tempted to abandon her general exams, the key to a master's degree, for the job. It would have paid sixty dollars a month, ten months a year, for two years, researching for Parsons. Hesitating, she went "down to see Taylor who thot the job keen but insisted I take my generals in the fall first—I said 'nuts' so we went out & smoked & talked and he said—'Your real trouble is Diplomatic History & I think you know plenty but don't know it, Go down & talk to Langer as he's the stiffest you could have & make him tell you what to expect.'" She did and was astonished to report that Langer said, "'I sort of hate to see you go out of history[.]' Well I just looked at him—I didn't think he even knew I was around—then he started talking about how busy he'd been, how he'd had all sorts of people in & had to do their work over in past years—how this year it had piled up." Langer, the rising star of Harvard's history department, had been promoted to associate professor in 1931 and taken on the revision of Carl Ploetz's *Epitome of Ancient, Medieval, and Modern History* in 1930. He asked Betty to put off accepting the Parsons job until they could talk further. She "fell over two chairs getting out—and was in a general tiz until 9 when he came." They walked, chatted, smoked, drank port, and played with kittens until at 10:30 p.m. Langer broached "this business of ours."[79]

Langer wanted a research assistant, and Betty told her parents how he described "what sections I should do—proof—publishing—other things for which I'd clean up on the research." Langer, expert in Bismarckian and later diplomatic history, had published his second book in 1931, would get out a third by 1935, and edit what would become the new *Epitome* by 1940. Betty may have worked on all of them. At ten minutes after midnight, she "staggered up the walk & stairs & phoned" her parents "as soon as I could borrow a nickel" to tell them that she was apprenticed to one of the great historians of that generation, committed to his work and to what would now be her own.[80]

Betty, fiercely independent about earning her way, was "working like the devil—getting my reading done & trying to find a job to sit on babies or something next year." She also mentioned moving in with friends, "as it'll be cheap." In October 1932 she worked on articles for something she and her father called "the Digest."[81] By 1933, while settling into her work with Professor Langer, she worked at the *New York Times*.[82]

She was committing to Langer, and to history, but her parents' lives, full of politics, also beckoned. Late in 1933 her father asked, "Were you surprised at H[enr]y Jr's going into the Treasury? You can imagine the excitement & joy in the Morgenthau family. Uncle H[enr]y & Aunt Joe went to Washington to see him sworn in." In the same letter he asked Betty about "the Russian recognition . . . the trade should prove helpful."[83] Engaged in politics, Betty wrote an urgent postcard to her parents late in 1932: "Please write to Governor A. Harry Moore not to extradite R. Burns. Know story is true through B. Matthews who knows B & his brother the minister—Please get others too—Conditions even worse than in movies & public opinion will help—Am absolutely positive of facts!! Betty" There is no mistaking the authority of her voice. Robert Burns had exposed conditions on southern chain gangs, escaped from them twice, and hoped to avoid extradition to Georgia, which was illegally pursuing him in 1932. Her family, like but unlike that of Agnes Fox, was engaged in politics. In 1933 her father told Betty that he and Elsa were "thrilled" to see their daughter Helen "casting her first vote."[84]

And then in 1934 Betty and Edward met, probably through Betty's brother Robert, in the same class at Harvard as Edward. The first surviving letter from her father to mention Edward is dated March 15 and is full of delight. By November, on the eve of her parents' first meeting with Edward, her father's letter and her reply suggested that the Simons' visit to Cambridge would be "trying for Ed." Neither explained why.[85]

Betty Married

Marriage in 1935 changed little for Betty and Edward. Betty was in the midst of her graduate work, Edward about to begin his, paid for in both cases by various assistantships. They had been inseparable before their marriage and committed to their work. What changed were matters beyond their control. Late in 1935 Betty's father died in his sleep. In 1940 they became pregnant, probably unintentionally, and Betty chucked her work, but not Edward's, for motherhood. She continued to type and research for him. Perhaps most important was the war, already real in Europe late in 1939, with fairly obvious omens before that. World War II would take Langer away from Harvard by 1941, when he headed to Washington, DC, to serve on the board of analysts in the Office of the Coordinator of Information. In 1942 he would move on to the Office of Strategic Services (OSS), precursor to the CIA, as chief of the research and analysis branch.[86]

There is no explanation in the surviving papers for Betty's decisions, only dates and facts. Every sentence we could write about her choices would begin with the word "perhaps." Upheaval abounded.

Edward would finish his dissertation in 1941 and look for jobs; he was physically unfit to volunteer for service. Friends and relatives were having babies, and Betty may have thought that she would keep working with Edward as she had been: typing, editing, researching.[87]

The life she imagined for herself may have resembled the working partnership of their friends Frank and Fritzie Manuel, noted intellectual historians. In November 1940 Edward left to do some reading at the Library of Congress and visited the couple in Washington. Betty, pregnant, stayed in New York City with her mother and kept busy identifying articles that neither Harvard nor the New York Public Library held, articles that Edward would have to read in Washington. He spent election night with the Manuels, bantering about pregnancy, delighted with Roosevelt's victory. In an odd letter from Edward that followed, he wrote, "My own Betsy," and by the second page was instructing Betty to "take care of Betsy for me (and Anne too!)."[88] What they had in mind we cannot know, but clearly the Elizabeth Ann of the old Ford was alive, and Betty was, for the duration of her pregnancy, inhabited by and sharing the persona of their unborn daughter. They seem to have been sure they were having a daughter, encouraging Edward to treat his wife as a child, not the slightly older and well-trained historian she was.

Elizabeth Ann Fox

Elizabeth Ann Fox was born in 1941 in a country on the verge of war, as her father finished his dissertation and her mother, prompted by some sort of revelation, gave up her career. It cannot have been an easy decision for Betty, but the fact that William Langer's preface to his revised edition of Ploetz's *Epitome,* published in 1940 after ten years' work as *An Encyclopedia of World History: Ancient, Medieval, Modern, Chronologically Arranged,* referred to her as a secretary responsible for tidying up loose ends may well have contributed to her revelation about motherhood.[89]

Elizabeth Fox, or Betsey Ann or B.A., as she appears in family letters, was born on the 28 May 1941, almost exactly two weeks before her father's accepted dissertation went off to the bindery. Betty had been typing the last of it six weeks earlier.[90] Agnes, indefatigable, arrived in Cambridge immediately. Betty wrote later, thanking Agnes for a letter: "It meant more to me than I can ever tell you—I reread it several times . . . since you left." Betty, unwell, had given up trying to nurse and consoled herself with how Betsey "seems to thrive on a bottle." Edward, on the other hand, was clearly a man who had finished his dissertation: "His eyes are twinkling & smiling just the way they used—I can't believe he's really free at last."[91]

Betty was still in bed, "fairly horizontal," as she reported to her father-in-law that Ed was out for supper with her mother and her sister Carol. Taking him out to eat would be Elsa Simon's usual means of helping when children were born, in contrast to Agnes, who would visit, cook, clean, and watch the children. After the next child, Betsey's brother, was born, Agnes would report to Philip: "Mrs. Simon & Carol were in here off and on and Betty sent them home, which will not add to my popularity. . . . She wanted to nurse the baby and they did not approve." But Agnes's real complaint came later, as she wrote edgily: "They came in at noon to feed and put to bed. But the dishes and washing they did not see or previous plans interfered." There is no mistaking Agnes's tone, that of a woman who has washed and wiped and cleaned for many years.[92]

When Elizabeth Fox was born, Betty was no longer the fiercely independent young woman who was thrilled to work with William Langer in 1932. Tired, typing, driven by hormonal changes, she chose to try amiable once more, rather than brilliance.[93]

2

Fitting the Child to the Childhood

A WASP, CANONICAL, AND GENDERED EDUCATION, 1941–1963

> This whole "exceptional" question is hard for me. Scared to death not to be best for fear of not being loved, scared of being best for fear of being hated.
>
> —Betsey Fox-Genovese, 29 April 1972

In 1942 when Betsey was one, Betty was struck by her daughter's ear for authority: Betty wrote to her mother that Betsey, "having observed that I got better results calling 'Ed' than she did calling 'Daddy,' . . . tried 'Daddy' once or twice & then looked at me & raised her voice & called 'Ed . . . Ed.'"[1] Betsey understood. This glimpse of her as a toddler, using her voice and choosing her words, is our only record of her until she was much older and much less sure of herself. When she traded the word "Daddy" for "Ed" she laid a foundation for her own later interest in Sigmund Freud, particularly in his description of that mythic crisis in a young girl's relations with her parents, the Electra complex.[2] Her close relationship with her father and discomfort with her mother mimicked the awkward triangle of Betty, Elsa, and Robert Simon, and probably persuaded Betsey of the importance of Freud's and Carl Jung's Electra. Derived from Sophocles, Euripides, and other ancient Greek (and later) presentations, Electra symbolized for the founders of psychoanalysis a young girl's competition with her mother for her father's attention.

Betsey's father became the rock on which she built her early life, although her mother fostered her love of literature and close reading. Betty's uncomfortable relationship with her own mother must have suggested that mothers were best kept at a distance, and fathers adored.[3] When Betsey was seven, Betty neglected to call her mother, then wrote to her: "Friday I have to have Benjamin Fine who writes educat. stuff for the *Times* & will be here for a conference. . . . I'd have phoned you Sun but by that time I thought you must be mad & didn't know what to do—I was sick about not being with you or talking to you & thot of you all day."[4] Betsey must have noticed the chasm between Betty and Elsa.

1944–1946: Washington, DC, and Ithaca

When Betty wrote that letter, Betsey was in public school in Ithaca, New York, after Edward took a teaching job at Cornell University. Two years earlier, the family had lived in Washington where her father worked in the State Department. As the war wound toward defeat of the Axis powers in 1944, Ed "left [Harvard] to seek my own adventure in the new phase of the peace." Almost undoubtedly with the help of his friend Kim Roosevelt, Betsey's godfather, he quickly found a niche for himself in the State Department as chief of a policy analysis group. The Foxes moved to the capital within two months of his appointment, but it was not just for the brief stint in the State Department that appears in Edward's vita. Following in Langer's footsteps and probably hired by Roosevelt, he was drawn into the branch of the OSS that moved to the State Department at the end of the war, as it transformed into the CIA. Although he left Washington eighteen months later, in 1946, taking the job at Cornell in French history, family recollections and the nature of his research trips to France make it abundantly clear, as his students at Cornell had assumed, that he remained a CIA officer for many years.[5]

By 1948 Betsey had a younger sister, Rebecca, born that year, as well as her brother Edward (or Teddy), closer to her in age. The family enjoyed a comfortable middle-class life, marked by education and connections in politics and, through Simon relatives, to the culture of New York City.[6] Edward was in Paris for the first time that summer, shortly after Rebecca's birth in April. Leaving Betty with Rebecca—Betsey and Teddy spent several weeks at Annisquam on Cape Ann in Massachusetts with Philip and Agnes—he enjoyed himself, writing just before his return to thank Elsa Simon for money sent and revealing what he had been observing: "The fall of the [André] Marie government is really very bad & almost certainly means trouble ahead. It is hard to understand why a people as intelligent & goodhearted as this has to make such a mess of its a[f]fairs. In all honesty much of the trouble must be attributed to the unutterable knavery of the communists & stupidity of the socialists—the latter perhaps being the more dangerous."[7] Utterly sure of himself, there is no hint here that this man was a junior faculty member. He was, instead, thinking as a Cold War liberal, assessing current political currents in France. What he was not doing was thinking as a historian and friend to leftist politics. Meanwhile, Elsa was scribbling on the back of a letter addressed to Betty: "Can B.A. use some of my ribbons for her hair or would that be sending 'coals to Newcastle'?"[8] Betsey heard both strains of concern and understood enough to tell where authority lay. She moved toward her father, probably without grasping that such work was what her mother had once intended to do as well.

Betty did not handle the change in her life from graduate student and wife to mother and wife very well. During her first pregnancy, she referred to herself as Betsy Ann, and Edward called her Betsy Ann until 1944. Edward had two Betsey Anns in his life in the early 1940s. The name "Betsey Ann" first appeared in November 1940, when Edward visited Frank and Fritzie Manuel in Virginia. Letters between Edward and Betty were frequent. Betty was doing research for him in the New York Public Library and signed her letters to him "Your Betsy Ann."[9] He replied, closing with "Be my own good Betsy. Take good care of Ann."[10]

Betty, pregnant, was no longer Betty, even though she worked through journal articles and sources of diplomatic records in three languages for Edward's dissertation, seemingly in her element. Then they named their little girl Elizabeth Ann. After the birth of their second child, Edward, Betty signed a letter to her husband "BA," the abbreviation he used for their daughter.[11] During Edward's Washington interview, Betty wrote, "I haven't made the transition of the last few years very well I guess, but I feel like your wife exclusively & it's the job I'd rather do best than anything in the world—Your Betsey Ann."[12] Betty was, if with difficulty, coming to terms with her decision, back in 1940, to quit her dissertation and work for Langer. For a while she surrendered her name as well.

Yet Betty did not give up history easily. In 1944 Edward wrote to Elsa, thankful that she appreciated the clarity of a recent book review he had written, pointing out "that a large part of the credit for that goes to your daughter."[13] Earlier, Betty had been a serious and competent research assistant, writing in November 1940, "Went thru' all the British Docs & got a general impression & 2 good quotes—Also a marvelous lead if we ever get to England & if you want to make a book of this."[14] The distance from this kind of work to baby foods was great, and Betty's comment about not making the transition well should surprise no one.

By 1945 Betty had turned her undivided, if still alloyed, attention to the children. She reported to her mother that "BA now has a full set of braces—with elastics—is getting sinus treatment & is improving I think."[15] Betty had earlier complained, while still living in Cambridge, that Betsey had been well for only twelve days out of eight and a half weeks and was to have her adenoids removed. Betty had time to take the children to doctors, entertain—Agnes and Philip came to stay for a week—and borrow a Victrola from Kim and Polly Roosevelt.[16] If Betty had the ideal of Fritzie and Frank Manuel's working partnership in view, Edward's administrative work at Harvard and intelligence work in Washington left little for her to do.

Betsey in Family and Household

In *Within the Plantation Household,* Fox-Genovese noted that planters' daughters "received much of their care from slaves," and later wrote, "manners and literacy became the earliest claims of the slaveholding mother's empire." Then, "fathers took charge of their daughters' formal education."[17] Betsey did not live that childhood, but she read those planters' letters and journals in light of her own experience: Betty read aloud to her, correcting grammar and recommending books, and at least by 1953, Edward decided on schools for his children.

There would be many schools. One source of stability became the summer weeks Betsey spent with Agnes and Philip, perhaps in

Northampton but more likely at their cottage at Annisquam on Cape Ann.[18] Agnes became a familiar relative, a source of stories about her lineage, the Whiting family, stretching back to Reverend Samuel Whiting.[19] From the ages of two through ten, Betsey visited and Agnes taught. Betsey wrote in 1992 that she "adored" Agnes, who "told me wonderful stories about the family and her own life growing up."[20] Agnes lingered in Betsey's memory, and in later years Betsey remarked that she thought she might have liked Agnes because her father had insisted on it.[21] Yet, reaching for a church in the 1990s, Betsey snubbed the Protestants, and neither Agnes nor Edward would have appreciated her Catholicism.

Ithaca, Princeton, and Europe

As Betsey turned nine, the family left Ithaca for Princeton, where Edward had a fellowship at the Institute for Advanced Study. It allowed him to spend part of 1951–52 in Europe, and the family followed. In all, they had six months abroad. Betsey turned ten while Betty drove her and Teddy "on a number of trips to England, Wales, Italy, Belgium, and Holland."[22] It was the first time Betty had been back since the war and the Holocaust.

Betty kept a notebook, filling thirty-five pages with the names of hotels, restaurants, and pubs and details about landscapes, stately homes, cliffs, friends, and relatives who joined them occasionally, and a few notes on what the children did. Like Agnes in Florida, she seemed to want to keep every moment for herself; unlike Agnes, she showed little of herself in her notes, cataloging the same respectable sights she had seen as a young woman. Nonetheless, the small notebook does reveal how much pleasure she took in driving almost every day, visiting places she had seen before, calling on friends, absorbing towns and countryside as they were before advertising and the tourist industry changed them. Her sister Helen and other Simons appeared briefly, as they often had during her European travels before her marriage and World War II. Betty introduced her children to Britain and reclaimed herself as a worldly person.

This was Betsey's first venture abroad. On April 16, 1952, she had her "first fish and chips" at St. Ives. Betty noted that it was "picturesque out of season—probably *awful* in," and that Teddy, riding home in a convertible that belonged to friends, was a "block of ice."[23] Shortly after, on the 18th, they visited Tintagel and the recently built King Arthur's Hall, where a Mr. Blake "talked w/ us and gave the children shields he'd made—Round table—Excalibur etc.—lunch at dairy out in sun."[24]

The notebook is exhausting to read. There were ponies on Dartmoor and tea at the thatched cottages in Bickleigh. Cornwall and Devon figured largely, while Scotland got about thirty-six hours of their attention. Betsey and Teddy "learned God Save the Queen & about cricket." They met up with their father in London at the end of April. They had tea at Selfridge's department store, and Betty "found BA's skirt & slacks." They watched Elizabeth II enter Buckingham Palace for the first time as queen and toured a grand Elizabethan house, Betty writing that they had gone "up further stairs found by children who found skeleton of woman in cavelier [*sic*] boots—secret stairs & doors." At another stop, "T & BA sat in Victoria's coach." Betty took Betsey to Knutsford, the village Elizabeth Gaskell used as a model for her novel *Cranford:* "Shopped & walked around . . . w/ BA & listened to gossiping women." Teddy seems to have missed Knutsford.[25]

It was a detailed, personal tour, reminding one of the expatriate Americans who lived comfortably all over Europe before World War II. Betty had been raised to be worldly, Edward quickly learned to be, and they encouraged their children to live much as cosmopolitan Americans had in the 1920s and 1930s.[26] The big difference, as Ed and Betty knew well, was the Cold War and the shadow of the Holocaust. Betty's rapid buzzing back and forth across Britain in 1952 replicated her wide-ranging tour after her first year at Vassar, when she roamed Britain and some of the continent, finding friends and relatives everywhere. Postwar Europe, however, was different, particularly so for Jewish families that no longer had networks of relatives in place. They did get across the English Channel to Belgium, Holland, and Italy but went no further east, despite Betty's perfect command of German.

A rare surviving letter from Betty to Betsey suggests that Betty wrote serious, which is to say literary, letters to her daughter:

> I miss you but now I can tell you because I'll see you soon. I miss you when I find an old Puffin or when I see a watermelon (½) all ripe in

> the market & wish I could buy it for you or when I see 2 little girls on a Sunday afternoon sitting in the corner of a narrow Paris street and one is about 6 and cutting the hair of the other who is about 4—and I'm sure neither mother knows a word about it. . . . Meanwhile I work for Daddy & have been to a couple of movies.[27]

Another letter, written seven months earlier, suggesting that Betsey did not join her parents immediately, reminds us that she taught Betsey what it meant to be a woman of letters:

> Dear Betsey,
>
> There certainly is a resounding silence from your side of the Atlantic. However, I forgive you for not writing very often because that means you've got too many other things to do, and if you've got so many other things to do, you're very busy, and if you're really very busy and have so many other things to do, that means you're very happy, and if you're happy, that makes me very happy, and if we are both very . . . well, one way or another it works itself out.[28]

Planning Betsey's Education

Ed, the chief architect of Betsey's education, left a trail of letters and records about and from the schools to which he sent Betsey, Teddy, and Rebecca. Writing in 1960, well after Betsey had been away at several private schools, he complained about the "manifest and all but universal deterioration of our educational standards." Continuing, he amplified his complaint: "It hurts when it forces you to send children away from home and the public schools of a university community to get a reasonable preparation for college." For a young man from Central High School in Springfield, Massachusetts, Ed's plans for his children were ambitious, and there is perhaps more of the Simon to them than the Fox. By 1953 Edward was unwilling to bear with the Ithaca schools.[29]

Those schools were ultimately in good company, because not many were acceptable to Ed and Betty. As Betsey and Teddy verged on secondary school age in 1956, their parents turned down Abbot Academy, separate from Phillips Academy but essentially its girls' annex, for Betsey, and Deerfield Academy for Teddy, settling instead on what were arguably the two best private schools in the country at that time: Concord Academy for Betsey and Phillips Exeter for Teddy. Ed wrote to a friend, complaining: "Of course, what we really want is a small New England school without the trimmings, but the ones that are left seem either to have gone up into something fancy or down into something deplorable."[30]

Ed's secular Calvinism was never clearer than in his choices of schools, and before Betsey entered Concord Academy, she would be sent to North Country School and Collège Cévenol. When Edward and Betty inquired about North Country School, they were reassured by a friend of a friend that the teaching in English and Latin was good enough to get their son through his first year at Phillips Exeter with honors. Their correspondent added, "My wife and I were won to the School in spite of our allergy to most 'progressive education.'"[31] So we know what Ed sought: he wanted a canon-bound education for his children but, in keeping with his own illness, a disciplined physical rigor as well. The Latin was well-taught; the skiing, hiking, art, and riding healthy; and the shared work of cooking and cleaning demanded discipline.

North Country School, 1953–1955

And it was progressive, after a fashion. Ed and Betty found it acceptable even so; they placed a deposit by the first week in August 1953. Teddy had already been at the associated Camp Treetops that summer, so it was a familiar spot, earthy and about 180 miles away in Lake Placid.[32] The school was a bit like a Shaker community and even more like a Waldorf school, integrating work, life, study, and nature. Along with academic subjects, Betsey as a seventh grader fed chickens, dug ditches, skied, knitted, painted, practiced piano, and explored the Adirondacks. Because it was quite small, supervision and reporting on student development were far more detailed than at most schools. Both Edward and Betty were the products of determined, interventionist parents, and it would be Betsey's challenge to survive even more intense attention.[33]

On September 12, 1953, Betsey began her first year at North Country School. The director, Walter Clark, sent a note to her parents soon after, describing her as "a strong, lively, natural girl" who was happy to be there. French lessons, he wrote, were unfortunately impractical, as Betsey would have to give up either typing or piano for them, and Ed and Betty agreed that she would have informal lessons at home during vacations. They were hoping to be in France within a year or two and wanted Betsey "to get into school there without undue difficulty."[34] She shared a large room with four other girls, one of whom spoke more French than English, and Betsey was assured, in a handwritten note sent out before the start of the term, of "lots of closet space." Also, as the bulletin noted, the corn and pumpkins were ripening, 150 cockerels had been slaughtered and frozen, a new horse had been added to the string, and a new piano teacher had been hired. There is no indication of what Betsey made of this, but corn, lots of mud around campus, and slaughtering chickens must have been utterly alien to her.[35]

Clark's impression notwithstanding, Betsey was not happy. The director's first report to Ed and Betty was carefully phrased: "Working with Betsy [*sic*] is a real challenge and a privilege." She had "tremendous strength and ability." But she was not happy or comfortable. She lied, stole candy, hid her own, and took on the management of the chickens but then failed to give them food or water, although she typed out a lengthy treatise on chicken management. Egg production suffered until adults discovered the problem. She was, to paraphrase her housemother, scornful and unkind to children her own age, repulsed by them or afraid to be associated with their immaturity. With adults, according to Clark, she was poised, pleasant, and understanding, but she lied to them and refused to do her share of housekeeping.[36]

The director and housemother felt that Betsey did not know how to be a twelve-year-old girl, could not admit to making mistakes, and worried too much about what adults thought of her. Caught in transition between what her parents expected of her at home and the very different expectations of the school staff and children, not to mention the chickens, she was left struggling.[37] She used to joke that she was her father's oldest son, pressed into a precocious maturity. In 1992 she wrote, "My father talked seriously to me from about the time I was two years old, and being taken seriously had a lasting influence."[38] But perhaps not a comfortable one. No wonder the director noted "how clever she was in covering up her shortcomings with the most convincing front."[39] She endured. Many years later she wrote, "I loved to read myself to sleep at night for as long as I can remember. (I think I survived many camps and boarding schools because I believed that you could get through anything if you had a good book and a chocolate bar for first thing in the morning and before you went to sleep.)"[40]

Her English instructor commented that Betsey preferred to read the same books over and over, rather than anything new. Her best subjects that semester were mathematics, science, and, fitfully, piano. In English and social studies she did enough to get by. There was more to North Country, however. Betsey enjoyed skiing and worked with hand tools, clay, and felt in shop, fine arts, and crafts classes. She was an intelligent listener in music appreciation, showed some skill at soccer, and did well at bridling and saddling horses but was "stiff and tense" when she got on one. She slept out one night and hiked a difficult trail on Pitchoff Mountain in the Adirondacks. Not all was fraught, but the marks of her serious upbringing were evident in her first few months at North Country. When she was home, Edward habitually woke her before sunrise to discuss books. Betty read to her from serious literature, exposed her to stories about women, and helped her select books.[41]

In the next report, from May 1954, Betsey emerged as "a genuinely honest, sincere, dependable person" who "has found a satisfaction and happiness which is wonderful to see in her." The director suggested that she should skip one or two years of high school. A standardized test had just ranked her at grade 12.3, and she would begin first-year high school work in the fall. Learning came easily; happiness perhaps not. Too much of it was built on meeting others' expectations, which she was certainly doing at school. I was never present at one of her later lectures without Betsey asking immediately afterward if she had "been good enough?" Precisely the "strength and ability" her teachers had noted in the fall of 1953 would have put subterfuge well within her grasp.[42]

Betsey continued to excel in math and science and now paid attention in the general music class, practiced piano diligently, and showed occasional "brilliant flashes of talent" but could not play when asked, or for others. Skiing and riding interested her; team sports, which she tried, did not. She addressed envelopes for the school's office, helped with the class newspaper, played jacks, traded cards, visited with friends in their rooms, tried basketball, knitted a pair of mittens, camped out, swam, and watched birds. She continued to work with the chickens, and she continued to have trouble with them, leaving the eggs in her locker, not the pantry. Her control of food, both the eggs and her candy, hint at the anorexia to come and underline the possibility that her glowing reports were more stagecraft than development.[43]

By the midpoint of her second year, Walter Clark wrote, "I don't know that a more glowing report on any child has ever gone out of our office. She is a truly amazing girl—highly sensitive and able . . . socially strong, popular and happy, and to top it off, a beautiful, delightfully charming girl." Nonetheless, "she sometimes exhausts herself out of her sheer enthusiasm for living and doing." In the director's words, Betsey "works at a higher emotional pitch than most of us realize."[44] By the end of her time at North Country, Clark observed with some joy, "Betsey is becoming more relaxed and more at ease. On a recent weekend, she spent the better part of half a day just loafing and chatting with a group of girls. We had never before seen her do this."[45]

To put this afternoon of loafing in perspective, consider what Betsey had mastered by the end of her second year's subjects: she did well in algebra, although she no longer led the math class; she was an excellent writer, outstripping her classmates in her poetry and essays; she took the lead in social studies; she mastered Latin I; she slipped to "good" in science; she was serious about her music and quite good at the piano, with a preference for the baroque; she abandoned shop and crafts for fine arts, and her instructor called her designs "powerful." Betsey continued to love skiing, took to track, enjoyed the jumps, threw a discus well, and was quite good in softball. She did her share of the work as headwaiter in the morning, as well as getting hay for the horses, cleaning one of the classrooms, and helping with the sugaring that spring. She headed the student council, planned student parties, played canasta and chess, was learning bridge, and put in "many extra hours on her music." These first two years away from home were hard, and Betsey established two patterns. First, food mattered, a sort of barometer of something she did not name. Second, in childhood her best subjects, intermittently, were math, science, and music. As they were displaced by history and literature, the scientist in her would survive through her attention to political economy and in her exhaustive knowledge of cooking, computers, and baseball. If her interest in the humanities was driven by her parents, it was probably abetted by awareness of the fields most likely to tolerate women in the 1960s.[46]

Collège Cévenol

As Betsey put it, "The year at College Cevenol [in Le Chambon-sur-Lignon, in the Auvergne region of France] was very important, primarily because it was so demanding. French Huguenots are a tough breed and ask as much of others as they ask of themselves."[47] Betsey and Ted—no longer Teddy—left New York in June 1955 with their father, spending the summer in boarding schools in Arveyes in the Swiss Alps while Edward settled in Paris. Betty and Edward had planned everything, including their return to the states in a year: Betsey had visited and been accepted at Concord Academy, outside Boston, and they had applied to Phillips Exeter for Ted.[48]

Cévenol, like North Country School, was yet another tough school in a cold climate. The boys' dormitory had no heat; the girls' did. Founded in 1938 by French Protestants, it was located in a region long associated with Protestant resistance to Catholic oppression, and locals had protected thousands of Jewish refugees during World War II. Begun by pacifists as an educational experiment based on nonviolence, cooperation, and internationalism, the school only offered classes in the French language. Betsey had to be fluent, not merely for conversation but for algebra, geometry, history, French literature, geography, and more. She did well in English and algebra, then French, geography, and history, with a bit of physics, geometry, and chemistry. Instructors noted in March that she worked hard and was a "bonne élève." By May she was also doing very well in physics.[49] In an undated letter she told her father, "I wouldn't leave if [Ted] did because I am having fun and *do* need to do the work for Concord!" Ted was unhappy, spirited, and probably unwilling to accept the discipline, not to mention the lack of heating in the boys' dormitory. Betsey worked hard and wrote to her father about her work.[50]

In one letter, she congratulated Edward: "You win about 'the ode to a Grecian Urn!'" And then she asked about Algeria, adding, "that's all anyone talks about these days. What is going on there?" She had landed in France early in the summer of 1955, eight months after the Algerian War began to fill the newspapers. Curious, she asked her father, "Can something be done about it or is France going to lose it?" With hindsight, it is now clear that France would "lose it," but that was not obvious then. Algeria was a small harbinger of the world in which Betsey would become an adult, but then Algeria gave way in Betsey's letter to one last, pressing question: "What do you think about my drinking French cider? Do you want me to or not and if so how much?" One other aspect of Betsey's and Ted's lives at Cévenol is worth noting. Presumably both children kept—although only Ted's survive—careful running accounts of their expenses. One of Ted's accounts, sent to his father in May 1956, lists pocket money, tea, food, cakes, pants clips, a brake cable, lost cash, money lent to Betsey, and a few more expenses. The tidy list on lined paper was included in a note to his father, estimating expenses for the remainder of the term, train fare back to Paris, and laundry, which together Ted estimated at 11,000 francs, or $31 in 1956.[51]

They were aware of money, of costs, and of the care they should take in judging their needs. They were not denied: Ted wrote enthusiastically to his father, describing the kind of bicycle he would like and later telling his father that Betsey would like one as well. But they were clearly expected to be aware of the cost of everything. Betty deferred to Edward in paying bills and making purchases. Ed's early training showed in Agnes's lists of the prices she paid for oranges, dishes, meat, and vegetables in Florida in 1929. A tiny slip of paper survives, printed neatly by Edward, on his notepaper, giving Ted a format for his accounts: "Spent: Date, Amount, Balance." Underneath, Ted had filled in a few expenses from his 1955 Christmas holidays in lira, suggesting a family trip to Italy.[52] By then, Betty had joined Edward in Paris, and seven-year-old Rebecca was in school at Sainte Marie des Invalides.[53]

Much of what we know about Betsey at Collège Cévenol comes from the postcards she sent to her mother in autumn 1955. Many of her early messages were about warmer clothes, classes, teachers, and pocket money for the after-class snack—*goûte*—which she shared with friends. On August 20, she wrote her first letter to her mother in French, a schoolgirl's letter, carefully phrased, very social. But she was clearly impressed with herself even as she asked her mother, still in French, to please excuse her errors. As she settled in, she reported "oodles of devoirs," or homework, and asked her mother to send particular food for *goûte:* "bisquits," jam, butter, Nescao (a chocolate drink), and "Dijon mayonnaise in a tube." And perhaps best of all, she could announce to Betty: "You remember that I said the girls weren't nice to me? Well now they want me to do things with them and I have *goûte* with them here now (Janine has special provisions)." On October 12, she wrote, "I really love it here!" She needed a duffle coat with buttons, not toggles, and was terribly pleased when a senior teacher gave them "tea in the bureau" and let them play records. Betsey did well in math, especially algebra, sometimes geometry, and Latin. She wrote, "I'm doing my Bible for Concord in my spare time, which isn't much, we have tons, literaly [*sic*] tons of *devoir.*"[54]

She was happy, although as October wore on she wrote anxiously, asking Mummy and Daddy to visit for a week, not just a few days. As at North Country School, their visits were rare and short. They came early in November, staying for one night. Betsey asked them to bring "biscottes & those *delicious cookies,*" her black loafers, and a green jumper. In November she celebrated a "divine Thanksgiving" and thanked her mother for snow boots. Her best grades were in Latin and algebra, her worst in French, and she was consistently better in her spoken than her written work. She labored at the French, and she was often ill: swollen glands, stomach complaints, a sprained finger, colds.

It was not an easy year, yet her frequent cards to her mother convey a strong impression of a happy, active fourteen-year-old, turning fifteen as she left in the spring. She planned to take piano and modern dance and spent much of her spare time in the spring learning to play guitar. She wrote about skis and ski equipment and frequently told her mother how much she enjoyed her cards and letters. She lived well, worked hard, traveled, learned. She found that her bond with her mother was always a negotiation, made out of words and sealed with gifts: snow boots, raspberry jam, a duffle coat.[55]

1956 in Concord

The year at Collège Cévenol prepared her for Concord Academy. Newly under the headship of Elizabeth B. Hall, a historian by trade, Hall was in the midst of transforming Concord into one of the best academies in the country. She was quirky and energetic. Her own patchwork academic past—she graduated from Radcliffe as an older adult—demonstrated that she knew the difficulties of higher education for women. The four letters and one or two expense accountings of Betsey's that survive from Concord show a mature young woman in her last year there, writing polite and cheerful notes to her mother and collegial, far longer letters to her father. Betty was thanked for food and asked for money: "I called Polly last night and I'm going to stay with her at Smith next weekend. I need $25 air mail special delivery. You can tell Daddy I'll keep accounts and send him the remainder but I need money for train fare, subsequent transportation food (we have to pay for all our meals) etc." Betty also received a smoking permission slip, with a request that it be sent back by return mail, and a careful last word: "Tell Daddy I won't smoke much at all; if I did I'd stop." She would come to smoke incessantly, stopped only by multiple sclerosis.[56]

Other than that, she mentioned playing tennis with seniors, which was significant in that highly stratified world because Betsey had been advanced from junior to senior in the summer of 1957. Elizabeth Hall wrote to Edward, explaining, "We were forced to put her in senior classes all along the line. There seemed to be no other way to give her the academic program she needs. . . . When it became apparent that she would have all her classes with seniors it seemed to us impossible to rank her any longer as a Junior."[57] Hall defended her decision, noting, "Betsey seems to have grown a lot since I saw her last and so I no longer have the fears for her social adjustment that I had formerly." Nonetheless, Edward, unconvinced of Betsey's maturity, decided that she should postpone college for a year and use the year she had gained to take his classes at Cornell and live at home. He reported to Hall that Betsey had been "a most satisfactory member of the family" during the summer but also "vulnerable to the social sophistication of the girls and boys of the community who were a few months her senior."[58]

Betsey was growing up. She was sixteen that summer, Rebecca was nine, and they were on their own in Ithaca while her father worked in England and her mother visited Ted at Phillips Exeter Academy. Friends in Ithaca provided dinners, and Betsey went out on a date with "an Ithaca boy who is Cornell Pre-Med (dean's list)." Betsey was careful to point out that he was a good driver, responsible. She also noted that she would be "in early" and that a sitter named Liz would stay until Sunday morning. More to the point, she seemed to be occupying her father's Cornell office and acting as his steward: "Moyer was in today and he really is an odd duck—wanted to know how much he was going to have to work—ha! ha! I tried to gently warn him." And then, "Sandy [Elwitt] is trying to be very officious & take over the whole office & 103 & 401 & your mail. We discussed this—I was quiet, dignified & firm and now he knows that Dick is doing 401, I'm doing the office—he is doing 103."[59] Presumably the numbers refer to courses that her father would not teach while away. A sixteen-year-old daughter handling her father's graduate students would certainly pass for maturity in the twenty-first century but for the fact that she was addressing her father as Uncle Rover and signing this and other letters as Fido: trusting, in Latin, like a good puppy.

Sanford (Sandy) Elwitt, her father's graduate student in modern French history, who later would be a colleague of Betsey's at the University of Rochester, compelled Betsey to detail

> a long argument I had with him as to whether one could be a good historian and still believe so firmly in Judaism that it made one "hot under the collar" to read about Catholicism in the Middle Ages, or to read Aquinas or Maritain. He wouldn't listen to me when I told him that he couldn't write history without these prejudices showing through. At the end of the argument (1½ hrs worth) he told me that you had argued the same thing with him. Just like my father again![60]

Before the exclamation point, she drew the head of a small dog, presumably Fido.

Betsey became dependent on her father, despite references to dates and boyfriends. She told Edward in 1957 that his office was full of books "I have to & want to read. I really must come back & study with you."[61] She had gotten good grades on three papers she had worked on with him the year before at Concord, asked him for a reading list, and mentioned that she was really enjoying Vera Brittain (presumably her World War I memoir from 1933, *Testament of Youth*, or successor testaments). Yet she had another voice, not that of Fido at all: "The more I think of it the more I don't want to go to Bryn Mawr but I suppose I'd better. Buzz Eberly (the Ithaca girl there) transferred out & the Cardozas met a brilliant beautiful girl who'd had some years in a French school who hated it. Encourageant, n'est-ce pas? I don't mean to end on such a grim note—I'm sure it will be 'good for me.'"[62] Bryn Mawr, like much of her education, was her father's choice, although it was a wise one. She applied to Radcliffe and Bryn Mawr, was admitted to both, and perhaps in deference to her father, enrolled in the latter. Much later she would write,

> Looking back, I think that Bryn Mawr was decisive. I had a number of extraordinary professors who took me seriously, stretched my mind, and encouraged me. . . . But, above all, I still believe that, in my generation, had I gone to Radcliffe instead of Bryn Mawr I would have been engaged or married by the time I graduated. A woman's college simply gave me more space and encouragement to develop my own talents.[63]

Betsey's teachers' reactions to her at Concord are useful. Her tenth grade English teacher wrote, "I am concerned at times by her ease in verbalizing about a subject without anchoring her ideas in facts." Her history teacher noted, "She still cares a great deal about her performance and still tends to think of the 'grade' as an end in itself." Her "native ability" and the "superficial maturity which travel and European schooling have given her" worked against focus, depth, and discipline. She was concerned with others' expectations. In November 1956 her advisor wrote, "Betsey's potential capacity merely makes more graphic what is less noticeable in the student of average ability." She was quick and ambitious to do well.[64]

Moving up a grade early at Concord appeared a success: "Betsey seems to thrive on work and enjoys the pressure of many demands," and she relished her choices.[65] She had, as she told her father in a brief note, decided to replace the usual senior history course with math. She did well, although her instructor reported that she was so quick in reasoning that she made errors of calculation. Her best class in her last year at Concord, however, was biology. She so impressed a Miss Morse, who was one of the best teachers in the school, with her enthusiasm, maturity, comprehension, and thoroughness, that Morse scrawled this final comment: "I do hope Betsey will go into 'the sciences.' She has done *superior work*."[66]

Betsey tried. She applied to a special program that summer at the Worcester Foundation for Experimental Biology, won a scholarship, and attended. Her parents declined to attend the closing dinner and probably had little interest in the program.[67] With this background, it is easy to appreciate the brief lines in her letter to Betty enclosing the smoking permission slip: "I'm having a wonderful time. I looked at hydras under a mic. in Bio today."[68] Her interest in math and science never left her, but it was displaced.

Edward's need for control never left him either. On the account Betsey submitted to him of money received and spent in January 1957, her last semester at Concord, he carefully noted the date on which he received the slip of paper and then made corrections on it with a finely sharpened red pencil. He no doubt believed that he was teaching her rudimentary accounting and attention to detail, but he also left a memorial to his expectations: her carefully ruled pencil lines superimposed on lined notebook paper, with double lines every six or seven lines; explicit categories that he probably expected to see repeated every month; and on the back a list of each purchase that fell under "Extras." Next to "1.00 for mints for Mrs. Smith" is the one line of text written against the lining on the paper: "Detailed account of what I spent your money on."[69]

There may not have been a hint of defiance in that line when it was written, but there should have been. It is starkly reminiscent of British feminist Millicent Garrett Fawcett's recognition that the money in her purse was legally the property of her husband, not hers. Fawcett was shocked by the insight, and it led her to agitate for property rights for married women. But why is this remnant of the life of a mid-nineteenth-century feminist relevant to the life of a young woman, legally a dependent, in 1957? Because it is not pleasant to have one's dependence rubbed in one's face, and Ed, having been quite dependent as a young man, wished to savor being on the other side of the equation as his child moved rapidly and successfully through years that had been difficult for him. And perhaps those accounts explain in part Betsey's pleasure in "verbalizing about a subject without anchoring her ideas," because she lived with constant anchors, constant demands for facts.[70]

Before Bryn Mawr

Betsey entered Bryn Mawr College in the fall of 1959, graduating in 1963. It was the most intellectually demanding of the Seven Sisters colleges. She never forgot her work there with "Isabel MacCaffrey in English, Felix Gilbert and Caroline Roberts in History, Mabel Lang in Greek Literature in Translation, Dorothy Marshall as my Dean, Mario Maurin in French."[71] In that biographical sketch she wrote in 1992, she said nothing about the year she spent at home, taking her father's History 103 and 104 courses at Cornell. She was assigned to Sanford Elwitt's discussion section for 103 and showed little interest in memorizing Greek, Hebrew, and Roman terms. A year earlier she had been arguing with Elwitt about his religious beliefs interfering with his ability to write history; now she was being graded by him in what would seem an awkward arrangement. But perhaps it paid off. She did write to her father from Bryn Mawr in the fall of 1960: "103–4 is coming back to me this year as wonderful background. It is an excellent course, Daddy!"[72] Betsey, in other words, was taking the same courses her father, and before him William Langer, had taken at Harvard and now taught, the same courses her mother had taken at Vassar—the canonical Western education. Betsey would defend that canon, with the addition of writings by women and people of color, Western and beyond, until the additions threatened to swamp the ancients. She also studied German, completing the languages trifecta that had made Betty so valuable to Langer.[73]

At Bryn Mawr, although a women's college, her path lay in her reliance on her father. Her interest in science took a back seat. Instead, she discussed a wide range of subjects interesting to her father, including Cornell office politics, how her instructors dealt with various schools of interpretation, the moment at which she understood that literary criticism was interpretive, not factual. Yet most of her letters seem preoccupied with detailed accounts of money spent and requests for more, often with apologies for the cost of books or food. She assured her parents that she was not overworking and was eating well.

The letters are deceptively simple, but there is an edge to them that suggests more beneath the surface. They were painstakingly written, and in reporting every penny spent, Betsey revealed much to her father about where she was and what she did: bus fare for a weekend away, lunch at this or that restaurant, every book bought at the beginning of a semester.[74] Sometimes she included receipts, justifying her expenses. Edward expected these accounts every month, and without them he would not have sent her monthly allowance. It was a short leash, but Betsey, at both Concord and Bryn Mawr, encountered many young women who had more money than she did, and perhaps he wished to impress on her the older theme of bourgeois virtue as opposed to the wealth and display of the elite. He referred to "Society" disparagingly to Elizabeth Hall, the headmistress at Concord Academy, and she had concurred: "Reflection since our conversation has made me wonder more and more if your fears about Betsy's social involvement (with a capital S) via C. A. is not really at bottom responsible for your urgent wish to move her ahead in school, perhaps more so than you realize. I can sympathize with you so strongly in your desire to keep clear of Society."[75]

Edward feared the influence of others over Betsey, even as his palpable control of the money in Betsey's pocket was also meant to teach self-control. Old New England families had cherished discipline and frugality as they made their bourgeois revolution. Agnes Fox and Edward taught these values to Betsey, and when Betsey came to study these ideas near their point of origin in eighteenth-century political economy, she would be in familiar territory. Yet, she also would rebel, later in life constantly lamenting her compulsion to spend unnecessarily.

As a sophomore, Betsey described working with Felix Gilbert. She was a bit mystified by his course, for he had "just plunged into sources and documents, and to me this suggests that he presupposes a chronological framework." Initially puzzled, she concluded that the course "was really fun." She preferred heavy workloads and long reading lists; she disliked a professor who was "coy and whimsical." She decided to spend her junior year in France, wished to go independently, and a year in France was "the only plan which makes sense in the light of any job I might want, or graduate school," she told her father.[76] Her surviving letters at this time are to her father, and she signed herself "your devoted Fido." She apprenticed herself to her father until she left for France.

Betsey worked too hard at Bryn Mawr, perhaps knowing that her father thought her bright but certainly not brilliant. When she was at Concord, he had argued for more work, harder work, and higher standards, writing that she only overcame weakness "when she has been most taxed by quantity & quality of demands." Betsey absorbed this, writing to her father from Bryn Mawr: "Please, convince Mummy that I'm not likely to work too hard—the real danger lies in my not working enough." She also tried to please her father by scrimping, reporting to Edward in 1960, "I haven't bought anything for my history courses. I spend industrious evenings in the library."[77] And then there was food, another expense: "The food is just for things Mummy wants me to eat. I haven't missed a meal in the dorm except for weekend breakfasts. This is all extra." On another occasion she noted that the dorm food was "inedible" and that her mother had offered to pay for better food.[78]

More contentious than money were her relationships with men. Betty and Edward seemingly had little memory of their own impulsive attraction, and they, or perhaps only one of them, flew into a rage over someone named Howie, Betsey's boyfriend the year before she left for France. Her calm response to them suggests that she was well-practiced in standing her ground:

> As for Howie I wish you and Mummy would trust me a little. I am silly sometimes, yes, but I am not quite as young as you seem to think. I am not going steady, nor have I the foggiest intention of getting married. I am just beginning to get excited about graduate school. Last semester was the first time I have been anywhere near feeling any academic control or having any sense of what I might do if I worked. I am not going out with other people, not on principle, but because there is no one else around. I spend more time working than dating these days—believe it or not! . . . Please give me some credit. I am growing up, and I have thought a fair amount about what I am doing. Daddy, I am working hard, I am happy, I am not planning to get married. There is nothing desperately immature in the life I lead.[79]

It was a manifesto from a nearly adult sophomore daughter, signed "B. A.," not Fido. But she appended the word "woof!" next to the signature, then added two postscripts, both signed Fido. Old habits died hard.

Edward had never had to defend himself, his academic choices, or his infatuation with Betty—at least not in surviving letters to his parents. Neither is it simply a matter of male prerogative, for Betty also moved through her college and graduate school years unleashed and uncorrected. They had been different in the 1930s, and their expectations, especially Edward's, were now baroque.

The Institut d'Études Politiques de Paris

Her parents' fears about men, marriage, and her career came to a head during the junior year Betsey spent abroad in France. She began a journal calmly enough on 7 December 1961: "Starting a journal has, somehow, an air of presumption. There should be an event, a beginning, a new love: something monumental, in short, to justify an undertaking of this sort. But there is no such reason now. Simply, Daddy asked me yesterday if I was keeping a journal of my reading, and suggested that if not I should begin one."[80] She immediately plunged into dutiful summaries of her reading, beginning, "Sartre says in *L'Age de Raison* that. . . ." By January 23 this exercise had worn thin, and she wrote, "I am turning this into a personal journal. It is time that I kept some record of my thoughts and tried to impose some order and discipline on my existence. The vagueness, the shapelessness of my thoughts is not only frustrating, it is frightening."[81]

Whether the discontent and dissatisfaction that followed were those of an ambitious undergraduate or of a truly lost young adult is not clear. Betsey recorded, "I shrink from writing" and "I am going on 21 and have done nothing." Neither sentence seems remarkable at the age she was. She read Simone de Beauvoir, Albert Camus, Marcel Proust, Jean-Paul Sartre, and at twenty was not like them. She worried that she was not a good friend, that she was "moping" and thinking too much of herself—and we might see little unusual in it. But she told us more: she wished for structure, for absolutes. She found writing "difficult" and almost "impossible" and concluded, "and yet I must write." She was torn between continuing at Sciences Po, as the Institut d'Études Politiques has been known for years, and reading on her own, perhaps only in literature. She had "attained a new degree of freedom in the course of this year" and wished "to free myself from the mess of my adolescence."[82]

And then, on January 24, she hit upon something important. She had been, she thought, living "largely in relation to other people" but now lived alone. From her new position in Paris—even with her father and mother apparently coming by at intervals—she saw her parents at a distance: "Daddy is undoubtedly a comfort, but I can't bear to have him tell me what to do, and I am frightened of remaining too dependent on him morally and intellectually. On the whole, the thought of Mummy, and particularly her presence makes me very uncomfortable. . . . If only she could let me go gracefully, without the necessity of more fights."[83] By the next day she was admitting to bridling at her mother, writing, "My feelings toward her are hostile. Perhaps that is too strong. Nevertheless I don't trust her." Betty, she thought, "loves me, but she has no sense of privacy." Later, former students would say that Betsey in turn lacked that sense. Her father was no more comforting. She wrote, "Nor do I know how to deal with Daddy whom I want to trust," adding, "I don't know if he repeats our conversations to her [Betty]—as she said this afternoon he did. . . . I am much too prone to visualizing a relationship between us which in some sense excludes her."[84]

She was alone, was no longer in love with Howie, cried when talking to her parents, and still needed her father's approval.[85] Thoroughly self-critical by late January, she turned resolute: "I am not rich and my purpose in life is not to be a clothes horse. I must learn to live with people who have more than I do." She worried, as she would continue to do throughout her life, that she spent too much money on clothes, boasted, competed. She was becoming an adult, taking up space in the world, and fearful that she was too visible, too loud, too prone to argument. She was, she wrote, insecure and wondered if the root was her "total lack of success as a child."[86] She was too big, too loud, and yet too small, too poor, too insecure. Only Alice in Wonderland changed size so rapidly.

In February her father's work disrupted hers, but by the 12th she was "settled in at the Beaujolais and again have the privacy necessary to keeping a journal." She was making progress. She described brother Ted as her ally "on the side of those who '*mettent tout en question*.'"[87] She visited more often, and happily, without self-critical rants. And on February 15 she wrote about a party: "I really met Jacques there (which I had been wanting to for a long time . . .) and miraculously enough we seemed to get on very well. We talked together most of the evening, and then he brought me home. And I think he liked me (smiley face drawn) I hope so."[88] Making her way into a new life, Betsey finished that entry: "I feel good. I love the Beaujolais & having really and truly a home of my own." The journal ends at that point, with a quotation from Proust's *In the Shadow of Young Girls in Flower.*[89]

She found Jacques Toyou, fell in love, and considered marriage. She spent the academic year at Sciences Po and remained in France during the summer of 1962. In August she was traveling with the Toyous and sent her father a postcard with details of swimming, visiting abbeys, reading Proust, and taking Jacques to see places important to her. It was idyllic but brief.[90]

By November she was settled into her senior year at Bryn Mawr while her father traveled in France. She intended to marry Jacques after graduation, despite opposition from her parents. Both, or perhaps just Edward, had traveled to France the summer before, met with Betsey and Jacques in June, and concluded that Betsey was not in her right mind. He engaged a therapist, probably a psychoanalyst, to interview both young people. They agreed to meet with Brunetti, the analyst, and he sent a six-page letter to Edward early in August.

After two interviews with Betsey and one with Jacques, Brunetti concluded, "They are both very serious and 'engages' in their relationship," and he was convinced "they can be happy together." But he also noted that Betsey had more doubts than Jacques, particularly about whether "the kind of life she will have in France will really be suitable for her personality and background." He then suggested "less conscious reasons: her strong attachment to her father, her fear of being hurt by a man inculcated by her mother." He described Betsey as ambitious and brilliant, deeply dependent, and angry with her mother because of her mother's belief that Betsey would forget Jacques once she was back in the United States, a belief that might ring true to her. Jacques, on the other hand, was the product of a traditional, authoritarian French family but claimed that "he will be happy, as he states now, about Betsey's professional activity." But he was also given to outspoken attacks on intellectuals, driven, Brunetti surmised, by jealousy over Betsey's attachment to her father. Jacques suggested that they marry without much delay—he did not want to wait more than a year—and that Betsey consider an English degree. "Betsey," Brunetti wrote, "needs to acquire a feeling of independence from her parents and the security of a stable relationship with a man of her choice." And in response to a direct question from Edward and Betty, he replied, "As to the question whether Betsey needs therapy or not? I would answer: no more than any American college girl."[91]

Brunetti was not telling them what they wanted to hear. Betsey was in love, she was considering acting on the fact with some maturity, she was too dependent on them—in short, it was time for them to let go. Edward and Betty were not like Agnes, who apparently had calmly accepted Edward's decision to marry Betty in 1935, even though she had reservations. Ed, with his own history, expected children to need care and control, and Betty, if Brunetti reported accurately, was angry, although with what man or men is not clear.

What happened over the next year bears directly on the degree to which Betsey fit or broke the mold her parents set for her, and there is little evidence to help explain her decision or how she made it. In the fall of her senior year at Bryn Mawr, she wrote long letters to her father about Jacques, yet in the spring seemed more focused on her thesis and other work. She still intended to marry Jacques and mentioned studying German and getting a graduate degree at the Goethe Institut in Berlin or Munich. Then, in the fall of 1963, she began classes at Harvard as a graduate student in history, and Jacques disappears from the story.[92]

If this was what her parents wanted, it was necessarily also Betsey's decision. Her father worked in France during the fall of her last year at Bryn Mawr, and two of her letters to him survive from November. She asked him about Jacques and urged him to act as proxy for her and "see what is bothering him." Clearly, she was still much in love. When her father asked if there was anything she needed him to do for her, or bring back, she asked him to "go to the B. N. [Bibliothèque Nationale de France] and look at *Combat* from the liberation to '47 when Camus leaves. I need to know what kind of headlines they used—anything of political significance about their format." This was an important part of her thesis, and she told her father that she trusted his judgment more than that of Jacques, although she was sure that Jacques would love to help her. But what she really wanted, she told her father, was "less portable—Jacques and a glimpse of the Louvre on a gray day, all shapes and black trees and lamp-posts, or perhaps a view of the Grand Palais from the Pont du Carrousel—a walk from the Beaujolais to St Germain and lunch with you at the Holy Fathers [she drew a smiling face here]." Then, with some fervor, she discussed her work:

> My history is going very well, and, Daddy, I am really loving it. For the first time I feel some control and some honesty in the work I am doing. It is extremely exciting. It is highly improbable that I [will] be able to use history much professionally in France, but it is not withstanding the most valuable feature of my education. Who knows, maybe I shall feel obliged to write something some day.

Not stopping there, she told him that she was "beginning to feel deeply *engage* and most importantly to care for what I study in itself."[93]

Two days later she was happy after receiving a note from her father telling her that Jacques "seemed well." But she immediately urged her father to see Jacques alone again and "do all you can to see what is bothering him." He was "tense and nervous," his mother worried about him, and Betsey wrote two pages analyzing Jacques's personality. She pointed out, "He is very different from you or me, Daddy; and that some of it is just plain youth or even immaturity, I don't doubt." Jacques did not wish to study, he wished to do things, to get on with his life, she wrote. Betsey sensed from Jacques's mother's anxiety and from his letters to her betraying "questions and uncertainties" that waiting for her was difficult.[94]

Her decision to give up the person she had loved to pursue a study she was coming to love was, in the end, not just her own but her father's. Whichever she chose, she lost. And if Brunetti was right about how much she needed her parents' approval, history was the better choice, especially as she confronted the practical details of study, career, and life in France. But it must have been a late, last-minute decision. In February, well into her final semester at Bryn Mawr, she told her father, "my plans for next year look promising." But she also told him, "The French course is interesting and it is very exciting to find myself doing well in it. Up until this year, I really hadn't grasped even the elementary subtilties [*sic*] of literary criticism. It took me a long time to stop looking for answers and start looking at the text and trusting my own observations."[95] As she learned to interpret texts, her February letter appeared ingratiating and more reserved than letters written before she met Jacques. She congratulated her father on a presentation, asked for a copy of his paper for Jacques, explained her accounts without apology, discussed her work, and closed by signing herself "Your devoted, Fido." But the smell of devotion was lacking. And by April 1963, her last year at Bryn Mawr, Jacques Toyou was also in the past, a casualty perhaps of his immaturity, her indecisiveness, and her father's willfulness.

Betsey's time with Jacques was like her father's drive to Florida. She did not return from France mature and independent, but Jacques allowed her to see herself as a woman whose parents were edging into her past. Once she had pushed them aside, if only briefly, she found a new relationship to her work at Bryn Mawr and dared to move on to Harvard. Nonetheless, much of her life from seventh grade through that last year of college rested on her sensitivity to authority, from the child calling "Ed!" to the young woman playing Fido to her father's Uncle Rover.[96]

3

From Fido to Fox-Genovese

CONFRONTING PATERNALISM'S AND ANOREXIA'S SWAY, 1963-1969

> Oh shit.
> I am a prisoner.
>
> —BETSEY FOX, 1966 Journal

IN 1940 Betty Fox, Radcliffe student of Harvard's star historian William Langer, abandoned her Ph.D. studies. Betsey, who must have known something of her mother's choice and her talent, almost did the same in 1966. Betty, full of restless intelligence, had once expected to have "a position," and Bianca Simon, her aunt, wrote to her in 1932: "I have learned with great joy that you have achieved this interesting post in Washington; it is really wonderful that, even long before the conclusion of your studies, you have the prospect of a secure position."[1] Betty ended up accepting other choices. She took the job after quarreling with her father over money, reconsidered, and settled into graduate work at Radcliffe, as the caption under her wedding photograph in the *Springfield Republican* made plain.[2]

In her turn, Betsey sailed through Bryn Mawr in 1963, finishing with a thesis on the Franco-Algerian writer Albert Camus's work in the 1940s. Camus suited her double major in literature and history. He also embodied the divided consciousness that would fascinate her: Algerian by birth, he was troubled by the Algerian War, sympathetic to both sides, unwilling to speak out against French rule, leftist but not communist, often identified as an existentialist yet confounded by that label. He was as well, in hindsight, a telling model for Fox-Genovese, given her habit of embracing contradictions, the spoken and the unspeakable.

She was settling into Boston in 1964, becoming a habitué of various ice cream shops in Harvard Square. Cambridge—Harvard Square in particular—was the target of massive rebuilding in the 1960s, so that much of the area that Betty and Ed knew was disappearing. Neighborhood shops—hardware dealers, grocers—were replaced by large office blocks, bookstores, and restaurants.[3] Nonetheless, it was far from completely changed. Ed and Betty's old brick apartment building at 1306 Massachusetts Avenue, finished in 1883, still stood, and if it was not the same Cambridge, two of Betsey's professors, Franklin Ford and David Landes, were family friends.

The first years at Harvard proved comfortable: the courses, work, and scheduling agreed with Betsey.[4] But by the summer of 1965, as her coursework ended and the choice of a dissertation topic loomed, she began to lose weight, to control her life by controlling what she ate. In Ithaca that summer, she prepared French gourmet food, feeding the family but eating none of it.[5] Her parents were oblivious until her sister, Rebecca, intervened, compelling them to notice. Her father believed Betsey was reacting to Agnes Fox's death that spring. He was ignoring his imminent departure for a year in France with Ted, just as Betsey faced her dissertation. Edward would soon panic at the thought of Betsey's controlling her trust fund in a year. He was quite sure that at twenty-five she would be too immature to be let off his financial leash. None of this seems likely to have inspired confidence in a young woman already trespassing on male territory at Harvard.[6]

Facing the question of her thesis, Betsey was determined to secure fellowship funding. Her husband would later write about her struggle:

> Then she was told that, to win a teaching fellowship in history, students had to take their comprehensive examinations by a certain early date. She did just that—something not expected of women. Having worked herself into the ground at the expense of her health, she passed with flying colors. Elated, she went to see the departmental secretary, whom everyone considered pretty much the department's boss. She replied, "But dear, you know we don't give those positions to girls."[7]

Nonetheless, Betsey got one. She taught. The urgency was less academic than a reaction to her father's tight control of any cash she had.

After her summer of avoiding the French food that she had cooked, she wrote to her father that autumn about sleep and food:

> I am enjoying my first real dip into Machiavelli & More. I find that I am still somewhat tired and vulnerable from last year. Although by no means unhappy I suspect it takes a long time to relax from the kind of state I had gotten myself into (what sentence structure!). Hav[ing] failed to take full cognizance of just how much I needed in the way of sleep & food, I never really stopped to get it & so I never really started over fresh. Now, I finally have my mind on getting as much as possible that is compatible with my minimal obligations.

She described food and sleep as a matter of cognition, of reason rather than sensory awareness. In the same letter she told her father, still Uncle Rover, that she was getting "my AAUW [American Association of University Women] application off," so she or Edward hoped for further funding.[8]

Money and her status at Harvard were continuing problems for her, captured in her oft-repeated story of the male graduate student who asked her "how in good conscience she could take a spot at Harvard and thereby deprive some man with a family to support."[9] Money plagued her. In a letter from December 1965, she thanked her father for a check he had sent from Paris and then apologized for an earlier letter:

> I am terribly sorry for that letter I wrote you. That was a particularly black moment and I should have resisted the temptation to dump the whole thing on you. Please don't tell Mummy—she'll only worry. Actually I'm feeling much better about life. Cambridge isn't gay, but when I wrote you I was in the depressing stages of a long dragging cold-flu-virus bug, and feeling terribly inadequate generally. By now even my financial state looks better. I had been trying to keep a reserve but all at once I had to pay a huge bill for boarding Peter, Harvard wanted some loan money back, it was expensive to be in Kitten's

> wedding & I could find no way to object when her sister was the only other bridesmaid & to top it all off, I had skipped a page in balancing my checkbook (for the first time) and so had neglected three checks I had written in establishing my balance several months ago. Over the weekend I slept, ate, (and I am finally gaining—promise [smiley face]) and worked happily.[10]

Harvard was demanding. Betsey, however, was also pummeled by her father's demands and his fear of expense. A terribly bright child, she had had little childhood, and her identity was at least as much her parents' creation as her own self-realization. Unsurprisingly, she took revenge on it.

She scrimped on food through the vocabulary of money, perhaps to make room for other obligations, like being Kitten's bridesmaid and upholding the social position she believed she must. Betsey's parents, ostentatiously preparing her for some "position," deprived her of intellectual and financial independence. Her response was to grow smaller instead of growing up, to retreat into a carefully regulated world in which she ate only desserts, almost only vanilla ice cream. She was five feet nine or ten inches tall and weighed a bit less than ninety-seven pounds as she began a journal in 1966. It fed and fed off of the first of two analytic relationships that would last for years.[11]

Dr. Galdston and the Journal

In January 1966 Betsey started keeping a journal, often of dreams. This was almost undoubtedly at the suggestion of Dr. Richard Galdston at Children's Hospital Medical Center. About forty, Galdston was a Harvard psychiatrist, recently qualified in psychoanalysis, whose published work demonstrates some interest in poor parenting skills and children abused in complex ways.[12] While that hardly makes Ed or Betty Fox poor parents, Betsey Fox did not reach a near-fatal stage of anorexia by herself. The first substantive entry in her journal: "Daddy called to tell me Mummy was seeing a psychiatrist. Immediate reaction—jealousy and fear. I construed this as a personal threat. I think I feared that this is something we would do together."[13] Apparently hers was not a happy family in 1965. These talented women found themselves dominated by a man made more patriarchal by his need to win out over his illness. Further, he apparently expected Betsey to imitate his drive to Florida at the age of eighteen and make herself well.

Betsey's journal gives us glimpses of Harvard: grading essays, teaching, reading English novels. Her foreground, however, was filled with dreams, food, Dr. Galdston, Mummy, Daddy, and a young man, Arthur, who remains unidentified. Much of her writing mapped walking to restaurants: Brigham's, Cardell's, the Ritz, and driving to Hartwell House in Lexington. Making some slight progress, she set out on her own, bought a bike, left Harvard to work in publishing for a year, and supported herself. She fought gaining weight by moving on to bulimia, got worse, spent time in a hospital, and then slowly fought her way out. By 1967 she was less thin, had fixed on a dissertation in French intellectual history, and in 1969 she married. In her therapy, she developed her growing sense of how the words she used were directly related to the reality of her life. She taught herself that those words now could free her from what she frequently described as her prison, by making audible her parents' voices in what she had innocently taken to be her thoughts. As she studied her dreams and heard her parents, she learned about hegemony years before reading Antonio Gramsci.

The 1966 Journal

The journal Betsey began in 1966 covers 162 pages and continues to 1969. The first line, from January 21, "Can I go on seeing you even if I gain weight?" conveys with simplicity and naiveté the state of Betsey's mind: that gaining weight could only have bad results; that the purpose of this treatment was to gain weight, not understanding. It was a response to her first meeting with Galdston. When she wrote again on February 19 her tone had changed; she had a deep interest in a dream, which she remembered in detail. She noted, "I ended up married to an older man—maybe 50—who was, I think, crippled." She recalled that she had thought she loved him, but once they were alone in their apartment, she "felt trapped & miserable & panicked." As they walked downstairs to go shopping, "he ran his hands down inside my blouse and started talking lecherously about my breasts." She was "physically repelled" and "caught in a situation I hated." She recalled that she "felt like crying, and running away; running home to Daddy and having him get me out of the whole thing." But she, still in the dream, "pulled [herself] together," determined "to stay and learn to be responsible," because "you can't go home to Daddy."[14]

Her father was fifty-five in 1966, intermittently troubled by the arthritis of his childhood, and in France. He fits the bill too well to be ignored—the old man who trapped her and the father who was not available to save her—but we have no grounds to suspect him of anything like this scene with the older husband, although he was close to his young daughter. Betsey often recalled with some pride the way her father took her seriously, his early morning visits to her room when he talked to her about history and politics or got her up to play tennis or baseball. No matter how these visits were meant, Betsey was, as Brunetti had written several years before, much too dependent, too attached to her father, and accustomed to his borderless intellectual intimacy.[15] As Betsey swam against the tide of that attachment, we can recall Brunetti's other comment, about Betty's warnings about being hurt by men.

The dream opened into a second episode: "This one involved Mummy. I first saw her at some dinner party which may have included other members of her family. She looked much younger—very thin, conceivably taller—and her hair was smoother, shinier, blacker." Betty seemed to be thirty, "supercilious, ironic and cold." After the dinner party, Betsey met her mother at a bookstore run by an old woman; this part of the dream "was shot through with latent rivalry between the two of us—about books maybe and certainly assertion of supremacy." At the end of the dream, she "returned to the book shop alone and found the old woman sleeping on her feet—I had taken her for a statue." This was the first dream Betsey recorded, one of the longest, and it mattered to her. She translated it into words. The first half was male, the second female; the first was private, the second public; the first sexual, the second cold, distant, combative, and literary. If Daddy weren't to save her, a very stern Mummy was to show her books, books where an old woman came alive. Betsey wondered, noncommittally, "if remembering dreams has any relation to my therapy."[16]

She had, with flourishes, outlined the family triangle that troubled her, complete with emotional shading for each parent. Her father was uncomfortably close but not present, her mother absent despite her proximity, present only in books. Those who find Freud's or Jung's discussions of Electra useful will consider them so here; those who do not should remember that Betsey would study and use Freud for the next twenty years. I have tried to keep readings of dreams close to literal: who appeared, invoking what emotions, in what context, as if it were a story that had slipped out in an unguarded moment.

Ice Cream

Still writing on February 19, she moved from dreams to eating: "Walking to Harkness [a new Harvard dining center] with Meg, Becky and Judy and afterwards eating a vanilla ice cream cone that wasn't soft enough and was smaller than everyone else's. Ate all my swordfish without scraping the butter off. Ate a good deal of ricotta impulsively." Food mattered, and her description suggests the perspective of a child compelled to eat. "The anxiety resulting from the conjunction of food with uncongenial circumstances" was how she introduced the Harkness episode, as she noted that she had been able to "master" that anxiety. Eating all her swordfish had been a triumph in "uncongenial circumstances," and the ice cream had been terribly wrong, but she ate it anyway. She ended this entry, a few weeks into therapy, with an ultimatum: "If I can't let myself eat what I want, then I'll have to go on eating ricotta and ice cream. It doesn't matter to anyone but me what I eat so long as the pounds go on."[17] Still materialist and uncomprehending of any higher goal beyond regulating her weight, Betsey had reduced her diet to white food. This was a diet of sickness: sore throats and school infirmaries come to mind, as when she had been cared for during her illnesses—enforced vacations—at North Country School.[18]

Daddy

Four days later, in a dream set in her parents' house in Ithaca, Betsey discussed history with her father. After a disagreement, she "may or may not have stood up to him. . . . I left him and went to his bathroom for some reason. Wanted to be alone. Can't remember why but think I wanted to do something secret." After inadvertently suggesting her later bulimia, Betsey noted parenthetically: "Uncle Rover is how I thought of him and then censored it—must tell Dr. Galdston about those names."[19] Her dependence was, barely, starting to be visible to her.

The dreams matter because Fox-Genovese saved them, incorporated them into her journal, made them part of what she would later call the story of how "I became myself."[20] That she took them seriously is clear from her subsequent study at Columbia's Center for Psychoanalytic Training and Research in the late 1970s.[21] Her engagement with her becoming herself never led to an autobiography, although she took the genre seriously and used her complex understanding of it in her later work on women and the prerevolutionary French economist Pierre Samuel du Pont de Nemours.

By 3 March 1966, almost two months into analysis, Betsey was writing more freely about herself. She began with her weight; she had gained a bit and weighed 98½ pounds. "So far," she wrote, "I haven't paniced [*sic*]." At that moment, she still had little sense of who she was: "I wish I knew more, if I were being spontaneous, if my reactions are genuine, & if I am over-reacting, if I really want what I think I want etc. There is no reason to believe that publishing will be a picnic, but I do hope that I like it and that I will be less lonely than I have been in graduate school."[22]

Unsure as she struck out on her own, taking a job at Houghton Mifflin, she pondered her "infatuation with English" and her "warming up to Arthur." Used to her father's household, she asked, "What external standard as to what my life should be could I accept? What criterion besides my own desires will ever bring me peace or fulfillment?"[23] She questioned whether she liked Arthur, whether her feelings were hers, and whether she truly felt at all. Still determined to find new rules to substitute for her parents' criteria, she approached her twenty-fifth birthday that spring.

Not that she was alone in asking such questions at that age. The film *The Graduate* would come out in a year; the book had been published in 1963. Lest Betsey appear as an extraordinarily isolated and distraught young adult, it is important to place her at the edge of a generation that thrashed mightily as members felt both the hooks pulled in by their elders and the allure and challenge of dramatic social, cultural, and political change. And equally important to note: in the film, it was Benjamin who questioned and Elaine whose questions had not yet surfaced. Betsey faced her questions mostly on her own, with just her family and Galdston as touchstones: "What chance have I of shaking parental standards and freeing myself from the image they and I have created over the years without plunging gratuitously off in the opposite direction. Am I headed on a path of repudiating or fulfilling myself?"[24]

Still questioning any new direction and hesitant to turn against the world her father had built, Betsey slowly moved on to admitting her self-destructive behavior. Letting herself note that she simply wanted a bicycle, without needing to justify the desire, she admitted that she wished to write. She could not, however, want for herself: "I need people." Specifically, she needed approval from Galdston, even as she wrote, "The therapy is mine to do with as I choose. Believe this, Betsey. That is the first step. Faith really."[25]

Bicycles, Arthur, and Independence

Choosing remained hard, and her worries about buying that bicycle figured constantly in her journal: "Yesterday I bought a bicycle. I had really wanted it, but actually choosing, ordering, paying scared me. No matter. No justifications needed. I want it. Since I have it, why not let myself enjoy it. Like eating—I don't deserve all this punishment." If the bicycle was easy to want, Arthur was more of a problem. She frequently noted affection for him but was always wary of confusing a need for him with a need for company, approval, or pleasant dinners. On one occasion, she recorded "a movement of affection towards" Arthur but quickly concluded that this was a result of feeling "let down about the hour with Galdston." Needing the support of one or the other, Betsey insisted, after the passages about the bicycle and Arthur, "I do want my independence and need it. That much should be clear."[26]

She framed independence as a rational choice, even as she hinted at the undercurrents of emotional dependence on Galdston and Arthur.

Independence was also about money. Knowing what one would like for dinner and paying for it are different but related. All of her writing on 3 March 1966 was finished before breakfast, and if coffee and hunger can shape prose, they probably did here. In the last page of the entry comes clarity:

> I can't have both what I want and what I could justify to Mummy and Daddy. Like the anxiety now in the pit of my stomach about what I should eat for breakfast. Eating economically & trying to save money on food, or at least to use up what I buy is fine, but I don't need to make it into yet another external control. The goal is still to find out what I *want.*[27]

Wanting

The day she began with the lengthy entry above, March 3, was a particularly hard one. A special delivery letter from her father about money came at breakfast. Without elaborating on it, she immediately noted that she had called for four job interviews with publishers, going to one the next day at Ginn and Company. Responding to her father's letter by turning to her search for a job made clear what she thought of her father's control. She followed up by attending Monroe Engel's class on British literature. He "lectured brilliantly on *Passage to India.*" There were "errands in the Square" then "a visit to the old Brigham's to get a vanilla ice cream cone I wasn't sure I wanted."[28]

This was one of many difficult encounters with ice cream: difficult and public. "It wasn't large enough so I ditched it in my coffee cup and went to the new Brigham's where I got another one. This time I ate it and even enjoyed some of it—particularly the cone part which I ate biking home—but I didn't really love it. That has to be neurotic behavior." Another description of her eating all her meat and some of the sauce sounds like a child trying to please her parents, and her father's letter about money was almost certainly the mainspring of this awful day. Once Betsey got home, she undressed, "promised myself a choc[olate] graham [cracker]. Waited for it until Meg et al got home from their lectures." In the presence of her friends, she ate "2 gingersnaps & 2 grahams & enjoyed them & was full."[29]

Her rationing of food, listing each shred of dessert, reflected the accounts her father insisted she keep. She still did, but now they were of calories instead of dollars and cents. And the two categories overlapped: she tried to save money on food and thus bought, so she often complained, things she didn't like just to save money. Not eating allowed her both to ration calories and to reject what she had purchased to please her parents. She avoided fats like butter and mayonnaise but ate cookies, chocolate, and ice cream. She "bought" calories to spend on these treats by eating fish, lean meat, and ricotta, without sauces; bread without butter; and a small number of other foods. Galdston urged her to try more foods, to find what she liked, not what she should eat.

She became the accountant her father had encouraged her to be while refusing the food that makes up so much of the nurture parents offer. Two grahams and two gingersnaps, together with the claim that she undoubtedly wanted to make herself believe that she "was full," fits Hilde Bruch's 1978 description of anorexia perfectly.[30] Much more fits with Bruch's case studies: upper-middle-class educational advantages, ambitious parents, high expectations, daughters treated like sons. And in Bruch's paradigm, one or both of Betsey's parents would have been too close, too controlling, and too present in her life. I mention Bruch's work—*The Golden Cage*—because Betsey assigned it in undergraduate women's studies classes in the 1980s, and she recognized herself in it.

March 1966

Returning to March, we see Betsey eating chocolate-covered grahams as a fellow student, Steven, "started in by saying the department would probably give me money—that my generals ranked with his and Charlie's as the best in the decade. Panic. do I dare get out?" The money, a grant or fellowship, would support her while she wrote her dissertation. It is not clear which she feared more, losing the money by taking a year off or getting the money and being expected to write. But she was comforted when Steven went on to say that she could easily take a year off and then switch to British intellectual history with Professor John Clive. Relieved and feeling worthy, she ate another chocolate graham without acknowledging that she was hungry and commented that Steven "evinced no surprise at what Daddy has been doing."[31] She did not elaborate, but she had no trouble talking to friends about her father.

The Bicycle

Comfortable with the choices she discovered she had, Betsey read Charles Dickens's *Our Mutual Friend* until well after midnight, then fell asleep pleased with Steven's report. She had not turned to that novel by accident; it was on Monroe Engel's reading list, and elements of the story—money, power, class, inheritances, and the young woman, Bella Wilfer, who defies her society—were a means of reflecting on her situation. She recorded happily the next morning that she had lost weight and was back under ninety-seven pounds. She feared, she said, "a steady gain of a pound a day." Success, control, making her life hers had become very much about refusing food. She reflected again on her new bicycle: "I think I really wanted it." It gave her freedom, a mobility her father could not control, and an excellent way to burn calories.[32]

Anorexia, Tight Lacing, and Other Double-Edged Weapons

Anorexia nervosa is a self-destructive behavior. But it is not simple suicide, because it endows its practitioner with illusions of control, power, and superiority. It is particularly appealing to young women because it disrupts a fundamental aspect of parental control: eat this now. Betsey wrestled with replacing her parents' extreme control with her own.[33] As with Isaac Newton's third law of equal and opposite reaction, the force of her parents' will to shape her provoked opposition in equal degree. So, she ate little, became emaciated, and slowly, with a great deal of writing about what she wanted and what her parents wanted, grew up enough to survive.

What has this to do with the extreme tight lacing of corsets at the turn of the nineteenth century? Women have abused their bodies to grasp shreds of power, and historical debate over the tight lacing of corsets emerged in 1977.[34] Betsey, engaged in women's studies by then, would have read it, drawn by her interest in fashion and culture. Having survived 3 March 1966 and feeling quite drained by it, Betsey spent many pages trying to figure out "why yesterday was so hard." She weighed 98½ pounds that morning and did not "want to gain." Still uncomfortable, she wrote six pages, most of them about food. Once she started writing about "doing a big shopping at Sage's," she had plenty to say: "I have picked this particular juncture to develop obsessions about what is good for me, and to start economizing. I think I'm trapping myself so that I can't have what I might want, but have to have what I have bought. On the other hand I clearly don't know what I want and think I'm enjoying what I eat. But I still half diet. No butter." No jelly, honey, cakes, pies, or soda either. She was buying "too much and things I don't necessarily want and choose with calories in mind." In utter frustration: "But how in hell am I to tell?"[35]

Betsey had stumbled on to another aspect of anorexia. It is learned, it is social, it is an aspect of fashion and taste, a means of representing oneself, of being present, expressing tastes one should have. Betsey reflected, "I wish I knew why I was doing it to myself and what it represented. Clearly an extension of some kind of Mummy's old concerns. I suppose I really could eat apple pie & ice cream instead of cottage cheese. I don't know, but I'm sure this is worth understanding. And what about the bloody bicycle?"[36] Presumably her parents had taught her to control her appetite, not indulge it, and now she knew only what she had learned.

The Bloody Bicycle

By March 5, after biking part of the way to her job interview at Ginn & Company the day before, she was cursing: "And what about that bloody bicycle[.] What in hell does that represent[?] How dangerous is it to ride it? I think I'm trying to seriously injure, if not kill myself, with it." She called her accident the day before "so perfect as to be eerie." She was on her way to the subway, headed for her "first serious job interview," when she ran into "some lady" on the sidewalk, fell, hit her head, and scraped and bruised her legs. Ranting about her "commitment to self-destruction," she noted that she got new stockings, "cleaned myself up," and got to her interview on time, paying for a cab to do so.[37] The irony was thick. The bicycle was dangerous; her intermittent attempts to starve herself to death did not figure. Her anger and probable embarrassment notwithstanding, the bicycle was the first in a long line of vehicles that she would want and drive with more passion than precision. Being in the driver's seat mattered to her, as it had to her father in 1929. Later, being her passenger could prove terrifying.

The Words and the Cage

Betsey recognized that she was in a cage. The names she had for her prison—"super-ego" or "the role of language," and "I often think and talk in formulas of Mummy's and Daddy's"—spilled out on a page as she concluded,

> Oh shit.
> I am a prisoner.

In the same two pages, all coming from the 5th of March, she wondered, "Is it too farfetched to think that my concern w/ writing and style has something to do w/ wanting to break this syndrome?" By syndrome she meant "formulas of Mummy's and Daddy's" and her elaboration of them: "I have to justify everything in the same old terms; accept the same old patterns." Coupled with this adult voice was that of a child. "Am I reacting to knowing Mummy is in the area (at Alice's) [?] Yesterday, at some moment I really missed her, wanted to call her, to cry, to be comforted. Daddy writes dear Betsey, signs love Daddy. He's probably trying to take his cue from me, to be good. But I think it hurts."[38] Recognizing that her words were often their words was her first brush with hegemony—and paternalism: precisely the fiery sense of paternalism that she would bring to her marriage, informing the change in Eugene Genovese's use of paternalism in the early 1970s.

The journal exposes us to the details of anorexia and graduate student life, a materialist message about sauces, cookies, dinners with Arthur. The materialism underpinned Fox-Genovese's Marxism and her later traditional conservatism. She was working and putting food on her table. Later she would take Virginia Woolf's *A Room of One's Own* very seriously, attending to Woolf's dictum: "A woman must have money and a room of her own."[39] Like Woolf, she attended to words, she survived, she learned the rudiments of psychoanalysis: "Think happy. There are things to live for—Pollyanna trash. The thing is to know why yesterday was so hard."[40] She scrabbled to make sense of her profoundly self-destructive behavior and her parents' voices. Unlike an academic subject, this was one she had to master or die trying.

She filled all 162 numbered pages of the hardbound journal, writing well into 1969, and then began writing in blue books—blue-covered eight- and sixteen-page stapled booklets of lined paper used for student exams in most U.S. universities—ending later in 1969 with dreams about her mother. Along the way, she learned from Galdston that "symptoms have meaning and integrity and can be understood in a nonpathologizing way."[41]

Psychoanalysis and Fiction

Betsey learned to read herself as she learned to read those novels on Professor Engel's list. She turned to Engel's lectures on nineteenth-century British fiction to learn how people, perhaps particularly people to whom she was not related, treated each other. It is worth excavating in Engel's 1959 *The Maturity of Dickens* for a sample of what Betsey heard in his lectures. On *Our Mutual Friend*, which Betsey read with great attention in 1966, Engel wrote,

> The relations between parents and children in *Our Mutual Friend* afford not a single example of the healthy, natural, or useful. Lizzie loves and is loved by her father, to be sure, but she must prove her love by aiding him in his preying operations on the river, and for so doing she has to do guilty penance after his death. Between Hexham and his son there is only distrust. Old Harmon drives his wife and daughter to

> their deaths, and all but does the same to his son. Mrs. Wilfer is either a joke or a trial to her children, and Mr. Wilfer, though he loves Bella, is fully as much her child or her proxy lover as her father.[42]

Engel talked about individuals, families, and society. And he was something of a character, a Harvard man about ten years younger than Edward Fox. Betsey found his lectures on Dickens brilliant, but Dickens, his dissertation subject, was almost peripheral to his life. Engel also taught creative writing, published a handful of novels to varying reviews, and had earlier been Lionel Trilling's editor at Viking in 1947 for *The Middle of the Journey.* He wasn't just teaching criticism; he was a working writer. Given her earlier remarks in her Paris journal about literature, Camus, and Simone de Beauvoir, it appears that in 1966 Betsey was turning her head toward a career as a woman of letters, an author—not a scholar. On March 9, she

> went to Engel who was great on Our Mutual Friend. . . . Spoke w/ Engel after his class: asked him for bibliographical material. He was charming—gave me names of works, and even asked my name. "That will be easy to remember," says he. I found him very encouraging about working with novels and doing English intellectual history. He really seemed to accept the idea of a switch and suggested that I see John Clive—which I think I shall.[43]

This change of direction to British intellectual history and literature was a big deal, and probably a reflection of her work with Galdston. John Clive, the professor to whom she might have migrated, was barely forty in 1966, promising, quiet, watchful, and noted as a terrible lecturer. His 1973 biography of Thomas Babington Macauley was important, and Clive was attentive to the biographical in all things, including his own life. Despite the veneer of a WASP name and Harvard degree, he was German, Jewish, and his family was allowed to leave Berlin in the late 1930s because of his father's distinguished military record in World War I. Clive, like Engel, was aware of himself in his work, and both might have helped Betsey find her way to a topic that would serve her purposes.[44]

Writing in her journal, wrestling with her parents' words, led Betsey to imagine writing no longer tethered to assignments: "To write. This I really want. Could I ever? Can I even make myself try? Can I not relax and let myself try things out without having to see every passing enthusiasm as the ultimate and right solution?" She concluded that she could not "abandon old compulsions, can't relax, seem compelled to live according to the dictates of my super-ego. What is the role of language in all this? I often think and talk in formulas of Mummy's and Daddy's." It was not, as she wrote, "too farfetched to think that my concern w/ writing and style has something to do w/ wanting to break this syndrome?"[45] Her sensitivity to the hegemonic, ideological, formulaic—to cant—had begun as a child, when she called out "Ed." She never wrote a novel, but she left one poem, about words, written in the 1970s.

Arthur

Throughout Betsey's hard winter and spring of 1966 someone named Arthur was always on hand, and Betsey enjoyed his company. In early March she recorded a lovely meal at the Ritz, ending, "After dinner, Arthur and I came back here. For the first time in ages I felt some stir of sex when he hugged me. I felt sort of warm and good and close. I do wonder just what my relationship with him is all about." A few days later, after a day of cottage cheese and melba toast, she wrote, "Began to feel better (improvement started shortly before he came)."[46] They went to the Sheraton, Betsey ate fish, some of its sauce, a little Russian dressing on her salad, and all of her ice cream.

After dinner they "went to a bohemian-type party upstairs in his house for a while. Neither of us knew anyone, except he knew the hosts, and we sat and held hands mostly. I felt blissful. The people seemed nice and there were lots of pretty, long-haired girls around all of whom had curves. Almost made me want to get fat." Aside from the shock of her association of a curve with "fat," the passage is a happy one. She "kissed Arthur nicely and meant it" at midnight, then read for a while, fell asleep, woke at 3:30 a.m. and ate cookies, went back to sleep, and woke at 7:00, writing, "My good mood holds." She weighed a bit over ninety-eight pounds that day, felt good about gaining weight, and ended with, "I want to learn to read better and to write. Learn to be happy and engage (engagée?)."[47]

Two days later, still feeling good, Betsey went to the Hartwell House in Lexington for lunch with Arthur "and had a wonderful time—peaceful, relaxed, I felt well-disposed. Mozart piano concerto played driving back—sleepy, warm, happy. I wonder if this could go anyplace." In the midst of more job interviews, they went out to dinner again—and disagreed. Arthur "proposed" some place Betsey noted as W.S., while she "favored" the "Chez" [Chez Jean in Cambridge]. He parked too far from the building, and "he wasn't feeling very well." Nonetheless, Betsey called it agreeable and ate her turkey, "played w/ some of the stuffing not to mention eating gravy and a single cranberry." Back at Betsey's apartment for coffee, he was melancholy; he wanted to marry Betsey "or at least get engaged in June." She wrote that she was too far "from the decision-making stage."[48] And too ill, something Arthur could not, or was not allowed to, see.

This was in March 1966, and Betsey was also relying on her friend Judy, and on Fritzie and Frank Manuel, noted intellectual historians. She wrote, with some joy, "Judy is coming Friday," and a few lines below it, "Fritzie called! God, how much they [Fritzie and Frank] mean to me, how much I'd like to adopt them as surrogate parents."[49] Comfort and discomfort played havoc with Betsey's ability to eat, and Arthur, Judy, and the Manuels seem to have brought comfort. The Manuels also brought a web of intellectual interests beyond that of her father. So, also, did editing bring intellect and comfort that spring. She

> settled down in the kitchen to work on the manuscript. It went slowly, but I think I really worked well. I was interested and concentrated hard—felt no nerves, no tension. Although not frenetic—euphoric I was very content. And while I worked I ate about 10 cookies (I love those cocoanut choc. chips) and 4 cheese and crackers. Granted I had just seen Meg & Jess finish off 1 lb bags, but even so, I felt neither panic nor compulsion. I wanted to eat cookies while I worked and so I did.[50]

Houghton Mifflin

Two days before the melancholy evening with Arthur, Betsey interviewed with several people at Houghton Mifflin's educational division. She liked the young woman she first met and the head of the college division, a Mr. Thoma, but she didn't like Matthew Hodgson, the history editor. He gave her a manuscript to edit and discussed salary ($5,000–6,000) for an editorial assistant. Pleased with the day, Betsey wrote, "Their enthusiasm for my resume gave my ego a huge boost. Imagine me getting a real job on my own. It's something to have gotten even this far: I haven't usually shown such initiative. Today I go to Little Brown. Life feels so much better. Warmer weather, maybe a job in the offing, a warm psychiatrist."[51]

Unlike the case of the bicycle that she wanted then feared buying before falling off, she was unequivocal about her desire for the job at Houghton Mifflin. And when she got it on March 15, she talked to Galdston about money and about her parents as "social climbers" who had given her "a strong sense of who's important, who's in," and a "desire to succeed socially." Her outburst on this had been triggered by a visit from her good friend Judy. Her parents did not think Judy was her "true peer" and believed Betsey was "selling herself short." The dissonance was useful. Where her parents saw the absence of social position, Betsey saw "quality, guts, and talent." Judy had been at dinner and lunch with Arthur and liked him, which encouraged Betsey to see him with renewed interest. But she also admitted, "I fail to trust men, in particular, unless they have certain external qualifications."[52] So even if Arthur was suitable in that sense, which Betsey amplified as "wealth, social standing," he was more valuable seen through Judy's eyes. Coupled with the job, which her father probably saw as beneath the abilities of his eldest child, Betsey was bucking her parents' views of society, life, and status.

The coming crash, taking shape during Judy's visit before Betsey got her job, began as a response to a letter from her father: "Uncle Rover stinks. Got a letter yesterday telling me how good I was at teaching—how much my students would miss me. Shit on him. Still, things look up—Here's Judy." More importantly, she talked to Galdston the next day about money, "and as I was talking, it became clear to me that I must write Daddy and tell him that I want my trust fund and that I want to assume full responsibility for my medical bills. It's called girding yourself for battle." The full dimensions of the struggle are not clear, but Betsey knew her father well. She continued, "I am so very vulnerable here, but now is the time to cut through a lot of nonsense." She ended, "I hope, out of sheer cowardice, that Daddy doesn't force me to fight about it with him."[53] Her father had no intention of allowing her any independence; he took her illness as evidence of her irrationality and inability to take responsibility for properly directing anything: food, money, or career.

Daddy

Taking his sabbatical in France with Ted, Edward Fox left a trail of letters to Betty from 1965 to 1966, so we have a more than adequate record of his responses to Betsey. Caught up in the French elections in late 1965, Edward was vexed and impatient with Betsey. He asked Betty what she thought of his analysis of "BA's crisis" in April 1966: "In December [1965] she told me she stopped eating because I went to Europe & also made vague charges about being left with the responsibility for you (which you found most upsetting). But as I thought this over it didn't fit because she had already stopped eating—not only before I left but even before she came back for the summer." He located the "actual start of her hunger strike during the school term & probably in the middle. . . . it coincided with the death of her grandmothers." Agnes Fox had died in April 1965, and Elsa Simon about a year earlier. Edward thought that his mother's death coupled with his imminent departure for France had filled Betsey with dread: "Since she can no longer count on me, she realizes the necessity of striking out on her own, but she also feels betrayed & resentful."[54] Uncle Rover had tired of the dependence he had created, a dependence he had also fostered in Betty, calling her a "little girl" after their marriage.

Ed wrote to Betty: "My instinct tells me that this 'crisis' has essentially the same 'anatomy' as a child's tantrums but on a grown up scale. When she found too much conflict between reality and her desires she quit trying & forced everyone around to concern themselves with her problems."[55] Fighting to find himself blameless in Betsey's illness, he worried about the expense of therapy. In good form as patriarch, he told Betty, "I see no reason why she shouldn't have the help & comfort she needs but with the clear understanding that it is a costly business in every respect, time, money, reputation etc. & that the sooner she gets up & on the better."[56] Later in April he complained to Betty that what she blamed him for was not his fault and then returned to Betsey: "What I will not find amusing is if BA's trying to develop a horror story. I am more & more of the opinion that she wouldn't spin this business out if it weren't too easy & intriguing."[57] He was angry that Betsey spoke to her sister, Rebecca, about him and believed that Betsey was trying to provoke him into some "slip" that "she can seize on."[58]

Some of Edward's fury and defensiveness were triggered by Betsey's request, put timidly in late March, to take over her trust fund and pay her own bills. Edward reported to Betty, "My only communication from BA when I returned was a card—very sweet—but uncommunicative—except for an urgent little statement that she did want to handle everything. The context, too difficult to reconstruct here, suggests that she is thinking not in terms of mere cash—but ultimate solutions. I'll stall by missing the point but I suspect I may need to know where we stand."[59]

When Edward wrote this letter to his wife, Betsey was about to turn twenty-five. In talking to Galdston, she had hit on the necessity of taking over her finances, not only the apparently modest trust fund set up from some distribution of Simon money but all her bills. Her father guarded these funds zealously; the checks were locked in his desk in Ithaca. While he was in France, he gave Betty careful directions to get checks out and send them to him. He managed all the family bills and taxes through endless letters to Betty, whom he apparently did not trust to pay bills. He found the thought of Betsey as an adult impossible.

It is no wonder that Betsey wrote "Uncle Rover stinks" in her journal. He asked Betty to find the "original trust" so they would know "at what age B.A. gets full legal control." He thought it might be twenty-five but hoped "at the last minute that I changed it & raised the figure."[60]

Wishing Betsey would get up and on, as Ed put it, he nevertheless fought to withhold her money from her.

Edward complained several times to his wife about the "sweet formal little notes or cards" that Betsey was sending him every day, writing cheerfully about her life. Betsey clung to him while complaining about him to Galdston and in her journal. Had she known how repelled he was by what he saw as her weakness, she might have used a stronger word than "stinks." Ed was frank to Betty: "Clearly she is indulging in gestures. These are going to hurt her more than they are me & while I can't interfere I don't see any point in aiding or abetting the process by providing extra cash that would facilitate larger & more damaging gestures. If you think she should be financed to live in New York that's fine with me. But I think you should write her a check."[61]

Edward calculated Betsey's illness in dollars and was determined that it would cost him as little as possible. He saw no bad consequence to his control and wished to be in the driver's seat. In a long letter to Betty in early March, he explained that he intended to force Betsey to cover all her expenses from her trust fund, freeing him from her bills: "I did tell her that if she had real emergencies, extra money could be made available, but only with detailed written estimates of what it was for & the possibility of review of its necessity." Ed continued, admitting that "in her present state" her expenses might outrun the trust fund, "but if she does, it has to be explained, justified, & paid back."[62] He failed both to grasp the correlation between the leash made of money and the leash made of calories, and to understand that his hand was on both.[63]

Caught up in his own rules of survival, Ed could not let Betsey off lead. Consciously or not, he reverted to what had made him happy in Florida in 1929. While abroad, he bought himself a new car, a Lancia convertible that he had painted a special color. If Betsey was "indulging in gestures," so was he. Cars meant for him freedom through control, and he cherished the fact. He and Betty were barely speaking at the time, and there are hints in those short-tempered letters that Betty was acting as an advocate for her daughter. Ed, angry with both of them, bought his car.[64] On May 4 he wrote to Betty, "Don't shush me," and just before that, "Do you think I am only 6?"[65]

And then on the 11th of May, Edward wrote to Betty, greatly relieved. He had received "your joint card—with BA. What a wonderful surprise." He was "happier than I can tell you that things went well and that you think BA is making progress." He was also delighted to get a "big envelope with bills, tax materials & your note."[66] A week before, in a letter to Betty, Ed commented that Betsey "is now supposedly handling" her account. That probably meant that he could not keep Betsey's trust fund from her. So, Edward had a new car, and Betsey had friends, money, a job in the offing, and the option of returning to Harvard in a year.[67] She had been replaced.

Although fortified by gaining control of her trust, Betsey was not saved. She described herself as "still singularly resistant" to the idea of gaining weight and asked, "How do these mechanisms of self denial work?" She could, she noted, "to some degree master bad moods when I'm with A[rthur] if I really make the effort. Lord helps those who help themselves." Two days later she "made a scene" in a restaurant, suddenly deciding that she did not want the fish she had ordered. She then commented that she was afraid she would become like "Mummy and Grammy." And she dreamed that she was at a funeral, a man had died, and after she woke, "I thought it might be Daddy for some reason." That was almost the last sentence she wrote in 1966 but for a brief mention of plans to go to Martha's Vineyard that weekend with Arthur.[68] Arthur did not reappear in the journal after March 1966, and the trust fund, a marked step away from her father, preceded the worst of the anorexia.

Betsey, noting that she weighed 101 pounds, stopped writing until late February 1967 when she began the journal again by describing a binge: "ice cream and marshmallow fluff—then cheese tidbits, then more ice cream & marsh, then finally rolls. Weighed 130 this morning, could have expected worse."[69] Gaining weight alone was not the answer. Bruch argued that anorexics who turned to bingeing and purging were using deceit "to avoid exploring the deeper problems."[70] Betsey had abandoned the journal for eleven months. In March she recorded a dream in which she and Galdston both stayed after hours in his office. At first she was lying on his couch, and "then he was in the next room lying down on the couch and I went in maybe to try to wake him. Knelt down beside the couch w/ my face close to his. Told him he had to meet his wife. . . . Feelings of warmth and trust associated w/ all this."[71]

She followed her warm dream with bitter comments on reality: "I'm running away from myself, from people, from situations. Want to cop out on life." Two weeks later she recorded, "I'm running from my own thoughts and what I need above all else is to think." She actually needed to feel, not think: "Perhaps I do feel anger at my analysis and him [Galdston] for showing me I feel caught, but tonight at least I'm moving beyond sheer angry retreat to some possession of the feeling of my own entrapment. By God it's real and I can do something about it."[72]

Two weeks later—she probably saw Galdston every two weeks—she was outlining a novel about "a worker-priest (an outlaw from the Catholic hierarchy) who tries to help an impoverished community." The hero does well until a petty conflict leads a villager to kill him. "Meanwhile, either the church, or the local Communist cell succeeds in establishing something of permanent value." She toyed with making the hero a "girl—teacher or social worker—in a big city." Quite possibly she may have read some of the Don Camillo books by Giovannino Guareschi, about a priest and communist mayor in a Poe Valley town. She certainly had been reading Michael Harrington's *The Other America,* and something of his discussion of alienation struck her. Galdston told her that no one is God, "no one has truth, no matter how right, influential, persuasive they may seem." Frustrated, or at peace, she wrote, "Marking time. This is birth. Leaving home." Then Betsey added, "I do have things to say. I can't take them to the grave with me."[73]

She very nearly did take them to the grave. On May 13, she recorded "a real bender after relative abstinence for a couple of weeks." She had been bingeing and purging the night before, falling asleep at nine in the morning and dreaming:

> Was going some place with the whole family. We ended up stopping for the night in some ramshackle cottage beside a lake. Becky and I were sharing a room. Sometime early morning I think, I ended up talking w/ people. For some reason I think it was Daddy. Felt like same quality as when he and I used to discuss Mummy. (I had fallen

> asleep wanting to call Galdston) Only part of discussion I recall: he & I were lying on a couch together and he was whispering to me, "but you should see your father w/ desserts."[74]

It was much like the dream with which Betsey had begun the journal: first her father, or an older man, and then the second half of the dream shifted to her mother:

> Suddenly everything had changed. Mummy was there, like an avenging fury in a long white night gown. (I must have felt very guilty about her for some reason although it was Daddy under discussion.) Daddy seems to have vanished for the moment, and a huge bee flew into the room (3 or 4 inches long anyhow) Becky was already in our room, and I retreated there leaving Mummy to cope. w/ a piece of paper she tried to shoo it out a window.[75]

Betsey, Daddy, and Mummy, the triangle in which the anorexic often finds herself. The dream mattered; it was followed by violent bingeing. The next day, May 14, at 3:45 in the morning, she wrote, "Went on a real bender yesterday the likes of which I've maybe never seen before. Eat, be sick; eat, be sick, all day & night." Betsey landed in the venerable Newton-Wellesley Hospital.[76]

She wrote her next entry from that hospital on July 1. Heading the page "July1—Newton-Wellesley Hospital" she continued, "Something's changed. Reading John Hersey's *Too Far to Walk*, I find myself spontaneously thinking like a mother. I see the adolescent hero as a potential son. I want to be a mother. I'm not really happy about my job at ABCD [Action for Boston Community Development]. I'd much rather teach." The next morning she was reading John Holt's *Why Children Fail*, commenting, the book "made me want to teach and that may really be a genuine impulse. Mobilized all my maternal feelings. Want kids, want to give them a decent break. Understanding imprisonment of education. Have always been an answer getter, afraid of reasoning—incapable thereof."[77]

Something had changed. She expressed shock at her friend Ellen's sympathy for psychiatrists, "hearing so many problems and all. I would not have looked at it that way: they don't feel." Nevertheless, she was waking to find that not only did psychiatrists have feelings, so did she. Her response to hospital food that she didn't like was "panic and fear," but she also cried about it and reported: "Numbness wearing off. Despair nearer the surface." And finally, on the same page, "Oh Galdston What shall I do? Why live? I'm scared and unhappy. I can't face my ap[artmen]t. I can't face ABCD. Why am I shaking things up so? I don't want to live for myself."[78]

Fearful of living for herself, wanting to be a mother, she said things consistent with her later critique of systematic individualism, her repeated questioning of the results of Europe's early modern exploration of the individual as the foundation of political society. But there was an element of herself in what she felt and a maternal identity that was new, good, and protective. If Betty was not the mother Betsey wanted or needed, she nonetheless had taken from Betty that dream, ending, "leaving Mummy to cope." If Betsey could see herself nurturing others, she could nurture herself, and that would seem to signal that she now not only would have some control over her anorexia but that she was no longer a daughter in thrall to her father. How she had come to change in that miserable summer we can't know, but she had.

On the same day, July 4, a day to celebrate independence, she transcribed a dream, noting that she was "willfully letting last night's dream escape me." Buying candy for others, she found herself "eating a piece of candy w/ no memory of having put it in my mouth or how many I'd eaten before." To eat something spontaneously without calculation broke the rules of anorexia. To recall it without comment suggested a new life, even as she continued to complain about her situation. "Part of me," she observed, "doesn't want to get well. Why not lie and rot in this hospital. I don't want to face my job, I don't want to face my apartment. I don't want to go back to Ithaca & be trapped." And then she responded, "By God, I want to do things for me. To read, to have time. I want children. I want to entertain (do I really?) I don't want to be a human dynamo (was I ever?)." And then, a few lines later, "I will not eat compulsively again. I have no idea if I can keep this promise but God I would like to."[79]

Feeling returned and surfaced. When her father called, she was not awed or at a loss for words: "Daddy just called good-night. Well good-night to you and fuck you. He's been drinking again, I swear that's not just fatigue. To have him try to be sweet and talk in that swaying drunken, oh so logical, and reasonable, well we're all men together fashion just kills me. Maybe I can write it out of my system. God it hurts in my gut." She followed by writing, "Mark you there are days in which I'm deciding, have decided to return to graduate school and to write the bloody thesis. I shall be working not for my father but for me." She was determined not to fall "back into the comfort/hell of parental dependence."[80]

The journal, now in its last few pages, becomes an intermittent record. A dream in October 1967 suggests progress: Betsey, her father, and sister were trying to get over the wall of a medieval fortress without success. "Finally I stripped panties, stockings & shoes & heaved myself on wall, and then very precisely gracefully sommersalted [*sic*] off. Apologized to Daddy 'cause he should have been able to get us out of the situation."[81] The apology merely pointed to his inability to get them out.

Authority

Balancing between her father's authority and her own in the fall of 1967 and spring of 1968 was complicated by the demonstration against Dow Chemical Company's recruiting at Harvard and the Columbia University student demonstrations in April and May. The students in the streets raised questions that uncomfortably echoed Betsey's struggle with her family. "Obviously," Betsey wrote, "the students are unhappy." She had just lunched with two friends who "reacted unfavorably" to the Columbia students' occupation of campus buildings. She was sympathetic but distant, admitting "that kind of resistance to authority is threatening."[82]

Betsey Fox, Fido, was not a 1960s kid. She was reticent. "For me," she continued, "the dilemma lies in the validity of the protest and must hinge on my own ambivalence towards authority. Students should have positions, but should not indulge in meaningless confrontations." She continued, "They have to make themselves responsible and independent, or accept the price of the moratorium. All that bothers me is whether I'm not being unduly harsh, gratuitously moralistic."[83]

On the brink of independent adulthood, she sounded much like a parent, her parent, setting limits on her peers in a voice she probably grasped as that of her father. The last sentence from this entry on 2 May 1968 reads, "Generation of rev.—relationship to McCarthy campaign—conflict betw/ generations."[84] She was writing this on the heels of an almost week-long occupation of Columbia buildings by students. Administrators called in police and the subsequent eviction of student and community protestors was violent, "triggering a campus-wide strike that shut down the university."[85] Students had been appalled to discover Columbia's ties to the war in Vietnam, and local residents, many African American and Puerto Rican, were protesting plans by Columbia to build a new gym on a public park without offering local residents equal access to the facility. Known as "Gym Crow," the facility sat between Harlem and Morningside Heights, on an incline, and access for Harlem residents was planned for a basement level only.

Spring 1968

On the same day, Thursday, May 2, the University of Paris at Nanterre shut down after weeks of student protests. May and June saw France rocked by university demonstrations culminating in workplace protests and a general strike that made the antiwar movement in the United States look tame.[86] The United States, a profoundly individualist and ultimately conservative society bereft of widespread socialist underpinnings, saw protest but at least as much resistance. Civil rights activists were in danger. Martin Luther King had been shot and killed about three weeks before the Columbia takeover began; less than two months earlier three students were killed by police while demonstrating at South Carolina State College. Students and workers came out in numbers across Latin America, France, Britain, Spain, Italy, and Poland. Economic demands were jumbled with civil rights, the war in Vietnam, and various issues ranging from utopian to communist.

The resistance to authority that Betsey found threatening would reach global proportions that spring. She was not unsympathetic, but she was guarded. "Needless to say," she added parenthetically in her journal, "horrified by barbarism of police brutality." The student protests irritated her, and she could not equate her complaints about her father's authority with their fury. She sided with her parents' generation, equating what she saw as the students' alienation and frustration with an admission that they were powerless, impatient, unable to project themselves as equal partners at the table. She did not want to see the authority that she believed would one day become hers challenged. It was a remarkable position for a young woman to take in 1968 and tells us much about why she would not discard her attachment to her father, for all the difficulty it brought her.[87]

Returning to Harvard

The next entry came on September 23 as classes—teaching—began for her, "and a life of some discipline." She gave herself an ultimatum: "I work and do not eat compulsively. That must be a promise." "I must," she continued, "be able to do this. I must see clearly how close it is to alcoholism." After a few more lines she concluded, "I needn't fear starvation. I can manage this."[88] The severity of her anorexia was underscored by the hepatitis from which she was recovering in 1968. It had been a terrible two years, and she had nearly died.

Recovering but looking worse than she had in 1966, she returned to French history, her father's field, settling on her dissertation topic while still in the Newton-Wellesley Hospital. She had not abandoned Dickens, English novels, and the biographical bent of John Clive. Her work on the French economy of the *ancien régime* also would lean toward the biographical, focused as much on the men who became Physiocrats as on their philosophy and political goals. Under the humanist surface, however, ran the old scientific and mathematical currents from her youth, from Concord Academy, from her father's strict accounts, a current that would carry her on to Marx's economic interpretation of history. Beneath the calculations of the Physiocrats lay an implicit joke: they dealt with the distribution and price of grain, the staple food of most French people in the eighteenth century. Betsey had chosen the supply of food as her dissertation topic.

After her ultimatum to herself on the first day of classes, she did not write a word in her journal until January 1969, and by then she was well on her way to marrying the already well-known and contentious Marxist activist and historian of slavery, Gene Genovese. She embraced Genovese's interests, moving rapidly beyond her unease with student activism. She recorded meeting "Mark Smith (black freshman, friend of Howie Sweibel's, apparently of NY Negro bourgeoisie)" in January 1969. He and a friend had "started an organization called FIRST for rehabilitating ad[d]icts." She was drawn to their method, to "encourage their ex-ad[d]icts to [write] apparently on the very good grounds that writing frees." She recorded waking to remember, "it made me want to write." But she was also reflecting on Smith's larger plan, for a street academy, a magazine, and economic self-sufficiency: "The ideological basis of his project seems quasi-Marxist, but more derived from Malcolm [X] without the Muslim or rabid nationalist overtones." She was relieved that Smith was "willing to recognize whites as human beings." And she examined her own interest in FIRST: "This is Gene's thing and I want a base in it."[89]

Gene Genovese

It was the first time she mentioned Genovese in the journal, and it is worth comparing her comments to his reminiscences. She had known him for several months in January; he left a detailed story of their first meeting, a blind date. He described her as "Death Warmed Over," with "yellowish-green skin taut on her sunken face." What drew him to her was her conversation, and that first date lasted from 5 p.m. to 1 a.m.[90] She told her good friend Nancy Wilson and, eventually, Gene that she knew that night that she had finally met the man she would marry. But it was not simple. Trusting Gene did not come easily to her and raised specters of her difficult ties to her mother and father. Betsey wrote,

> Gene I have to learn to trust him. I do feel occasional waves of hostility he doesn't need me as much as I need him. But there is no point in testing. I have to be able to feel that our need is mutual. The whole eating thing must be related to that & self-hatred. There seems to be

> no dealing w/ the eating. No rules count, no resolutions hold. But I feel what is going on. I eat to escape, for love, for security.

Like the young Betsey Fox at North Country School, she was still hiding, stealing, and otherwise manipulating food. She still battled binge eating, commenting, "I can call Gene and should, but resist it. Probably I don't want him to know I need him now." "He is," she continued, "my man, my rock, my anchor. There I'm safe. If I could fully feel that, I should be able to call."[91]

Gene thought, she wrote, that she was "getting cold feet about marriage," and she ended with a parenthetical aside about her mother: "I wish I could really talk to Mummy about this, she must have gone through some of it. She is certainly capable of those cold rages I feel at times."[92] Betsey never showed this journal to Gene.

In the winter before her marriage in June, she fretted. Money, compulsive buying, and eating in the middle of the night vied for space in the last four pages of her journal. Using Gene's money felt like theft, and she worried, "How can I start a marriage by stealing from him? Old feelings *re* Mummy & Daddy of not having what I need." Gene forced Betsey to confront old questions of trust, dependence, and "being good." She wrote, "Why not have my own standards for being good—then feel secure if I meet them. Like I feel when I don't eat."[93]

In 1969 not eating remained the one sure standard by which she measured herself. As she fretted over all this, she blurted out: "I must tell Gene about not being able to have children, but that means talking to Aisner."[94] This was striking. Genovese later reported, "When Betsey accepted my proposal of marriage, she made it clear that she wanted a large family." And she was prepared to give up her career for the children, much to her husband's dismay.[95] There were no children. Her eating disorder made conception unlikely at best, and she knew that when she married. Nonetheless, she did not tell Gene, and near the end of her life she wrote, "As a child, I dreamed of becoming the first woman president of the United States and of having twenty-three children."[96] Protectively, Genovese claimed to be sterile in a memoir written after Betsey's death, but she had also consistently thwarted pregnancy with her eating disorders.[97]

Betsey nonetheless found Eugene D. Genovese at the right moment. He was a workaholic, first-generation Sicilian American from Brooklyn, a kid in the Communist Party, a young Marxist with degrees from Brooklyn College and Columbia, and a prominent historian of the South and slavery. He had had two marriages and a reputation as a womanizer and chauvinist when he met Betsey. Edward and Betty Fox heard about him from colleagues who spotted Betsey and Gene together in Toronto. Edward and Betty, especially Betty, were furious.[98] They intervened. Betsey stood her ground, sure of her choice, although Genovese could not have been further from the Foxes' orbit. One need only remember Agnes Fox's concern over her son marrying "a Jewess" and her friend's comment that at least the intended bride was not a Catholic.

Gene Genovese was the perfect man for Betsey Fox. He was brash, sure of himself, and wrote beautifully. He required, and accepted, taming. And he worked ceaselessly, initiating her into a world where writing could replace not eating as a means of liking oneself. Betsey had been searching for a long time, dithering, leaving notebook pages like these: "How long can I hold off. If I wait forever to keep my hands clean, to choose a suitable expression of my soul, my personality may I not be left with no soul, no personality? Not to get too hung up about choosing, to somehow feel master of my choice. To try."[99] Over the next seven years she would try and succeed: she would master her choice and use the solid ground it provided to calm her still-fraught personal life.

PART II

INTELLECTUAL ORIENTEERING WITH FREUD AND MARX

4

The Quiet Voice

PSYCHOANALYSIS AND ENLIGHTENMENT, 1969-1976

> The gap and the ties between civilized expression and primitive feeling haunts me. Language is a taking possession.
>
> —ELIZABETH FOX-GENOVESE, London, 26 August 1976

IN THE 1920s British intellectual Vera Brittain wrote about the "quiet voice" of Oxford dons that her brother and his friends acquired before the war.[1] That voice maddened her because she heard in its very softness a limitless self-assurance from which she was excluded. Fox-Genovese heard this too in her father and, rather than discard it, fashioned a version for herself, trenchant, less dry than that of Oxford, with "primitive feeling" underneath. She learned its dimensions from her father, and she heard it all around her at Harvard. As noted previously, she complained bitterly in the summer of 1967 about her father's tone: "To have him try to be sweet and talk in that swaying drunken, oh so logical, and reasonable, well we're all men together fashion just kills me. Maybe I can write it out of my system. God it hurts in my gut."[2] It bears repeating because twenty years later, one of Fox-Genovese's graduate students would complain that her advice was similarly double-edged, brutally critical followed by ill-advised attempts at physical kindness.[3] What Betsey complained of in 1967 was a small piece of the iceberg of her father's cutting assurances of her immaturity, followed by engulfing and infantilizing warmth. Betsey hated it, learned it, and made it part of her legacy of paternalism.

Years before reading Gramsci, Betsey understood the pull of hegemony and responded viscerally. Yet rather than reject authority as others did in the late 1960s, she weaponized that quiet voice, thoroughly appreciating language, the value of good form, and restraint in the male academic world in which she matured.[4] Like many of the eighteenth-century scholars whom she read, she was at her best in debate and discussions, whether over coffee or, ironically, at dinner. She also learned to write, from Genovese and from H. W. Fowler's *Modern English Usage,* but reading her without having heard her speak is to know only half of her voice. Between 1969 and 1976 Betsey Fox-Genovese transformed herself from student to working, published, literary woman.

Her husband was so struck by her self-possession on their first date at Restaurant le Maître Jacques in Boston that he told the story countless times and included it in his memoir of their marriage:

> I inquired about her doctoral dissertation. She identified her subject as the Physiocrats—eighteenth-century pioneers of political economy. I took a long swig of gin. I had taught medieval and early modern political economy and knew much more about the Physiocrats than she was prepared for. "So, you think you have something to add to what Marx, Schumpeter, Weulersse, and the best modern scholars have said about the Physiocrats?" She replied without a moment's hesitation: "Yes." Not another word.[5]

What she thought as she said "yes" we do not know. Betsey Fox was twenty-seven, a student recovering from anorexia and hepatitis on a blind date—suggested to Genovese by Edward Fox's former student Sanford Elwitt—with a nationally known scholar. She had been stunning before the anorexia; she would never look like that young woman again.[6] Nevertheless, she stopped Genovese, who was by then a rock star among academics, in his tracks. He recalled thinking at that moment: "Gene, you just met a big winner or a big loser."[7] As it turned out, both won, but not in the ways they led us to believe. Without addressing the well-known disparities in their backgrounds, perhaps best understood through a photograph of Gene at the Harvard Club in New York cutting their wedding cake with a cigarette hanging out of his mouth, it is clear that Betsey found and made something like the working partnership that her mother craved and that her beloved friends historians Frank and Fritzie Manuel had.[8]

Her period of tutelage—but never partnership—with Uncle Rover was almost over. Indeed, she had been moving away from his politics throughout the 1960s. Edward Fox was sufficiently provoked by Adlai Stevenson's endorsement of John F. Kennedy in 1960 to write him a furious, ranting letter. In it he denounced Stevenson for leading Betsey away from Edward's carefully inculcated worship of Stevenson and encouraging her to respect Jack Kennedy, whom Fox saw as "a ruthless young man."[9] That Edward preferred the WASP to the Catholic echoed his parents' belief that Catholicism was the root of all evil.[10]

Throughout her years of anorexia in the mid- and late 1960s, Betsey Fox had been reading, thinking, talking, fully aware of the world around her, Stevenson and Kennedy included. If her body had been in peril, her mind had grasped that illness and her attendant therapy as part of her education. She recorded more of her disease than her intellectual life in her 1966–69 journal, but both were intertwined. She emerged with the eating disorders under some control, a dissertation topic about the politics of food supply, and a marriage that gave her the companion her father was not, either to her mother or her. It is impossible to overstate the importance of her illness and psychoanalysis as part of her education. They provided skills that took her beyond what Bryn Mawr, Harvard, and her father had taught her.

Other, practical attainments stemmed from Betsey's work at Houghton Mifflin in 1966–67. Matthew Hodgson became her mentor and colleague, and she remembered him, writing when he retired as director at the University of North Carolina Press in 1992:

> I like to think how it would read in a novel, but then some critic would probably dismiss it as improbable. The rather lost and confused woman graduate student stumbles into the College Division of Houghton Mifflin in search of a job. There she is interviewed by a bemused, deceptively relaxed, and almost willfully unassuming editor, who concludes their conversation by asking her to try her hand at editing an "impossible" manuscript on the history of the ancient world.

She brought it back after "two weeks, countless pencils, erasers, and cups of coffee" and got the job. In a third paragraph reminiscent of

Betsey Fox on her wedding day, June 6, 1969, wearing a Pucci dress that Genovese loved. Her sister, Rebecca MacMillan Fox, provided the photo, remarking that it "shows her at one of the last times in her life that she was really healthy." (Courtesy of R. M. Fox, used with permission)

Mad Men and the male culture of white-collar business in the 1960s, she captured her experience:

> Gently, unobtrusively, he taught her the business. Editing for sure, but also layout, design, and marketing. And then there were the lunches.

> In those days, girls did not normally attend the lunches that kept the male editors out of the office for three hours and sent them back good for little but wandering around the corridors to gossip. She had been so sheltered she almost did not know what she was seeing. But she did know that member-in-good-standing of the luncheon club that he might be, he was also different.[11]

Hodgson included Betsey Fox in lunch meetings, remembered her interests in history, treated her as a colleague. When he announced that he was leaving Houghton Mifflin in May 1967, she "suddenly decided to" return to graduate school.[12] And the letter she sent him years later reminds us that she could have written the novel she often contemplated; the letter is a perfect vignette, a voice not apparent in her scholarly writing. While she wrote nothing in her journal about Houghton Mifflin after getting the job, she was hard at work learning her trade from a useful angle: how to make the work of a single mind accessible to a wide readership. When Hodgson moved on, Betsey was far better prepared to write her dissertation, if not to eat enough food to enable her to do so. And in roughly another year, she met the man she called the best line editor she ever knew, Gene Genovese.

In the spring of 1969 Betsey Fox finished her third year as a teaching fellow at Harvard and, according to her mother's wishes, married Gene in June at the Harvard Club in New York City. Her husband brought his records—the Shirelles, Beatles, Four Tops, Jefferson Airplane, Booker T. and the MGs. As he recalled, "the Harvard Club rocked."[13] The wedding didn't make Betsey a historian; it made her the wife of the newly hired chairman of the history department at the University of Rochester. But Genovese may have negotiated an untenured position for her there, since she began teaching, possibly as early as 1969 or 1970, according to Robert Kreiser, the early modern French historian—Betsey's field—there who remembered her teaching before 1973. Also Richard Kaeuper, who would be history department chair when Betsey received tenure later, recalled that she "entered full-time teaching by stages."[14] Throughout this period as chairman's wife, graduate student, and possible part-time instructor, then junior faculty member by 1973, Betsey lived in Rochester, entertained with

Gene, worked in roundabout ways on her dissertation, attended to her ongoing psychoanalysis, and probably taught a mixed bag of humanities courses, possibly through the university's adult education school, then through the history department by 1973. In a letter to an inquiring student, she wrote about those years:

> After our marriage, we moved to Rochester, NY, where [Gene] became chairman of the history department. I spent the next few years being a very good chairman's wife and continuing with my own work. But I was scared of finishing. Instead of my dissertation, I finished a short book on Bordeaux and the Origins of the Girondins, which I still plan to publish one of these days. Gradually, with a lot of support from my husband and a wonderful (woman) psychoanalyst, I came to recognize that I would have no real choice about what I wanted to be when I grew up until I finished the dissertation.[15]

There was some irony and a little sarcasm in that last line, a touch of wry self-criticism, and much left out, especially any reference to her early teaching. She was aware of just how long her childhood had been, even as she was a very good chairman's wife. Paula Gordon, writing about their friendship, remembered Betsey's arrival at Rochester: "I had never seen a person actually beam before watching Gene introduce his beautiful young scholarly wife to his Department. And I had never met anyone like her—elegant, smart, lanky and sophisticated with memorable hair, the consummate hostess welcoming incoming graduate students."[16] Gordon was the wife of one of those incoming graduate students, and Betsey was still a graduate student as well. Gordon, among others, invited Betsey to join a women's consciousness-raising group; Fox-Genovese accepted. Those conversations, coupled with the work she did with the woman therapist she began to see in Manhattan, may well have allowed her to express the anger she recorded in journals in the 1970s. There was stress. Women were scarce in academia in 1969, Fox-Genovese responded with armor, psychological and sartorial, and that would have provoked negative reactions to her among colleagues. One such colleague from Rochester described her as exuding "an air of arrogant haughtiness." That perception and her reality may not have matched.[17]

Dissertation

In 1971 Edward Fox published his one monograph, *History in Geographic Perspective: The Other France,* advancing a description of France that emphasized the division between the agricultural regions underpinning the monarchy and long-distance commercial centers, including Bordeaux. He acknowledged his daughter "Elizabeth F. Genovese" for her "unstinted devotion," which "made it possible for me to bring my project to a coherent conclusion." Both Betsey and Gene assisted him in bringing out the book at age sixty.[18]

And it must have been at this time that Fox-Genovese wrote her "short book" about Bordeaux and the Girondins, delving into the commercial side of matters she had just discussed with her father. Her dissertation took up the other side: agriculture, monarchy, and the Physiocrats. It would seem that father and daughter could not resist one last intellectual struggle, arguing back and forth over rural and commercial areas of France. A generalist, he focused on geography, while she, a specialist, saw human agency. Yet, he presented the "endless conversations" that "helped me develop my ideas" as driven by his book.[19] However the conversations began, father and daughter prodded each other, and when Edward's book came out in 1971, Betsey was at work on a lengthy essay, almost a book, about Bordelais merchants, a distraction from her dissertation that might have been one last short-lived debate with her father.

1972

In early January 1972 the distraction ended. On January 11, Betsey's first moments of wakefulness were filled with letters: "A.R.T.I.C.L.E. D.I.S.S.E.R.T.A.T.I.O.N. Woke up this morning counting those letters on my fingers to see which fit into the space allotted. Sort of like a crossword puzzle. Somehow I seemed to expect they were the same length. Working backwards I remembered fragments of a dream." In the dream, she was "boarding a plane or boat" and "had to declare things." She noticed that those who declared were allowed to board first, and then she was back at home, talking to a man, "maybe Daddy, who was telling me what to do and I was saying I know, I've done it, I've declared." That she cast her decision in the form of a customs declaration, making it a palpable choice to move on, to board the plane, fitted her life perfectly. So also did dreaming the moment as another argument with her father. As she wrote a few lines later, "Doing my work is the only way to beat Daddy."[20]

That comfortable, shapeless, sometimes fraught interlude between Harvard and an established professional life was winding down. In January 1972 Betsey started a new journal after beginning with a new therapist, Nini Vas Dias. She ended her first entry: "Finally decided yesterday. new year, new book."[21] She chose to write. She went to France for six weeks that spring and to Eleutherian Mills—now the Hagley Museum and Library—in Delaware that August.[22] Her own later words are as spare and direct as the drive to finish her dissertation must have been. "At Thanksgiving, I joined [Gene] at Palo Alto [Center for Advanced Study in the Behavioral Sciences, Stanford] and started sorting my notes. On January 1, 1973 I began to write and by April had all but one chapter completed. I spent May back at Eleutherian Mills, where I finished the last chapter."[23] Betsey completed her dissertation in a little over a year. She was more than ready to write, had a permanent position at Rochester waiting, and emerged more firmly into public life just as she turned thirty-two.

If Fox-Genovese appears to have had an easy time of it in an academic world where women were still both rare and unwelcome, that was and was not true. She was offered a job at Rochester in "Liberal Arts and History" in 1972, before her dissertation was written, contingent initially on many things. Almost certainly Genovese broached the subject of her job offer; administrators feared he would leave if no offer were made to Betsey, and difficulties ensued. Policy allowed spouses in the same department but not when one was chair. Documents show alternatives were considered: positions in economics, political science, and the humanities program at the university's Eastman School of Music. There was discord. Support came from the administration, and some faculty advanced seemingly valid criticisms: there should be a national search, is this the next position the department would wish to create, requests for new positions should emanate from the department, not the administration. In December 1972 Fox-Genovese received an offer of a tenure-track appointment in liberal arts and history, with conditions. Her dissertation had to be finished, read by her advisors, and approved by 1 September 1973. Substantially finished in May, her final version was accepted by Franklin Ford over the telephone on 27 August. On September 1 she entered into a tenure-track assistant professorship. There must have been some sparring, but before leaping to imagine this an operetta of Genovese's cantankerous managerial style, there were other contexts.[24]

Her dissertation irked her. She clung to the idea of publishing her short manuscript on Bordeaux, which was an escape from her dissertation, possibly a response to her father, and an alternative route to that tenure-track position. Harvard University Press rejected the book manuscript in September 1973, although by then it was irrelevant because her dissertation was finished. She and her husband suspected dislike of their Marxist politics. She sought advice from noted British historian and editor J. H. Plumb, ignored it, sent the manuscript to Yale, and got a longer and even less sympathetic rejection.[25] She was loath to abandon that first manuscript—*Social Origins of the Girondist Bourgeoisie: A Contribution to the Marxian Interpretation of the French Revolution.* She ultimately used some of it in *Fruits of Merchant Capital* and still alluded to her intent to publish it as late as 1992.[26] At the same time, she was aware of the early ripples of second-wave feminism, as her consciousness-raising group affirms. It is worth remembering that she was hired as a woman at a time when this was becoming both controversial and expected, and that is the larger context for her determination to write a book instead of a dissertation, for Genovese's commitment to getting her hired, and for the administrative push to ignore customary hiring procedures. The early 1970s were years of cultural flux, confrontation, and movement; Betsey and Gene were alert to the moment and deploying two strategies to get that tenure-track job.

Betsey and Gene tried to have children in the early 1970s and failed, and that may have helped Betsey reconcile herself to an academic career. Whatever she said to her husband about wanting many children, she had clearly suspected her inability to conceive in 1969. Apparently, Betsey's difficulty included a complication of her anorexia, her relationship to her parents, and her view of her professional self. Consequently—somehow—it also became intrinsic to her critique of individualism.[27]

Complications abounded. Betsey expressed anger, much of it directed at one parent or the other, in her journal. Early in 1973 she wrote: "Getting a lot done—for me. But I am fearfully angry—at almost everyone. It is a lonely and a scary feeling. I can take it, but it's hard when I'm angry at Gene too—which I am. It's not really his fault, it's just that I hate men."[28] This was adulthood speaking, with a bit of feminism thrown in, with the weight of her dissertation on her shoulders. Having just turned thirty-two, Fox-Genovese was better able to verbalize anger. Times were changing, but slowly. She had ridden into Rochester on Genovese's coattails, with those coattails serving feminist purposes.

Daddy

Fox-Genovese began this second journal for her therapist Nini Vas Dias in 1972.[29] She was determined to write, and her father figured frequently in her life and dreams: "I was in New York, it was summer. Somehow Daddy came to see me and was very nasty about my seeing Nini. It was like Christmas all over—I was no good, or I should come some place with him and Mummy, or something. Main thing is that he was very unpleasant—nasty & shouting. I walked out and along 86th St, by Sophia's to Nini's."[30]

Complaints about her father and Gene flowed. Able and willing to record her dreams, she noted her fury with another man who was "a perfect stand-in for Daddy." She damned him, as well as her father, as "WASP" and impugned their masculinity to boot. Later in the journal she would admit to fantasizing about making love with the same man while with her husband, which makes those dreams hilariously Freudian and underlines the complexity of her relationship with her father.[31]

In June, after sending her essay on Bordeaux and the Girondins to her father for his comments, she dreamed that she was her sister's mother and in bed with her mother and father—"if I was Becky's mother I should have to be Daddy's wife." But the dream dissolved into reality: "Daddy's comment on my Bordeaux paper arrived today and that fucking bastard is unbelievable. (Did you know Virginia Woolf was a Lesbian? She hated her father too, but her husband doesn't let it show in her diaries.)" And Betsey had a subsequent dream, titled "The War is On!" about Edward's comments.[32]

If one presumes some connection between Fox-Genovese's work on Bordeaux and her father's book on "the other France," his criticism seems all the more curious: Did Edward Fox object to her Marxism, or Gene's, given Fox's insistence on a different material determinism? Or did it endanger him, given his ties to the CIA? Meanwhile, Sanford Elwitt's manuscript was coldly received by a press, and Genovese, who was Elwitt's friend, was furious. Edward, Elwitt's mentor at Cornell, called Betsey every day to insist the poor review of Elwitt's work was justified: his Marxism was impossible, and he didn't follow the Fox thesis. Fox-Genovese thought the manuscript not good but found her father's comments extreme and the criticism of Marxism directed at her.[33] Elwitt was dear to Betsey and Gene then, having introduced them, but Genovese would end that friendship abruptly.

The anger toward father and society that she combined in the word "men," anger not expressed directly in the 1960s, was coming out, and it was necessary and good. Invited to Ithaca by her mother for a weekend with her brother and sister, Betsey refused to go. Her sister reported that "D[addy] hands down opinions, dictates and won't let T[ed] get a word in." Relieved to have stayed in Rochester, Betsey recorded having marvelous sex with Gene. It marked the beginning of growing self-confidence and pleasure in her work and herself. By the end of July, she was working well, wanting to write a *bildungsroman* about her new intimacy with Gene, and noting, "I clearly don't want an actual baby now."[34] Yet her anger at her father was not over.

In this same triumphant mood, Fox-Genovese had what she believed to be a "breathtaking intellectual insight" about Marx. "Property," she wrote, "is a hegemonic ideology." Her description for Vas Dias was much more detailed, but that line was the key. Genovese "grumbled about my being smarter than my husband, but was generous." Yet her father "didn't say anything—not one word." She feared or hoped that her father would steal her idea, and she would have to argue with him publicly.[35] Perhaps she wanted just that; she was certainly ready.

Mummy and Nini

Neither did her mother escape Fox-Genovese's anger. In a dream from March 1972, an unpleasant woman whom Betsey had met at a conference, reminded her of her mother: "Clearly I registered castrating, German—jewish bitch, ie Mummy, ie my female role model."[36] Not to be misled, one should remember that the anger she expressed was "at almost everyone." Nini came in for more of it as 1972 wore on and Fox-Genovese prepared to pause her analysis and leave for Eleutherian Mills, feeling less than independent.

Her journal writing in 1972 was confident, angry, introspective, full of motives, and a bit smart-alecky. The anger she had turned on herself and that had nearly killed her was now flowing out. In a scene at the end of the journal, Fox-Genovese rued an outburst in the office of Arthur Goldberg, an associate dean for arts and sciences at Rochester. "I've sure as hell revealed my hatred of men and authority," she recorded, although what she said to the unprepared dean revealed both her need to accomplish what she thought Gene expected of her and her dependence on him.[37] She believed that Gene thought she should come home with a faculty appointment in hand, without any contingencies. As with most recent graduate students, even with just finished dissertations, that was almost impossible, and she found she had to write her dissertation and have her advisors approve it. Although that angered her, she avoided the usual hoops: there was no search, no competition among candidates, and the departmental expectation that spouses not be hired when the other spouse was chair was worked around. After some years of contention within the department, she just had to write, get approval, and accept Rochester's offer.[38]

Genovese no doubt helped ease in the history department's third woman faculty member, but his influence in Betsey's hiring mattered less than an uprising spearheaded by Willie Lee Rose at the 1970 meeting of the American Historical Association, sparked by the discrimination women historians faced. This led Rochester's history department, like those at other universities and colleges, to look for suitable women. And a woman who was the daughter and wife of known historians reassured the less willing among the faculty. By late 1972 Betsey had an offer, albeit conditional.[39]

Fox-Genovese finished the first draft of her dissertation at Eleutherian Mills, living in rented rooms and surrounded by eighteenth-century books and manuscripts. It had been a long apprenticeship, marked, as her old friend from Bryn Mawr Nancy Wilson wrote, by the problems of "free choice and responsibility." Nancy understood: "You didn't have much trouble doing history when it was your father's; the trouble started when it became yours."[40] Nonetheless, it was Betsey's now.

Recognized as an expert on the Physiocrats before her dissertation was done, Fox-Genovese was asked to review the first volume of Margaret Kuczynski's translation of *Quesnay's Works.*[41] Before that she had written her first published essay, "The Many Faces of Moral Economy: A Contribution to a Debate." She was pleased with it, noting in her journal, "And I finished the piece (short contribution to a debate) for Past & Present today. I had an idea & sat down & wrote it up—over a crowded weekend no less—and am sending it off. They may well reject it, but at least I wrote it—and enjoyed the writing."[42] She was primed, even over-ready, to write by 1972, and perhaps her Bordeaux manuscript should be counted as a sign of overflowing ideas even more than as a symptom of struggle with her father.

The short "Contribution to a Debate" is important, not only as a first flight but because it signaled Fox-Genovese's interest in the essay as a form that suited her.[43] As earlier instructors had noted, she liked abstraction and ideas, not details; she saw the structure of a mathematical problem so quickly that she made errors of computation. She wrote many more articles and essays than books and wrote more books with Genovese than without. Essays were like conversation. Her first publication was even more so, as part of a debate between the British Marxist historian E. P. Thompson and his critic A. W. Coats over Thompson's "The Moral Economy of the English Crowd in the Eighteenth Century."

Thompson was a prominent left-wing historian, an ex-communist like Genovese, and, over his life, one of the founders of *Past & Present* and a string of other leftist journals. He was sufficiently important that a young scholar would think twice about criticizing his work, especially in a journal in which he had a hand, but Fox-Genovese was intellectually white-hot from her research in Physiocracy, agriculture, and the distribution of food in the late eighteenth century. Food riots, food prices, and the emergence of rural capitalism were her subjects; her wide acquaintance with historians, not only of her father's but also of Genovese's as well as her own generation allowed her to stand on equal footing. She was a firmly social being, and it is not surprising that her first published piece was written in the midst of a busy weekend, and intellectually in the midst of a debate.

The Moral Economy

Thompson saw the moral economy—the expectation on the part of the poor that their social betters should take responsibility for provisioning them in times of dearth—driving riots over food prices in the late eighteenth century. Betsey flatly declared this impossible. Her rejoinder was sharp and to the point: there were no traditional peasants in late eighteenth-century England to advocate for a traditional moral economy because England had seen the triumph of agricultural capitalism well before that; those protesting food prices were caught up precisely in that new market economy, and their howls of anger were loud but new. Traditional peasants, if one went far enough back to find them, had had far less need of any kindness on the part of local elites simply because agricultural capitalism and the pull of markets had been absent. And in the face of old-fashioned famines, rooted in weather, elites had been powerless. The notion that one's betters could help relied on the capitalist truth that they controlled the markets, the shipping, and the supply of grain. Marxists like Thompson, she added, had little business pinning their hopes for social or economic justice on landlords or merchants tempted to see themselves as the heirs of antique, possibly imaginary, and originally Christian communities.[44]

It was the voice that would become classic Fox-Genovese, gently and respectfully suggesting to Thompson and Coats that they ought to know better, that work existed making clear the complexity and chronology of the transition to agricultural capitalism, and if they reflected, they would remember the roots of the argument they were having. And with her penchant for saving the best for last, she closed by recommending to Thompson that he take seriously Coats's defense of classical economics, "for Mr. Coats is right in defending the moral intentions of the classicists. If the rise of a market society brought indisputable horrors, it also brought an emphasis on individual freedom of choice, the right to self-betterment, eventually the opportunity for political participation. The values of Liberalism should not be reduced to nought simply because their practice has historically been so shoddy."[45] So she boxed the ears of one of the most prominent British Marxist historians alive at the time, gently and respectfully, suggesting something of how she taught her classes. That she advised a respect for liberal individualism should not startle us in the face of her emerging critique, not only of liberalism's shoddiness but of its inadequacy in the face of societal needs. She always recognized the beneficent changes individualism produced but at the same time excoriated the negative consequences.

In this period, which might be broadly called her dissertation years, even Betsey's letters to her best friend glowed. Uncomfortably treated as a faculty wife in need of tea parties at Stanford, Betsey heard from her friend Nancy Wilson: "As you know, I have often admired your ability to survive in atmospheres that, if not all so aggressively hostile (as you so aptly put it) as Stanford's, have at least been lacking in any degree of support or even acceptance of your person and purposes."[46] Nonetheless, Wilson wrote,

> Your letters are unbelievable! They seem to get better and better, or maybe we are just figuring out better how not to let the paper get in our way too much. This last one I have read and reread: I don't know where to begin to tell you what I enjoyed most about it, except maybe to start backwards, with style instead of content. . . . At one time I was sure that if we ever exchanged letters regularly they would be small masterpieces of elegance and wit: a correspondence between Lady Mary Wortly Montague and Madame d Sevigny (with one eye, certainly, on posterity) and here we are, writing so clearly not for posterity but for each other—and oh, my friend, I like it so much better! . . . But mainly I get such a clear sense of the unedited you through these letters, and wouldn't have dreamed it was possible.[47]

Elizabeth Fox-Genovese was coming into her own, writing her "unedited" self and a 733-page dissertation—"The Forging of a Bourgeois Ideology; a Study in the Origins of Physiocracy."

Moving beyond her dissertation, if her later habits are any guide, she worked hard at teaching, preparing far more material than most undergraduates could assimilate in a class period. She would have developed this approach at Harvard, where women teaching fellows were scarce and young men were unprepared to respect them. True to form, she exhausted herself that first year, landing in a Rochester hospital in the spring of 1974.[48] She rebounded quickly, gained four pounds, bought two large bound journals a week later, and left thirteen pages of occasional, reflective writing from 1974 to 1977 in one.[49]

Much of that journal shows how quickly and with what determination Fox-Genovese moved from French history to women's history and, most particularly, to the close examination of women's fiction. She had been, she wrote of her hospitalization, "riding high and then bang—out flat." She had written a poem just before this illness and within weeks of coming home finished a review essay, begun just before, on Jacob Price's *France and the Chesapeake*. It is worth pondering how close she was to leaving history to become a woman of letters. While she never again wrote a poem, she pored over women's writing, journals, letters, and fiction for the rest of her life.[50]

The poem marked a step into women's lives, utterly different from the review of Price's work on the tobacco trade between France and the Chesapeake. Intensely personal, sensual, private, and female, it is a voice unlike that of Fox-Genovese in print. And it illustrates just how far outside the familiar she was willing to go in 1974, searching for the center of her life as a writer.

For Juliet

Seeing with words.
Words focus my sight on yours.
Jennifer stirs; the heat of summer shimmers in the lot;
The cape furls
Raising generations by the lake.
The bell cord summons dolls to tea,

To open presents
Wrapped and rewrapped—
Papers once used, now reused.

Conceits unjustly tarnished,
Wasted when they could
Have served.
The pleasure of them lived suspended
Between giver and receiver
Uniting sights.
They forgot their roots,
Shimmering spun their own reflection:
They lost connection.
Loss of meaning,
Baubles gracing shells.
No wonder meaning fled—
"Take me naked or do without."

But the echoes were lost too.
Presents without wrappings
Too blunt
To summon the guests,
Shattering
the privileged space
Between you and me.[51]

"For Juliet" reminds us that Fox-Genovese was never reconciled to her father's version of his trade, to being a historian who argued for geographic determinism. Family determinism too was to be resisted, not just accepted when the bell cord was pulled. She tried out a voice that was opalescent, full of the moment, testing the potential of two minds to connect and, ultimately, the potential of language itself. Wrapped, rewrapped, unwrapped—gifts, connections, conceits, reflections, language with the promise of sensual force, bringing body and mind together. The subject of the poem—which I suspect is language, the power to connect—shimmers between the allusive lines, never fully visible, almost seductive, until they "lost connection" and "meaning fled." Full of what a colleague called "fragility and longing," the poem reminds us of Fox-Genovese's years of analysis, her confidence as a writer, and the thin line between.[52] Even more, it suggests the tension between "primitive feeling" and "civilized expression" that she pondered in those words in 1976.

Stretching in another direction, she drafted a paper for Genovese's 1974 *Time on the Cross* conference, a gathering of two to three hundred scholars in Rochester to generate discussion of Robert Fogel and Stanley Engerman's controversial and prize-winning *Time on the Cross: The Economics of American Negro Slavery.* Genovese found funding and recruited speakers; Betsey Fox-Genovese gave a paper that, as a colleague present at the conference recently recalled, generated "widespread agreement among many of us that her paper was the best paper of the conference and raised a lot of issues historians and others ignored."[53] She published "Poor Richard at Work in the Cotton Fields: The Psychological and Ideological Presuppositions of *Time on the Cross*" in 1975 and expanded it for *Fruits of Merchant Capital* in 1983.[54] She was staking out territory, much as she would declare her interest in psychohistory in 1975 with "Psychohistory versus Psychodeterminism: The Case of Rogin's Jackson."[55]

Genovese's conference on *Time on the Cross* drove two other collaborative projects—both Betsey and Gene's *Fruits of Merchant Capital* and the journal *Marxist Perspectives.* The latter sprang from a meeting "after the conference." Finding money to start the journal was not hard. Louis Ferleger, who came to the conference and stayed for the meeting, later commented, "Gene had contacts with foundations, he knew NY folks who were thrilled at the idea of the journal, who offered help both financially and otherwise. We had fundraisers to support the journal—organized by Gene through his vast contacts in the world of academia."[56] Those contacts are evident if one reads the acknowledgments in the front of Gene's *Roll, Jordan, Roll* and the extensive masthead in any issue of *Marxist Perspectives.* Betsey appeared there, taking responsibility for international affairs.

As Betsey moved from graduate student to author in the 1970s, her journal changed. It was no longer part of her psychoanalysis. Even when she recalled her recent bout of illness, "bad nights with Gene away," and some awkward social incident involving her mother and her mother's prized friends Kim and Polly Roosevelt, Betsey was happy. Never mind the anxious dreams and sleeplessness triggered by the incident with her mother. She was pleased with her poem and with the Jacob Price essay. She had been reading Quentin Bell's *Virginia Woolf,* noting, "Writing was much on my mind. For a while (probably since I wrote the poem the week before I got sick), I had had my eye out for an appropriate journal and when I saw this one I knew it was what I wanted. Funny how they must be bound. Permanent. I bought two."[57] She was now both a diarist and an author, and this freed her authoritative voice.

As Betsey found the right journal—it was a traditional, hardbound black ledger—she would have read that Virginia and Leonard Woolf bought their own press and handset the type. Woolf mattered at this point in Fox-Genovese's life, as she and other modernist women emerged in biography and reprints just as young women like Fox-Genovese sought jobs and incomes. Reading Quentin Bell's thorough but biased version of Woolf's life in 1974, Betsey found it reason for self-reflection. That life too was of an intense, talented woman, somewhat left-leaning, troubled by but attached to her father, married to a politically adept scholar, talented from childhood, iconoclastic, a great reader, literary critic, and anorexic.[58]

Fox-Genovese emerged as women of Woolf's and Agnes Fox's generation were hungrily rediscovered, but she also had a husband who could open doors for her, giving her the best of both worlds. Few had her advantages, and as historian Linda K. Kerber, hired in 1971, remarked in 1997, "I have lived my professional life in an academic world from which women ten and twenty years older than I have been virtually absent."[59] When Betsey published her dissertation in 1976, she acknowledged her sister, Rebecca, and her good friend Nancy Wilson for "a steady acceptance and support that eased my way to participating actively, as a woman, in what is still a man's world."[60] Silent on Gene's support and her father's influence, she nonetheless chose to turn to Cornell, where her father had taught since the 1940s, to find a publisher.

The book was precise, closely argued, with a nod to her 1972 phrase "property is a hegemonic ideology." Physiocrats argued that land, the preeminent form of eighteenth-century property, could far more profitably be nestled in a free market in grain, produced by capitalist farmers. Most importantly, they thought it could become so profitable that it would save the absolute monarchy by improving its chief source of income. What Betsey saw was that the model they had in view, that of the agricultural capitalism that had taken hold in the United Kingdom, could not work in France without a similar social revolution, turning either peasants or aristocrats into capitalist farmers who would ultimately hold a whip hand over the monarchy. The Physiocrats remained willfully blind to the political ramifications of their economic plan, a blindness Fox-Genovese called "their particular intellectual hegira." Betsey found their blindness to monarchy's mutability telling and sought its source in the lives of François Quesnay and Victor Riqueti, Marquis de Mirabeau, the two men at the core of Physiocracy. Quesnay wished to save the absolutist state by increasing the taxable basis of that state; Mirabeau, a landed aristocrat, wished to restore "the traditional French community (resident nobles and serfs)," with little regard for the absolutist monarchy. Both thought they had found the means to their ends.[61]

Tackling the intellectual dilemma at the heart of Physiocracy, Betsey examined Mirabeau's and Quesnay's "dialectic procedure," attending to their silences, contradictions, and failures to comprehend the dangerous implications of their emerging ideas. Blindness to obvious conclusions was something she understood. With no visible nod to anorexia, she grasped how destruction can appear salvific. Having learned to see the psychological mechanism by which refusing to eat had become a comfort and a refuge that had nearly killed her, she viscerally read the intent and practical failure of Physiocracy.[62]

The book's subject and Fox-Genovese's life played off one another in other ways. The agrarian roots of the problem the Physiocrats addressed brought her face to face with people's need for food. The personalities of Quesnay and Mirabeau, especially in conflict with the authority of the king, drew on her years of analysis, conflict with her father, and interest in biography, and the *Tableaux*—tables showing the circulation of impressive wealth that the Physiocrats envisioned—resembled in spirit the laborious accounts her father had demanded from her. Her readings of the writings of Quesnay and Mirabeau often caught the awkward word, telling absence, or tone of correction. She still used her child's ear for the difference between calling for Daddy and calling for Ed.

Fox-Genovese wrote her longest chapter on the *Tableaux*. For almost sixty pages she examined, compared, and noted variations in the three versions and otherwise made obvious that she liked economics, systems, and abstractions. If Ed's disciplined red-pencil corrections of her monthly statements had in part prepared Fox-Genovese for the *Tableaux*, she also had always loved mathematics and science. The same impulse, which likewise led her to Marx, later fortified by a summer seminar at the Newberry Library on econometrics, shaped her analysis of *Time on the Cross*.[63] She was at home with numbers and systematic analysis from early in her life; one must remember the Concord teacher who had advised her to go into "the sciences."[64]

Fathers and Kings

Lurking in both Betsey's dissertation and her powerful introduction to her translation of the autobiography of another Physiocrat, Pierre Samuel du Pont de Nemours, was the early modern metaphor of king as father. Explicitly evaluating Du Pont's motives and dissimulations as an autobiographer, and his relations with his mother and father, she restored the dimension of personality to her larger story of the Physiocrats' inability to admit they were breaking with their father-king.[65] She worked to connect the hard numbers of the several *Tableaux* and the convoluted lives of their creators. Not exactly Marx and Freud harnessed in tandem, but close, akin to what Karl Miller had written in 1976, using Freud in his incisive biography of the Scots Whig Henry Cockburn. Cockburn, Miller argued, was not simply a Whig reformer. He was, like many Whigs, the son of Tory parents. For such men, political reform was a deeply personal break. In Cockburn's case, it meant separation from his parents and his extended, influential family. Reform was inseparable in the late eighteenth century from kings and fathers, sentiments Betsey knew well.[66]

Fox-Genovese's revelation of Du Pont de Nemours's struggle in his autobiography to identify himself to his sons—he wrote expecting imminent arrest and execution during the French Revolution—marked more than a continuing interest in the Physiocrats. Her introduction to her translation and reconstruction of his autobiographical writings, published in 1984, tipped her hand. She would claim both liberal individualism as topic, and its genre, the essay, as the weapon with which she would attack it.[67] In her early years, however, she first sought to understand liberalism's genesis. She used what she had learned in psychoanalysis and from her careful study of Freud in examining the lives of the Physiocrats. Du Pont de Nemours's autobiographical writings were perfect for her purpose, uniting political economy with family dynamics. As in her study of Freud, she came to see his writing as autobiographical, much like Jean-Jacques Rousseau's work, and as revealing much about the political and economic transition not of late nineteenth- but of late eighteenth-century Europe.

In an unpublished essay, "Freud and Womankind," Betsey set out Freud's Oedipal, competition-driven male individual in terms of the transition from feudalism to capitalism:

> In my judgement, the particular problems of Freud's vision of women result not so much from the rigid, secure, smug domination of patriarchy as from the nerve-wracking assault upon patriarchy, from conditions of existence within the brother band. The violent dismantling of institutional patriarchy bequeathed the brothers not merely that guilt which Freud stressed, but the pervasive competition between themselves as well.[68]

She was deeply engaged in making the political personal, and her insights into Freud, men, and women as mirrors owed something to Virginia Woolf's earlier statement of the problem, her "very elementary exercise in psychology, not to be dignified by the name of psycho-analysis." Betsey called Rousseau's Sophie a "domestic mirror," and Woolf wrote, "Women have served all these centuries as looking-glasses possessing the magic and delicious power of reflecting the figure of man at twice its natural size." So, they differ—Woolf lacked Fox-Genovese's historical framework of feudalism and capitalism, of a difference between patriarchy and the brother-band—but the link between them remains, and the passage in Woolf, full of anger and reason, remains instructive.[69]

1976

Betsey's scholarly work was flowering: the first three reviews of *The Origins of Physiocracy* called it "excellent" and "outstanding," a "major contribution."[70] Two nights before her birthday in 1976, about a month before her book on Physiocracy was released, she had a dream: "My book. At first I did not recognize the title." In her dream, she had given the book a hilarious new title: *The Natives Are Restless*.[71] If this described the prerevolutionary intellectuals of France, it did nicely as a description of the book's author as well. As a colleague remarked, "Her anorexia was the analog of [her father's] arthritis," and put in his position, she adopted the coping skills she had seen him use: impatience, determination, and a fierce disregard for limits.[72] "Language," as she wrote, "is a taking possession."[73] So was tenure, perhaps even more so, which she had received, anxiously, from a department no longer chaired by Genovese. The new chair, Richard Kaeuper, remembered several late-night phone calls from her.[74]

Fearless in her writing, she had begun edging beyond eighteenth-century France before she had established herself as a French historian. Her rejoinder to Thompson on moral economy was followed by her critique of Fogel and Engerman's *Time on the Cross*, and then by a scathing review of Michael Paul Rogin's highly regarded *Fathers and Children: Andrew Jackson and the Subjugation of the American Indian*. It was embarrassingly easy, as Fox-Genovese criticized Rogin's work, for her to give examples of paternal and patriarchal metaphors for political and economic rule ranging beyond the Jacksonian frontier to Europe. Rogin's reference to paternalism, for that is what his *Fathers and Children* implied, coupled with what she saw as his less learned use of Freud, drew Betsey into battle. Rogin's claim that Freud was central to U.S. history while Marx was irrelevant struck her as a foolish denial of class structure, and she, determined to combine Marxian and Freudian analytic tools, asserted a different version of psychohistory. She was quite serious about Freud in the 1970s, as is evident also from that unpublished paper she wrote while at Rochester, "Freud and Womankind." She followed this furrow thereafter, writing a brilliant introductory essay to her translation of Du Pont de Nemours's autobiography in 1984.[75]

Patriarchy

Genovese's interest in the paternalism of southern planters matched her interest in fathers. In the 1970s she was, for all her intellectual power, a girl, Mrs. Genovese, an outsider, and her father's daughter. That liminality must have rankled Genovese, who was an acute observer of social relations. Gene undoubtedly saw how she did and did not get along with her father, heard what she was willing to say about it, and knew from his life the hegemony of the old WASP elite. Betsey's interest in the paternal and patriarchal, in John Locke, Thomas Hobbes, Robert Filmer, Sigmund Freud, and her father had been simmering since her first analysis began in 1966, and it was Fox-Genovese who amplified Genovese's paternalism into the complex, vicious, attractive, and powerful form it took in *Roll, Jordan, Roll.* Fathers for Betsey and then for Gene were not necessarily good, kind, or decent.

Filthy Paternalism

Genovese's *Roll, Jordan, Roll* begins with the words "On Paternalism" in a large font, words that were in part a product of his marriage to Betsey and her life with the father she called "an iron fist in a velvet glove."[76] He wrote, "Cruel, unjust, exploitative, oppressive, slavery bound two peoples together in bitter antagonism while creating an organic relationship so complex and ambivalent that neither could express the simplest feelings without reference to the other." The catalog of vile and complex attributes that Genovese assigned to paternalism ends, somewhat, on the next page, where he quotes Imamu Amiri Baraka's equally grim assessment of slavery, ending with Baraka's words: "filthy paternalism."[77]

Subsequent readers have often equated Genovese's paternalism with the most superficial dictionary definition—for example, a government or employer exercising authority over individuals in the manner of a father over children, benevolently and intrusively. They have not understood how Genovese used the word, and how his usage changed.[78] His fathers are cruel and deadly as well as deceitfully kind, pushing both extremes. Genovese used Marxian dialectic and Gramscian hegemony as tools to reveal the complex nature of life lived in close interaction with others, who were, always, on both sides, present and dangerous. Genovese's paternalism in 1974 was a constant state of negotiation, trickery, self-deception, force, and almost inexplicable sentiment, rolled together and proceeding day after day. From an article dismissing Genovese after his death as too fond of the planters, we hear this defanged usage of paternalism attributed to Genovese: "While 'some paternalistic planters endeavored to encourage their workers through an array of rewards, a far greater number resorted to harsh physical punishment to keep their chattels in line.'"[79] In Genovese's far more complex, Marxian—his word might have been tragic—South, the masters who rewarded also kept the lash in hand, always. The paternal masters were the harsh masters.

Genovese's amplification of paternalism, more suggestive early on of social structure than of power and psychology, did not emerge as fully dimensional and vile until *Roll, Jordan, Roll,* published in 1974. The word didn't appear in the index of either *The Political Economy of Slavery* (1965) or *The World the Slaveholders Made* (1969); his usage was simply as the dictionary indicated, and often in tandem with "patriarchal." The word did appear in the index of *In Red and Black* (1971), and in one article title, "Black Culture and St. Gronlesex Paternalism," but with its most complex although still brief development in "The Legacy of Slavery and the Roots of Black Nationalism."[80] This was originally published in *Studies on the Left* in 1966, and while Genovese revised it for *In Red and Black,* the passage on paternalism was present in the original, which began as a talk delivered at a meeting of socialist scholars in 1966: "Paternalism did not mean kindness or generosity or love, although it embraced some of each; essentially it meant a special notion of duty and responsibility toward one's charges. Arbitrary power, harshness toward disobedience, even sadism, constituted its other side."[81] This may be the earliest, still incomplete, indication of where Genovese would take the concept of paternalism. Nevertheless, in the late 1960s he could still use the word gently as well, speaking of "a benevolent paternalism" in a 1967 article on U. B. Phillips.[82] In the same year he qualified that in a foreword to a reprint of Phillips's *American Negro Slavery,* writing, "Phillips's view of a patriarchal plantation dominated by a spirit of paternalism, which of course may be either benign or cruel, should be taken into full account by any theory of infantilization of the dependents." On the next page Genovese made clear that "paternalism necessarily involves harshness" as a facet of a father's "duty" and "concern."[83]

Why describe Genovese edging toward the fully developed usage of paternalism that he delivered in *Roll, Jordan, Roll* in 1974? Because between these brief asides on paternalism, these minor indications of a dualism not to be found in the Oxford English Dictionary's equation of paternal with fatherly—the first example of usage is from Shakespeare's *King Lear*—and the dramatic, dialectical, perverse, and full-blown paternalism that opens *Roll, Jordan, Roll* came his marriage to Elizabeth Ann Fox. And, ironically, Genovese's early years of tutoring his wife in his authoritarian, absolutist managerial style.

London

By August 1976 Elizabeth Fox-Genovese was a tenured professor, in London for a year, married, influencing Genovese, buying a new fountain pen.[84] The years in and out of Harvard had not been easy, and she had wrestled with demons to become the woman who finished her dissertation. And it was more than finished, because out of that work, and her two periods of psychoanalysis, had grown much of the scholarly agenda that would absorb her life: biography, autobiography, individualism, paternalism, and moral economy. In the next year she would be free to add women, fiction, feminism, and culture, remaking herself.

5

Woman of Letters

BECOMING A MARXIST BOULEVARDIÈRE, 1976–1983

> Most important, [language] represents what I most (I almost hesitated in writing that superlative) want to be—a writer, an intellectual, a literary woman.
>
> —ELIZABETH FOX-GENOVESE, London, 26 August 1976

BETSEY'S 1976–77 YEAR in London was her first sabbatical, a reward, an opportunity to write, and a chance to stretch. Genovese had an appointment at Cambridge University, and Fox-Genovese had a fellowship from the National Endowment for the Humanities. As she wrote "language is a taking possession," she was sitting in a comfortable flat at 22 Park Crescent in London, facing Regent's Park, claiming the life of a literary woman.[1] Still fraught, still beset by her usual demons—feeling fat, compulsively eating, arguing with her mother, uneasy with Gene's moods—she was well aware of the good work she had produced and, cautiously triumphant, ready to try her hand at contemporary women's culture.

Sitting down to write in late August 1976, she noted that she had not used her journal since 1974, keeping notes of dreams instead in blue exam books and "a French school child's exercise book." She had separated her psychoanalytical habits from her journal and her work. Finishing her analysis that summer, she could resume keeping a literary journal: "But I did lug this journal all the way to London with me and actually have some hope of keeping it up. I have been fantasizing so long now, although with increasing intensity and purposefulness in recent months, about keeping a journal, writing a novel, preserving impressions and so forth that perhaps this time I will." And she recorded, "Now, with my analysis done, taking possession of my own life—verbally at least—seems more pressing, or perhaps simply desirable and manageable, than ever." Her "immediate impulse" for taking out the journal that morning had been to think about the piece she would write for *Partisan Review:* "The Ambiguities of Female Identity: A Reading of the Novels of Margaret Drabble." But Drabble didn't appear. In her stead, Fox-Genovese dwelt on language and ambiguity, herself, and her father.[2]

Daddy and the Typewriter

Because she wrote so little about herself, publishing almost nothing, it is worth reviewing her two-and-a-half-page journal entry in detail, especially as it comes just as she had established herself, balancing between the shell of herself as apprentice and the mature author she had become. Her journal, she wrote, "lies so central to what I expected and wanted—expect and want—of this London year." Doris Lessing's *The Golden Notebook* came to mind, and Fox-Genovese wondered whether she too wished "to compartmentalize" the "strands" of her own personality, as the character Anna had done in the novel. Lessing's 1962 novel was remarkably apropos, about a woman writer, men, feminism, notebooks, London, race, and the Communist Party. With Lessing in view, Fox-Genovese saw her own language spreading out before her in the journal and commented that it "is more literary than it might have been a few years ago and yet not strained in the writing." She next brought up "the gap and the ties between civilized expression and primitive feeling." "Language," she wrote, "is a taking possession." Refusing to see language as "purely artificial," she implicitly evoked Scottish School Common Sense understanding and acknowledged her engagement with the social linguistics of the circle of Mikhail Bakhtin, noted Russian proponent of dialogism in reading texts. She knew Bakhtin from Gene's Rochester colleague Paula R. Backscheider and even more so from Backscheider's graduate students.[3] "Maybe," Fox-Genovese ruminated, "I cling to the notion that human nature is in part (or more) social and, therefore, verbal. In any case I could not accept that this kind of expression is fundamentally untrue to me."[4]

Fox-Genovese put her faith in language, as an intellectual and analysand, and her literary journal kept taking psychoanalytic turns.

Language, she wrote, "anchors the escape from childhood terror, from primitive drives. It captures and makes sense (some sense? a sense?) of a life. Most important, it represents what I most (I almost hesitated in writing that superlative) want to be—a writer, an intellectual, a literary woman."[5] Almost hesitated. These two words, after the didactic anchors, escapes, terrors, and drives, suggest the hesitation of the anxious child, and student, that she had been.

Trying on her new identity, Betsey wrote, "London, my book, my tenure, the Drabble and St Laurent pieces, writing on women for *Partisan* all bring that aspiration home most forcibly and help to make it real." That aspiration—to be a literary woman—became more real as she described buying a fountain pen:

> No accident, surely, that I could not even begin to settle down to work here until I had bought a new pen—deep symbol of my new (not new but renewed, invigorated, or matured) intention. The dream, at the end of my analysis (in the last beautiful sequence, of which more over time) about Daddy and the typewriter, left little doubt about the phallic, masculine, mastering implications of writing for me. And to how many others of those literary sisters over time?[6]

Betsey never returned to that dream, but "Daddy and the typewriter" and the funny and troubling "phallic . . . implications of writing" show us how a young woman with a fountain pen saw the male academic landscape. Without knowing more of the dream, we are left to conclude that Fox-Genovese survived—with the exception of a brief hospitalization in 1974—and sometimes mastered her compulsions in the 1970s. She wrote, taught, published, and found distance from her parents, and London, an even greater distance, was her reward.

Concluding the passage about Daddy and the typewriter by proposing a gendered intervention, or perhaps exile, Fox-Genovese wrote, "But the women and fashion, culture and literature are ways of feminizing it, making it my own."[7] She wrote nothing more in the journal until after December, apologizing: "Fall was so terrible is so many ways." She wrote letters, read fiction voraciously, and gave herself no credit for what she was learning. She read Margaret Drabble, discussing how she and Drabble would place "finally" very differently in a sentence. Despite her apology, Fox-Genovese was hard at work: "At the moment I am deep in literature (women's novels, literature?) and literary criticism in view of writing the Drabble piece."[8]

That parenthetical doubt peeking through echoed her parents' fear that Betsey was—as she had written in the 1960s—throwing herself away on books or friends who were not important in her parents' eyes.[9] But it was a parenthetical aside, no more. She continued writing that Drabble "makes me think how much more such writing would be for me which makes me think how much my scholarly work remains for others: exhibitionism, virtuosity, quest for approval. Also, in all fairness, the real pleasures of objectification. The distance has its virtues. The externality, the curiosity, the pleasure of how does it work/how it does work are all quite genuine."[10] Hired to teach early modern French history, in competition with the early modern French historian hired in 1969, Fox-Genovese was about to spend her sabbatical on something completely different, women's fiction. Having her book, her tenure, and a slew of essays done meant that she had established herself, and this new stability freed her.

1977

By January 1977 Fox-Genovese had published or had in press *The Origins of Physiocracy*, two review essays, and six articles, one coauthored with Genovese.[11] Four of the essays were directly relevant to her book, extending her expertise on the Physiocrats and demonstrating her competence as a historian of early modern France. The fifth, "Poor Richard at Work in the Cotton Fields," overlapped; Fox-Genovese wrestled with Fogel and Engerman's path-breaking quantitative study of plantation agriculture as essentially capitalist, teasing out differences between capitalism and plantation agriculture. Studying Physiocracy had prepared her for the quarrels that followed the publication of *Time on the Cross*. She had no difficulty wading into southern history, Genovese's territory, clarifying the ideological bases of the book's authors and critics as she calmly explained what made capitalist agriculture different from the slave-based plantation agriculture of the South. It was much like what she wrote in "The Many Faces of Moral Economy"

(1973): taking to task authors from left and right who failed to grasp the implications of the words and frameworks they used.

Fox-Genovese brought human nature, morality, and psychology to bear on authors invested in numbers and statistics; she brought hard numbers and structure to bear on those who wrote about emotion and culture. As she mastered the Physiocrats' balancing act of old and new, seigneurial and capitalist, she moved beyond France easily, reviewing Jacob Price's book on France and the Chesapeake and debating Thompson and Coats on English grain riots. "The Psychological and Ideological Presuppositions of *Time on the Cross*" was no great leap at all; these were all variations on the profound Marxist theme of how humans managed, profited, survived, or attempted to avoid various aspects of the transition from feudalism to capitalism.

Betsey and Gene avoided direct confrontations with urban industrial capitalism in their work and had instead come to the transition debate by the more subtle, older back road: the land, the laborers, the owners of one or both. They were agricultural historians of superficially or deeply traditional societies eroded by capitalist innovation. Genovese brought Marx into southern history, and Fox-Genovese brought Lord Kames and other Scots, Thomas Hobbes, John Locke, Herodotus, Freud, and Bakhtin into Marxist history. As I and other students teased at Binghamton, Betsey was a transition junkie, and the transitions were economic, social, political, and psychological. That moment, or process, was her touchstone in every sphere, and the Scots had lived through it, wary, balancing between the new individualism and the still lived community. She particularly valued Adam Smith's fabric of community in *The Theory of Moral Sentiments,* so densely intrapersonal, and the writings on agriculture of Henry Home, Lord Kames.

One of the lessons of Fox-Genovese's early work from the mid-1970s, as she ranged beyond the Physiocrats and France to discuss *Time on the Cross* and Michael Paul Rogin's *Fathers and Children,* was that her education prepared her to work not just in Europe but in the Atlantic world. She had a broad vision that could quickly narrow to a critique of one character in one novel, one autobiography. That close psychological focus, supplemented by what she knew about grand theoretical structures—patriarchy, liberal individualism, and capitalism—prepared her to act as historian, literary critic, and public intellectual in the last quarter of the twentieth century. Writing about Margaret Drabble's fiction was her first step toward her later books probing feminism.

Betsey's journal echoed her father's early complaint that she lacked discipline: "Too much rushing and devouring of reading w/o enough real assimilation of what I know. But I am not putting myself down: my progress has been reasonably okay and my methods not so much more slipshod than those of others." She responded in the next line, "It is only that if I really do want to write, particularly novels and criticism, I must keep at it, and writing the foregoing makes me think how much more such writing would be for me."[12] She wanted to write fiction and quite possibly tried to do so in London.

Perhaps the anxiety and eating difficulties Betsey recorded tell us that, as with her dissertation, she was trying to cross into new territory. After "taking a slug of [her] already lukewarm tea," she described her struggle:

> Last night was bad—I ate an extra (i.e. after allotted dinner) half pound of digestive bisquits and subsequently a can of cream of chicken soup. Of course it could have been, and frequently has been, much worse, but since I have done nothing remotely comparable since we came to England it was distressing. On the plus side, when I later woke in the middle of the night I did not eat. On the minus, I spent most of the day feeling very fat and spent at least an hour this afternoon trying on all my clothes, sucking in my gut, and hating my thighs.[13]

The battle was likely triggered by reading fiction with an eye to writing it, and a few lines further on she noted, "So much of my sense of health turns on being able to be thin and in control. Not, bien entendu, on being *too* thin, but a little thinner than I need to be (i.e. 130 lb)." By current standards, 130 pounds is at the very low end of a healthy weight for a woman of her height, so, like most anorexics, she still ached to be thinner than everyone else.[14] She blamed her eating that winter on "two weeks in the States" and "Mummy and those last dreadful phone conversations," along with other family crises that fell around the Christmas holiday.[15]

For good measure Fox-Genovese threw in troubling old wounds: her inability to accept Agnes Fox's death in 1965, having distanced herself from Agnes to spite her father; marrying Gene as a means of "having Daddy," coupled with a still unsettled question of having children with Gene and his "ferocious" anger at being deposed, as he apparently saw it, after two terms chairing his department, although department rules made clear that no member could be tenured while their spouse was chair. She concluded with her use of training as an analyst "to make more trouble for myself." Analytic training, she wrote, "is rather perfect: it draws on the maternal/female—nurture, caring, people, identification w/ Nini [her therapist]; it ups the ante on the paternal/masculine identification—intellectual sophistication, success, etc.; and it reinforces my daughterly dependence on Gene." In the next few lines she wrote that her training as a Freudian analyst "anchors me more firmly than ever in all my existing patterns from which bearing a child would help to free me."[16] That training was proceeding, she wrote to friends, in London at the Tavistock Clinic and then at the Institute for Psychoanalysis, and if it was irritating her, that would explain why she never finished and why neither institution now has any record of her attendance.[17] Not surprisingly, the fraught January 1977 entry ended with Fox-Genovese simply returning to the necessities of life. She began "rereading Drabble whom I do not like and am determined to be hard on. Gene home."[18]

"The Ambiguities of Female Identity"

When the essay on Drabble appeared in *Partisan Review* two years later, Fox-Genovese damned Drabble as "a cheery and talented magpie." Worse than a magpie, she was a bourgeoise whose female characters were streaked with more than a little narcissism, whose empire was built of amoral personalism, and who betrayed the novel's tradition:

> And the bourgeois novel, that great tradition Drabble reveres, similarly focused upon the individual destiny. But traditional modes of

> salvation, like so many bourgeois novels, assumed that the destiny of the individual had a higher purpose with respect to the community at large. The marriage of a Jane Austen heroine contributes to a vision of proper social order, independent of whether or not one shares the politics or ideology upon which the vision rests.

In short, she preferred Doris Lessing's notebooks to Margaret Drabble's narrow, middle-class world; preferred Lessing's political and historical specificity to Drabble's "quasi-photographic" and "neo-mannerist" sketching of a world where women wanted what men had and disliked other women, especially those to whom they had biological ties.[19]

The ambiguity Fox-Genovese highlighted in the essay's title reflected her sense of Drabble's women as insubstantial and almost interchangeable with the men, as she complained about Anthony Keating in Drabble's *The Ice Age:* "Anthony Keating functions as the structural successor to Frances Wingate. He presents a rather androgynous figure. Not merely could his Oxbridge background and early-television career serve as well for a woman as a man—they have so served in other Drabble novels—but his gentleness with children explicitly evokes a maternal dimension." Fox-Genovese disliked Drabble's characters' petty femininity—narcissism—but bridled at their slow drift toward masculinity: "to find a human identity only by becoming men."[20] She preferred Doris Lessing's Anna and Lessing's edginess to Drabble's unquestioned success.

This was a subtle, sophisticated, but unsurprising socialist response to a mainstream bourgeois novelist. She did admit that Drabble had "considerable" talent but thought it "waste[d] on complacent, life-denying mirrors for middle-brow, middle-class women, who themselves deserve something better."[21] Fox-Genovese worried about the culture in which women—herself included—had to make their lives, and the roots of her 1990s critiques of feminism—which I suspect Betsey saw as middle-brow—were in this confrontation with Drabble's individualism, narcissism, and masculinization.

Genovese

Genovese appeared in Betsey's journals in the 1970s as something of a worry. In 1974 she wrote, "And this evening returning from a drink (water) at the Elwitts, all the[ir] misery & worry about him: he is old, tired, dying; I am forcing him into a life which has none of what he really wants, none of the rewards it has for me." What that life was Fox-Genovese did not say. Perhaps the Elwitts were referring to the beginning of her teaching career. Genovese was forty-four, neither old nor dying. In a phone call, he "sounded as if he was ready to take over the history-psychology seminar. I reacted by feeling threatened." She concluded that she was too strong and independent "to make an issue with Gene."[22] She had, however, influenced his use of the word "paternalism" in his 1974 *Roll, Jordan, Roll* and would dominate the work that they wrote together, from *Fruits of Merchant Capital* in 1983 to the much later first two volumes of *The Mind of the Master Class* trilogy. His voice would emerge again, clearly, only after her death, in the last volume of the trilogy, *Fatal Self-Deception: Paternalism in the Old South.*

Both were working brilliantly in the early 1970s; both were branching out in 1976, Betsey into women's culture and Gene into preparations for the journal *Marxist Perspectives.* Nonetheless, Genovese's growth was haunted by the loss of his chairmanship, marked by the smoldering rage Betsey noted in her journal, and that loss was not completely eased by the Pitt Professorship at Cambridge which he held by commuting from London that year. A few months before they left for London, in February 1976, toward the end of her analysis, Betsey "had a long dream": "Near the end, I had Gene on one of those high hospital beds that rolls, only it was more like a table (no bedding or mattress) and I rolled him under a faucet to wash him? At any rate, he was on the table, which I was pushing, & under a heavy stream of water."[23] At best, Genovese was in a hospital, at worst in a morgue. We cannot know why Betsey had this dream; two years had elapsed since the Elwitts claimed he was dying, and it may have been no more than an unconscious remarking on his finished chairmanship, a bureaucratic death and rebirth that was, after two terms as chair, an ordinary process in academic departments.

Betsey at thirty-five had a lingering desire to have a child, and her last years of childbearing were closing in on her in London. She did write, on the 12th of January, that she was unwilling to let go of the "substitute gratifications" she had found to replace a child—her early productive years in the 1970s—and if Gene knew then that he was troubled by a low sperm count as he later wrote in his memoir, children were a conundrum. Whatever the vicissitudes of their psyches over this, the world was their business that year, and they were internationalists at home in the Atlantic world.[24] They met with Italian communists in Rome and Bologna with an eye to including them in *Marxist Perspectives,* and Genovese later described the meetings—suggesting he was, if only much later, awed by his wife—in his memoir, *Miss Betsey.*[25]

Betsey worried about Genovese, writing, "I do know on some level that nothing is resolved w/ him. The better mood, the prospect of the journal, all of that makes things look better, but the underlying anger is pretty ferocious, and I only did do my extra eating after he called in the middle of my second (i.e. last) piece of bread and cheese to announce that he was coming home today—i.e. a day earlier than expected."[26] She and Genovese were still learning to work together, and much as she depended on him, one can see why pushing a silent husband on a gurney might have appealed to her occasionally.

In the winter of 1977 her journal ended after fourteen pages, and she would not, with the exception of a brief few pages in the early 1980s, write like that again.

The Women's Liberation Movement

Second-wave feminism was all too obvious in London by 1976, and Betsey, wary of the student movement of the 1960s (and the mix of love, peace, anarchy, and students at the 1968 Democratic Convention), would have avoided it as it raged around her. The magazine *Spare Rib* sold on street corners, and marchers, shouting "Take Back the Night" and "Free Abortion on Demand, a Woman's Right to Choose," gathered without warning and blocked traffic. There were feminists, radical feminists, bourgeois feminists, socialist feminists in several varieties, anarchist feminists, lesbian feminists, separatists, and permutations of all of the above.[27]

Most certainly their demand for abortion would have rankled Betsey. Some of them already had children, and most knew that having a child would not free them from "daughterly dependence." They would have struck Betsey as anti-intellectual, troubling, ill-educated, inattentive to Freud. Most worrying would have been the anger that was visible in their faces. If Betsey sensed and then described Gene's "underlying anger" in her journal, that was probably where she let it lie.[28] Her parents' anger was worse. The feminists' anger, confrontational style, and dismissive attitude to childbearing no doubt appalled her. Legal abortion in the United Kingdom and in the United States had coincided with the early years of her marriage.

A new friend at Binghamton University, Sarah Elbert, wrote to Fox-Genovese in September 1976, giving her the means to contact socialist feminist scholars—Anna Davin, Sally Alexander, and Lenore Davidoff—through the Women's Research and Resources Centre in London. Elbert recommended them as "the kindest most simpatico women I know" and hoped Fox-Genovese would "become an integral part of the supportive, though far-flung, network of sisters." But Elbert also noted that Fox-Genovese did not seem likely to enjoy the "late night, grubby suppers & cheap wine drinking" that marked the network.[29] That sisterhood had not existed at Harvard in 1963, and Betsey, coming from her parents' circle of friends, had been raised to avoid anything that could be called grubby. In his turn, Gene had long since declared war on the New Left.

It might not, however, have been the grubbiness that put Betsey off. Fox-Genovese had turned toward teaching about women several years before, and her published work would reflect that soon, but she was known in Europe for her French economic history work. What she had done at Rochester in women's history and women's studies was a beginning and not known in London. While she might have joined the discussion of patriarchy—the word was much debated among feminists in the 1970s, and her article on property and patriarchy would appear while she was in London—she held back. After all, she had come to get away, to write, and to spend time with her old friend Nancy Wilson, also then in London.

Betsey's essay on Margaret Drabble appeared in *Partisan Review* in 1979, but it was her "Yves Saint Laurent's Peasant Revolution," published the next year, that established her as a woman of letters.[30] The essay was by turns funny, timely, learned, and so broad that the reader is swept up in a whirlwind. Thomas Carlyle rubs shoulders with Roland Barthes, Marie Antoinette with Jackie Kennedy, narcissism with capitalism. Betsey knew fashion, she knew about revolutions and transitions, culture, commodities, seamstresses, trade, and psychology. And she enjoyed herself in the writing.

Of all the work Fox-Genovese published, this essay still comes nearest to capturing her dinner conversations, her mind at work, her range of interests. As in her response to the Thompson-Coats debate and her dissertation, she wrote quickly. The *New York Times* announced Yves Saint Laurent's peasant collection in July 1976, a revolutionary reference not lost on Fox-Genovese. She had written about those clothes by early 1977 and had the essay in print by 1978. Patriarchy and Margaret Drabble lurked in the wings, one essay informing another. The Drabble piece led Fox-Genovese back through the eighteenth-century tradition of women novelists to social order and marriages as a personal and social good. Jane Austen's Elizabeth Bennet and Charlotte Brontë's *Jane Eyre* returned her to patriarchy and marriage in Locke, so over the same ground, albeit in earlier and rougher form. The social implications of marriage buzzed loudly in the late 1970s, and Fox-Genovese would examine Kate Chopin's *The Awakening* next. Through apparently disparate pieces she created a broad synthetic historical narrative from which women were never absent.

In a brief autobiographical letter she wrote in 1992, Betsey noted, "By the time that I started teaching at Rochester, I was interested in women's history, largely because of the women's movement. I taught the first course in women's history at Rochester and designed the Women's Studies program there (although it was not implemented until the year I left for Binghamton)."[31] When she arrived in Rochester the Susan B. Anthony Center and the beginnings of women's studies, including a good deal of women's history in the women's studies' introductory course, were up and running, vociferously feminist, organic, and nonhierarchical.[32] Fox-Genovese may have taught the history department's first women's history course, probably did not find the open-ended leaderless women's studies program very congenial, and undoubtedly observed the history department's "very strong Marxist streak."[33] Fox-Genovese was making use of her year in London to develop new pedagogical as well as intellectual territory—women's novels. These had been known to her "very early" with her mother's help but without any sense that they rose to the level of literature.[34]

In the 1970s Fox-Genovese took up women's studies—the expression "with a vengeance" would not be out of place—but she did so with other women, both at Rochester and at the State University of New York at Binghamton. She might have entered academe more safely by never reaching too far beyond the Physiocrats, a bit of Marx, and wearing simple suits. Instead, her armor of choice was expensive, tailored clothing, still feminine but redolent of power and money beyond the reach of most academics. And once she had tenure, she wrote on what pleased her, moved freely across the Atlantic world, crossed disciplinary lines, always working within larger syntheses.

Timing was everything. Just as important as her training were the women scholars she found as she began to write, particularly Sarah Elbert in Binghamton and Mary Young in Rochester. Letters from both make up most of the correspondence Fox-Genovese saved from her year in London, along with a few aerograms from her parents. Young commented on drafts of essays; Elbert did the same. But Elbert had a wide acquaintance among women scholars, especially left-leaning historians, and she pressed Fox-Genovese, who was hesitant, to join the community. But which community?

Fox-Genovese worried that *Radical History Review* had not received her piece on patriarchy or did not like it. In a 1977 letter from an unidentifiable editor there she was assured that Molly Nolan's Boston group, who read and recommended articles, in no way overlapped with the journal *Radical America* or its parent group, Students for a Democratic Society. Fox-Genovese feared "ideological 'correctness'" on the part of *Radical America*'s New Left folks.[35] The editor's letter makes clear the factions that she, as a socialist feminist academic, thought she had to navigate in order to publish—factions rooted in the old left, or Marxists, and the New Left, born out of the waves of student protest in the late 1960s, and compounded by Gene's acute fears of faction and betrayal. In the United Kingdom—where Betsey might have been more at home—the old left held sway, particularly through the work of the well-known Marxist historians Edward Thompson, Eric Hobsbawm, and Christopher Hill, and Marxist and socialist women tended to dismiss the work of indigenous radical feminists.[36]

The order was reversed in the United States, where Marxists and socialists were considerably scarcer and the cultural radicalism of the student movement of the 1960s predominated. Not that Marxists were invisible, but Eugene Genovese was one of very few to hold an academic appointment, and he was argumentative, combative, and irascible. The work of Joseph McCarthy and the House Un-American Activities Committee had made them an endangered species. Genovese had been discharged from the U.S. Army during the Korean War when the government figured out that he had been a member of the Communist Party as a young man. The background to Fox-Genovese's worries about how her work would be read by various factions of the left no doubt grew from her sense of marginalization at Harvard, and Genovese would have fed her fears, given his own and also his tendency to suspect conspiracies. Despite her anxieties, she had colleagues and friends who wrote, discussed work, and gossiped about the women's movement and office politics, and her work found journals eager to publish it.

Sisterhood

In 1973 Fox-Genovese joined a history department faculty committee writing a proposal for a women's history program. Mary Young remembered her participation in the committee and her willingness to write up the "final proposal."[37] Hired as a French historian, Betsey taught courses in women's history, the survey course in European history, and "co-taught a seminar on psychology and history with Bill McGrath." When she left Rochester in 1980, she was replaced by Bonnie Smith, a French historian with an interest in women's history and global expertise. As Genovese moved on from chairing the department and focused his attention on *Marxist Perspectives,* the journal's early organization put Betsey in touch with socialist women academics, particularly Sarah Elbert at the State University of New York at Binghamton.

A glance at the list of editors, designers, contributing editors, and organizational representatives for *Marxist Perspectives* suggests the extent of the Genovese, if not Fox-Genovese, network of leftists in the late 1970s. There were 103 people on the masthead; 25 were women.[38] These latter represented Genovese's colleagues on the left rather than Fox-Genovese's, but they can stand as a known universe. Some were congenial, some were not. From the particular lens of later years, Genovese recalled a shared distaste for some of his political bedfellows:

> When Betsey met my radical left-wing political associates in New York, she rubbed her eyes. Some of the men and most of the women hated her on sight. Their hostility did not bother her much since she judged most to be overgrown junior-high school girls. After awhile, she asked "Am I wrong in thinking that your radical friends in New York do not have the slightest idea of who or what you are?"[39]

From Genovese's perspective, especially later, there was little love lost among the New York left radicals of the 1970s, and Betsey, an old-school scholar to the core, would have been anxious about associating with radicals who did not define themselves as she did, by scholarship.

Sarah Elbert, a former Cornell undergraduate familiar with Edward Fox, had also survived Harvard and probably met Fox-Genovese for the first time at the Berkshire Conference of Women Historians at Bryn Mawr in June 1976. Elbert studied Louisa May Alcott, and her interest in Alcott's novel *Work* made her a good companion as Fox-Genovese took up fashion and women's fiction. The reverse was also true. Elbert was writing to Betsey within weeks of Fox-Genovese's arrival in London, confessing,

> As you probably have guessed, I like both you & Gene very much—on top of, around & underneath the enormous respect I have for your intellect & work. I would like to see you, especially, become an integral part of the supportive, though far-flung network of sisters. . . . Like—at the Berks [the Berkshire Conference], I so wished you'd been staying in the dorms, sitting out under the trees at lunch & at night & sharing the personal & the intellectual struggles.[40]

Fox-Genovese, as Elbert would learn, did not share "struggles" or dorm camaraderie. Elbert identified herself as a New Left Marxist. While admiring "Gene's real 'political' experience," she nonetheless situated herself differently. She wrote, "Of course Gene is Gene is Gene & I don't imagine that he's going to be transformed into a pot smoking Almaden drinking choc chip cookie freak! Nor for that matter do I expect you to become same! Nevertheless I wish there was a way to bridge the gap between our lives." She concluded wistfully, "Gene has many children—in a funny sort of way." At the very end of the letter, she threw in a remarkable announcement. She believed the chair of Binghamton's history department, Thomas Africa, with the support of a Binghamton vice president, labor historian Melvin Dubofsky, and world-systems sociologist Immanuel Wallerstein, intended to make "you & Gene a lush offer—really seriously."[41]

If that was true, the offer apparently evaporated. In a subsequent undated letter, Sarah Elbert added as a postscript that Dubofsky was sure that Betsey and Gene could not be lured away from Rochester and was now trying to hire Herbert Gutman instead.[42] Gutman had been at Rochester, where he and Genovese agreed and then disagreed, but by 1977 he was teaching at the City University of New York Graduate Center, where he received a major grant from the National Endowment for the Humanities to teach labor history to union members. He drove upstate for an interview but must have decided to stay close to New York City and his National Endowment for the Humanities lecture series, which he developed into a major archiving and preservation effort, the American Social History Project.

Whatever hiring efforts were afoot at Binghamton, Elbert also read the essays Fox-Genovese drafted in London. So too did Mary Young, William Leach, and a Rochester student. In an undated letter, Elbert recommended that "your fashion piece should go to either to *Feminist Studies,* or to *Signs,* probably the former with a little scholarly beefing up and nice French footnotes which always impress the hell out of Americanists like me!"[43] Responding to Fox-Genovese in another letter, she began, "Your St. Laurent piece is just too good for *Atlantic,* but I should imagine they'd love it." She complimented the essay but suggested adding "one more dimension," the marketing of fashion to "different classes of women." By different she meant middle- and working-class women, and she provided Fox-Genovese with lists of the appropriate magazines, from *Vogue* to *Family Circle*.[44]

In the same letter, Elbert broached another dimension of what she experienced as a difference between herself and Fox-Genovese:

> I was very moved by your answer to [unreadable] suggestion that you join us plebes. . . . I really am dopey sometimes when I assume that elegance, flair and seeming poise and self confidence for women are not grounded in painful personal history. I DID not, of course, know much about your past history but that should not have led me to objectify you as a classy broad—that was a damned male thing to do and I hereby apologize. I certainly can relate to the burden of a mother who denied her daughter womanhood and even personhood.[45]

This may not have been the cheap-wine-sipping sharing of struggles that Sarah had earlier hoped for, but it was close. Fox-Genovese did not want to be understood as merely the well-dressed, smart, confident Europeanist she now appeared to be, and she wanted to fashion how her underlying troubles were understood.

By 1977, as Elbert's letter shows, Elizabeth Simon Fox emerged as the villain after Betsey's analysis was complete—but not in the journals Betsey kept during analysis. Most of those who knew Fox-Genovese well heard similar stories about her mother. Genovese, when asked about Betty, said simply, "She was crazy." When pressed, he gave as an example a memory of Betty's sudden rage at finding some friends of Betsey and Gene in their—not her—kitchen one morning.[46]

Yet her daughter's anger, directed at her mother's imperious bearing and pride, is a small part of the story in Betsey's journals, where most of her quarrels were with her father. Perhaps she came to hate her mother because Betty did not save Betsey from Edward's need to control and dominate. Because she did not save Betsey, she bore the brunt of Betsey's anger at both parents. And Betty, watching her daughter's attachment to her husband grow, understood the irony: there was little profit in an attachment to one's mother in the 1940s and 1950s and much to gain from emulating one's father. Betsey may have been given two godfathers, after all, and quite possibly no godmother.

Most of the letters to Fox-Genovese that survive from her year in London are amusing, professional, concerned with her articles—she was also working on a version of the Bordeaux study and a critique of Herbert Gutman's work.[47] Others addressed Genovese's new position as president-elect of the Organization of American Historians, as well as the question of how to pack his tuxedo for the presidential ceremony. One other subject lurked. Fox-Genovese wished to become a psychoanalyst. Three letters suggest that she had plans to enable her to practice, two from Mary Young, one from an unknown woman, and a less specific, fourth letter from Jacques Marchand, the soon-to-be managing editor of *Marxist Perspectives.* Young mentioned the Tavistock Centre and the Psychoanalytic Institute. Marchand thanked her for her "brilliant analysis" of a personal situation and suggested she "ought to go into this work since you have such a sensitive grasp of inner and outer realities." The unidentified woman wrote that she "was thrilled to hear you enjoy your work at the Tavistock clinic."[48] Neither the Tavistock Centre nor the Institute for Psychoanalysis has any record of Fox-Genovese training or working, so her association must have been informal.[49] What bears remembering is her commitment to psychoanalysis as an undercurrent in her persistent dialectical thinking.

1980

In the fall of 1980, Elizabeth Fox-Genovese accepted a job in women's history at the State University of New York at Binghamton. It was an auspicious year for the field. Gerda Lerner, who had developed the first graduate program in women's history at the master's level at Sarah Lawrence College in 1972, moved to the University of Wisconsin at Madison to build a Ph.D. program. Linda Kerber, hired at the University of Iowa in 1971, became key in developing women's studies. Fox-Genovese was hired at Binghamton to do the same in history. There were two other women in the department at Binghamton when she arrived, Sarah Elbert teaching nineteenth-century U.S. women's history and Deborah Hertz in eighteenth-century German and European women's history. Betsey came as a tenured full professor and was hired to put the program on the map, much as Lerner was hired to do at Madison. If the demand for women's studies and women's history grew out of the activism of the 1970s, women's history developed deep roots quickly because the archival material on women existed, in far greater volume than anyone suspected, opening doors to interpretation and reinterpretation.

Students entering the program in 1980, as I did, or at any time in the next several years had no idea of how new and fragile the experiment was or of the hostile comments women professors faced. "The ice," one woman teaching at the time remarked, "was really thin" for women professors.[50] The miracle that Binghamton produced was simple, and it was Elbert, Fox-Genovese, and Hertz who somehow managed successfully: students in women's history rarely glimpsed what was behind the curtain. We had financial support, serving as teaching assistants in undergraduate courses in women's history. We found ourselves welcome. We dominated a good many of the courses we took, and we—students and faculty—achieved critical mass quickly.

There were problems with transplanting Betsey, a product of elite private education, to a public university. She negotiated larger stipends for two incoming students, and penurious Binghamton graduate assistants living on less were outraged. Adjustments were made. Worse was the later tension between Elbert and Fox-Genovese as the latter began teaching in nineteenth-century U.S. women's history, Elbert's field. The resulting edginess was no greater than that between men in many programs and exceptional only if one assumes that women are not also serious, competitive, and territorial. That most students only occasionally sniffed brimstone owed much to both the women teaching us and the egalitarian seriousness of the men, many of whom taught in the women's history program. Nonetheless, some students and some faculty fell afoul of Fox-Genovese's expectations.

Thin, elegant, well read in the specialties of several of her colleagues, commanding in four-inch heels, Fox-Genovese brought a legitimacy to the program that was grounded in her particular mix of conservative, almost aristocratic outward persona and—still—leftist interpretation. Her Marxism was that of Marx, Gramsci, Bakhtin, and the literary turn, and she was a rigorous systematic thinker of the very late Enlightenment, not a late twentieth-century radical. When combined with the passionate work of Elbert and Hertz, both products of the New Left who came of age with the demonstrations of the 1960s, the result proved a heady, unstable mix that drew good work from good students until too many sparks flew.

That it was such a fragile combination of personalities and intellectual agendas had, of course, something to do with the people themselves but also with American intellectual life in the last quarter of the twentieth century. That world shifted throughout the 1980s. Ronald Reagan led Republicans to a landslide victory in November 1980, and John Lennon was shot to death that December. The dissolution of the Soviet Union was on the horizon, but the end of the Cold War was not yet in sight. Reagan's Star Wars initiative was.

1975–1983: Writing

In the fall of 1980 Elizabeth Fox-Genovese started commuting to Binghamton. Working against the grain of her parents' aspirations and her own upbringing, she began teaching in a state university where many undergraduates were the first in their families to continue their educations beyond high school. She was outspoken in 1980, insisting that the best faculty ought to teach in public institutions. She had not been happy at Harvard, had wanted to leave Rochester, and was determined to make a virtue of moving to what the English called a redbrick university.

The job talk Fox-Genovese gave in the spring of 1980—the lecture historians deliver during interviews—was on the eighteenth-century French fashion industry. Seamstresses, shop windows, and French cities combined French economy, culture, prerevolutionary politics, and women's work, leading to and from her other interests. She collected a great many prints from the period on a research trip to France and framed and hung them in her house. She was interested in the images by which clothing survived its period, and she was immersed in work on women. This grew from her analysis of Saint Laurent's peasant outfits but disappeared as she began work in southern history, in the collaboration that eventually became hers and Gene's trilogy, *The Mind of the Master Class.* But that work on the South first took a detour into the worlds of southern women, and Betsey was engaged with this by 1980. Her hallmark pattern as a scholar had emerged: she would have a big project, a book, while at the same time writing a score of essays, related and unrelated, always watching for her next new interest.

Teaching at Binghamton

As her teaching assistant, I can remember Fox-Genovese writing on blackboards, sometimes for many minutes before a class, until there was not a square inch of space left. One surviving image of Genovese in the classroom—probably at Rutgers—shows two titles scrawled on the blackboard and a lot of empty space.[51] Gene brought all his voices, manner, learning, and personality into the lecture. He was at home. Betsey's undergraduate lecture style developed at Harvard, where she always said she enjoyed teaching, despite the fact that she was one of very few women teaching fellows standing in front of young men. Genovese's teaching more likely—and I am imagining this—grew out of his early work in the Communist Party, out of passionate debate and argument. In the 1960s and 1970s Gene could be comfortable in the profession in ways a woman could not.

Fox-Genovese and Genovese shared an interest in early capitalism when they married, but they worked separately and did not begin to collaborate until the mid-1970s. *Roll, Jordan, Roll* and *The Origins of Physiocracy* show no overlap. The authors worked hard, but not together. Both wrote with discipline and speed, but Fox-Genovese and Genovese were still far from equal in the profession, as Lawrence Stone's stinging and pompous response to Betsey's criticism of his review of Barbara Tuchman's *A Distant Mirror: The Calamitous 14th Century* demonstrated. He referred to her as Mrs. Fox-Genovese—oblivious to the fact that there was no Mr. Fox-Genovese—ignored her criticisms, lectured her on genres, and mocked Marxism.[52] There was no level playing field in 1978, although those who knew Betsey could probably scent desperation as well as arrogance in Stone's response.

Nonetheless, Betsey and Gene collaborated as equals, despite the fact that the academic world that would see them as equals had barely begun to emerge by 1980.

The collaboration included great doses of solitude. Betsey's parents had left her little privacy, and she longed to be alone. She once remarked to me, "In the end you marry the man who leaves you alone." Gene did and did not. Beginning with *Marxist Perspectives* and the essays that became part of *Fruits of Merchant Capital,* Genovese and Fox-Genovese collaborated repeatedly over thirty years. The volumes of *The Mind of the Master Class* series were the culmination. That two such tempestuous people could work together so well in the face of their differences of background, intellectual makeup, and style is remarkable. How did they?

Fox-Genovese left a clue in one of her earlier journals, writing that "Gene is my rock."[53] His stability—if not his operatic fits of temper—gave her the peace she needed to establish herself, not so much as a historian but as she preferred, "a woman of letters." And his utter joy in exploring the field he had chosen for himself gave her a model that fed her own single, central concern in virtually all her work: her consistent critique of liberal individualism, those it benefits, and those it does not. This preoccupation stemmed from her own struggle for individuation, for separation from her parents, especially her father. As contradictory as it may seem, she relished dissecting the individualism that made her life possible. At the same time, she shared Gene's concern with power's role and consequences.

If Genovese's stability anchored her explorations, their collaborations owed much to another stability, that of their educations. When they published "The Political Crisis of Social History: A Marxian Perspective" in 1976, it was a short, seamless collaboration blending many conversations. They had debated Marc Bloch's value during their courtship, with Genovese defending Bloch and his wife claiming Georges Duby as the better medievalist. Genovese later wrote that it was "one of the few such disputes with her I would ever win."[54] Much of that essay demonstrates how well served and firmly anchored both were by their educations: Gene had a substantial background in European history, and Betsey had no trouble moving around the Atlantic world.

Neither were they bound by period or method. From Herodotus to *Annales,* back to the Scottish Historical School, on to socialist social history and then contemporary social-historical practice, including quantification, anthropology, sociology, psychology, and a derisively named neoantiquarianism, they cast aspersions, made connections, and brought order. In fifteen pages they set the stage for *Fruits of Merchant Capital,* including the use of Ernest Vogelin's line, "The order of history emerges from the history of order," which would reappear at the front of the chapter on domestic economy in *Fruits.* When "The Political Crisis of Social History" came out in the winter of 1976, Fox-Genovese was already at work on essays for *Fruits of Merchant Capital.*

Fruits

The book still strikes me as a spectacular and innovative collaboration, not of two specialists in the same field but of broadly educated people in related fields, joined by congenial preoccupations with political economy and culture. Genovese, ever the rock, brought his profound knowledge of the South, the literature on slavery, and human nature; Fox-Genovese brought her early work on Bordeaux, her predissertation insights about property as ideology, her command of theory and structure and all things quantitative, her grasp of psychology, and her growing interest in women. Both turned old school canonical educations to good use in breaking new ground in their fields, testing the limits of those educations and using them as anchors in later life.

Between them, Genovese and Fox-Genovese extended the critique of social history that they had begun in the initial version of "The Political Crisis of Social History." They did so by providing their own best efforts as examples of an Atlantic world reaching not from New England to England but from the slaveholding states to France, focusing on the origins of capitalism. Between 1976 and 1983 they worked together and apart on a set of loosely connected essays that would stun, baffle, and delight a range of reviewers, many of whose comments are discussed in the next chapter. Yet *Fruits of Merchant Capital* was merely part of a bigger, more complex process of untangling. In *Fruits,* Fox-Genovese was still an economic and intellectual historian, working somewhere between 1750 and 1850 in the Atlantic world. Her path forward in the 1980s was more complex.

The Awakening

Not for nothing had Betty taken her to Knutsford in Cheshire, the model for Elizabeth Gaskell's *Cranford.* After slogging away in London on her Margaret Drabble piece for *Partisan Review,* Betsey published "Kate Chopin's Awakening" in *Southern Studies* in 1979, followed by "The New Female Literary Culture: Tradition and Innovation" in 1980 and "Scarlett O'Hara: The Southern Lady as New Woman" in 1981. Her essay on *The Awakening*—or, as she put it, Kate Chopin's Awakening, possibly a different subject—is by far the most important.

Fox-Genovese innocently told readers that *The Awakening,* published by Kate Chopin in 1899, "presents a brief twenty-eight-year-old married woman's discovery of love and sexual passion and her rebellion against the marital codes and institutions of her society."[55] Then, as she had warned readers in the preceding paragraph, she demonstrated that every feminist reading of the heroine, Edna Pontellier, is wanting. In a densely argued twenty-five pages, she peered beneath the trope of a nineteenth-century woman married to an older, patronizing man, finally in love with a young man more suited to her but out of her reach, given the "marital codes" of her society. She was not persuaded that Edna drowned herself for love of Robert, in the tradition of cheap novels and ballads written by hacks. Fox-Genovese's eye was not drawn to Robert but to the women of the novel's New Orleans. All older than Edna, her acquaintances made room for themselves within the codes, laws, and paternalism of the nineteenth century. They lived comfortably at Grand Isle in a world reminiscent of Cranford. Edna's ties to these slightly older women, especially Edna Ratignolle, who could be a mother to her, were more important to Fox-Genovese's reading of the novel.

With great precision, Fox-Genovese reevaluated the suicide after the ostensible triggering event, an affair, and found a deeper cause than the protagonist's flirtations with men. With some deep resonance in her own life, Fox-Genovese pointed out that Edna's mother died when she was young, and that without her, Edna could not become a woman. Even though she had a husband and children, some means of finding maturity and authority were lost to her. It is Edna's growing awareness of this absence that drives her to seek out the sea, a common symbolist representation of mother in the period. And, so, she swims out, seeking a love denied her for many years and not to be replaced by husband or lover.

Elizabeth Fox-Genovese was about twenty-four when her anorexia showed itself and twenty-seven as she came to control it. Her mother had been absent, and her father overwhelmingly omnipresent. She was no stranger to the reality of young women in their late twenties taking their own lives. It was a powerful reading of *The Awakening,* full of the lessons that the young Betsey Fox had wrested from Freud as she fed herself a diet of ice cream, soft cheeses, and chocolate biscuits. Her version of baby food had sufficed; she survived, and she saw the absence of Edna's mother and her attraction to mature women immediately. The year after Betsey published the essay, she took a new job, far from where her husband taught, and moved to a house in Ithaca less than a mile away from her parents' house. In 1980, hired to teach French history at Binghamton, she had other plans.

6

Returning to Ithaca

BECOMING A WOMEN'S STUDIES SCHOLAR AND SOUTHERNIST, 1980–1986

> Here is my lord Odysseus' hunting bow.
> Bend it and string it if you can. Who sends an arrow
> Through iron axe-helve sockets twelve in line?
>
> —*The Odyssey*, translated by Robert Fitzgerald, book 21, lines 78–80

BETSEY WAS well aware of *The Odyssey*, of the resonance of returning to Ithaca, of reclaiming her place in the family. The daughter whom Edward Fox tried to create in his image was now stringing her bow. On her return to the town in upstate New York where she had lived as a child, she was not quite as old as Odysseus on his return to that other Ithaca. Neither was she male. Yet she too had voyaged out and faced temptations and challenges. Often having called herself her father's eldest son, she otherwise could not have moved practically next door to her parents. She did so in the summer of 1980, just after Ed's retirement.

At the time, Betty Fox was seventy, Edward sixty-nine, Gene fifty, and Betsy thirty-nine. Betsey and Gene bought a house less than a mile from Betty and Ed. But while physically closer than in years, Betsey was intellectually moving farther away from her parents than ever before. She had just taken a position at Binghamton University as the senior member of a graduate program in women's history. Hired as a French historian, she would teach no French history. She would instead emphasize comparative women's history, which gave her room to teach an Atlantic world that included work on Latin America and Africa. Her recognized specialty in French economic history, prominent in her written work through 1984, was rapidly retired, although not abandoned, as she shifted increasingly into U.S. women's history and the antebellum South.

Fox-Genovese's move to Binghamton advanced her to the rank of full professor. She certainly looked as if she were coming home victorious. Yet moving back to Ithaca had not been her goal; finding a job away from Rochester had. Before taking the position in Binghamton, she applied for a position at New York University as a senior Europeanist. Carl E. Prince, a professor there specializing in revolutionary America and the early republic, urged her on. It could not have hurt that Betsey shared his love of baseball. Despite his support, Fox-Genovese did not get an offer. Probably not senior enough for New York University (she had only had tenure at Rochester for three years after all), she took the job at Binghamton.[1]

Eight years earlier, in 1972, when she negotiated her tenure-track offer from Rochester, she had judged that "there are problems with Gene and me working at the same place."[2] By 1980 and with a new job in a different place, she no longer felt the pressure. If she was abandoning her father's France to take up her husband's South, she was, more importantly, legitimating women as colleagues and subjects of study. Immaculately and fashionably dressed, wearing just enough gold and just the right watch to make it clear that she was well-dressed, in good suits or warm skirts and beautiful sweaters, Betsey undoubtedly staged herself as carefully as the French women in the antique prints she collected. She was dressed for Paris in upstate New York. At the time I write this, there are women in Paris, on the Metro, with Betsey's sense of style, a self utterly interwoven with la mode, who sit the same way and convey nuance with similar facial expressions. This fierce French essentialism, the French feminine, was reinforced for Fox-Genovese by Freud, and she never left it behind, a security and identity she kept wrapped around her.

The authority she expressed through clothing was constructed, and there was more anxiety than conceit in her wardrobe. She chose clothing a cut more professional than the things she had asked her mother to send her when she was a student in France at Collège Cévenol: the ubiquitous plaid skirts, woolen sweaters, blazers, and, for university life, suits that echoed them. She had chosen to teach at a public university where no one dressed like that and where neither her husband nor her father had ties, where she would be alone. In her last year at Rochester, she had defined herself as a Marxist feminist in an essay published in *Marxist Perspectives,* "The Personal Is Not Political Enough."[3] Four years earlier she had described herself as a Freudian with an interest in psychohistory, and both Marx and Freud would hold her interest through the 1980s and, in certain respects, much longer.

In 1979 she received an important six-figure grant from the Organization of American Historians and the U.S. Department of Education, becoming project director for "Incorporating the History of Women in America into the Broader Curriculum."[4] Funding several conferences, extensive bibliographies, and teaching guides over the next three years, the grant further recommended Betsey and women's history to Binghamton.[5]

The Physiocrats were slipping into the background. Betsey, however, deployed her intellectual strengths carefully. Her job talk at Binghamton considered French fashion and the economics of the clothing industry in revolutionary Paris. With hindsight, the calculation is palpable: even a department seeking a senior woman scholar in 1979 and welcoming women's history as a field wanted someone who drew on her specialization—in Fox-Genovese's case, eighteenth-century French economic history.

Moving to Ithaca meant that both Betsey and Gene, more so Gene, faced lengthy commutes. Gene never drove, so he relied on Greyhound buses and occasional rides to reach Rochester.[6] Betsey drove her dark brown Audi Fox too fast and sometimes got speeding tickets on the back roads leading from Ithaca to Binghamton. She would mutter over them, insisting that she knew what speed the roads would bear. She learned to drive on those country roads during her gap year at Cornell, back in 1958–59, and even earlier with her father.[7] She liked fast cars, and like her father and mother, was particular about what car she drove. Hardly surprising given that she was named after the Fox family car that her father had learned to drive in 1929.

What Betsey brought to Binghamton and to women's history was a jarring, effective combination of haute bourgeois style and patrician manners with solid Marxist credentials. She had read Marx, all of Marx. She was a Marxist intellectual, but unlike her husband's, her Marxist credentials were scholarly while his originated in leftist activism. She had read Freud, all of Freud. She owned and read the collected works—the James Strachey edition. Hired as "an able French historian" who would help establish the new program in women's history, she was seen as a French historian like Edward Fox and a Marxist like Genovese.[8] Her interest in women's history made her different from both. It is worth noting that she fit into no particular box in 1980 but was the humanist, the woman of letters, and eventually the public intellectual that her mother could have been. In a briefly kept journal from 1982, Betsey wrote, "The impulse to begin again has been mounting steadily for the last few weeks, months, but has less to do with introspection than ever before. Increasingly, I feel the need to capture thoughts that will otherwise be lost. I want to hold the fragments for different projects—that ever possible novel and my work on women's history especially."[9]

The desire to write a novel notwithstanding, Betsey defined herself in 1979 in "The Personal Is Not Political Enough" as irked by the contemporary feminist slogan "the personal is political." Defending her irritation, she listed a host of family metaphors for political life reaching back to patriarchy, paternalism, Locke's husbands and wives, the brotherhoods of revolutionary societies, and the sisterhoods of nineteenth-century feminism. Ironically, she rejected those sisterhoods, insisting that they reflected only the shared experiences of white, middle-class, northeastern women. Worse yet, sisterhood was limited, charming, homosocial, apolitical, somehow individualist, and finally damnable: "Sisterhood essentially identified itself as the egalitarian distribution of powerlessness." Her main argument was that common to nineteenth-century socialist feminism, sisterhood and independent feminist movements invariably inclined to "the ideology of the dominant class . . . where propertied individualism has afforded the historical and social basis for freedom and equality."[10]

The exclusion of the poor, the immigrant, the Native American, the enslaved, and the free African American in the name of securing reforms that would benefit women who yearned for the rights their men had gained would continue to irk Fox-Genovese. For her, the old

Cartesian assumptions of equality had run into a material world full of class antagonisms that could not be healed by treating women as men. Sylvia Pankhurst had broken with her mother, Emmeline, and sister Christabel over the needs of working-class women, and Fox-Genovese continued that socialist critique of feminism and its slogans, including Robin Morgan's "sisterhood is powerful."[11]

Earlier socialist feminists, such as Sylvia Pankhurst, Aleksandra Kollantai, and Rosa Luxemburg, had grappled with the liberal, bourgeois components of feminism, so it is no shock to see that repeated. Betsey had, however, defended liberal individualism in its male guise in 1973. Remember she then lectured E. P. Thompson in her first published essay: "The values of Liberalism should not be reduced to nought simply because their practice has historically been so shoddy."[12] There was something about the word "sisterhood," surely a communitarian idea, that irked Betsey and led her to insist that it was synonymous with individualism for white women from the Northeast—her home. That old socialist trope of Betsey's would outlive her socialism, and it had a propulsive energy for her, sending her into the writing of both *Feminism without Illusions* and *Feminism Is Not the Story of My Life* in the 1990s.[13]

What sisterhood—also known as collaboration—she had known hardly survived the contentious breakup of *Marxist Perspectives*, and that fact would make her future tenure as director of women's studies at Emory very difficult. Her connections to feminism were scholarly and shaped by her readings of Locke, Hobbes, Smith, the Physiocrats, and women's literature. Summers at Annisquam on Cape Ann in Massachusetts, hearing stories about the Whitings and the Foxes from Agnes Fox, gave her roots, but she was also a Simon, a nonpracticing German Jewish woman. Eric Hobsbawm's flight from Berlin in 1933 would have resonated with her in ways that her father's roots in Springfield and Annisquam did not, much as St. Teresa Benedicta of the Cross—Edith Stein, also Jewish—would matter to her in the 1990s. Her possible godfather, the noted intellectual historian Frank Manuel, was Jewish but not Jewish, living in a circle of Jewish intellectuals in Cambridge, Massachusetts.[14] In 1997 Manuel wrote about Marx's self-hatred as a converted Jew in *A Requiem for Karl Marx*, clearly having thought about the complexity of being Jewish yet not Jewish.

In the early 1980s Betsey remarked that she felt like an impostor, meaning, as she explained at that moment, she did not feel like the scholar others saw when they looked to her. She drew on a variety of identities in the course of her life—her father's eldest son, almost Jewish, almost the wife of a French civil servant, a leftist scholar, wife of a working-class Sicilian, and feminist, as well as a French historian, southernist, cultural critic, conservative Catholic activist—ultimately consistently living only as a haute bourgeoise, her armor of choice. In the early 1980s, however, she seemed to be reflecting on arriving at Binghamton without Gene's assistance, with doors open to her: seniority in women's history, moving to U.S. history, working on antebellum southern women. It was all new.

I have no idea how she saw us, the usual ragtag bunch of preprofessionals, including the usual mix of conservative, moderate, and well left-of-center graduate students at Binghamton. For the most part, our jaws dropped in the first seminars. Professor Fox-Genovese was nothing like the socialist feminist women I had known in London in the 1970s. What she said, which was as little as necessary to move discussion along and lead us to water without forcing anyone to drink, was so concise and learned that we forgot the four-inch heels and listened. She brought order, theory, and structure to an emerging field and made that field seem centuries old. She allowed us to take for granted, in a profoundly positive way, that women's history was respectable, serious, and established. In 1980 that was a miracle, albeit an imperfect one. She did not do this on her own. Sarah Elbert and Deborah Hertz were already in the department, and Hertz, a recently hired Germanist, put up with disparaging remarks, including comments that would now no longer be tolerated. Lord knows what Elbert had had to put up with.

If Fox-Genovese faced similar flack, she rarely mentioned it, but there were friends and enemies of women's history, as well as those she perceived as personal friends and enemies. My own sense at the time was that supportive history faculty outweighed other voices, as they must have to build the program. Nonetheless, Fox-Genovese's elegance and *sangfroid* would have discomfited men and women used to the old ways. She did not socialize with the faculty but instead had lunch with her students. She also had parties for her students. After one remarkably inept gathering at her house in her first semester at Binghamton, to which she invited her parents, distinguished faculty from Cornell, all men, and her students, mostly women, she gave up that approach. It was uncomfortable, reeking of *Susanna and the Elders*—the 1610 painting of the biblical Susanna by Artemisia Gentileschi captures the lewd (and puzzled) male gaze perfectly—and Betsey thereafter produced more congenial gatherings.

Other dynamics proved challenging as well. In the late summer of 1981, Fox-Genovese fell out with Sarah Elbert. Elbert and other women connected with the journal *Marxist Perspectives* had complained that Genovese exercised too much power and that Fox-Genovese failed to support the women on the masthead of the journal. Yet, Genovese had pulled the plug on *Marxist Perspectives* the winter before, so the journal was unlikely to have been more than background for their quarrel.[15] If their argument had immediate roots, it would have been over the two colleagues' support for different candidates in the upcoming election of a department chair.

Marxist Perspectives

Marxist Perspectives was an extraordinary journal, born in a hotel room immediately following the 1974 Rochester conference Genovese had organized on Robert Fogel and Stanley Engerman's *Time on the Cross.* A handful of participants met in that room: Christopher Lasch, Betsey Fox-Genovese, Gene Genovese, Warren Susman, Eric Foner, Jay Mandle, Jack Womack, and Lou Ferleger. The small conference had been extraordinary, and the energy carried a growing core of editors and organizers through four years, until the first issue appeared in 1978. While this was Gene's project, it mattered greatly in Betsey's life. Her paper at the conference was one of two that, to quote a listener, "dazzled the audience." The other was Warren Susman's "compelling critique of the conference."[16] So, even as a junior professor in French history in 1974 Fox-Genovese was able to impress a select audience of southern historians, economic historians, historians of slavery, some of the best in their fields. The paper, "Poor Richard at Work in the Cotton Fields," appeared the next year in *Review of Radical Political Economy.*

Fall 1980

The demise of *Marxist Perspectives* was ultimately Gene's doing, following a heated meeting in Eric Foner's New York apartment in late 1980 with a good many of the organizational secretaries and area editors in attendance, including Sarah Elbert and Ann Lane, Genovese's former wife. Genovese, recovering from signs of a heart ailment, did not attend. Betsey represented them both, and after much heated discussion, an agreement was reached to share power among a group of editors, taking a burden off Genovese that he could perhaps not afford to bear at the time and resolving issues of authority and control. The journal had become influential, respected, and remarkably solvent in its first two years, and decisions about its direction mattered as its audience grew.

It remained for Betsey to report the resolution to Gene, and she left believing, with those at the meeting, that the journal's future had been secured.[17] As she later told a colleague, she admitted to her husband that at the meeting she had felt alone, attacked, and without support. She had had support, but it was not universal. Betsey wanted to be treated as an equal among her *Marxist Perspectives* colleagues—she couldn't stand being pushed aside, ignored, omitted from private conversations, thought of as merely Gene's spouse, as she sometimes had been. Others ignored her path-breaking work and continued to insist that she was new to leftist circles, which was true but irrelevant. Neither would they consider her as the editor. Genovese's dissatisfaction settled the matter, and the journal died at his hand.

Gene told a friend that he acted for three reasons: the way others at the journal treated Betsey; his distrust of others' editing of his project; and his increasing distrust of much of the left for supporting the new, and to him, apolitical approaches in social history.[18] The episode permanently discolored Gene's and Betsey's notions of the left. They did have good friends, serious colleagues, and defenders at *Marxist Perspectives,* but both preferred to see them as exceptions to a left they now distrusted. Fox-Genovese's sense of her marginalization at *Marxist Perspectives* tells us much about her later shrugging off of the left, or what she imagined as the left, especially the feminist left. Betsey and Gene could collaborate with each other, but, despite occasional one-offs and a few deep friendships, over the long term with no one else.

Eva Hoffman, writing in early 1981 for the *New York Times,* quoted Genovese as saying, "We had a chance to create something really good—and we blew it."[19] A staunch ally of theirs remembered the meeting at Foner's apartment in New York:

> It was a very contentious meeting where we finally agreed on a solution to save [*Marxist Perspectives*], something that everyone wanted, including Betsey. But after the meeting Gene decided, based on Betsey's interpretation of what happened at the meeting (for the record, I, as well as others strongly disagreed with Betsey's interpretation of events which I repeatedly told her), to shut down the project. Gene, without consulting others, decided that project should die. Many of us, to this day, were stunned and very unhappy about the demise of the journal and how their views were misrepresented.[20]

Both Betsey and Gene were quick to feel themselves attacked and to construct motives and see underlying causes in others' behavior. These skills may sometimes have served them more than well in their scholarly work, but not in life. Genovese's description of the wretched position of overseers in *Roll, Jordan, Roll* reverberates with that oversensitivity to human relations, and Fox-Genovese, in her powerful introduction to *The Autobiography of Du Pont de Nemours,* shows a similar sensibility in unraveling Du Pont's fears during the French Revolution.[21] But with people close at hand she and Gene easily overreacted, and like the Russians facing Napoleon, burned their towns to keep them out of others' hands.

Summer 1981

Stemming presumably from the fallout over the election of a new department chair at Binghamton, the break between Sarah Elbert and Fox-Genovese became a catastrophe. Betsey stopped eating, slept little, and paced the house for several nights. She was shaken. Whatever had happened, she was, like her old alter ego Fido, experiencing this as a betrayal. It unnerved her. Friends from that time reported that Genovese and Elbert disliked each other.[22] Genovese, good Sicilian patriarch that he was, responded to whatever was going on with fury, and Betsey found herself caught in another triangle, reminiscent of mother, father, and Betsey. Her old, self-destructive anger and anguish returned, perhaps reminding her of her years in Cambridge. The episode proved short-lived, but Betsey very probably began plotting her escape from Binghamton then, letting this coalesce with her work in southern history.

She carried on, perhaps more committed now to her work on antebellum southern women. I was a student in both Fox-Genovese's and Elbert's seminars, and although I sensed the separation, I kept to myself and had very little curiosity about the distant affairs of the faculty. I was older than other students, had done graduate work in Scotland, and spent a number of years in the grassroots women's movement in Britain. I did not expect women—feminist women in particular—to get along any better than anyone else. Fox-Genovese spent more time with her students over lunches and dinners. In another year or two, Fox-Genovese brought home a puppy, defying her husband and bearing his undisguised anger for several days to keep the dog. She built a family that suited her, and Genovese acquiesced.

Marxist Perspectives had been superb, and Fox-Genovese had served as its international affairs editor. Genovese remarked on her comradeship with members of the Italian Communist Party in his memoir, noting that they trusted her discretion and insisted on her as the journal's international representative. The journal, her position there, and the Italian trip she and Gene took during that year in London allow us to remember that Genovese intended the journal to resonate with communist movements current at the time. He and Fox-Genovese were Marxists, and Betsey got on better with Italian communist leaders than with leftists in the United States.[23]

1982

Elizabeth Fox-Genovese survived, despite pacing the floor for several nights. Graduate students were coming to Binghamton for women's history; her undergraduate courses filled large auditoriums. With *Marxist Perspectives* gone, she was free to work with Genovese, whose heart ailment forced him to take a year's leave from Rochester, thrusting most of his share of editing *Fruits of Merchant Capital* on Fox-Genovese. By April 1982 the book was finished and Betsey was in France, although whether she was doing research or visiting friends is not clear. She returned with an armload of early nineteenth-century fashion illustrations, which suggests she was continuing her work on fashion, as well as preparing her essay on women's work and an introduction for Samia I. Spencer's *French Women in the Enlightenment.*[24] Betsey was still, and would remain to some degree, a Europeanist, even as she began sketching out early chapters of *Within the Plantation Household.*

Genovese wrote to her. He worried about "Oxford [University Press] . . . undergoing a major shake-up, with the Limeys moving in in a big way." He was concerned because the manuscript of *Fruits of Merchant Capital* was in their hands. And he worried about an incoming department chair and his salary: "But the salary bit is chilling because it means that I shall have to earn some outside money if we are to stay steady. And that is what I had hoped to avoid. In any case, I do not intend to develop another heart flutter over any of it and am even slowly beginning to assert a sense of humor."[25]

Gene had begun the correspondence in April by joking: "Back from Hamilton, so now you get a letter, even though I do not know why I should write to someone who deserted her loving family for a frog pond. The cats, at least the two males, are in open rebellion against their mother's absence." He quickly continued by detailing what he had heard of a department meeting at Rochester, which he recounted as a battle, or at least a coup, after which he wrote, "Quick, get a Paris Tribune. The Red Sox are in first place. God knows how long they will stay there."[26] By May 6 he was writing that he loved her "and would continue to do so until May 24," when she was due home. He concluded, "Please come home. Bellevue [the 'insane' asylum] does not appeal to me much."[27] The letters are long and illustrate both his anxiety and the degree to which Betsey managed the house. On one letter, Genovese had scratched out some questions about paying bills and scribbled in the margin, "ok—just read your note over."[28] Although he insisted after Betsey's death that he was a natural solitaire, Genovese was lonely while his wife was busy in Paris, and on May 14 he wrote with pleasure about her phone call, letter, and two postcards. She no doubt understood from his single-spaced, typed letters, full of worries and hilarious cat fantasies, that he needed her.

Fruits of Merchant Capital

Gene and Betsey had worked on the essays eventually included, sometimes in significantly modified form, in *Fruits of Merchant Capital* in various iterations for almost a decade, beginning with Fox-Genovese's 1974 paper for the Rochester conference on *Time on the Cross.*[29] Five other pieces of hers on France included a revised version of her 1974 review essay "Jacob Price's *France and the Chesapeake*" and chapters on Bordeaux, the social history of the French Revolution, Physiocracy, and domestic economy. These were undoubtedly drawn at least in part from her early unpublished work on Bordeaux, completed before her dissertation.

While a quick reading of the "Authors' Preface" in *Fruits* makes clear that the coauthors edited every chapter, it also reveals Fox-Genovese's hand at work in much of this book. Gene and Betsey did collaborate, living with each other's ideas, discussing work as they read, ate, and shopped together. This is why their discrete essays cohered. Drawn up in those essays were the forces of merchant capital, arcing across the Atlantic world yet focused on terrain that had been revolutionary in the eighteenth century. According to that preface, Elizabeth Fox-Genovese was the primary author of six essays and Genovese of three, with four coauthored.

Reviewers, mostly southernists familiar with Genovese's work and not Betsey's, and almost all oblivious to the depth of their collaboration, persisted in treating the book as Genovese's, but they were wrong, underestimating both the power of the collaboration and Fox-Genovese's contributions. Not all made that error. One reviewer who fathomed the collaboration, Lawrence T. McDonnell, wrote,

> *Fruits of Merchant Capital* passes . . . to its second major contribution, a brilliant analysis of the psychology of slavery. Genovese has offered important insights into this problem throughout his career, crowned by *Roll, Jordan, Roll,* yet the authors surpass their own achievement in this volume. Fox-Genovese's theoretical prowess, one suspects, makes the difference. The expanded version of her essay, "Poor Richard at Work in the Cotton Fields," here provides an essential point of departure for all future work on slave psychology. Placing Freudian object-relations theory in a context of Marxist social analysis, the authors convincingly argue that slavery's paternalist imperatives caused "tremendous ambivalence and a constant internal struggle, at a high level of tension, for spiritual survival."[30]

That Fox-Genovese used object-relations theory in rewriting the paper she first presented at the 1974 conference—"Poor Richard at Work in the Cotton Fields"—makes perfect sense of a remark she made in a seminar in the early 1980s, just as she and Genovese were revising essays for *Fruits of Merchant Capital.* That remark, remembered roughly thirty-five years later: how often was the first loving face encountered by a planter-class child a Black face? This surely indicates her engagement with Freudian—or not so Freudian—object-relations theory, which posits that the first disembodied objects a child encounters—a breast, a hand, a face, slowly pieced together into humans, most likely parents—structure the child's relations with others forever after, through those first experiences of kindness, feeding, pleasure, consistency, or pain and unreliability.[31] It contributes to our understanding of Fox-Genovese as historian and literary critic—think of Edna's missing mother in Betsey's essay on *The Awakening.* It also suggests just how different Betsey's New York psychoanalysis in the 1970s with Nini Vas Dias was compared to her work with Galdston in Boston.[32] Both analyses testify, however, to an extraordinary degree of privilege, not to mention self-absorption: when in analysis with Vas Dias, Betsey would visit New York City for a week every month, talking with Vas Dias for four or five days in a row.

Committed to using psychoanalytic insight after her years of analysis, Betsey promised a book on Marx and Freud in the preface to *Fruits* in 1983, having warned in 1975 in her review of Michael Paul Rogin's *Fathers and Children* of ways in which psychoanalysis was incompatible with history.[33] With "Poor Richard at Work in the Cotton Fields," Fox-Genovese came as close as she ever would to demonstrating the combined power of Marx and Freud for historians. By the mid-1980s she was still using this matrix: the original subtitle of *The Mind of the Master Class* was *The Psychology of Southern Slaveholders.*[34] By 2005 Betsey, shaping the work, had changed that subtitle to *History and Faith in the Southern Slaveholders' Worldview.* Psychology, which Genovese had deployed brilliantly in *Roll, Jordan, Roll,* was preempted as a principal avenue to understanding. That mind of the master class became an intellectual construction rather than a psychological puzzle.

Working Together

Both Genovese and Fox-Genovese were fond of the essay form, conversations, arguments, and gatherings, and their marriage was always an astonishing intellectual collaboration, always full of words.[35] Essays worked for them, and perhaps especially for Betsey because she worked quickly, spurred by reading and conversation, always overcommitted, always short on time. Ironically, the essay form, as David Moltke-Hansen has shown, was a powerful medium for bourgeois liberal individualist reform in the eighteenth and nineteenth centuries, but at the same time, in the hands of Betsey and Gene, for those debating liberal individualism's ascendancy.[36]

The distance between Betsey's agricultural France and Gene's antebellum South was not great, and reading Betsey's and Gene's dissertations in succession makes clear that both were agricultural historians, intellectual or mud-caked, and both were caught up in the Marxist debate over the transition to capitalism. Gene certainly knew more about the import and distribution of guano by southern planters and Betsey more (but not as much more) about Physiocratic thought. Nevertheless, they recognized each other's worlds from the beginning. Betsey did not have her father's interest in geographic determinism, yet she intentionally placed her chapters on the Chesapeake and

Bordeaux next to each other in *Fruits of Merchant Capital*, recognizing the importance of the Atlantic world, including, through the tobacco trade, Glasgow. Gene benefited from Betsey's Atlantic perspective; she learned from his extensive knowledge of New World slavery.

Both were interested in interior life. David Brion Davis, reviewing *Roll, Jordan, Roll* for the *New York Times* in 1974, wrote, "Genovese's great gift is his ability to penetrate the minds of both slaves and masters, revealing not only how they viewed themselves and each other, but also how their contradictory perceptions interacted."[37] Fox-Genovese could have been at home in that contradictory southern world of unacknowledged half-truths, the "fatal self-deceptions" of their—really Genovese's—last volume, much as she had been delighted to discuss the Physiocrats' blindness to the implications of a free market for *ancien régime* society thirty years earlier. But she veered away, avoiding both psychology and religion in *Within the Plantation Household*, while Genovese held his course into *Fatal Self-Deception*.

1983

Fruits of Merchant Capital was an exceptional and innovative project created out of congenial obsessions with political economy and culture. Extending the critique of social history that they had begun in the initial version of "The Political Crisis of Social History," Genovese and Fox-Genovese provided their own work as examples. Unfamiliar and challenging, their efforts ranged across the Atlantic world puzzling many of the reviewers, much as the Marxist framework irritated them.

The reviews that appeared in the wake of *Fruits* are instructive. They were mixed, ranging from bemused and angry to appreciative and impressed. As most reviewers remarked, some essays were clearly Gene's, some Betsey's. It was striking that the urge to separate the essays drove some reviewers, obscuring any sense of the book as a whole. The reviewer for the *Journal of Social History* despised the book, calling it irrelevant to non-Marxists. Readers of *History Teacher* were told that it was "excessively argumentative" and "hard to read," not to mention "disjointed," but the essays nonetheless did "converge on important themes." The *Political Science Quarterly* reviewer was appalled at Marxists writing with "sectarian assurance." Lawrence T. McDonnell, a leftist writing for *Labour/Le Travail,* valued Betsey's contributions and with a few others saw the larger narrative so clearly that he could criticize aspects. The *Journal of American History*'s review judged, "Together [the essays] constitute an impressive effort to formulate a Marxist synthesis of European and American history from the sixteenth to the nineteenth century." The reviewer for the *Virginia Magazine of History and Biography* was impressed by the work's complexity and continuity. Roughly fourteen years after Gene's and Betsey's marriage, this book was evidence of how each had influenced the other, how their work was, by 1982, synchronous. The book appeared as Fox-Genovese was building her own house, metaphorically, at Binghamton.[38]

"Poor Richard at Work in the Cotton Fields"

Fox-Genovese grew between the first and last iterations, in 1974 and 1983, of "Poor Richard at Work in the Cotton Fields." The conference paper seems not to have survived, but the 1975 article covered seventeen large pages, and the 1983 chapter, although printed on forty-eight much smaller pages, was roughly 40 percent longer. Betsey kept the first half of the title, which was a pointed reference to Benjamin Franklin's *Poor Richard's Almanack,* full of choice, economically rational advice. It was cruelly clever, because Robert Fogel and Stanley Engerman were arguing precisely that: southern plantations were rationally run businesses, more like northern capitalist enterprises than not. When Betsey embodied their argument in the northern, urban figure of Poor Richard hoeing weeds in a cotton field, she gave readers pause. Poor Richard, like Ben Franklin, looked out of place, and this was a clever way of advancing Gene's as well as her argument that plantations were in but not of the capitalist world.

The early version was a critique of Fogel and Engerman's *Time on the Cross;* the later version extended the critique to the works of Stanley Elkins, Sydney Mintz, John Blassingame, Herbert Gutman, Kenneth Stampp, and Gilberto Freyre. In both essays, however, Betsey tackled the point where economics merged with psychology. Making room for references that would present her as an Americanist, she left out of the later version precisely what had concerned her in the 1970s: France, feudalism, and elements of a deep view of the past that were of everyday utility to her as a teacher of Western Civilization at Rochester. The earlier version is a more accurate representation of the breadth of her mind, the essay in *Fruits* more driven by a precise focus on the psychology of slavery in the work of U.S. historians. The transformed essay served notice in 1983 that she was working as a southern historian.

Betsey knew Poor Richard well because Benjamin Franklin corresponded with Pierre Samuel du Pont de Nemours. Concerned with efficiency and economy in all things, Franklin was favorably impressed with Physiocracy, and he was also the author of one of the first modern autobiographies, addressed to his son. Presumably, because she had invoked it in her 1974 paper, Betsey had read his autobiography earlier, and she likely did so again in the early 1980s, as she translated, edited, and introduced the autobiography that Du Pont de Nemours began just as Franklin finished his. Franklin demonstrated Betsey's Atlantic world nicely by crossing and re-crossing the ocean, and contributing both to her understanding of individualism, with the birth of modern autobiography, and to her understanding of Fogel and Engerman's error in seeing the plantation through the modern, calculating eyes of Franklin's Poor Richard.

The upcoming bicentennial of the French Revolution loomed large in 1983, and Fox-Genovese had no interest in it, or perhaps in a new generation of French historians, many of them feminist. She left with a flourish, however, editing Du Pont de Nemours's autobiography, written, much like Franklin's, for sons (or a son) who would grow and live in a very different, postrevolutionary world. And in 1995 she would write, "Far as I have moved, I still credit 18th century France and the physiocrats for having taught me to think about the real issues under the play of contemporary events."[39]

The Autobiography of Du Pont de Nemours

Fox-Genovese's interest in Du Pont de Nemours's personal writing was grounded in her curiosity about her own life, a curiosity flowing out into others' lives. She introduced her reconstruction of his text and the role of autobiography in the growth of individualist ideology, and then returned to argue, for the last time, the usefulness of Freud. Her introduction was an impressive essay on changing conceptions and articulations of the self in the eighteenth century, and it stands as another fragment of her long-intended work on how Marx (economics and politics) and Freud (consciousness) grew out of that revolutionary moment and could, in turn, be used to gain insight into it.

Du Pont, an eighteenth-century Physiocrat who had first appeared in her dissertation, now reappeared as a son, father, autobiographer, man of letters, and reforming monarchist not yet fully reformed into a moderate republican. He first wrote some of his autobiography in 1792 in revolutionary France, while in hiding and in some doubt about his own survival. Weighing Du Pont's difficult language and his intentions, motives, and possible lacunae in the manuscript, Fox-Genovese developed that exceptionally long introduction of seventy-four pages. She presented Du Pont; she demonstrated her own ability as a humanist, Freudian, and literary critic, painstakingly aware of nuance, structure, word choices, absences, and the position of autobiography in the developing Western political theory of individual rights.

Du Pont, Betsey reminded readers, was a product of the *ancien régime,* struggling to describe himself in 1792 in the midst of the French Revolution with little more than Jean-Jacques Rousseau's *Confessions* and Benjamin Franklin's autobiography as examples. She described Du Pont writing then, making something of himself on paper—undoing ties to his parents, reinforcing his ties to his sons should he be executed, making a conservative bourgeois of himself as he entered a new ideological epoch.

Du Pont and the Terror of History

Fox-Genovese used Mircea Eliade's phrase "the terror of history" in writing about Du Pont's decision to compose an autobiography in the form of what was possibly a last letter to his sons while he hid from the Jacobins. He wrote in full awareness of his possible, imminent demise and probably, Fox-Genovese thought, because of it.[40] The historical moment mattered, perhaps all the more so to Fox-Genovese because she too had faced down a form of terror. She made clear that Du Pont's narrative was that of the making of a very moderately liberal individual, forced out of the *ancien régime* by the revolution. The revolution made men revolutionaries, she found, not the hoary textbook opposite, that revolutionaries had made a revolution.

Du Pont was, Betsey argued, establishing himself for his sons as he was before they were born and before he became a notable, public figure. He adored his mother and struggled bitterly with his father, and for an orthodox Freudian like Fox-Genovese, this was "a classic study of the oedipal conflict in action."[41] Du Pont's journey from son to father of his own sons gave Fox-Genovese ample room to investigate paternal authority and patriarchy, and she undoubtedly meant to oppose this essay to Michael Paul Rogin's *Fathers and Children.*

"I Am My Father's First-Born Son"

Her father had cast a long shadow. Even in 1972, ninety miles away from her parents, her father's criticism infuriated her. The anger Fox-Genovese saved in journals and letters was substantial. As she shed the emotion, she found herself able to finish a draft of her dissertation quickly. That work brought her into contact with the Du Pont papers and drew her back to write about his path to independence from his father and then to Du Pont as a father. Perhaps without irony, Betsey dedicated the book to her brother and thanked her family for their help, writing, "If I think I have some empathy for Du Pont's investment in his family, I can only hold my own responsible." She thanked her mother for her "research skills, and sheer deductive brilliance" and her father for, among many things, "wonderful conversations about this point of telling detail and that."[42]

Abandoning Binghamton

By the mid-1980s Fox-Genovese was publicly successful; she and Gene would spend the fall of 1984 and the spring of 1985 at the National Humanities Center in North Carolina. Her letters by the mid-1980s marked a professional success that had not been documented in earlier papers. Friends, publishers, students, and colleagues sought advice, criticism, recommendations, and other favors. She was asked, thanked, and solicited by friends and strangers. Little of it would surprise anyone familiar with the service expected from academics—a manuscript reviewed for a publisher, an essay solicited to celebrate the fortieth anniversary of Herbert Aptheker's book *American Negro Slave Revolts.* She wrote "Strategies and Forms of Resistance: Focus on Slave Women" for the Aptheker volume, probably Fox-Genovese's first essay on African American women.[43] By the fall of 1984 both Betsey and Gene were settled in Chapel Hill for their year at the National Humanities Center. They were there to begin work on Gene's *The Mind of the Master Class* but Betsey was almost immediately drawn away to southern women's writings.

A Year in North Carolina

In North Carolina, many of Fox-Genovese's letters were about antebellum women's journals, diaries, and letters, and once she began reading these writings by southern women, she would not return to the intellectual history of southern men for fifteen years. As she well understood, work on the master class meant reading the letters and essays of the almost entirely male intellectual leadership of southern agricultural society. These men resembled her Physiocrats, and she turned her back on them, for the moment. Her disinterest in Gene's project was painfully obvious, as was Gene's eagerness, in an interview on *Soundings,* a weekly radio program produced at the National Humanities Center and digitally archived.[44]

Betsey was riding high that year. In March 1985 she wrote to then Secretary of Education William J. Bennett, former head of the Humanities Center and then at the National Endowment for the Humanities, hoping to engage him in a conversation about the canon. The great tradition required the restoration of its orphans, she argued, as did the common culture, if it were to be common—widely understood—as eighteenth-century Scots had used the word.[45] She sent Bennett a copy of her "The Great Tradition and Its Orphans," noting, "I share your respect for the Great Tradition and only hope that, along with Jacob Neusner and others, I can interest you in some degree of reformulation. You will recall the wisdom of Lampedusa's *The Leopard:* 'If things are to remain the same, things will have to change.'"[46]

This dialectic of new and old was central to Fox-Genovese's sense of herself. She was forty-four in 1985 (almost the age of Odysseus on his return), established, adult, professional, and mercurial in the full, mythological sense of the word: fast-moving, quick-witted, unpredictable, edgy, and unsettled. In letters written during that sabbatical, Betsey reflected on who she believed herself to be: "I am not, you will say, a proper child of my time. But I do have a deep sense that, however out of tune with the times I may be, I am less interested in acquiring new selves than in enjoying the old."[47] In her forties, she gave up the pressure to become and instead assessed who she was. She was no baby-boomer. She had deep roots in the 1940s and had been shaped by her family, by profound intellectual ties to Frank and Fritzie Manuel, who, like her father, were grounded by the great Western tradition. Frank Manuel left bibliographic notes that reflect Betsey's mainstays: in Locke and Hobbes and C. B. Macpherson, in discussions of patriarchy, individualism, and utopias.[48] Comfortable with the New York Jewish voices of the Manuels and their interest in Freud, along with her father's voice, so familiar to her, and their colleagues, she emerged a precocious graduate student, but not of her generation—of theirs. It was a blessing and curse: to be a child of those who had taken degrees in the 1930s and to become irrelevant in her prime. An old friend of Fox-Genovese's reported, "Now that I come to think of it, Ed [Fox]'s accent resembled that of the New England elite who were 15–20 years older. Eliot Perkins and Samuel Eliot Morison, both Harvard professors born in the 1890s, had precisely that accent, but I don't recall it being common among professors born in 1911."[49] Betsey chose a husband who was eleven years older, who recognized the class structure of the East Coast and, as she admitted in the 1970s, represented her father.[50]

With time to reflect, which Fox-Genovese rarely allowed herself, and archival work to do, she wrote two letters to Nancy Wilson, her close friend since their days at Bryn Mawr. The first letter reported desirable jobs that were out of her and Gene's reach. When they inquired about two jobs at Duke University, the chair of the search committee told them they were too "visible." Betsey explained, "It was a bummer for Gene who was beginning to think about the joys of retiring near these archives, of being able to do the work he loves and forget about academic politics. I could have died for him." She continued,

> I have reached the point at which I really do not expect much acceptance from the "establishment." I know that my work is good—forgive the arrogance—and that they know it. You will see the notices on the cover of my *DuPont* (and I have requested that a copy be sent to you). But I do not expect them to want me around. I never did, as you may remember from Bryn Mawr, Harvard, and all the rest. I think I got more of a sense of being an outsider from my father's experience than Gene did from his background and politics. When I married him, he enjoyed more of the world's attention than I had ever expected to in my life. And I still don't, and don't regret it. Family, real friends, my life matter more and more to me and the rest seems more and more unreal.[51]

Plagued with the sense of "being an outsider," she followed her father, who felt his outsider status keenly at Harvard, which no doubt was aggravated by his parents' relative poverty during the Depression. He sent his daughter into the same devil's den, and her sense of exclusion as a woman joined her discomfort, visible since North Country School, firmly woven into her reality. No surprise that she moved from one field to another, one university to another.

If this letter seemed grim, her isolation in an unfamiliar neighborhood, with Gene ever present, chafed. She needed to get out, to chat, to shop. She wrote in January that "this has been a year of togetherness with a vengeance." She complained that the house "is neither laid out, nor set up, for individual space. For normal purposes, there are no doors to close in the main areas—and no phones at all behind doors that can close." She had had no privacy at home as a child and now, again, less than she needed: "His constant presence restrains me in intangible ways. I like to read and to write with spaces of silence—no other presence—around me. I even like to be able to walk around the house, to putter—alone." However, she took comfort in accepting her discomfort:

> A lot has jelled for me this year. I do feel that I am who I am, am who I will be. And I do not expect to be a member of the "in" group in my profession, or anyplace else. I suspect it is a good deal the way I was at Bryn Mawr, if I have any clear perspective on myself as I was then. I know that I am not now, nor was then, the shadow, the "non-person" I have so frequently felt myself to be—and still do, although in a much happier and resolved way than ever in the past.[52]

The passage is much longer but the confession is the same. Elizabeth Fox-Genovese was profoundly uncomfortable and yet, as she approached her forty-fourth birthday, was able to say so and live with it. Sort of. She would never resist making that sense of being excluded her reality, as she had with *Marxist Perspectives.* Neither would she ever be more included or at the center of her profession than she was in the 1980s. Her lifelong dislike, or critique, of individualism, which she often understood historically as the triumph of the male individual, stemmed from her own—intermittent—absence of self. Having no individuated, independent self, she detested it where she saw it, thinking it false, clinging to her sense of herself as a shadow figure, quick to take offense.

As usual, her ruminations did not overshadow her joy in her work. Fox-Genovese was moving to the history of the antebellum South, and she shared her joy in what she was reading with her friend:

> One of my great pleasures—and one that I would love to be able to share more immediately with you—is reading the diaries and journals of my antebellum southern ladies. I have been reading slowly and luxiouriously [*sic*], taking copious notes, trying to get inside their heads, and to learn all the details of their world, to understand

their presuppositions. What has, perhaps, struck me most—and pertaining most directly to you—is my own response to the different kinds of diaries. I am especially drawn to the mature women—the women in their thirties (you could have had ten kids, and buried three or more by then), forties, and early fifties. No surprise, right? They are at our stage of life. The surprise for me has been that I am suddenly having trouble in not dismissing the adolescents as boring. And they are not, and I can still be charmed, or even, momentarily, drawn in. But the stories that interest me are no longer those of becoming, they are those of being: Not how you choose your life, but how you live it; not how you choose your mate, but how you love and live with him. And I find the love stories of the settled, married people inexpressibly moving. And I think I understand them. And I think I understand what no young person ever can—or probably should—that the great loves and tragic losses concern people who have lived together for a long time. I am hard pressed to choose a favorite, but Sarah Gayle is a strong contender. She married, in her teens, John Gayle, lawyer and politician. His career frequently took him away from home. She raised their numerous (six) children, kept their household in Greensborough going, worried about money, tried to justify buying something for herself or the house by saving elsewhere, read, thought, concluded delightful letters to him "oysters! oysters! oysters!" (she wanted him to bring her some from Mobile or wherever), enjoyed and agonized with her friends, reminisced about her family, fretted about handling the difficult servants, and more. He was eleven years older than she and they loved each other devotedly. She recounts, in her diary, how during a trip to the dentist she was almost glad that he was not there, because his absence removed the sense that anyone could save her and permitted her to be brave. All except for one instant during which the dentist, after a particularly violent assault, paused and patted her hand. Immediately, she thought of Mr. Gayle, and, briefly, cried. Later, she writes of nursing Rosa, an old servant (slave), through tetnus [*sic*] to her death, and describes how towards the end Rosa clung to her hand and would allow no one else to nurse her. The chunk of her diary that I have ends with John Gayle's traveling in Cherokee country to buy lands and planning to return so that they can move together to a

> new home in Mobile. They miss each other. I learned from some letters and other sources that she died shortly after the diary breaks off, of tetnus that she had contracted through a trip to the dentist—and that John Gayle did not make it home in time to see her alive. I cannot bear her having died alone, his not having made it back in time.[53]

As she read "slowly and luxiouriously," she drafted much of her prologue in this letter to her friend, and in that prologue, as in much of the book that emerged several years later, she prepared readers for her later work on marriage, family, and opposition to feminism.

By the end of her sabbatical, she was a southernist, firmly settled into a social history where personal writing would bear much of the weight of political and economic explication. By 1985 she was able to lose herself in women's words while keeping in view the larger structures shaping societies. Given her anxiety during her first sabbatical, about whether women's fiction was or was not literature, her respect for what she saw in Gayle's diary demonstrates how much she had grown in a decade. And white southern women's letters and diaries invited her to continue her interest in life-writing. She found the papers "escapist" and familiar, and just as she took on Kate Chopin's mothers and daughters, and Du Pont's fathers and sons, she used many of the same family papers that Genovese had read for *Roll, Jordan, Roll*—for instance the diary of Meta Morris Grimball—but used them very differently.

Betsey's interest in biography and autobiography went back to her days at Harvard, when she had thought of leaving history for fiction, autobiography, and biography. Monroe Engel and John Clive encouraged her to move to English, just as her first therapist, Dr. Richard Galdston, urged her to consider her emotions and dreams.[54] By 1985, testing the narrative of Sarah Gayle's life with which she would begin *Within the Plantation Household,* Betsey finally satisfied her dream of writing, if not fiction, biography, in a near-poetic voice.

What she wrote about her response to the diaries remains haunting and bears repeating: "There is something unrealistic, almost escapist, in my response. But they ring true to me. I am not, you will say, a proper child of my time. But I do have a deep sense that, however out of tune with the times I may be, I am less interested in acquiring new selves than in enjoying the old."[55] Grimball, Gayle, Louisa McCord, Mary Chesnut, and other literate, privileged antebellum women resonated and satisfied her long-established escapism—reading favorite novels over and over at North Country School, eating chocolate; reading shelf after shelf of murder mysteries; watching baseball games; needlepointing during faculty meetings; and buying clothes, cosmetics, pens, and paper in shops and online until she had enough for nine lives.

By the time Fox-Genovese and Genovese returned to Ithaca in June of 1985, they were seeking a new home. Betsey would have one more year of teaching at Binghamton, Gene five more at Rochester. From her correspondence for 1985, we see that she hit the ground running. Colleagues requested letters of recommendation, reviews of manuscripts, graduate students capable of teaching for a year here or there. Journals called for papers. Both Betsey and Gene had essays in the slowly forthcoming collection celebrating the fortieth anniversary of Herbert Aptheker's book on slave revolts.[56]

Betsey applied for other jobs, now in women's studies rather than history. In the fall of 1985 or perhaps later, she interviewed at Emory University, which was far from a hotbed of radicalism and newly endowed with a large sum. Invited to develop an existing women's studies program at the undergraduate and graduate levels, she and Gene got ready to move to Atlanta in the summer of 1986. She would finish *Within the Plantation Household* there and, not long after, abandon history for a time to take up the life of a public intellectual, tangle with feminism, face a lawsuit, and discard Freud to become a Catholic and an advocate for unborn children.

She had not become those things in 1986. Then, she was intermittently confident, deeply engaged in writing a book about women that was difficult, conceptual, driven by a new economic paradigm. She also was pushing her earlier engagements with women writers and autobiography in her historical rather than literary and editorial work, writing intensively and descriptively about women's experiences and thoughts. The book would be a blockbuster. She had moved slowly toward this concentration since her early work on Physiocracy and the Atlantic economy, and now she was carrying out the ambition. Buoyed by this, she moved herself and her husband to the South, declaring herself for women's history and women's studies. Neither field would remain her intellectual home, but in 1986 they were, and she wanted to leave Binghamton and administer a program of her own. As she moved to Emory University that year, Binghamton's newly hired director of women's studies arrived, which suggests Betsey did not want or was not offered this directorship.

PART III

REFASHIONINGS

7

Leaving Home

A FEMINIST CRITIC'S MOVE SOUTH, 1986–1992

> Anger lies at the heart of the matter, for without anger, there is no feminist consciousness at all.
>
> —Elizabeth Fox-Genovese, 1991

Anger was almost impossible for Fox-Genovese to express openly. Yet it, along with a genuine joy in southern women's history, led her to leave Binghamton in 1986. She and Genovese were both drawn to the South and had sought southern jobs while they were in North Carolina, and ten months after returning to Binghamton, Fox-Genovese took one at Emory University as director of women's studies and professor of history. Her years at Rochester and Binghamton moved her to accept women's history as her own, to identify with a field that came of age as she matured. In 1986 she leapt at the chance to direct a program, now in women's studies, and to do so in the South. She was leaving a department where a senior professor estimated that half the faculty were relieved to hear that she was leaving, and one of her graduate students contacted a friend at Emory, warning that Fox-Genovese might provoke a lawsuit.[1] Within six years, the job she so eagerly embraced would turn to ashes. Fox-Genovese was adhering to a six-year pattern. Earlier, Genovese had chaired the history department at Rochester for six years; then Betsey and Gene had spent six years with *Marxist Perspectives;* not counting four or five years as an adjunct or lecturer, she spent six years at Rochester on track to tenure or tenured in the history department; and finally six years at Binghamton. Later, she and Gene had an equivalent run with The Historical Society. In each case, the rupture reflected not only an immediate, triggering event but deep psychodynamics.

Like Rochester, Emory was a monied, private university. Genovese, whom Emory's history department refused to hire, would now commute even further, from Atlanta to Rochester until 1989, when he made arrangements to teach at a consortium of Georgia campuses.[2] Fox-Genovese did worry in her journal that "he has no context" as a result of her move but added, "I am solid. Somehow during the past months the last traces of the old demons seem to have faded away."[3] She was referring to food, her need to remain thin, and perhaps the pleasure of teaching at Emory.

Betsey was elated about her new world. She delighted in taking command, as her letter of acceptance shows. It is a model of contractual precision combined with a gracious yet iron-tough will—and she made it quite clear that she expected her conditions to be met:

> The terms of the appointment set forth in your letter and in the accompanying memorandum of agreement correspond to the agreement that we reached before I left Emory with the exception of $15,000 for faculty development for the Women's Studies Program and an IBM PC for the Women's Studies secretary. I accept your assurance, given yesterday on the telephone, that you have budgeted for those items and do consider them part of the terms of agreement.
>
> You surely know that it would have taken a special job at a special institution to persuade me to move at this time. You and your faculty have convinced me that Emory offers both.[4]

The job was special because Betsey had been hired to shape a program represented by courses already being taught, working with a committee of committed faculty, some of whom would have preferred a feminist studies focus. Her new dean understood that by 1986 it was no longer desirable to avoid women's studies, but if the feminist faculty were eager, older members nevertheless were appalled.

An editorial had appeared late in 1985 in the *Emory Wheel.* There, medieval European historian George Cuttino declared, "Dear Mr. Woodruff must be turning in his grave like barbecue on a spit! And what will alumni, alumnae, and parents think of a university that underwrites pseudo-academic avant-garde rubbish instead of buttressing proven academic disciplines?"[5] Letters from students and faculty supporting women's studies followed in the next issue, and it is worth remembering that, just as at Binghamton in 1980 and Rochester in the 1970s, the study of women, with roots in second-wave feminism, was still on the margin. Women's studies programs balanced between the activism of women's centers and the scholarly expectations of academic departments, and if Fox-Genovese was prone to suspicion, if not paranoia, she sometimes had reason.

Professor Cuttino was a serious scholar working in medieval diplomacy and enjoying his reputation as a "gruff academic curmudgeon." He was sufficiently alarmed to include a joke in poor taste: "What would you call one thousand feminists at the bottom of the ocean?—A start." Yet he was no simple chauvinist; he had abandoned his desire to be a diplomat for a career in history after taking Mary Albertson's seminar at Swarthmore College many years earlier.[6] He approved of Eleanor of Aquitaine and Blanche of Castile but detested feminists and "tiresome Marxists."[7] Cuttino ranted and raised questions of faculty governance, yet the tide was now against him.[8]

What changed everything was a gift to Emory from the Woodruff brothers (Coca-Cola heirs) of $105 million in 1979, the largest single gift ever made to a U.S. university at that time. It spurred growth and competition for those resources on campus. In that setting, the plan Betsey inherited from the Emory committee made sense. The recommendation was that women's studies faculty have joint appointments to avoid the marginalization of women's studies and engage other departments. But this decision also gave those departments, rather than women's studies, a voice in tenure decisions, leaving women's studies faculty obliged to their disciplinary departments while they taught half-time for women's studies.[9]

Moving to Atlanta

Betsey sent more letters to the dean in June as her impending move loomed, and replies survive. One letter promised the shelves she requested for her campus office.[10] She loved starting over, and she requested an IBM computer for her staff, sure that such computers were the most powerful and fastest on the market. Throughout her life she showed similar taste in cars. She also insisted on faculty development money for the program, determined that women's studies would not be a poor relation on campus.[11]

Hired to develop the women's studies program, within a year she gave the university an Institute for Women's Studies. The change in name was her choice; no one questioned it when she casually mentioned it at a fall women's studies retreat, suggesting it would aid grant applications.[12] This was another sign of the free hand faculty and administration gave her in her first years at Emory, also an indication of her sensibilities. Her Latin was very good, and she would have known the root words, as well as traditional usage: an institute referred to a group of departments, not just one. As an old word too it reeks of solemn learning, foundational knowledge, and permanence, and using it was Fox-Genovese's way of nailing her flag to an interdisciplinary yet traditional mast.

Lurking behind this choice may have been the somewhat monumental figure of Gerda Lerner—married to a communist, very Jewish, ardently feminist, engaged in southern history and questions of race. Lerner "chaired The Women's History Institute at Sarah Lawrence College" in July 1979, where she, Alice Kessler-Harris, and Amy Swerdlow took turns lecturing to leaders of women's organizations every morning for fifteen days.[13] Fox-Genovese would have heard about it and perhaps admired the name. She also may have wanted to echo the naming of Emory's Institute of Liberal Arts, the ILA.

Since the early 1980s Fox-Genovese, joining other scholars, had argued the seriousness of women's history. In an early typescript lecture that later appeared in 1982 as "Placing Women's History in History," she acknowledged the newness, namelessness, and marginality of the field:

> These days, only the most skeptical would deny the emergence of a recognizable entity known as women's history. You will note that I refrain, at least for the moment, from calling that entity a field. For there remain those who would deny to women's history precisely the status of a field. Women's history lacks, I have heard, those monuments

> of scholarship that command inclusion in our great historiographical tradition. Women's history lacks, I have also heard, identifiable questions of world historical significance. For the historians who raise these and like objections, women's history ranks, at best, as a subset of that new social history which these same historians view with barely disguised contempt. But even these doubting Thomases—and occasional Susans—cynically support the inclusion of occasional courses in women's history—whatever it may be, preferably all taught by the same, underpaid, female assistant professor. After all, plentiful enrollments require certain sacrifices, and a few well-populated courses can support several less well-populated courses in serious topics: It is a hard truth that the piper must be paid—and the expense of a history faculty must be justified to financially hard-pressed deans.[14]

Arch and pithy, this early reflection betrays an impatience with those "doubting Thomases—and occasional Susans" and their self-serving use of underpaid female assistant professors. It may echo Fox-Genovese's possible early teaching experience at Rochester.[15] Nothing of this introductory paragraph survived in the later essay, but the commitment to turning "that entity" into an institute did. Betsey's attention to detail in the arrangements she made in her Emory office—the shelves, the books, bringing her dog to work—were a means of claiming the project as hers, something she had never done at Binghamton.

Moving in the summer of 1986, she did much of the same work in the new house: painting, having shelves built, making changes to accommodate the many thousands of books and journals she and Genovese brought with them. The warmth of Atlanta pleased her; the soft colors she chose for the house pleased her. Always under the cloud of anorexia, smoking, and drinking coffee and diet cola instead of eating, always a bit too thin, she found the warm air and open windows a pleasure. She recorded in a new journal how comfortable the move was for her:

> I have been handling old journals during the move to Atlanta, but have not read in any of them. I'm not sure why. I don't think that they threaten me. Indeed I think that I would really like to read them. But

> I haven't had the time to give myself over to going back. It would be a good time. I have never felt better in my life—certainly not my adult life.[16]

The colors on the walls of their new house echoed the light and airy pastels favored by French women of the Enlightenment, colors Fox-Genovese mentioned in an essay on Enlightenment women written for the 1987 edition of *Becoming Visible,* a European women's history textbook.[17] She was now in a position to realize what she had been writing about: the place of women's history, broadly interwoven with a women's studies field that would in turn enrich and thus maintain the canon. It would be a mistake to ignore Fox-Genovese's commitment to that greater canon, but it would be a greater mistake to neglect the dialectical nature of the commitment, driven by Gramsci and Bakhtin, full of hegemony, dialogism, and perhaps more than a hint of the communitarian, of the multiple voices Bakhtin found in Fyodor Dostoevsky.

The canon could be saved only by being questioned and elaborated, much as Fox-Genovese had written in "For Feminist Interpretation" in 1979: "Translation, transformation, appropriation: such are the elements of interpretation, the modes of engaging authority and tradition, the means of understanding texts, cultures, societies." In the same essay she cited Paul Ricoeur's phrase, "the intelligence of the double meaning," to emphasize the transformative nature of interpretation, and by extension, of canonicity.[18] What she valued in writing in 1979, however, was not echoed in the absolute authority she used in running her new program in 1986. The playfulness of 1979—Fox-Genovese was teasing readers with a variation on Susan Sontag's well-known "Against Interpretation"—should remind us that as an essayist Fox-Genovese was somewhat more closely akin to Sontag than to any French historian in the 1970s.

Perspective on Fox-Genovese's experience at Emory requires remembering that women's studies was a new venture undertaken by this staid, traditional, regional university. The undergraduate college had only admitted women since 1953, "in the face of declining [male] enrollment during the Korean War."[19] Bringing in an outside director in 1986, a recognized scholar in several fields, can be seen as a move intended to disarm the opposition and give leadership to campus feminists who had worked for so long to create a program that would be theirs. Problems would arise when their intentions and Betsey's—an old-school scholar—diverged.

If Cuttino resented the "tiresome Marxists" he saw demanding women's studies, folks at the Emory Institute for Liberal Arts, a home for interdisciplinary graduate work that was almost coeval with the admission of women, were also disgruntled. Emory's tree-shaded paths and manicured lawns were suddenly the backdrop for Betsey Fox-Genovese striding rapidly to her office with a bulging briefcase in one hand, a large purse over her shoulder, and her dog's leash in the other. With Josef's (ironically named for Stalin) prancing and expensively cut coat flying out behind her, she looked more like an American expatriate in Paris in 1924 than a late twentieth-century academic going to class. She was always more than anyone bargained for and in ways they did not expect. Her appearance, so carefully arranged, belied her need for approval, her fear of being discovered as an impostor: that tall woman striding across campus was still Fido, and her dog, like his mistress and his namesake, was always anxious.

As director of her institute and a southernist, Fox-Genovese faced two tasks in 1986. The first was to build a network of faculty at and beyond Emory who would take women's studies from a minor to a major area of study and then to a graduate degree. Perhaps because she saw the program as hers to build, she found it difficult to build on what was in place before her. The Ph.D. in women's studies, administered through the ILA, appeared in the 1988–89 academic year, and the first jointly appointed faculty, hired by both the Institute for Women's Studies and the new hire's disciplinary department, came the year after. In this, Fox-Genovese followed the plan set out by Emory faculty in 1985, insisting that both new faculty and students have a core discipline, however wide their interests might be.[20]

Her second task was the book she published in 1988, *Within the Plantation Household: Black and White Women of the Old South.* She finished it, proofreading all 544 pages in time for publication in December, while working on minor, major, and graduate programs in women's studies. By 1991 Fox-Genovese would publish another book, but in 1988 it was more than enough that *Within the Plantation Household* had appeared.

Within the Plantation Household

In an interview given at the time of the book's publication, Fox-Genovese recalled the childhood stories that her grandmother Agnes Fox had told about her own grandmother in the South: "She brought me up with extraordinary stories about what women's lives were like."[21] Those stories abetted her book, as did her marriage to Genovese and, more concretely, her participation with him in the *Time on the Cross* conference in Rochester in 1974. While a herald of things to come, that early foray into southern studies did not yet indicate an intellectual shift away from prerevolutionary France toward the antebellum South, from economic to women's history, and from the study of agriculture and merchant capitalism to the examination of literary and autobiographical texts. Nevertheless, looking back from 1992, Fox-Genovese told an inquiring graduate student:

> I had also always been interested in comparative slavery. One of my fields at Harvard had been the Expansion of Europe (at a time when no one else was doing it). . . .
>
> Meeting and marrying my husband reinforced my interest in comparative slavery. Since I was something of a perfectionist, I had figured out that to do French history the way I thought it should be done I would have to spend a lot of time in the French archives. After my marriage, it did not take me long to figure out that it would be more fun to go to southern archives with my husband than to go to French ones without him. . . .
>
> My article, "Poor Richard at Work in the Cotton Fields," is a good example of how I engineered the shift. And, in general, *Fruits of Merchant Capital,* shows the way in which I moved toward southern and women's history.[22]

Fox-Genovese used to say that historians did not do their best work until they were fifty—perhaps a consolation directed to her father—but she was still in her forties as she pulled together the material and perspectives that made *Within the Plantation Household* so rich, dense, contradictory, direct, and oblique. Outside of essays, it was, together with *Feminism without Illusions,* her best work. She wrote it when she was most at home in the world and when that world was still of a piece, with her parents reasonably well, her health bearable, her dog at her side, her husband cantankerous, her places at Binghamton and then Emory stormy but secure, and her identity as a Marxist, feminist, old-school scholar with Freudian inclinations largely if not entirely intact.

Behind the Scenes

Fox-Genovese's 1974 *Time on the Cross* paper marked the breadth of her attention to economy, agriculture, and psychology across the Atlantic world. It flowed from her dissertation and overlapped the editing of her first book. When she revised the published version of that conference paper in the early 1980s for *Fruits of Merchant Capital,* she was working on households and on slave women's resistance.[23]

Hiring Fox-Genovese, Binghamton engaged a French historian who never taught French history at her new university and who was following a fluid intellectual path on which *Origins of Physiocracy* was merely one step. She cared less about France and more about the South by 1980, although she told that student in 1992 that what consistently interested her was "the logic of social and economic structures."[24] She was still the scientist she had been at Concord Academy, very much also still the Marxist materialist. France, the South, her early work on Bordeaux were all about a transitional, no longer feudal, not yet capitalist Atlantic world.[25] Fox-Genovese and Genovese were kept from parochialism and prodded by their wide-ranging reading and international, leftist colleagues—Albert Soboul, Marguerite Kuczynski, and Eric Hobsbawm among many.

Temporal, structural borders mattered more than political ones; those boundaries echoed in Fox-Genovese's words describing the South as "in but not of the capitalist world."[26] Fox-Genovese's command of the agricultural old order in transition had been apparent in "The Many Faces of Moral Economy." When she began to work on southern households in the 1980s, the ground was familiar, through the Physiocrats, eighteenth-century Scots who wrote on agriculture and economy, and such more recent British agricultural historians as Eric Kerridge, Joan Thirsk, and E. L. Jones.[27] The last never used the word "household," but their books are full of the groundwork of households: the holdings, the manorial maps, the complaints of peasants about landowners, tenures, and leases. Fox-Genovese's view of southern households was grounded in her knowledge of French grain markets and the moral economy of the British grain riots. She read Anand Chiṭnis on the Scottish Enlightenment in the late 1970s, underlining and commenting on passages about the division of common lands, famines, and the provision of schoolmasters.[28] Fox-Genovese's research and writing of her dissertation had prepared her to see power in play on those green fields.

Households

At Binghamton in the early 1980s, the Households Working Group at the Fernand Braudel Center gave Fox-Genovese a community in which to shape much of her first chapter of *Within the Plantation Household*. In 1982 she and others at the Braudel Center coauthored a National Endowment for the Humanities grant proposal for the study of households, and in 1983 she published "Antebellum Southern Households: A New Perspective on a Familiar Question." Arguing for greater care in using the term "household," she wrote, "There is some irony in the dearth of household studies for the antebellum South, for it is peculiarly appropriate to describe antebellum southern society precisely as a network of households and thereby to cast the debate more fruitfully."[29]

The debate then was over whether households of the South, "spawned by merchant capital," were capitalist, precapitalist, or permutations of one of those systems. It mattered to Marxists and non-Marxists alike, for, in the midst and then in the aftermath of the civil rights struggles, the problem of slavery claimed attention: Was the institution old and incompatible with capitalism's thirst for free labor? Or could capitalism stretch to encompass slave labor? Betsey proceeded to draw distinctions, consulting recent work in West Indian anthropology, English demography, and the French *Annales* school. Households had definable qualities, with variation. Most explicitly, the household trumped family, pulling unrelated and profoundly unequal people together into an economic unit directed in the South by a white master.

The implications were "dramatic" for slaves when seen primarily as participants in this larger household, as individuals or families who were "hostage to the master's whim and economic needs." For Fox-Genovese, the plantation household was more than a social formation; it was a weapon used by masters to undercut kinship and "sub-household membership" as "reliable bases of resistance."[30] The debate was not about terminology; it was about power. It was also for Betsey about undercutting Genovese's argument about the slaves' role in making that southern world, advanced in 1974 in *Roll, Jordan, Roll: The World the Slaves Made.*

Fox-Genovese was more rigidly Marxist than Genovese, who had used her insights about the power and depth of patriarchy yet still granted agency to slaves. In *Within the Plantation Household,* she would grant none to women or slaves, seeing the household's material base and resulting psychological imperatives—the hegemony of class relations—as absolute. Bertram Wyatt-Brown, noted for his work on the code of honor that ruled planters' lives, saw what she was doing and commended her.[31] As Laura F. Edwards wrote many years later, Betsey remained "true to her Marxist intellectual roots, she subordinated women, race, and gender within an analytical framework rooted in the solid base of class relations."[32] Nonetheless, Genovese continued to argue for a more spacious and subtle understanding of will and psychology among the slaves in the last volume of *The Mind of the Masterclass* trilogy, *Fatal Self-Deception.* Yes, he insisted, the enslaved did not just accept and perform according to their masters' expectations: hegemony has cracks.

For Betsey, slaves had little control or space within the households she described: their membership curtailed their participation in any household of their own, and their masters were unreliable, for they in turn felt themselves ruled by the markets they confronted. The household—food, clothing, and power—were old and well-lived themes to Fox-Genovese, elements she was well aware of in her own life and could foreground in her work, for mistresses as well as slaves.

Within the Plantation Household is a curiously divided book, something Fox-Genovese acknowledged in her prologue, where she warned, "Those with no taste at all for theoretical arguments may choose to pass over [Chapter 1] lightly." That first chapter, with its roots in the skills that led Fox-Genovese to master Quesnay's *Tableau économique,* could not have differed more from the lyrical biography of Sarah Gayle. Many readers no doubt found the transition from Gayle's visions of her younger and older selves drifting on a river to that chapter on the household economy of the South jarring:

> Yet southern households, as the embodiment of a particular tendency within merchant capital, helped to endow southern society with its distinctive character as a specific social formation.
>
> By social formation, I meant the distinct crystallization of social relations, political economy, and culture that constitutes a subsidiary society within a dominant mode of production.[33]

Population, urban development, and the use and critique of aggregate statistics remind us of just what Fox-Genovese had studied and then taught in her summers at the Newberry Library institutes on quantitative methods for historians. If the preface recalled Betsey's attention to women's emotional worlds in her essay on Kate Chopin's *The Awakening,* this voice took root from her love of science, precise observation, and description of systems and physical structures that had persisted from her school days through the Physiocrats and her work on households at Binghamton.[34]

That first chapter also grew out of Fox-Genovese's appreciation of Eric Hobsbawm and her father's Western Civilization courses. It stands as Betsey's most carefully developed attempt to write like Hobsbawm, to take on the world.[35] Fox-Genovese never abandoned that overarching vision, even as she moved outside the Marxism that had framed it. Much of what she added to her 1983 essay on households in writing the first chapter of *Within the Plantation Household* she drew from the debates among Marxists, non-Marxists, and others, as Christine Stansell noted in 1989: "Southern history is a notoriously contentious field, and you can almost hear the feuds rumbling through the text even if you don't know enough to spot where, exactly, the trouble is coming from."[36]

Fox-Genovese quickly outlined the history of the South's development, drawing on her years of teaching and her scientific bent. Quickly sketching the North's and the South's "double indebtedness to Elizabethan and Jacobean legacies and to capitalist innovation," she differentiated southern from northern households, contrasting rural, urban, slave, free, industrial, and agricultural. She argued that plantation slavery in the South "evolved in conjunction with the development of the capitalist world market of which it was a product, but in its emergence as a social system it extruded social and political barriers to the working-out of the capitalist market."[37]

Fox-Genovese described the household by drawing on much of what she had, to my ear, been saying in classes at Binghamton for some time. Anyone who wishes to have taken a course from her could still do so by reading that chapter. It is redolent of her long apprenticeship in history and her arrival at a new conception of households, her contribution to economic thought. In writing it, she turned Genovese's famous subtitle, *The World the Slaves Made,* on its head. Her households were ruled by masters who were controlling, viciously paternal, and patriarchal; if slaves sometimes resisted, neither they nor white women made more than small dents in this oppressive order. The household mastered them. She was keenly aware of her opposition to Genovese's theme; for her, resistance was an illusion, hegemony was real, and ownership of the means of production was everything.[38] The 1960s were over, if she had ever acknowledged them.

That network of households was the stage on which Betsey set her southern women. She emphasized that southern women, Black and white, lived in a slave society while northern women did not. Those households allowed Fox-Genovese to repudiate the relevance of historical work on northern women to southern women and to insist there were few signs of bourgeois individualism among southern women. The household probably appealed to her authoritarian streak and pushed her toward wholehearted corporatism—unity within a hierarchical society—by the late 1980s, when she described herself as "a committed southern democrat" in a 1989 letter to Senator Sam Nunn.[39]

Fox-Genovese's demanding first chapter was a slapping down of credentials on the table, should anyone think she was out of her depth in southern or economic history. The anecdotal fourth chapter used other kinds of evidence. There Fox-Genovese exposed the gender conventions she found in the words of plantation mistress Meta Morris Grimball, as well as the prescriptive writings of George Fitzhugh and the Scots historian William Robertson, among many. Planter-class women were to be models of submission. As Fox-Genovese put it, "Above all, as the religious and secular proslavery polemics tirelessly declared, the subordination of women to the men upon whom they acknowledged their dependence confirmed inequality among all members of society."[40] She was brutal in opposing what she saw as women's subservience to Genovese's dialectical view of slaves' resistance: her dialectic was with Genovese.

Fox-Genovese's appreciation of order ensured that she would see no systematic critiques of southern social order from its wealthiest women, no abolitionism, no serious rejection of the hand that fed them, and no wrinkles in the patriarchy such as women managing plantations. Complaints were to be expected. Rejecting sisterhood with yeoman and slave women in the name of class and race and renouncing much of the superiority of class in the name of patriarchy, the white women of Fox-Genovese's plantation elite balanced precariously atop their denials. And who benefited from this, one might ask. Christine Stansell noted that Mary Chesnut and Louisa McCord do not compare well with Emily Dickinson or Elizabeth Cady Stanton: "If this is the best that privileged Southern womanhood could produce, what does it say about the Old South and the balance of its 'compensations' against the toll it exacted even from pampered female hearts and minds?"[41] Fox-Genovese, finding comfort in corporatism for herself, described the power of the southern slave economy to shape behavior and thought, implicitly affirming her rigid Marxism.

Betsey had one eye on social structure; the other followed the plantation mistresses who wrote. Her fascination with the women's texts she encountered in the archives was obvious, her quotation constant.

Well aware of the complexities of Mary Chesnut's editing of her Civil War diary, she nonetheless let herself be led by her writers. Less acute as a critic, she ignored the emendations in Sarah Haynsworth Gayle's journal and other, complicating voices in the plantation women's pantheon, preferring to take Gayle and her other favorites at face value. She chose women who would demonstrate hegemony at work, quoted extensively, and reinterpreted what did not fit. Mary Chesnut was not truly critical of men, she was irritated by her childlessness; Harriet Jacobs could not have refused her master's sexual demands because hierarchy and power inequalities made escape impossible.[42]

Familiar with Bakhtin, Fox-Genovese had an ear for voices and used a multivocal technique here, as she would again in *Feminism Is Not the Story of My Life.*[43] Designed to reveal hegemony, her love of the materials led her to include so much that, as her many reviewers noted, she undercut many of her points.[44] She mastered her intellectual, structural argument easily, but she avoided the control over her materials that Genovese had demonstrated in *Roll, Jordan, Roll.* The words of the dozens of women she quoted complicated her views, and she let them do so without adequately taking them into account.

Sarah Ann Haynsworth Gayle

What remains when we set aside households and gender conventions is an unfinished novel. As Fox-Genovese wrote, "Were Sarah Ann Haynsworth Gayle's story written as a novel, the interlocking themes would appear to defy real life. Sarah Gayle harbored a genuine literary talent. She especially developed an external perspective on her subjective experience." Gayle's story flows through the entire book. Only once is it possible to go as far as twenty-five pages without coming across her, until she vanishes after page 281, just before the chapters on women who did and did not oppose slavery. Gayle's ability as a writer held Fox-Genovese's attention, as Betsey's 1985 letter to Nancy Wilson, serving as a draft of the prologue, confirms.[45]

Fox-Genovese consulted two versions of the journal, distinguishing them in the notes as a journal held by the Southern Historical Collection at the University of North Carolina at Chapel Hill and a diary held by Hoole Special Collections at the University of Alabama in Tuscaloosa. The latter may have been the original manuscript, of which numerous transcripts have been made over time. All those transcripts, following the original manuscript that was increasingly defaced, replicate the intentional crossing-out of lines and removal of pages by family members who apparently wished Gayle had been less frank and more circumspect. Recent painstaking reconstruction of the original journal and study of Gayle's correspondence led her editors to suggest that the excisions were prompted by a desire to hide John Gayle's chronic troubles with money and drink and Sarah Gayle's probable opium addiction, but sixty pages now lost contained entirely unknown matter.[46] Betsey chose not to wrestle with the meaning of the emendations or the faulty ordering of some pages, and that was noted by one reviewer, Sarah Woolfolk Wiggins, coeditor of the scholarly edition of the Gayle journal, in 1990.[47]

Gayle was moderately educated but widely read, and Fox-Genovese recognized and responded to her voice, little surprised by the constant descriptions of deaths, unfortunate early marriages, sermons of varying quality, John Gayle's debts, and the importance of family, especially those no longer living. Sarah Gayle's literary craft attracted Fox-Genovese, and while she noted how Gayle's "vocabulary and formulations inadvertently betrayed her immersion in a broadly disseminated Romantic discourse," Betsey also found evidence of "Sarah Gayle's natural talent and a concern for craft, however hesitant she was to dignify her jottings by an official title."[48]

Although Gayle was in many respects a Romantic widely read in books also common to many British and northern households, Fox-Genovese insisted on treating her as a product of "her profound immersion in the specific social and physical topography of her own region."[49] From this perspective, Gayle's difficult relations with slaves, the roughness of life on the Alabama frontier, and the distance she traveled from her childhood home in Sumter, South Carolina, must have shaped her as much if not more than her reading and writing. Nevertheless, it was her writing that Betsey loved, especially the dream-like passages she quoted at length in her prologue. In them, Gayle recalled herself as a girl and young mother, drifting on a river, a near-perfect depiction of Romantic and—possibly specifically—southern womanhood.

Preserving Impressions

While chapter 1 and a bit of chapter 4 were the work of the economic historian, the prologue and much of the rest of the book belonged to the Fox-Genovese who wrote in 1976: "I have been fantasizing so long now, although with increasing intensity and purposefulness in recent months, about keeping a journal, writing a novel, preserving impressions and so forth that perhaps this time I will."[50] I think she did, surrendering to her early loves, literature, biography, and psychoanalysis. Christine Stansell understood, judging the book "an account that at times has the political and psychological resonances of a fine nineteenth-century novel."[51] In large part, *Within the Plantation Household* was the fruit of Fox-Genovese unleashed amid personal papers. While acting as literary critic, psychoanalyst, and preserver of impressions, however, she did not use the critical eye and distance that made her analysis of Du Pont's autobiography piercing. Instead, she responded intuitively, reveling in the letters and journals.

The novel I am thinking of does not exist, but Fox-Genovese peopled her plantation households, adding a good dose of description. She recognized the extent to which those depictions relied on transatlantic literary conventions. Nevertheless, she insisted that she found southern difference in the extended households emerging in the pages of her women informants—households where slaves lived inches or yards away from their owners. Christine Stansell emphasized the point in her review that Betsey clipped and saved: "Decency, God-fearingness, and attractiveness and warmth were also common literary tropes which privileged women in the nineteenth-century used to represent themselves in diaries and letters—just the sources Fox-Genovese depends heavily on."[52] Sarah Gayle may have appeared on more pages than any other woman, but Mary Chesnut, Louisa McCord, and Harriet Jacobs got significant attention as well. Other vivid women writers became part of the Greek chorus: Anna Matilda Page King, Meta Morris Grimball, and Eliza Clitherall. In the end, however, Gayle and the tragedy of her early death permeate the book.

Eliza Clitherall could ignore her life in South Carolina to describe her family ties to England: "My heart, thoughts, habits and approbation was all English—I was born, have lived, & shall die an

Enthusiast."[53] In sharp contrast, Keziah Brevard, a widowed, working plantation owner who had less time and style, began her one surviving volume with this: "At home with a sore throat." She went on to describe prices, bags of various qualities of flour, the weight of her peaches that year—1860—and her difficulties as a woman managing slaves. Of the two, Fox-Genovese used much more from Clitherall, and that choice speaks to many others as she sought to manage the voluminous material from elite planter women in the archives. Brevard survived a less than happy marriage and was a resilient, long-lived, terse manager of several plantations—and barely present in Betsey's book.[54]

Fox-Genovese's problem was that only a few planter-class women would or could put into words what was distinctly southern about their lives, as opposed to replicating the common, learned vocabulary of somewhat educated female life in the nineteenth century. Excepting Harriet Jacobs, slave women, although usually far less educated in the forms of nineteenth-century prose, were more likely to put into words the impact of slavery but much less likely to have their words either recorded or preserved. Teasing out elements of southern difference from endless letters and diary entries about sewing, weather, visits, relatives, and illnesses was a thankless, difficult task, eased occasionally by remarks about slaves. Had Fox-Genovese engaged more fully with what Stansell, quoting Betsey, called "explosive intimacy," she might have found something more southern. She preferred, however, to locate that telling difference from northern women in plantation mistresses' subordination to their husbands. That bemused those who judged submission to patriarchy elsewhere as a bond that elite women shared.

Reviewers also commented that *Within the Plantation Household* was a big, sprawling, internally contradictory, encyclopedic book with no simple punch line at the beginning or the end. It drew attention to the field, generated debate, and attracted review after review. Two years after the book appeared, Suzanne Lebsock published a twenty-five-page essay wrestling with it, insisting it was "driven by a quest for a certain kind of intellectual order" while also "curiously—but instructively—at odds with itself." "It is" she wrote, "a big book, packed with engaging characters, apt quotations, and interesting description."[55] Lebsock immediately saw that Betsey, by arguing the South was a network of households, put women—who were never leaders in church or state—at the center rather than on the margins of southern history. As Lebsock also pointed out, however, Fox-Genovese included so much that neither her argument nor her structure could contain it all: Betsey loved nineteenth-century novels, full of people.

What Fox-Genovese found but would not focus on within those households was, in Lebsock's words, "this powerful narrative of domestic wretchedness." Stansell agreed. Yet, she began her review by calling *Within the Plantation Household* "the first book of women's history to match in subtlety and rigor the best radical scholarship in 'mainstream' Southern history. The heart of the book is a rich, sprawling argument about how womanly identities, white and Black, served at once to strengthen, accommodate, and destabilize the slave regime."[56]

The book was a blockbuster. Fox-Genovese did not pay particular attention to C. Vann Woodward's edition of *Mary Chesnut's Civil War* diaries, reworked in the decades after the war, nor did she attend much to the Grimké sisters, those early abolitionists raised on a South Carolina plantation. Chesnut, Betsey had argued in seminars at Binghamton, was carefully representing herself as rather less Confederate after the Civil War; the Grimkés had fled to Philadelphia. She saw none of the three as true antebellum southerners. Betsey argued that plantation mistresses were just as much a product of their society as their men, racist and utterly dependent on others' labor, and that their position in the all-important household enforced this. It was clear enough that the *Raleigh News and Observer* ran a brief review in 1989, under the headline "Women of the House Were Racists, Too."[57]

Within the Plantation Household got reviewed by scholars in southern history, women's history, African American history, economic history, and various combinations of all the above. Only one reviewer declared the book a failure, as merely synthetic. Reviewed beyond the realm of historical journals, on the front page of the *New York Times Book Review* and in the *Nation,* the book made waves. Most acknowledged it as important, whether one agreed with Betsey's arguments or not. Bertram Wyatt-Brown wrote "impressive"; Wilson Moses, "compendious"; Margaret M. Caffrey, "major book." Catherine Clinton added "conceptual boldness," and Nancy L. Grant, "ambitious." Jan

Lewis thought Fox-Genovese's northern bourgeoise a "straw woman." Perhaps the main impression the reviews leave is one of widespread, serious engagement reaching beyond the various criticisms and praise, marking a book that had to be reckoned with. It mattered; it drove discussion.[58]

A few themes emerged. Several reviewers were pleased to see plantation mistresses admitted to full membership in the abusing elite; others questioned Fox-Genovese's choice to ignore abolitionists like the Grimkés. Some complained that Betsey had less to say about African American women than the title and book jacket promised, and Catherine Clinton and Ronald G. Waters caught a telling omission, something that must have, spoken or unspoken, riven the Black and white women of those southern households: "Her silence on sexual matters generally disturbs, however." These silences—on African American women and on sexuality—mattered, and Betsey returned to them, particularly prompted by Toni Morrison's *Beloved,* but she never completed her planned response, *Ghosts and Memories: History in the Fictions of African-American Women Writers.*[59]

Fox-Genovese did not read the words of slave women as well. Her chapter on slave women's resistance, based on an earlier article, both segregated those women within the book and, because they rarely participated in slave revolts, allowed Fox-Genovese to focus on their lone opposition to master or mistress or overseer: "The ultimate resistance lay in the ultimate loneliness—the absolute opposition of power and submission, of one will to another."[60] She would reiterate this loneliness and struggle in her epilogue on Harriet Jacobs's *Incidents in the Life of a Slave Girl,* while insisting that Jacobs had fictionalized one element of her autobiographical story, her ability to resist her master's sexual demands. Given her belief that the South's plantation society demanded submission, and ownership entailed it, Fox-Genovese found it impossible to accept that Brent/Jacobs defied her owner. Neither was Fox-Genovese willing to allow cracks in that social framework, and she was unshakeable in her belief that resistance was futile then and there.

Fox-Genovese returned to African American women's writing in the 1990s, but her enthusiasm for elite, and literary, southern women remained. In 1994 she playfully told Michael O'Brien, "Yes, I very much admire Miss Louisa [McCord], but have never thought she belonged to me, especially since, like the Gemini that I am, I identify just as much with Miss Mary [Chesnut]—and more than a little with Miss Sarah [Gayle]."[61] Between 1988 and 1996, however, Fox-Genovese read African American women's fiction and autobiography, producing a stream of significant essays, including "My Statue, My Self: Gender and Identity in the Autobiographies of Afro-American Women" and "Unspeakable Things Unspoken: Ghosts and Memories in African-American Women's Narratives of Slavery." Betsey reworked her thoughts on Harriet Jacobs as well and read Toni Morrison and Zora Neale Hurston. As she argued in "Unspeakable Things Unspoken," she found in Toni Morrison's *Beloved* clues to the silences in slave women's recollections of the horrors of slavery: rape, sexual abuse, infanticide.[62]

Betsey had always been loath to find or name sexual or physical abuse, at least of children. I and other students remember her insistence that the rape of Pecola Breedlove in *The Bluest Eye* was an awkward form of paternal love; that the physical abuse of young African American girls by their fathers, girls whose abuse emerged much later when interviewed as adults by one of Fox-Genovese's students, was not abuse. She was certain that threats and punishments meted out to children in fairytales were proper expressions of parental anger, fear, and discipline.[63] This free hand—in comments from seminars and discussions before and after 1988—given to fathers and mothers stands in contrast to the dangers she suggested in "Unspeakable Things Unspoken" that slave women faced from men who were not their fathers. Drawn to these stories, she would not be pulled too far; she invoked disguises, memories, and forgetting. The ineffable lingered in the titles she chose: statues, selves, ghosts, memories, a past barely remembered. The unspoken that Fox-Genovese avoided in Keziah Brevard's life and Sarah Gayle's journal she sought in African American women's words, writing about them for almost a decade.

By 2002, seven years after her entry into the Catholic Church, Betsey, driven by her corporatist perspective and disdain for liberal individualism, wrote to the then-besieged Boston cardinal Bernard Law.

Fox-Genovese comforted him as reports made it obvious that he had concealed the sexual abuse of children by priests for many years: "I can only begin to imagine—and barely at that—how painful a time this must be for you, and I am loathe to intrude, even by letter, on whatever privacy you may muster. I write now only to tell you that you are very much in my thoughts and prayers, that I cherish memories of your graciousness to me, and wish there were some way in which I could ease your travail." She closed by hoping "that in this very dark night it provides some shred of comfort to know that there are those of us who ache for your suffering, respect all the good work you have done for the Church, and think of you with love."[64] Her letter, coming near the peak outcry against Law by Boston Catholics, leaves us to contemplate her commitment to the privileging of fathers, the importance of order, the necessity of not seeing child abuse, and hers and Gene's visceral hatred of Anita Hill, the law school professor who insisted on bringing to light her complaints of sexual harassment by future U.S. Supreme Court Justice Clarence Thomas, a Catholic also.[65]

Bertram Wyatt-Brown summed up *Within the Plantation Household* nicely: "There almost seem to be two books here, one that explains the primitivism of the South's implacable social and racial order, another that celebrates the well-educated plantation women who so much benefited from it."[66] The first book was the Marxist economic history; the second marked Fox-Genovese's profound turn toward literary consciousness. And this second book was much like a novel.[67] This combination made *Within the Plantation Household* a curious, ambitious book, a culmination of Fox-Genovese's historical work on women from which her subsequent work would flow. It was also a tour de force of Marxist, determinist analysis, brooking no deviations in the culture from the rigors of the economic system. Yet many of her chapters overflowed with words, stories, accounts, memories of women, obliterating the bounds she had set.

The Idiosyncratic Marxist

In 1988 Fox-Genovese wrote at length to intellectual historian Michael O'Brien, examining her position:

> Your comments on the new historicism piece made me thoughtful, all the more so since I had received some very good comments that raised similar, although not identical, issues from my colleague Walter Reed in English, whom I hope you will meet in the spring. Without getting into specifics, you and he have brought home to me how idiosyncratic my own position has become. Last Sunday, Gene and I caught the last few minutes of 60 Minutes (I love Murder She Wrote, which follows it) and heard Andy Rooney say, "I am opposed to abortion, but don't like the other people who are," or something similar. That captures, in reverse, my own position vis a vis Marxism. Although I retain a serious commitment to what I consider social justice, and although I am convinced that ideas must be understood with some reference to context, and although I believe that context must take account of social relations of production (and reproduction) not just "economics," I am increasingly distant from others who call themselves Marxists, and especially distant from those who don't but claim for themselves the mantle of the left. Accordingly, I am very lukewarm in my identification with Marxism and probably even confusing in my attempts to make my own position clear.[68]

Betsey's letter sounds much like her rejection of the *Marxist Perspectives* group, reinforced by Genovese, an old leftist living in the midst of the New Left.[69] In explaining herself to O'Brien in 1988, the weight fell on her distance from persons, not ideas. Her intellectual framework remained Marxist, old school, determinist, theoretical, and structural, which explains why her voice and Genovese's in *The Mind of the Master Class* would be consistent with their earlier work. Those familiar with her later traditional conservatism will jump to say that this isn't possible, but her public, political positions, which struck many as hard right and which she defended as corporatist, were one layer of argumentation, while her underlying analyses were still driven by a Marxist understanding, something she was making clear to O'Brien.

Genovese and Fox-Genovese were iconoclasts given to argument, left and right were two ends of their playing field, and Betsey's happy prodding of the left is not news. In 1988 her idiosyncrasy was coinciding with the last days of the Soviet Union and with Genovese's decision (and also O'Brien's), around 1986, to write a novel. Genovese's—like O'Brien's, still unpublished—excoriated the left, which is something people on the left do all the time. There was no visible exit from the left: Fox-Genovese and Genovese were still Christopher Hitchens's "royal couple of radicalism" in *Vanity Fair*'s February 1994 issue, even though Betsey had by then broken with Emory's women's studies program.[70]

After 1988

In the wake of *Within the Plantation Household,* Fox-Genovese was sought after by other universities, nominated for other positions, including director of American studies at Vanderbilt and director of American studies at the College of William and Mary. Only William and Mary appealed to her. Genovese had been lecturing there, she had split her time between Emory and William and Mary, and she went as far as to set up interview appointments, only to withdraw after Emory countered with the professorship she held until her death.[71]

In 1994 Fox-Genovese wrote to Michael O'Brien, insisting, "You especially err in confusing me with 'our age.' I should have thought you would have learned better on that score by now. At the very least, you may be sure that most representatives of our age do not confuse me with themselves."[72] She was reiterating exactly what she had told Nancy Wilson in 1985: "I am not, you will say, a proper child of my time."[73] What she was refusing she would not say, but her persistence suggests both her ties to her parents' generation and her right to name and rename herself. She sought a new intellectual paradigm much as she sought new clothes. While the clothes, however, expressed elite classicism and anchored her as an haute bourgeoise, her self-description was both marginalizing and freeing: I am not—or, in the words of Odysseus/Ulysses in the cave of the Cyclops, "my name is nobody."

Feminism without Illusions

Feminism without Illusions came out three years after *Within the Plantation Household,* and it marked Fox-Genovese's transition from academic to public intellectual. Its rapid production also suggests Betsey's declining interest in administering the women's studies program in favor of writing, speaking, and teaching—being a woman of letters. She wrote from the left, and her criticism of feminism's bourgeois, individualist strands was not a criticism of feminism. It was an invitation to debate feminism. Enjoying the success of *Within the Plantation Household,* she brought into the present her unease with that nineteenth-century northeastern tradition, as she saw it, of Yankee women's arguments for rights as individuals. Those doubts about individualism were of long standing, much older than Fox-Genovese, and it should be no surprise that, having chided those feminists in *Within the Plantation Household,* she turned to feminism, to the present, and to life as a public intellectual.

Originally titled *For Feminist Interpretation*—a response to Susan Sontag's much earlier *Against Interpretation*—the book had been under contract with Jeannette Hopkins at Wesleyan University Press since 1986. Fox-Genovese's proposal listed thirteen essays, eleven published earlier:

Introduction:

I. Women, History, and the Politics of Individualism

1. Gender, Class, and Power [1982]
2. Placing Women's History in History [1982]
3. Property and Patriarchy in Bourgeois Political Theory [1977]
4. The Personal Is Not Political Enough [1979]*
5. Women, Affirmative Action, and the Myth of Individualism [1986]*
6. Pornography and Individual Right: The Issues [?]

II. Women, the Canon, and the Politics of Representation

7. For Feminist Interpretation [1980]*
8. The Claims of a Common Culture: Gender, Race, Class, and Canon [1986]*
9. Gender and Discourse [?]
10. Kate Chopin's Awakening [1979]
11. Scarlett O'Hara: The Southern Lady as New Woman [1981]

> 12. The New Female Literary Culture [1980]
> 13. To write Myself [1986]
> Conclusion.
>
> In the introduction I would layout the general argument as we have discussed. In the conclusion, I would pull together the essays on baseball wives and men and feminism into a new piece on women and power.[74]

It was never published. Hopkins left the press, and instead came *Feminism without Illusions* from a different press and editor in 1991.[75] The alterations reflect how Betsey had changed since 1986, possibly driven by her teaching experience in a women's studies program and her own willingness to offer a leftist—perhaps more corporatist—critique of feminism.

Fox-Genovese ultimately chose to use only four of the thirteen essays she first proposed, marked above with asterisks, and rewrote those extensively. Between 1990 and the book's publication in 1991, she altered her older essays almost beyond recognition, often not for the better. Clarity and style were sacrificed to complexity in the later revisions, as she piled analyses of recent work on top of what had interested her in the 1970s. Occasional bold statements, in the French style of her early education—for example, they abound in Camus's *The Rebel*—are sometimes striking, sometimes banal.

Of the four essays she kept, "The Personal Is Not Political Enough" and "Women, Affirmative Action, and the Myth of Individualism" marked her interest in public policy and a public voice. Given these impulses, she cut her early historical pieces and rerouted her literary criticism to *Ghosts and Memories in the Writing of Southern Women,* under contract by 1991 with the University of Virginia Press. By early 1992, an explosive period in her life, she had an outline in place for something she called *Feminism Is Not a Story about My Life,* which she described as "suggestions for public policy" based on conversations with women about "their disaffection" with feminism.[76] *Feminism Is Not the Story of My Life* took shape for her amid professional defeats and crises, but the publication of *Feminism without Illusions* came first and deserves careful attention.

Betsey left a valuable trail as she revised. "The Personal Is Not Political Enough" had originally begun, "Advanced capitalist society has stripped away the veils of neutral, natural-rights politics."[77] It is a play on Marx's words from the first chapter of *The Communist Manifesto*, about stripping away veils, and the following paragraph is underpinned by a Marxist worldview. Thoroughly emended, the essay opened *Feminism without Illusions*. Betsey liked her critique of sisterhood, the core of both essays, but now began the essay, renamed "Beyond Sisterhood," very differently: "Contemporary feminism has emerged from the crucible of the extraordinary economic and political developments of the twentieth century, especially since World War II. And high on the list of the many gains and casualties of these developments stands the erosion of our inherited doctrines of neutral, natural-rights politics."[78] Her 1979 references to "an autonomous women's movement" and "a strong socialist movement" disappeared.[79] Instead, we have an oddly wistful erosion of natural rights politics. However, Marx and perhaps Gramsci persist—in the "Illusions" of the title, which replaces the allusion to veils in the earlier essay, a joking play on Marx's words.

The biggest difference between the 1979 and 1991 iterations lay in Betsey's conclusions about sisterhood. In 1979 she ended hopefully, with a penultimate line: "even as sisterhood itself helps to shape the theory and practice of Marxism." In her 1991 version, the end of the story had altered: "The most daunting challenge remains to develop a new vision that underscores the claims of society as a whole. For without such a vision we risk a radical fragmentation that realizes the most Kafkaesque nightmares of solitary individuals at the mercy of sinister, faceless power."[80] Presumably this shift to a nightmare vision owed much to the collapsing of the Soviet Union, but Betsey was increasingly driven to exaggerate the horrors of an individualism most women had not yet found.

The last essay in *Feminism without Illusions* began life in 1979 as "For Feminist Interpretation," a remarkably beautiful echo of late 1970s feminist scholarship, from the days before acute specialization and academic jargon, a time when Fox-Genovese's broad range was both stunning and viable. Read with her sly, rousing condemnation of Margaret Drabble's fiction, written in the same year, it gives a good picture of Betsey in 1979.[81] It began with some of her best writing:

> Translation, transformation, appropriation: such are the elements of interpretation, the modes of engaging authority and tradition, the means of understanding texts, cultures, societies. Such also must be the intellectual foundations of feminism—or, at least, of that feminism which, in the spirit of what Rosemary Ruether and Eleanor McLaughlin call "radical obedience," seeks to press the tradition to the fullness of its meaning, and womanhood to the fullness of its being. If interpretation is, following Paul Ricoeur, "the intelligence of the double meaning," feminist interpretation must aspire to be interpretation *par excellence.*[82]

Filled with energy, Betsey was writing from the edge of a new paradigm in the late 1970s—not the edge of an abyss. She addressed the duality of women's position in society as insider and outsider, and at the same time the accrued dualisms from various disciplines: Hegel's master and slave, Sherry Ortner's nature and culture, histories of women's oppression and histories of great women. And, yes, the male privilege of individualism as a snare and a delusion to women, who "as potential experts on the double meaning" could see the apparent male privilege of a unified self as a false front.[83] This essay was and is a gorgeous piece of writing, a white-hot insight from an expedition into the new territory of women in 1979.

Tillie Olsen had published *Silences* just the year before; other feminist work in the notes came from the 1970s, with only Hegel, Ricoeur, and Sontag coming earlier—in Hegel's case, much earlier. Two years before Fox-Genovese's essay, in 1977 Luce Irigaray had published *This Sex Which Is Not One.* Betsey would deny this, but the female identity Irigaray, a Freudian psychoanalyst, described as rooted in a sexual multiplicity, stemming from an anatomical materialism, resembled Betsey's dualisms and multiplicities. Irigaray and other French feminists had been omnipresent in the 1970s, and Betsey must have known them or at least their work.

Those double meanings and translations underpinned Fox-Genovese's communitarian sensibility. So also did her earlier reading in the Scottish School thinkers, Adam Smith, Lord Kames, Thomas Reid, Francis Hutcheson, communitarians all. In their emphasis on commonsense—understandings shared in common—they were a powerful antidote to the individualism of Locke and Hume, and not long after she read the Scots she encountered the Russian literary critic and philosopher Mikhail Bakhtin, popularized in France in the 1970s, with his collective sensibility and his description of a self that existed through discourse with others. Reinforced with a dose of Gramscian hegemony to invest those discourses with power and complexity, she interlaced the Marxian dialectic with the Freudian latent and manifest, rooted in her own sense of the impossibility of the isolated individual. It was already evident in her description of Du Pont de Nemours's coming to terms with himself in his autobiography—he evolved as France did, in the midst of, while caught up in the latter days of the *ancien régime* and then the revolution. When Louise A. Tilly, reviewing *Feminism without Illusions,* complained about "Fox-Genovese's lack of precision about what a community is," she was right.[84] Betsey's communitarian world was one of intellect and words; her emerging corporate world was public and social.

The 1991 version of this chapter is less elegant, more determined to propound, more obviously written by an established scholar. But it was not, as Ellen DuBois described the book, "a thorough-going attempt to reconcile contemporary feminism with traditional conservative thought."[85] How could it be when it contains, in place of an earlier formulation, this line: "Anger lies at the heart of the matter, for without anger there is no feminist consciousness at all."[86] In 1979, amid the heady years of feminism, Fox-Genovese had written, "Sooner or later, all feminists must face the inescapable, gut-wrenching angers that inform the aspirations of women too long cast as impure, inferior, and inadequate, and cast out from the sanctuaries of truth, law, knowledge, and the Word."[87] She set aside the bitterness of those "cast as impure, inferior, and inadequate," but she opened the door to righteous anger, much as Christine de Pizan and Virginia Woolf had done in earlier, profoundly feminist texts: *The Book of the City of Ladies* and *A Room of One's Own.* If the *Querelle des Femmes* is alive in *Feminism without Illusions,* the latter is hardly at one with traditional conservative thought.[88] When I first read the book in draft, in 1990 or so, I read it as a leftist critique of individualism. I now read it as the work of what

I would once—in my old days as a grassroots member of the women's liberation movement and a socialist in another country—have called an academic feminist but still one rooted in the left.

Fox-Genovese wanted to make readers reconsider their ties to each other and, especially, to children. That she chose to cloak or ignore the socialist antecedents of her argument against individualism as the foundation of society tells us that there was little basis for a socialist critique of feminism in the United States in 1991. So too does Betsey's peculiar positioning of herself as a Red Tory. She was enjoying some extraordinary middle ground, swinging at every pitch, unraveling every new feminist position, as she had been doing in her feminist theory seminar. She was also doing so as the Soviet Union collapsed.

In late 1991, after *Feminism without Illusions* had appeared, Fox-Genovese was interviewed by Jennifer Hyman for the Rochester, New York, *Democrat and Chronicle.* Hyman wrote,

> But before hardline anti-abortion activists begin celebrating a new convert, they had better listen carefully to what Fox-Genovese is saying.
>
> She opposes an outright ban on abortion. She has few problems with terminating a pregnancy in the first trimester—provided it is "socially sanctioned" and is not used as a means of birth control. However, she has "a major moral problem" with aborting a fetus after it has demonstrated signs of life.

The interview, given just before Fox-Genovese spoke in Rochester at the invitation of the local chapter of *Feminists for Life,* highlighted consensus and social sanction. More important, Hyman opened the article by paraphrasing Fox-Genovese: "Society, she insisted in a recent telephone interview, has a stake in children and families. For their part, women had better start thinking less of unfettered rights, and more about social responsibility."[89] So, yes, there was an edge of anger, a disgust with "unfettered rights," but yoked to moderate if reluctant acceptance of abortion. Fox-Genovese was battling Locke and Wollstonecraft, as well as *Murphy Brown* and the women on *L.A. Law,* and she mistook a narrow range of mass-market feminist literature and media caricatures for the reality of women's organizing.

Fox-Genovese did not understand that the roots that mattered in the formative years of the feminism she was writing about lay in the labor movement; Nancy Gabin's book *Feminism in the Labor Movement: Women and the United Auto Workers, 1935–1975* had just come out in 1990. By 1976 Betty Friedan was hinting at her past in the labor movement, which she had hidden in *The Feminine Mystique.* More recent work has made clear that the formation of the National Organization of Women had more to do with working-class women than with any feminist elite.[90] Had Fox-Genovese worked historically, had she read labor history, she might have found the origins of second-wave feminism in the United States were hardly antithetical to social responsibility.

Betsey's insistence that abortion was a means for career women to have the freedom of the male individual, and thus was antithetical to family life, mattered a great deal to her and fit her still-Freudian paradigm. Abortion became a highly cathected touchstone for her, having some deep personal resonance that we never find in her writing. For her, it linked feminism, individualism, and masculinity, and it struck her as maddeningly inconsistent with feminist reliance on an essentialism that described women as caring, maternal, and perhaps morally superior to men as a result. She was determined to point out this inconsistency in feminism—and shocked, I suspect, that other feminists were not interested.

In a sharply critical review of *Feminism without Illusions,* Ellen DuBois was quite correct in pointing out that Fox-Genovese was out to reconcile feminism with its own various strands: the individualist, the communitarian, the corporatist, and the Freudian/essentialist.[91] Fox-Genovese attempted an intellectual history of feminism's implications and contradictions, but her facility with ideas—always a strength—undid her. She was too impatient to unravel the chronological and material bases of the North American story. Her extraordinary command of what a colleague called "the effects of corrosive Lockean individualism" failed her in this project, although the potential of such a grounded history of the discourses Fox-Genovese sketched is haunting.[92]

At best, Fox-Genovese's voice was less rigid and determinist than what DuBois heard when she reviewed *Feminism without Illusions* for the *Nation.* Louise A. Tilly reported that Fox-Genovese "writes in the first pages that she offers no political program, and indeed she does not." Tilly continued, finding "great learning, good sense, and sensibility, but also a certain lack of closure."[93] The work was not closed; it was Fox-Genovese's voice from classes, from her discussions with students, from her thoughts as she drove home. Curiously, she missed entirely just how much that "corrosive Lockean individualism" had penetrated the right as well as the left in the postmodern world. Claiming to favor "social obligations, traditional, community values and limits on individualistic excess," Betsey also missed, or avoided making the point, that she was following in the footsteps of nineteenth-century socialist feminists.[94] Much of what she argued, balancing on the fence as a Red Tory, was their territory, but I suspect that they had not figured in her education.

The Red Tory

Hyman's interview survived as a clipping in Betsey's files. In it, Fox-Genovese described herself as a "former intellectual Marxist recently metamorphosed into a 'Red Tory.'"[95] So Ellen DuBois was right: Fox-Genovese thought she was halfway to being a "traditional conservative" thinker by late 1991. However, Red Tories fused paternalism with socialism.[96] It is arguable that Charles Dickens was a precursor, with *A Christmas Carol* as the best known, unrecognized presentation of Red Toryism in existence. That Betsey described herself as a Red Tory affirms her love of the dialectical, the two-sided, the conflicted.

Feminist Theory, 1991

In the fall of 1991 Betsey's overbooked feminist theory seminar, which became notorious in a 2015 memoir, irked and pleased students for many reasons that had little to do with Betsey's still embryonic excursions rightward.[97] Some were unhappy with the limited range of texts, some with the overpopulation, while others were pleased with the course. An advanced-level seminar that had been allowed to fill with fifty or so students would be rife with complaints. Sexuality theory was never on the syllabus. Fox-Genovese's own book was. She had inspired an array of negative reactions since Harvard; she knew too much, spoke out with a precision and calm her adversaries found unbearable, dressed in Ferragamo shoes from Saks, mixed her own combinations of Jo Malone scents.

If her blithely patrician manner, coupled with her increasingly visible discomfort with abortion, irritated people, some of what lay beneath her critics' outrage was good old sexism, drawn from the depths of male and female consciousness by the sight of a woman who over the years became more comfortable with her opinions, more authoritative, more elegant. She did not wear jeans. Her style was all wrong for academia in the late twentieth century. The sniping and irritation and disrespect had been there for decades, and while Genovese later created a mythology of radical feminist attacks on her, this only obscured the longer history of bitter learned men, older and younger, who could not abide the presence of an unapologetic woman.

The Institute

Nonetheless. The way Fox-Genovese ran the women's studies program provoked more serious criticism, and criticism from women. Determined to exercise the authority she was sure she possessed, she had little sense of how other faculty, especially those who preceded her in women's studies, expected to share responsibilities. Overcommitted, she made overarching decisions quickly to save time while she traveled constantly, edged toward life as a public intellectual, and wrote books. She disliked and distrusted, or did not understand, the collaborative nature of academic programs or the further reaches of shared responsibility typical within the women's movement. During her 1989–90 sabbatical, those at Emory directing women's studies in her absence discovered how much authority she had arrogated to herself and what the consequences of that were. While the drama of a lawsuit against her held center stage by 1992, the real nub of the problem was that discovery, and Fox-Genovese's fury with those women's studies faculty who were now raising complaints with the dean.[98] Once eager to challenge her father's authority, at fifty she sat on the other side of the table.

In the spring of 1991, Betsey framed a request for an associate director for her to hire. Rather than selecting from within the women's studies faculty, she wanted someone else, in this case her newly graduated student Dr. L. Virginia Gould.[99] In the fall of 1991, Gould took the job; later that fall she complained, citing a range of abuses from sexual harassment to sexual discrimination, then was fired in the midst of memos regarding her complaints. Betsey very probably expected Gould to be thankful and to take on the work of an administrative professional—in a position suited to a faculty member. By 1991 Fox-Genovese was turning toward the life of a public intellectual, not a program director, and wanted more time to travel. When Fox-Genovese resigned as director in January 1992 after arguments with the administration sparked by complaints from women's studies faculty and students, she was simply finding another exit from unwanted administrative work. That work entailed engaging with her faculty to develop the program, and that set the stage for a rerun of the *Marxist Perspectives* fiasco. That she and Emory University were sued by Gould in 1993, with Gould alleging sexual harassment and verbal abuse, both highlighted and obscured Fox-Genovese's difficulty with shared faculty governance of the women's studies program.

Moreover, Gould's complaints echoed those made by one of Fox-Genovese's graduate students at Binghamton in 1986. Stephanie McCurry had complained bitterly of being belittled, berated, and forced to hug Fox-Genovese. She had conveyed that warning to a faculty member at Emory, to no effect.[100] By February 1993 Gould's suit was news, leaving a trail in the press and in academic newsletters.[101] Gould's complaints brought various troubles to a public head; they were fairly spectacular, but they came after the crisis had burst. Nonetheless, the almost five-year long extravaganza of depositions for the case, which never came to trial, changed Fox-Genovese. Gould's legal team deposed Fox-Genovese's students and colleagues from Rochester, Binghamton, and Emory, drawing out a good number of complaints.

The ones I read are available to the public, and I have chosen not to rehearse them here. I have spent most of my career working in eighteenth-century Scots criminal trial records, and I am well aware of the caution with which I learned to read them. Eighteenth-century testimony, and the expectations of Scots advocates and judges was driven often by Enlightenment ideals of precision, of differentiating between assumptions and direct knowledge, awareness of community expectations, corroborating testimony, and, frankly, hellfire. Given that my ear is attuned to that culture, I choose not to recount what all those people had to say about Fox-Genovese. There are four points to be made, and made over again: Betsey aroused either love or hate; she learned from this legal experience, her scientific, systematic mind flourishing in argument and strategy; she took on legal expert status in defense of all-male education at The Citadel and the Virginia Military Institute because of it; and she moved further, and faster, to the right, defensively finding supporters there.

Betsey resigned over what she saw as the failure of the administration to back her against those she argued were politically motivated radicals within women's studies. To understand the genesis of the dilemma requires going back to 1986. Fox-Genovese had been hired at Emory for her extraordinary old-school bearing and sangfroid, as she had been at Binghamton, to lend respectability to a new venture. In carrying out the balancing of scholarship on women and the rejection of activist women's movement politics, she worked with the plan she was given, hiring new faculty for women's studies on a half-time basis, so each new hire would remain anchored in the department of their specialty. This created two kinds of faculty teaching in women's studies, the new hires and the older faculty, who had been at Emory before her, whose appointments were wholly in other departments. Perhaps no one had thought about the possible ramifications of these two levels of membership in women's studies. Fox-Genovese, who used to lecture students at Binghamton on our need to accept authority so we would understand it when it came our turn to hold it, found herself handed a means of marginalizing the early and overtly political drive behind women's studies.

Resignation

There are two points about the sudden end of Fox-Genovese's term as director of the women's studies program at Emory: First, Fox-Genovese revealed a good deal by choosing to shed the administrative work that brought her into contact with her faculty yet expecting the new associate director, a few months beyond being a student, to do this work. Second, as complaints about Betsey's management began to rise from faculty to senior administrators before as well as during the lawsuit, no one demanded her resignation. Five faculty did complain to George Jones, vice president for research and graduate studies, and David F. Bright, vice president for arts and sciences and dean of Emory College. They were followed by some staff and students, all dissatisfied with Fox-Genovese's structuring of women's studies.[102] There was no plot by radical lesbians to oust her, as Genovese often claimed, only what appear to be legitimate complaints, especially in women's studies, about her autocratic rule. That autocracy, as Danielle Balderas has argued, can also be partly explained by Fox-Genovese's awareness of the need to defend the scholarly legitimacy of women's studies by the end of the twentieth century, amid the culture wars.[103] Of course, her refusals to allow the politicization of women's studies were undercut by her entry into the abortion debate in 1991, and that double standard probably irked colleagues.

Letters flew from Bright and Jones to Fox-Genovese, her dean, vice president for undergraduate studies, and vice president for graduate studies respectively, and from her to them, in January 1992. She was, on paper, furious and defensive. She used a small font, single-spaced, and filled three pages. She enumerated her responses to their points, and she was right in several instances: a term had been set for her directorship when she was hired, directors of graduate and undergraduate study had been requested, discussions of other subjects were already initiated. Then she lectured the two administrators: "Careful reading of your memo suggests that you may not be entirely familiar with the specific issues. I very much regret that you saw fit to give me an agenda derived from complaints you have heard from people whose motivations and relations with the program may not be entirely clear to you."[104] What remains clear from her responses to their points—ultimately points raised by those disgruntled faculty—is that Fox-Genovese had made the decisions, initiated discussions, appointed committee members. It was a first-person narrative, a list of what she had done, in response to those who had been left out of the decisions, and it was much like Betsey to be oblivious to what was inappropriate about her response. She betrayed her deafness to the collaborative nature of faculty governance, defending herself with a list of her accomplishments.

Fox-Genovese presented her agenda, which was terse and limited, and followed it with three paragraphs that were her manifesto, ending with this:

> Almost from the beginning of my tenure, however, there have been concerted attempts to politicize the program. That is the root of our unnecessary but dangerous crisis. And it is clear that some faculty will continue to create tensions until they get their way. No, they will not tell you that their goal is politicization. They will protest one or another administrative matter—the "substantive concerns" of those whom you, in your memo to me, acknowledge as having a political agenda. In this instance, as in others, form and content are one. Apart from other considerations, the psychic cost of having to wage a constant guerilla battle has rendered the whole project "not worth it." The administration has a simple choice. It may, however, inadvertently and with whatever intentions, open the way to politicization, with results that may be seen throughout the country, or it may firmly and unequivocally declare its support for the program's principles and help the director to seal off this destructive effort once and for all.[105]

She experienced the call for collaborative faculty governance as a dire threat—a constant guerilla battle—from a coordinated opposition, no doubt with a nudge from Genovese, who had spent much of the late 1980s fighting depression while writing his satirical novel about faculty politics.[106] He had run the history department at Rochester with an iron fist from 1969 to 1975, rotating out of the chairmanship so that Betsey could, in accordance with university policy, receive tenure in the history department.[107] Genovese was elevated to a university professorship, which did not remove him from the history department, but he proceeded to organize the journal *Marxist Perspectives,* re-creating a similar level of control—like a chairmanship—for himself there.

Both Gene and Betsey were inclined to believe they lived in the midst of wars—of campus politics and ideas. Gene's toast, "Up with us, down with them," was always appropriate, and this was Betsey's war. She had married a man who echoed and magnified her tendency to suspicion and fear. And she was not only leaning to the right; she was turning her back on women. She despised Anita Hill—another complaining woman in 1991—sure that she was lying in the Senate hearings over Clarence Thomas's confirmation to the Supreme Court. Betsey and Gene celebrated Thomas, and Betsey refused to allow the institute to send a letter of support for Hill. This was more than the academic neutrality that Fox-Genovese claimed; it was personal. Genovese celebrated Clarence Thomas as a brilliant jurist and a Catholic. Fox-Genovese hated Anita Hill with a passion, repeating rumors about her from the gutter press as gospel. The old friend of theirs who told me this was appalled. I was reminded that Betsey's haute bourgeois armor sometimes cracked, allowing accumulated anger and hate, probably from other times, to burst out.[108] As one of her graduate students at Emory at the time reported,

> Her support of Clarence Thomas cost her even more credibility at Emory with women who had experienced similar treatment at the work force. I know Betsey mentioned working-class women's distrust of Hill, but this was about working class white women and not African American women. She never wanted to see this or tried to see this even when we mentioned circumstances from our lives. I was a flight attendant and told her about numerous incidents that happened to me. Other grad students did as well. When I look back at this, I also realized that we never read any theory in Feminist Theory about power dimensions in gendered relationships. Not one bit about abuse or rape. Crazy omission in a feminist theory course.[109]

Singularly unable or unwilling to perceive what others called abuse, she was likewise unable to sense the effects of her lack of empathy with faculty, staff, and students in women's studies, and with Virginia (Ginger) Gould. The student who believed Anita Hill also wrote, "I told her that she helped create the mess with Ginger, and of course, she didn't want to hear that. It was the truth."[110]

In the midst of complaints about her direction of women's studies in January 1992, Fox-Genovese may have been especially outraged, or dismayed, by her administrators' response regarding the complaining faculty, staff, and students: "However, the fact that we do not have a specific political agenda in mind for Women's Studies does not mean that we can ignore the substantive concerns of those who do."[111] Bright's and Jones's reply, following her demand that they "help the director to seal off this destructive effort once and for all," was considered, calm, and pointed. They listed the items that must be discussed by the full women's studies faculty and closed by asking her to remain as director through the rest of her seven-year term. She promptly resigned. Her war was ultimately with her bosses, over who was the boss.

"To the Surprise of Many"

Although Fox-Genovese could be fearless on intellectual grounds, facing the full contingent of core and associated faculty without the absolute support of Dean (and Vice President) Bright was unbearable.[112] Her resignation was unexpected by faculty and students, which tells us that it was not anyone's goal, but she had always been sensitive to criticism: there was Uncle Rover's approval, the dean at Rochester who refused to give her a tenure-track position before her dissertation was written, and the last meeting of the *Marxist Perspectives* group. Emilia Navarro, an established scholar, founder of the Emory Women's Caucus, and one of the associated faculty, was quoted in the *Chronicle of Higher Education:* "Basically Fox-Genovese does not believe, in practice, in the collaborative nature of a program." That was the problem, although Betsey's preferred narrative became one of a conspiracy of radical lesbians, combined with bias against conservatives on college campuses.[113]

As Susan Tush, adjunct professor and critic of Fox-Genovese, remarked in 1992, "For years, Bets[e]y has attributed problems in the department to the presence of radical lesbians. After a while, we started wondering where they all were. I mean, have you ever *been* to Emory?"[114] There was no conspiracy. The proof lay in her replacement as director by Martine Brownley, a serious scholar who had been in the United Kingdom the year before and who would not have agreed with

Betsey's administrative practices had she been present. She met with Betsey every month, tactfully but never seeking direction, after Betsey's resignation. Fox-Genovese was not replaced by the radical feminist furies of Betsey's and Gene's imaginations.[115] The problem, at the end of the day, was Betsey's unwillingness to meet with all the women's studies faculty to address what some saw as her failings, and so she framed the problem as a political agenda, not hers.

In this fiasco, the trial now loomed. The plaintiff's lawyers set about searching for a pattern of harassment on Fox-Genovese's part. They deposed her colleagues and students, reaching back to the late 1960s. Quite a few of those deposed expressed irritation and anger, and reading the depositions, as Betsey was asked to do by her lawyers, could not have been easy. Fox-Genovese argued that "women exercising a lot of authority" drew just those responses—but not from so many.[116] This is the stuff of student and faculty nightmares. The lawsuit demonstrated to Betsey that she did not have the unconditional support of others she had worked with and taught. Her reaction was defensive. The extended misery of it unraveled over the next four and a half years, as legal bills—all possibly handled by Emory after the first year or so—mounted.

Fox-Genovese read these sometimes-venomous reflections, and the years of trial preparation reshaped her in the mold of those arguments that she fashioned in her defense. Forced to confront, if she would admit it, just how unpopular her haute bourgeois persona had been, she embraced her deep sense of not belonging but learned to see herself as a devout conservative, not an unpopular person but unpopular politically. More remarkably, she deposited selected depositions and lawyers' queries in an open archive, which, if one reads the words left there for public view, is extraordinary. Gould was one of several students Betsey sought to employ as a sort of doppelganger, just as she wanted me to take over editing the journal of The Historical Society some years later. I was saved from that, but Gould was shoehorned into taking a job that did not fit, and she was old enough to express her anger and do it with lawyers. Women's studies tends to make women more aware.

Leaving Women's Studies

Between *Feminism without Illusions* and Fox-Genovese's rejection of feminism in 1996 in *Feminism Is Not the Story of My Life* came a powerful material reality, that of the impending trial. It impinged; it took money. Genovese heightened her distrust, and the depositions encouraged her to see the world even more in terms of us and them. The young woman who had signed letters to her father as "Fido" and valued loyalty found herself at sea, and for her, conservatism and learning to think like a defense lawyer would now develop in tandem.

8

Retreating and Regrouping

AFTER THE WALL FELL, 1992–1998

> What would you call one thousand feminists at the bottom of the ocean?
>
> A start.
>
> —PROFESSOR GEORGE CUTTINO, Emory University, 1985

BY 1992 Elizabeth Fox-Genovese had almost come to agree with Cuttino, although she qualified her disgust by blaming radical lesbians for her troubles. By resigning as chair of the Institute of Women's Studies in January, she finally reified her discontent with leftists, feminist and otherwise, that had been brewing since the *Marxist Perspectives* fiasco. She was cut from her moorings, soon overwhelmed with questions from her lawyers, increasingly wary of some colleagues—and yet she maintained friendships with some on the left and some lesbians. She was not in transit from left to right, which is too simple; she was shuffling, dealing, and getting ready to play a new hand, avoiding the New Leftists and the neoconservatives and libertarians alike. Not a child of her time, she was reimagining herself again and seeking an intellectual community.

Her wariness was abetted by Genovese; she had his full support in her anxieties, and now she was bereft of the feminist counterweight to him. Much of what had anchored her died between 1992 and 1996: her career (as she had previously imagined it), her health, her identity as a feminist, her father. How she rebuilt herself, her community, and comity through the 1990s was influenced by four very material factors. The unraveling of her administrative authority in women's studies was beginning; her parents', and especially her father's, health was failing; her continuing participation in the women's studies program became uncomfortable; and her own health deteriorated. Just as the Beaujolais Nouveau was released—the third Thursday in November—in 1992, Betsey collapsed in her kitchen during a party she and her husband were giving for graduate students. The students were stunned. It was, as one of them remarked later, a sign of "the perfect storm" in which Betsey found herself.[1]

Because she typically worked too hard, smoked and drank too much, ate too little, and had had bouts of serious illness before this, it is hard to know how perfect this storm was, but the collapse may have been the first serious manifestation of the multiple sclerosis that was diagnosed some seven years later, around 1999. At any rate, Gene claimed it began in 1992.[2] Betsey had been indomitable, her health had stabilized after the serious anorexia of the 1960s, and it would be wrong to overestimate the impact of this perfect storm, because she was resilient and tough-minded. Nonetheless, the collapse in front of students was new and must have appalled her.

Betsey's unrelenting appetite for work and multiple engagements became even more intense in difficult times, when she needed distraction. She and Gene also believed that they should involve themselves politically. In 1992, therefore, Betsey joined Gene in a political venture. Distressed by what they considered the corrupt choice between the Republican and Democratic front runners for president, George H. W. Bush and Bill Clinton, that summer they hosted a gathering of perhaps twenty intellectuals at their house. They wanted to accomplish several things.

One idea behind the meeting was that right and left had parallel structures, ranging from communitarian or corporatist at one extreme to anarchist or libertarian at the other. Therefore, Fox-Genovese and Genovese reasoned, these ideological divisions masked commonalities of priorities and perspectives. Might those, they asked, foster at least limited cooperation across the ideological divide? They aspired to forge such a coalition of right and left, excluding the liberal center, to support Patrick Buchanan for the presidency. Libertarian Lew Rockwell and Thomas Fleming, editor of *Chronicles of Culture* and president of the Rockford Institute, participated, as did *Washington Times* columnist Sam Francis and radical economist Louis Ferleger. Both critical and appreciative of Buchanan, Genovese and Fox-Genovese were searching for an alternative to the Hobbesian choice they feared voters faced in the election that coming November.[3]

The meeting was an abysmal failure. Unsurprisingly, neither left nor right trusted the other. The episode stands as a footnote to both Genovese's and Fox-Genovese's determination to bring ideological combatants together and their remarkably poor judgment of human beings. Genovese had hoped to do the same with *Marxist Perspectives* ten years earlier, and he and Fox-Genovese would attempt this again with The Historical Society, which launched in the spring of 1998 after a year of planning.[4] Throughout the years in between, Betsey and Gene became more insistent on asserting dismay at the way the world was going and more determined to find and follow an alternative path. They did so while returning to the scholarly collaboration that would crown their last years.

1993

Trial preparation impinged on Betsey's time by 1993 and undoubtedly shaped her writing of *Feminism Is Not the Story of My Life.* It also may have sped her discovery of the consolations of faith. She traveled a great distance intellectually between 1993 and 1995, when she entered the Catholic Church, profoundly influenced by the example not only of Edith Stein, later St. Teresa Benedicta of the Cross, but of St. Teresa of Avila and a Catholic student, Sheila O'Connor-Ambrose.

Intent on reorienting her life and transforming its meaning, as she had in the 1970s, Fox-Genovese was replacing her Freudian vocabulary and understanding of human nature with the Catholic Church's teachings on the human person. The shift came unevenly. When reading fiction and memoir, Fox-Genovese continued for some time to use analytical approaches that included Freud, long part of her bedrock understanding.[5] Increasingly, however, in her addresses and articles on contemporary issues, she deployed her church's teachings on the human person. These combined understanding of natural and divine law. Membership in the Catholic community offered more, however, than this understanding. It provided order, stability, and governing norms, as well as bonds that she had craved as a child and had never cultivated in women's studies.

Betsey was drawn by Edith Stein, a German, Jewish phenomenologist trained by Edmund Husserl: a woman, and a Jewish woman philosopher, living at a time when neither was welcome. Stein converted to Catholicism in 1922, became a Carmelite nun in 1933, and died at Auschwitz in 1942. She was beatified in 1987 and canonized in 1998. By 1995 Fox-Genovese, no longer a Red Tory, was more like Stein, a well-educated intellectual determined to bring Catholic theology into public discourse, especially as it touched on women's place in society. Stein was no stranger to the questions of women's nature and women's place; she was barred from an academic career in Germany by her sex and, ultimately, from teaching in Catholic girls' schools because she was Jewish. Like Fox-Genovese, Stein had to improvise, to rebuild her life several times, and Stein's version of squaring the circle, fitting careers for women into the church's teaching on women's natural vocation, and her experience of exclusion had a powerful appeal for Fox-Genovese. There is more to be said about this later, but Stein's example and eventual beliefs together served as an alternative to the demands of trial preparation.

Fox-Genovese inspired strong reactions, and there was little middle ground in students' and colleagues' responses to her. By March 1996, on the eve of the trial's start date, Betsey's lawyers had deposed 49 people and assembled a witness list of 189.[6] The plaintiff's lawyers had deposed many as well. Betsey would have read or at least discussed most, if not all, these depositions and was deposed herself: the documents and filings, faxes and phone calls, and mounting bills were ubiquitous in her life for years. Six months after hiring her own lawyer, Fox-Genovese wrote, responding to a bill:

> I am sorry to have taken so long to get back to you. My only explanation (I am not claiming excuse) is that this has been a rough period for all sorts of reasons, including elderly parents who are not doing well. In any event, an initial check is in the mail, sent on Friday, and I will have the account "current or near current" by the end of the year. Obviously, the amount is not trivial for us, and I do not want to run

> the account any higher than necessary, but Gene is adamant that I keep you (and would be even if the Braves were leading).[7]

Whatever the amount—no corresponding bill survives—it was more than she and Gene could pay from ordinary income. Afraid of being thrown under the bus, Betsey did not trust Emory's lawyers completely. Final settlement would come on her birthday in 1997, after a year of negotiation. In 1993 and 1994, those last years before email became common, the faxes and calls from her lawyers probably displaced much of her regular correspondence. In that process, she wrought a defensive narrative for herself, discovered allies among conservatives who also felt marginalized, and sought a new job.

In September 1993 Fox-Genovese applied for a joint position in women's studies and history at Harvard. In December David Brion Davis, a superb historian of slavery and Sterling Professor of History at Yale, wrote to Vanderbilt University, nominating Betsey for a "window of opportunity" chair in the Department of Political Science.[8] No jobs were offered, although the chairman of the political science department at Vanderbilt had invited her to apply for the position of director of American studies in 1988.[9]

This was unfamiliar territory; to be at sea and unwanted so soon after having been courted must have shocked. Meanwhile, Fox-Genovese continued working on the book that became *Feminism Is Not the Story of My Life*. Feminism had once mattered to her, but now, after the loss of her public persona as director of women's studies, she used this book to separate from it. And the book was helpful too as it brought her a handsome advance, possibly needed for lawyers' fees.[10]

While maintaining a professional mien with lawyers, Fox-Genovese wrote out her anger with feminism, with a perceived feminist elite, and finally over children deprived of their mothers' protection. She would not be literally deprived of her mother until 2004, but she had felt like a motherless child long before that. Her conversion to Catholicism gave her discomfort with abortion a new and firm context; it also gave her a holy mother. When she came to write about her conversion, roughly four years after entering the church, she described herself as receiving instruction: she had gone back to school, taken a class, done well. It was comforting to learn, to be a student again, to start over. When her essay "A Conversion Story" appeared in *First Things* in April 2000, she had finished her four or five years of instruction and practice and was ready to appear in public as a Catholic scholar.

Feminism Is Not the Story of My Life

Fox-Genovese started the new book immediately after *Feminism without Illusions,* as she began to question abortion and think about children, first imagining a book titled *What Do We Want for Our Daughters (and Our Sons)?*[11] As it progressed and students and faculty in the institute spoke out against her, and her sense of betrayal drove her disdain, abetted by Genovese's fury, she shifted from accusing radical lesbians to condemning a "feminist elite." In the process of working on the manuscript, she divested herself of most vestiges of typical feminism, finishing the manuscript as she was taking on her Catholic identity. As she finished, in 1994, she became an expert witness for The Citadel as the South Carolina military college sought to forestall undergraduate coeducation by fighting the admission of Shannon Faulkner. While she defended single-sex education publicly, her somewhat primeval disgust with Faulkner showed through in private.

In the summer of 1992 *Lingua Franca* had profiled her resignation in "Field Notes," highlighting her "conservative views" and students' complaints.[12] It brought her some sympathy from conservatives and drew her toward them. Nonetheless, late in 1993 Christopher Hitchens interviewed Betsey and Gene for *Vanity Fair,* where he referred to them as "the royal couple of radicalism." He wrote, "We are not talking here about some once radical couple preparing to enter mellow and mature retirement. They are serious and committed radicals, not neoconservative defectors."[13]

They seem to have enjoyed the interview, posing for Hitchens's photographer, providing a photograph from their wedding in 1969. Their radical pique—Hitchens's words—was directed to political correctness, which had come to mean many things. For them, filtered through the interviewer's prose, it meant a lowering of standards, a replacing of critical thought and debate by everyday shorthand. They were also cultural conservatives, open to the familiar, the canonical, and the respectable. At virtually the same moment, Michael Skube reiterated Hitchens in the *Atlanta Journal/Atlanta Constitution* book review section, referring to them as "old Marxists" and insisting that Betsey had been forced out of women's studies by "feminist fascists" for "failure to follow the party line."[14] This was the politically correct vocabulary of the right, or perhaps merely the shorthand of willful misunderstanding. By September a friend was writing in some alarm: "Yikes! Imagine my surprise when I opened up our local Conway newspaper, and found Paul Harvey quoting *you* [smiley face]! Say it ain't so, Joe!?!"[15] How much of Betsey's mid-1990s drift to the right was designed by her, or driven by media's prevailing winds, we cannot know. Both mattered.

The Oxford Amnesty Lecture

On 11 February 1994 Fox-Genovese spoke in England at the Sheldonian Theatre, Oxford. In her lecture, "Contested Meanings: Women and the Problem of Freedom in the Mid-Nineteenth Century United States," she challenged Orlando Patterson and any simple opposition of slavery and freedom, using the experience of slave and free women to muddy the waters.[16] She spoke to a thinly populated hall, where one of her students from Binghamton sat:

> The Oxford Amnesty Lecture in the Sheldonian was a marvelous experience and also an alienating and odd experience. It was cold and misty and late in the afternoon so the light was fading. I think it was February or early March. I was wearing a beat-up cast-off navy Barbour and sweatpants. I remember this because Betsey was always stunningly dressed and on that day, she wore her signature red and looked sharp and smart as ever. I noticed, though, that her face was a bit drawn and, if I looked past a convincing display of incredible strength, I could see between the interstices that she'd gone from fashionably tall and slim to the sort of gauntness that one would associate with ill health, with being in the wars. What struck me as totally odd was that the Sheldonian was not as full as it usually is for an Amnesty Lecture. Betsey was not playing to a full house—to me, that was a

> new experience. The hall seemed full of cold space and echoes—not friendly. Still, Betsey appeared to physically shrug this off her stylish shoulders and she gave a brilliant and searing lecture. So despite being the fag end of winter in a cold, damp, dim, and drafty space, there was a fire in the Sheldonian—it was Betsey. She fought the noble fight, her smile beaming, and her head inclined as if her desire to help you to understand was taking her mind and spirit straight past the podium and hotwiring your brain. A mighty wake-up call. When she finished, she straightened up her papers in front of her, gathered her material neatly and efficiently, then crossed up the main aisle with her characteristic panache—a fine and deliberate stride, lovely shoes, head held high.[17]

The half-empty Sheldonian was the result of rumors spreading about her move to the right and the lawsuit, abetted by her insistence on questioning abortion. In 1994 she had not rejected it on moral grounds but saw it as less useful than she had once thought, writing, "At best, access to abortion will permit a poor woman to re-engage the weary struggle for a more promising future without the encumbrance of a child, but it will not necessarily improve her education or her job prospects, provide her with medical insurance, or increase the likelihood that she will marry. And access to abortion does nothing for the poor woman who chooses to keep her child."[18] This was a materialist criticism, and it was published in 1994 in London by a left-wing publisher, Zed.

The Road Not Taken

Among Fox-Genovese's essays from the period following her resignation is her "Unspeakable Things Unspoken: Ghosts and Memories in the Narratives of African-American Women."[19] She first wrote it as the 1992 Elsa Goveia Memorial Lecture at the University of the West Indies, and the university published it as a pamphlet. She was attempting to track down some of what had eluded her in *Within the Plantation Household:* the voices of African American women describing slavery. For some years, she planned a book of related essays, tentatively titled *Ghosts and Memories: History in the Fictions of African American Women Writers,* but abandoned the attempt, finishing *The Mind of the Master Class* with Genovese instead.

She began her essay—her lecture—by reading from the end of Toni Morrison's *Beloved,* and commenting:

> The concluding pages of Toni Morrison's novel *Beloved,* from which these words are taken, evoke the difficulty of telling the story of women's experience of slavery—of the cost of slavery for enslaved mothers and their children. Beloved, the ghost of the "crawling already?" baby, remains not lost, but disremembered and unaccounted for, because no one is even looking for her. The story of her murder by her own mother, which implicated slavery in its entirety, including the other members of the community of slaves, was not one that anyone—black or white, slave or free—chose to tell. And their forgetting, even more than the original event, becomes a story that cannot be passed on.[20]

The story of Beloved, the lost baby, was for Fox-Genovese a means of redressing the missing stories in *Within the Plantation Household,* those of Black women and slavery. It was also a parable of psychoanalysis, of resurrecting a lost childhood or remembering that something was lost, through words and ghosts. It is finally a tale of fearful maternal power made more fearful by the mothers' helplessness: infanticide and abortion lurk in this paragraph, written in 1992, couched in the language of history, slavery, and loss.

If this was a story—about slavery—Fox-Genovese wished to recover, there was another she did not. *The Bluest Eye,* also by Morrison, includes another childhood story that Fox-Genovese wished to deny: the young girl Pecola Breedlove is raped by her father. Betsey, in my seminar experience, taught that episode in the novel as something other than rape, announcing at the end of three hours that it was not to be understood as rape but as the only form of love a poor man could give his daughter. Parents had their reasons and their acts are not to be questioned, she had insisted at Binghamton. At Emory, she advised one of her students completing a dissertation on Black and white women teachers, quite a few of whom had been physically abused by their fathers, that this was not abuse. Her extraordinary, perverse advice did not stick, but the memory of it did.[21]

Drawing the unspeakable and the unspoken into the light, especially the lost experience of Black women in slavery, was something Betsey had avoided in *Within the Plantation Household.* It was what she had attempted in her own lengthy psychoanalyses. She did, brilliantly, pull the unspoken in Du Pont de Nemours's autobiography into the light, as she had with the Physiocrats. She was good at this interior psychic anatomy, this extraordinary sensitivity to intimate language in historical context, and this capacity was at odds with her obsessive critique of individualism as an ideological delusion. She had been interested in biography since 1966, when she considered switching to English intellectual history and working with biographer John Clive at Harvard. Before Harvard, she had written a senior thesis at Bryn Mawr on Camus, and she had frequently told students at Binghamton that the easiest way to apprehend a historical period was through the life of one living it. So the constant references to Sarah Haynsworth Gayle in *Within the Plantation Household* should surprise no one, but Betsey's refusal to plumb the erasures to Gayle's diary should.

The Trial

When *Feminism Is Not the Story of My Life* appeared in January 1996, Betsey had very little time to reflect on it; she had a scheduled trial date set for March 20. She was busy returning lawyers' calls and finding colleagues to teach her classes during what she was warned would be a long trial, lasting at least four and a half weeks, if not six. Her emails were frantic, taking on the tone of an anxious person leaving on a long journey: "I am not in [*sic*] clear-headed enough to give it much thought right now. And the more I talk to lawyers, the clearer it becomes that I am going to be swamped for the next couple of months. Let's talk over the weekend."[22] She worried about her teaching, writing,

> I learned yesterday that the trial in the suit against Emory and me will begin on March 20 and that the lawyers want me in court every day. . . . As I predicted last fall, this does create problems for

> my teaching schedule, but the timing could have been much worse. I think the best thing to do is for me to ask my seminar to write a reasonably substantial paper and to give them the final month of the semester to do so—i.e., not to meet with them after the 20th.[23]

A few months earlier she had written to her brother about selling the family's summer house in Annisquam: "My lawyers' bills are crippling, and they will continue to mount steadily. We are talking about $30,000–$50,000, and my life is on the line."[24] She had told colleagues that Emory was, after the first year, paying her private lawyer, but perhaps not. In January 1996 she remarked to her brother, "We are now down to serious business."[25] A few days later, she wrote to another correspondent, "I am in for a hell of a semester since the . . . trial begins March 20, will run for four and a half to six weeks, and they want me in court every day."[26] The weight of the impending trial must have erased nearly all the pleasure of having the book come out, but not all. By the end of the month she had returned to Atlanta after talking about her book on C-SPAN's *Washington Journal,* introduced and perhaps invited by the Independent Women's Forum. She was pleased, writing, "I think everything went extremely well. Even Gene thought I was a '10' on *Washington Journal,* and everyone seemed pleased with everything else. And I even had a good time."[27]

As of this writing the *Washington Journal* episode is available, archived online.[28] Betsey looks much like herself, speaking earnestly with a compelling frankness and an emphatic clarity, as if she expected to be misunderstood. She was fully aware of the reviews already published in the *New York Times* and the *Nation,* both insisting that she was now an antifeminist, a point she would argue. As the camera pulls back, Betsey looks remarkably like Eileen Atkins in her one-woman performance of Virginia Woolf's *A Room of One's Own,* released six years earlier. Betsey seemed dressed to suggest a woman intellectual, perhaps explicitly European, from the interwar years. It was not her usual style, and she must have chosen it quite intentionally for this audience at this time. Betsey knew the power of Woolf's famous adversarial opening word, "But," and perhaps meant to position herself as Woolf, a modernist and member of a closed intellectual elite, ready to argue.

She was far more serious and less playful than one imagines Woolf to have been. Nor do they see history the same way. *A Room of One's Own* is history told through Woolf's consciousness, as *Feminism Is Not the Story of My Life* is history told through a diffracting prism, breaking Fox-Genovese's views into dozens of others' voices. The comparison is not far-fetched: Mary Gordon, the author of the important and negative *New York Times* review was also the author of the introduction to a then-current edition of *A Room of One's Own*. Both books were adversarial, and there is more to be said about the literary tradition into which *Feminism Is Not* fits.

With the trial weeks away, Fox-Genovese had little time to reflect, but she did note the importance of her conversion to Catholicism the year before, writing, "My being a Christian makes all the difference in the world, and I do know that I will be able to endure." She also noted that she "had to wrestle with the forgiving" and acknowledged that she was "not complacent about my own sinfulness."[29] Compared to the Marxist-feminist Fox-Genovese of the Binghamton years, who had told a student reporter there in 1984 that she was not "a believer in any normal sense of the word," this was an enormous change.[30]

On Tuesday, March 19, Fox-Genovese left the courtroom at nine o'clock at night after a day of jury selection. She sent her brother a quick email to say, "We have a jury we can live with, which is very important."[31] After the 19th, there was a day free, perhaps to give the lawyers time to go over their opening statements. And then, unexpectedly, the suit was settled. By the next evening, Betsey was back on email, advising a student but beginning, "Briefly, since I am wiped. We settled today. Thank God. I cannot reveal the monetary terms, but can talk to the press if I choose. The university was terrific, the lawyers even better if possible. I cannot begin to imagine what it will be like to get my life back. This has been more than four years."[32] And so it ended. Emory paid, and the legal costs began to subside. The great legacies of this lawsuit—setting aside Betsey's conversion for the moment—included her experience of reading depositions and of being deposed herself. She was familiar with the kind of talking she had done with analysts, but this was different, driven by the questioners and directed to different ends. What readers of *Feminism Is Not the Story of My Life* read was Betsey deposing witnesses and gathering evidence.

The sometimes thinly disguised women whose stories Betsey used to represent her views are effectively witnesses testifying to the rightness and normalcy of Betsey's arguments. While I appreciate her insistence on invoking the ties that bind women and children, husband and wife, and women who shop together, I see problems. Mary Gordon, in the *New York Times,* identified several: her stories were not quite to the point; she showed signs of being "trapped in an unhappy essentialist argument"; she was "far more pessimistic about men as moral agents than feminists are"; and she had, in attempting to tell a broadly accessible story, made the story too simple. Gordon had quickly identified one woman's story as strangely exaggerated, and she was right. Among Fox-Genovese's sometimes barely disguised women, this one's story, meant to "cite the dangers of the sexual revolution," was not true.[33] The character—"Tracey"—was a composite of several graduate students, probably based on confidences shared with her as a mentor, not interviews, and presented in a way that made Tracey readily recognizable to her family. Betsey used her confidences without permission.[34]

The book cost Fox-Genovese friendships and lost trust because she indulged in the great temptation of nineteenth-century oral historians and collectors of oral compositions of all sorts: she emended material she collected to please herself and her audience. As one graduate student wrote,

> About three of us were invited to lunch at her house, which was odd because she always wanted to eat at that restaurant at Phipps. When we sat down, she brought out a tape recorder. Never asked us for permission. Never asked us later. She asked us questions about our mothers and their work because all three of us had working mothers. Then she took my story (I was the wife of the pilot so everyone knew that was me) and really diminished what my mother did. I was furious when she sent me the monograph. I never really read it. She knew I did oral histories and that I carefully obtained permissions before recordings. I had all kinds of release forms from the Oral History Assn.

She didn't do any of that with us. She simply assumed we wouldn't mind.[35]

Feminism Is Not the Story of My Life was a misstep in unfamiliar territory that effectively ended what little was left of Fox-Genovese's reign as one of the lions of women's studies. The misstep was intentional, driven by her desire to mock women's studies with what she was sure was the truth. The claim was made worse by her old tendency to authority. She used and reshaped students' words at will; by contrast, she was more respectful of what she was told and how she used the words of friends and colleagues, even having some sign releases, and at the top, worked to please her editor at the commercial press.[36]

The book had two poles: feminism and essentialism. Her feminism was a two-dimensional characterization that had grown from her bitterness with her experience at Emory, had little to do with internal and academic debates in feminist theory, and had much to do with media mudslinging and soundbite characterizations of feminism. Betsey appeared on William F. Buckley's *Firing Line* in December 1994, agreeing with his proposition "The Women's Movement Has Been Disastrous."[37] She argued that feminism disregarded the needs of poor women, favoring wealthy career women. This was hardly true of the many permutations of grassroots women's movements.

Five years earlier in 1989, Betsey had given a speech to undergraduates as the director of women's studies, defending feminism: "For many of you, the very word 'feminist' probably has an ominous ring. In my experience, most undergraduates associate it with 'bra-burners' and 'lesbians' and especially, with dissatisfaction and anger. For most of you, the very idea of being a feminist probably seems puzzling. What do we need it for?"[38] Fox-Genovese was betraying her own impressions here, although they may have resonated with some Emory students.

Between late 1989 and 1995, when Fox-Genovese finished *Feminism Is Not the Story of My Life*, feminist theory had proliferated. The book's selected bibliography is telling, showing a handful of books from 1991 on and no articles. Feminism was not something she loved, it was something with which she was minimally conversant, interesting to her as an adjunct to the political theory she had mastered. What

Fox-Genovese advanced to replace feminism was in keeping with the eighteenth-century scholar she still was, a biological essentialism à la Rousseau: because women bear children, women should raise children. She had not believed that in the early 1980s, saying the exact opposite at Binghamton. She was not as heavy-handed in advancing that argument as Mary Gordon insisted, but she was certainly seeking clarity and order in understanding society and public policy that would benefit children, families, and especially poor women. Betsey was adamant about women's responsibility for children—without acknowledging what that said about her opinion of men.

She tried to make the book answer too many provocations, as her own life was pulled in many directions in the early 1990s. The title, *Feminism Is Not the Story of My Life: How Today's Feminist Elite Has Lost Touch with the Real Concerns of Women,* was an obvious, intentional slap in the face to women's studies, and it drove the book's reception before reviewers read a word of the content. Highlighting the word "Not" on the cover by printing it in red drew attention to her anger, which she could not easily express directly.

The strategy of spreading her argument through the words of dozens of other women, deposed, edited, and carefully selected, was less communitarian and populist than it was self-justifying. Toward the end of the book, Fox-Genovese referred to herself "as a woman of a transitional generation," and those women—their ages were not given—became both a supporting chorus and a means to speak for ordinary and poor women, which Fox-Genovese refrained from doing in her own voice.[39] How ordinary or poor some might have been we shall never know, but Betsey interacted with relatively few ordinary or poor women.

Fox-Genovese was not the only woman to criticize feminism in the early 1990s.[40] In 1994 Christina Hoff Sommers published *Who Stole Feminism? How Women Have Betrayed Women.* Daphne Patai and Noretta Koertge produced *Professing Feminism: Cautionary Tales Taken from the Strange World of Women's Studies,* and one year earlier Katie Roiphe had come out with *The Morning After: Sex, Fear, and Feminism on Campus.* Only Sommers's book was anywhere close to developing a similarly broad critique, but she and Fox-Genovese were, if anything, at loggerheads: Sommers wanted a return to liberal principles, a simple individual rights doctrine, letting the chips fall where they might. Fox-Genovese was advancing—albeit awkwardly, trapped by privilege and distance—the needs of working women, the poor, and children. Lurking behind her words was a faint recognition of the relative poverty of Agnes and Philip Fox, her father's penniless years at Harvard, and the Simons' tenuous status as wealthy Jews in the 1930s.

The *Querelle des Femmes*

The proper context for her two books on feminism, books that dominated her work in the 1990s, is a long tradition of writing in defense of—and against—women: the *Querelle des Femmes.* Beginning with Christine de Pizan's *The Book of the City of Ladies* and perhaps earlier with Jean de Meun's addition to the *Roman de la Rose,* this writing on woman's nature and place in society continued into the Enlightenment, through Mary Wollstonecraft's *Vindication of the Rights of Woman,* the first-wave feminists, Virginia Woolf, Simone de Beauvoir, and the second-wave feminists. What Fox-Genovese wrote, while not central, was nevertheless embedded in this discourse. She felt able perhaps to fall back to an older humanism while recanting her own feminism and still participate, a useful footnote to the state of the discourse in the late twentieth century. She believed she was working out a new way forward, a reconstituted feminism forged from something better than the pervasive individualism of the revolutionary era. Ultimately, her critique betrayed her unwillingness to abandon corporate authority; she may have become a Marxist historian, but she was never a socialist.

She found her materials in Catholicism, and in particular in the writings of Edith Stein. The phenomenology of Stein's chief professor, Edmund Husserl, had roots in psychology; she wrote her dissertation on empathy while serving for a time as a Red Cross nurse during World War I. She was briefly Husserl's teaching assistant but blocked from further academic advancement as a woman. Like Fox-Genovese, she remade herself through the church, writing eight essays on women between 1928 and 1932 from her new position as a teacher in a Catholic girls' school. These combined a secular commitment to women's education and exercise of professions with essentialist and Catholic beliefs about women's nature as empathic, nurturing, and devoid of any facility for the abstract.[41]

The fact that Stein wrote these essays just as Betsey's father and mother first met in the 1930s reinforces for us both just how comfortable Fox-Genovese was with her parents' generation and how ill at ease she was with her own. Betsey was greatly taken with St. Teresa Benedicta and with the recent saint's inspiration, St. Teresa of Avila, a late medieval Spanish mystic. Both Fox-Genovese and Stein read *The Life of St. Teresa of Avila by Herself*; Stein was moved to convert by it. Not far into the story Teresa of Avila recounted the loss of her father:

> I suffered much myself during his illness. I believe I rendered him some service in return for what he had suffered in mine. Though I was very ill, I did violence to myself; and though in losing him I was to lose all the comfort and good of my life—he was all this to me—I was so courageous, that I never betrayed my sorrows, concealing them until he was dead, as if I had felt none at all.[42]

Betsey, raised in the stiff upper-lip tradition of Protestant New England saints, probably found the words of this medieval Catholic familiar and comforting. And those words offered her a model very different from the constant digging and uncovering of Freudian analysis. It suggested that virtue lay in concealment, and the burden of knowing all was left to Christ. Freud's focus on childhood was displaced for Betsey by believing in original sin and the preservation of the traditional family. Catholicism gave her a channel in which her emotions could flow yet was also an intellectual enterprise, as her study of St. Teresa Benedicta and St. Teresa of Avila attests.

Edward Fox died in May 1996, a few days before Betsey's birthday. After so much writing in her journal about him, and so much time spent helping him with his work, there seems to be little surviving correspondence about his death. A few cards expressing sympathy came, most of them a few months later, suggesting that she had not spoken to many friends about him at the time. Perhaps it was a matter for the telephone. He had been unwell, clearly declining, his death no surprise. Genovese and Len Hochberg, a student of Fox, had published a volume of essays in his honor in 1989. Betsey planned to edit a collection of his unpublished essays but never did.[43] With her father's death she abandoned the Betsey who had railed against him and set about remaking him to her taste. Speaking at her parents' joint burial after her mother's death in 2004, she assured the audience that her parents would have understood and approved her conversion to Catholicism. Her father would not have.

Fox-Genovese entered the Catholic Church in December 1995 and the next year found herself free from the wearying lawsuit, experienced her father's death, and celebrated the publication of her one commercial book to some negative reviews, although not among conservatives. In the wake of its publication, David Burner at Brandywine Press wrote to tell her that he felt compelled to remove her name—as one of the authors—from a textbook, *Firsthand America,* as department chairs began calling him to say their faculty were reluctant to use a book by someone so antifeminist. Mary Gordon's review of *Feminism Is Not the Story of My Life* in the *New York Times* had consequences, but Burner assured her she would still receive her agreed-upon royalties.[44] Betsey argued, and Burner replied, with remorse, "It was purely a business decision, a mean one."[45]

Fox-Genovese, meanwhile, was using her exposure to legal methodology by testifying as an expert witness, defending The Citadel's and the Virginia Military Institute's exclusion of women. That legal experience had been another kind of schooling for her. She learned quickly and applied it to her subsequent writing about women's rights, equality, sexual harassment, and marriage. It drew her toward public policy but not completely away from southern women's writing. Two essays on African American women's writings, both from 1997, were the last signs that she might complete *Ghosts and Memories: History in the Fictions of African-American Women Writers.*

That unfinished book marked a profound change, from scholar to embattled warrior, determined to re-present herself as a Catholic scholar, addressing public policy, and still determined, with Genovese, to bring together left and right by 1997 in The Historical Society. She had spent a goodly part of the 1990s learning and studying, both

Catholicism and lawyers' ways of thinking, and both provided her with the opportunity to be a student again, something she relished.

Betsey was less exposed to the vicissitudes of fortune, error, and choice in the 1990s than the foregoing would suggest. She and Genovese, with Genovese always leading, were hard at work creating the kind of institutions he had always urged, crossing disciplinary and political boundaries. First came the St. George Tucker Society, initially an invitation-only southern studies group. No doubt after many phone calls, Genovese sent a letter to roughly forty-two proposed members in November 1990, suggesting a structure and some early meetings. It was full of his usual dry humor: "In deference to traditional republican and southern sensibilities, however, we agree that every so often—say, every three years—the Fellows will be able to throw the rascals [officers] out for incompetence, stupidity, sloth, and the embezzlement of funds."[46]

Creating this group well before Betsey experienced difficulties with the women's studies program at Emory, Gene built it for her as she established herself in southern history. Just before the first meeting in April 1991, Fox-Genovese was listed as program secretary, and membership had reached sixty-four.[47] Of all of Genovese's inventions, this one endured, giving both him and Fox-Genovese an audience for their work, especially as it emerged again in 2001 as they completed the first draft of *The Mind of the Master Class.* In the midst of this, they once again joined with friends across historical specialties to challenge the primacy of the American Historical and Southern Historical Associations and found a new society. Some of those people had been with them all along and had worked on *Marxist Perspectives* twenty years earlier.

9

Right with God

PUBLIC CATHOLIC INTELLECTUAL AND SOUTHERN SCHOLAR, 1998–2007

> Only the person blinded by the passion of controversy could deny that woman in soul and body is formed for a particular purpose.
>
> —EDITH STEIN, 1930

> The real point of homosexuality is to defy nature.
>
> —ELIZABETH FOX-GENOVESE, 10 August 1995

ENTERING THE Catholic Church late in 1995, free at last from lawyers' faxes in 1996, withdrawing from women's studies, working with Genovese on The Historical Society and on *The Mind of the Master Class,* Fox-Genovese began to accelerate shifts in her scholarly life. Her speaking engagements are telling. In 1996, except in the case of one conservative organization, she was speaking by invitation at a variety of universities and law schools, showing her interest in public policy, albeit conservative policy, as in her defense of the Virginia Military Institute as a male institution. The next year was much the same, but by 1998 Betsey was more often speaking to conservative Catholic audiences. By late 1999 her lectures were those of a Catholic public intellectual, addressing Catholic women. She seldom spoke any longer to non-Catholic audiences as a historian or literary critic. There was only one exception in 1999: "Proslavery: The Unremarkable Life and Violent Death of an Idea," which drew on her work with Gene for *The Mind of the Master Class.* However, she delivered the talk at a Catholic university.[1]

Fox-Genovese changed her teaching as well. Having retreated from women's studies to teach history and literature classes, she increasingly focused on male authors, possibly reflecting what she was reading for *The Mind of the Master Class.* At the same time, she became less visible in academia, presenting papers at only five professional conferences between 1996 and 2000.[2] What Steven Hahn referred to in 2012 as "Genovese's tragic self-marginalization" was Fox-Genovese's as well, and quite possibly hers more profoundly than his.[3]

Nevertheless, Betsey continued to organize formal and informal intellectual engagements beyond the church and to do so in familiar fashion. Toward the end of every decade of their marriage, Fox-Genovese and Genovese attempted the founding of an ideologically and intellectually inclusive group of some sort. For Betsey's part, these actions partially reflected a commitment to moral economy. But for Gene also, building these intentionally inclusive intellectual havens was necessary, continuous, and all too likely to fail. Fox-Genovese's and Genovese's angularities and what some considered paranoid tendencies got in the way.

The journal *Marxist Perspectives,* open to non-Marxists for debate, came first. While directed to Marxists and those who wished to argue with them, it included literary criticism and poetry. It was successful and financially secure, and Genovese shut it down after two years. The St. George Tucker Society, founded in 1990 as an alternative to the Southern Historical Association, has survived. It complemented the informal Southern Intellectual History Circle, started two years earlier by Michael O'Brien. Betsey designated it a circle. That too continues. The Historical Society, however, failed in its turn, despite receiving significant funding. Intentionally named to challenge the breadth of the American Historical Association, The Historical Society inevitably produced a journal, named with equal lack of subtlety the *Journal.* Editing that journal would drain Fox-Genovese, who was also working on *The Mind of the Master Class* as the twentieth gave way to the twenty-first century. The first issue of the *Journal* appeared in 2001, the same year Fox-Genovese and Genovese finished the first draft of *The Mind of the Master Class.*

Anyone who saw the coverage of the initial meeting of The Historical Society in the *Chronicle of Higher Education* may recall the photograph of some of the founding members with Betsey and Gene at the center. I remember walking with all of them from the conference building at Boston University to find a suitable ivy-covered wall and old trees for the photo, and I remember how difficult it was for Betsey, limping painfully, cane in hand, for twenty minutes to the spot the photographer wanted as a background. Yet, her pain was not apparent in that front-page photo—Betsey and Gene are beaming, confident, standing tall. Then Louis Ferleger brought a car around so Betsey wouldn't have to—and she couldn't—walk back.

Betsey enjoyed the new communities, but The Historical Society, especially the editing of the *Journal,* not only pleased but exhausted her. She had considerable help from Laura Crawley, her managing editor, and I pitched in at her request on the last issues she edited. Nonetheless, she was unable to meet deadlines; the publisher, Blackwell's, was often frantic. Facing multiple sclerosis, an unpredictable disease at best, and wracking, unpredictable pain from spinal stenosis, Fox-Genovese taught full time, clung to editing the journal, and continued to write. Seeing herself as exceptional, even as she fell asleep at her kitchen table during editorial meetings, she needed to work. Work was her drug of choice when faced with difficulty and her preferred means of dealing with her failing health. After the diagnosis of multiple sclerosis in 1999, she simply worked more.

Betsey's introduction to her last issue of the *Journal,* an introduction that she wrote and presented as jointly hers and mine, bears remarking. The articles were, as she framed them, about revolutions and the difficulties of freedom. It was very much her territory. She began her atypically short framing of the issue by invoking Mary Wollstonecraft standing on a London bridge and deciding to jump, and ended with Emmett Kennedy's essay on Simone Weil. Betsey wrote, "Bright, Jewish, talented, and well-off, Weil would spend the rest of her short life smoking, eating little, and searching in both socialism and Catholicism, the secular and the spiritual—for some means by which to live."[4] It could almost stand as Betsey's epitaph.

She wished to make me the next editor of the journal, and I knew she intended to put a new name on the masthead and retain control, much as she had earlier insisted on hiring Virginia Gould while retaining control of the Institute for Women's Studies at Emory herself.

Betsey fought with The Historical Society, I tried to back out, and she was relatively gracious as she tried to maintain her connection to the journal. Although Genovese blamed her old friend Louis Ferleger, who had made an argument about cost and circulation, it was Franklin W. Knight, the president of the society, who simply asked her to resign, and after some correspondence about files to be transferred and bills to be paid, she was writing amicably to Knight on 18 May 2005. On the same day, Gene wrote angrily to Knight, not about his request but about "the swinish behavior of the National Office."[5] Both Genovese and Fox-Genovese were, unknown to me, fighting to keep me on as a coeditor, something I felt unable to flatly refuse.

It ended badly in the summer of 2005. A colleague referred to her loss of the *Journal* as her defenestration. It was worse than the end of *Marxist Perspectives.* Not only did Betsey lose the editorship; Gene and Betsey found they were no longer on the board of governors or even members of the society. Gene wrote a dense, furious letter to Knight, concluding, "I herewith resign from The Historical Society—or, rather, I accept your decision to 'resign me.' Betsey authorizes me to communicate her resignation as well."[6]

What had happened at the Boston headquarters of The Historical Society probably was more complicated and has been lost in the mists. What matters is that editing the *Journal,* especially getting material to the publisher by deadlines, had become irremediably difficult for Betsey. A year and a half earlier, in February 2004, her mother had died at home in Ithaca, New York. Betsey had not gone to see her, telling me that the discomfort of the journey would have been too great. By 2005 the pain and the spinal degeneration were worse, and the side effects of the painkillers she needed could be overwhelming. That her last editor's introduction was so short—precisely on target but very short—is telling. Refusing to back down, she listed four books in progress on a 2005 curriculum vitae, books she had dropped from a vita written in 2000. Nonetheless, she was becoming estranged from life, not just because of the lost editorship but because the pain and the drugs that relieved it were pushing her away.

From 2003 until 2005 her managing editor and sometime personal assistant, Laura Crawley, spent a good deal of time calling various conservative groups, excusing Betsey from speaking engagements she was physically unable to attend. Crawley knew, as I intuited, that the one thing she could never say as she politely canceled one engagement after another was that Betsey was physically unable to travel. She did once, tired at the end of the day, say that Betsey could not come because she was ill. Betsey angrily demanded that Laura call them back and explain the situation differently.[7]

Betsey, who loved cars much as her father had, needed to travel, needed to get out of her house often, and clung to an image of herself as mobile—physically and intellectually quick. She would not admit to illness and immobility. That was unthinkable. In the words of the police procedural dramas and detective stories she loved to watch, to do so would blow her cover. If Crawley's small leak upset her, the loss of the editorship, rooted in the same illnesses, exposed her as someone no longer well. It was a truth she had pushed aside, and she needed her constructed identities as public intellectual and professor to obscure her lived reality, even as she recorded much of it in journals.[8]

Some of the story of her illness lies in the two journals she kept for religious meditation, where her writing often spills over from directed meditation to blunt comments on her shrinking abilities. Her conversion in part was a search for the right language with which to make sense of her life, the true paradigm. The language of Catholicism replaced that of Freud as a means of coming to terms with and recreating herself. Her conversion prompted her to write about herself in a new way, underlining how she had replaced her Freudian understanding of self. And it was a relief. She had always joked that she was good at being a student, at going to school, and she began her conversion, as she wrote in 2000 in "A Conversion Story," by attending Mass alone and asking to "receive instruction."[9]

Earlier, in 1997, she published one of her rare personal accounts, "Caught in the Web of Grace." There she described considering and refusing the Protestant religions of her childhood—not, notably, the Judaism of the earlier generations of her mother's family—choosing instead "an acceptance of mystery and a reverence for the sacred" that led her to Catholicism.[10] Judaism seems not to have crossed her mind, the evangelical churches she did not like, and the Episcopalian and

Presbyterian churches of her father's father and mother, respectively, would not do either despite Gene's assumption that she might adopt Presbyterianism. Catholicism was all that was left within the Judeo-Christian tradition. It is worth remembering that Agnes Fox had accepted Edward's marriage to a woman nominally Jewish far more easily than almost any Fox family member would have accepted his marriage to a Catholic—Catholicism, in Philip's words, being the root of all evil—in 1935.

As Genovese remarked after her death, Betsey as a convert was determined to be more Catholic than the Pope. Her desire to learn, to "receive instruction," was real. Late in 2002 she attended a retreat at Opus Dei's Murray Hill Place in New York City. Her first meditation, recorded in a new journal, sounds much like earnest note-taking: "Object is to get to know God = to know ourselves. How do we respond to God? How do we respond to the sanctifier—the Holy Spirit? The most important part of a retreat is our own—my own—dialogue w/ Our Lord. We all need renewal, change, conversion."[11] What followed resembles a commonplace book, full of quotations from St. Anselm, Pope John Paul II, Cardinal Newman, and St. Thomas Aquinas. By the second day, October 25, she moved beyond catechistic repetition to saying something of her own: "Cross I wasn't looking for: MS. Time, energy. Am I lying to myself, or truly trusting God? Sins of omission: I am behind on everything."[12]

Her work penetrated even Murray Hill, and her conversion was very much a means of righting herself, putting herself on a new footing, and getting back to whatever her work was to be after her professional disasters of the early and mid-1990s had shaken her. That second day she carefully copied down the words of St. Augustine of Hippo: "Our hearts are restless, Lord, until they rest with you," and "before I bring myself to God in prayer, I must know what I am bringing."[13]

As Betsey came into her own voice in these meditations, she turned to familiar themes: judgment, self-examination, pride, sacrifice, and the word "should," which reared its head constantly like a schoolmaster's index finger. Her last meditation was about moderation and the temptation of "worldly goods."[14] Her need to buy food and clothes, cosmetics and gifts for others had long troubled her, and this discourse on what is necessary and what is not was a tangled one. Back in Atlanta two weeks later, she began writing again, about "evangelical poverty," noting, "I fail woefully at austerity. Am I holding parts of myself back from Jesus?" She also noted, "Confession at Murray Hill—dismissive, deeply unsatisfying." She listed, either before or after her confession, her sins:

> Sorrow for sins: Mummy at Ed's death.
> Behind—always behind.
> Left retreat early.
> Ordering on line—buying too much.
> Impatience. Frustration.[15]

Most of these sins were immediate, but what disturbed her about her mother at her father's death, roughly eight years before, we shall never know—but we do know that she had not forgotten it. Betsey also wrote about Gene, ending the journal with "Gratitude for Gene—fear of losing him. But I get furious when he beats me at football."[16] Of course they did not play football; they belonged to a football pool with other historians. The fear of losing him (he was eleven years older) was not new; neither was her refusal to be second to him in anything.

In her second journal, beginning in 2003, Betsey continued to blend religious reflection with worldly matters. She began with "enjoy yourself here with Him," and then continued with a story: "The Hispanic woman who greeted me when I arrived—who heard my coming and opened the door for me and greeted me with a kiss. 'Knock and it shall be opened to you.' I didn't even recognize the miracle of the greeting until I started to write. How fitting on the day I am starting to use my new red leather book." It was an expensive Levenger journal, and within a few lines Betsey would be lamenting her habit of overspending. Before that, she noted that the week had been "non-stop worldly" and "impoverished for the lack of Mass & prayer." She listed the work that had taken so much of her time, ending with, "Do I have what it takes to exercise some self-denial?"[17] For a woman who had been, in varying degrees, anorexic since 1965 to ask herself to exercise self-restraint is stupefying and directs us to listen to these journals and understand that they were, like her long confessions, another form of therapeutic analysis, modeled on the years of Freudian analysis that she had used in the 1960s and 1970s.

I had known Betsey to spend an hour, and sometimes more, in confession. She would invite her spiritual director, a Father Lopez, to dinner, and he would hear her confession before the meal. It would take an hour. Gene would joke about his wife's many sins. I believe confession was much like an hour of analysis for her, and something she craved. She left a note in the back of her 2002–3 journal, carefully written on her personal note cards, beginning, "Value of frequent confession—one a month or every couple of weeks. J.P. II: Reconciliation & Sin. Seeing the face of Christ. God the Father [not] a harsh task master."[18] By 2003, in the second journal, she added at the end of her first entry, "But I can talk to You about things I wouldn't talk about to anyone else. I have been so dumb about money, spending on things I don't need."[19]

The problem of self-indulgence continued in Betsey's next entry, in April 2003—Lent: "It is hard to see this as a time of real penance—or even as any penance. The worst is that I have gone on buying things and pretty much eating & drinking what I want. TAXES!!! Fr. Lopez says that my pain is my penance, and there has been enough of that—more than usual, and I am not sure why—And so much to do."[20] She had an exact, scientific mind, and what she bought, aside from food, balanced her account when weighed against what she did not eat. She recorded that she had been "eating & drinking what I want," but she was not admitting that she had taught herself to eat within rules she had created.

There were moments of religious meditation. Betsey noted her pain and went on to describe that Lent: "I have not had a true retreat, have not really given myself over to contemplation & worship: I keep reaching for true holiness, charity, self-denial, and I fall woefully short." She had little sense of her worth, although her prodigious work, along with Gene's, on *The Mind of the Master Class: History and Faith in the Southern Slaveholders' Worldview*, was almost complete. She was pleased with the church she had chosen, writing out carefully a description of a recent service: "The anointing of the sick at yesterday's Vigil was beautiful." She was crying, as was a woman next to her, who "had come up to me from behind & said 'I will be your right hand.'" She wrote, "I feel God's love all around me—" and continued, "but I do so little in return."[21]

The little Fox-Genovese claimed she was able to do in 2003 included teaching; sitting on numerous boards of academic and religious organizations and publications; continuing to write articles, mainly for a Catholic conservative feminist audience; editing and introducing the *Journal of the Historical Society;* and working through material for *The Mind of the Master Class* with Genovese. There was a lot of her voice in that first volume of the trilogy, and in the second, *Slavery in White and Black,* which appeared in 2008. It would have been enough to exhaust a healthy scholar. She also had to attend to exercise and medication for multiple sclerosis, along with the shifting pain caused by spinal degeneration. That she persisted with her schedule, despite writing "the fatigue & the pain are overwhelming" in June 2003, was a sort of pathological response rooted in her particular needs and mental economy.

By August 2003 her journal was taking its final form, combining religious thought; recrimination, especially about her use of money; and medical notes. Betsey recorded in 2003 that she was taking Celebrex again—a pain-relieving drug—and it is likely that aspects of the journal were driven by pain, its relief, and the unpredictable nature of both multiple sclerosis and spinal degeneration.[22] Multiple sclerosis generates constant uncertainty about what part of one's brain might be affected next, a loss of control that would have been maddening for Betsey. She began to keep daybooks, listing people to call and work to be done. She exhorted herself to simplify, prioritize, and focus, suggesting that she was finding it difficult to keep her schedule.

With effort, Betsey remained happy. In August she reminded herself "that overall this has been a beautiful time, with great love, and I have so much to be grateful for in Gene—so generous and not pushing. I feel part of this book in a way I have not in years." She admitted her other reality immediately after: "Sadness—mourning about all the other things I will never do, or never do again."[23] The book she referred to was *The Mind of the Master Class,* and it was nearly done in the summer of 2003: floppy disks survive labeled "Mind of the Master

Class 12-2-2003 Done." Another set survive from September 2004.[24] In between, Betsey and Gene got a few colleagues to read the manuscript and make suggestions. In any event, the finishing of the draft in late 2003 pleased Betsey enormously. Well before those backup disks were made in December of that year, she wrote, "But there is this extraordinary gift of finishing MMC! I cannot even absorb it. And the summer is over, and I am rushing into term virtually unprepared. Gift of Gene—our gift of self to each other. This has been a real summer of grace—and marriage."[25]

Finishing *The Mind of the Master Class* stretched into September, as she and Gene "worked through final revisions" and copied everything to disks in December. Pressure to complete the manuscript having eased, she filled pages with lists of things she had not done and returned to religious thought. She wondered, in a way more Freudian than Catholic, "When did Jesus know he was God—the son of God? Did his consciousness develop like that of other children?" She may have been more comfortable with a failing she confessed, skipping Mass to go to Chateau Elan, a spa, but she ended by insisting that even "when we are doing what we should be doing . . . it never seems like enough—as if I were a spiritual fraud."[26]

By Christmas she was joyful: "Christmas week has been spiritually rich, at least in the sense that I have felt wrapped in a blanket of love. Meditating on Jesus's being crowned w/ thorns, I recalled Gene's waiting to be picked up to go to his first meeting with Dennis O'Brien (new pres. of the University of Rochester). Gene looked like a little boy—so good, so expectant. The image brings tears to my eyes. I wonder how much I have cost him things he should have had. I received those awards, which maybe he should have had."[27] I think there was no guilt here, no blame, just an awareness of what she had, including Gene, and what his support of her career had cost him. Her insistent use of the word "should" to structure her reality dated back to childhood.

By 2004 Betsey was writing very little in the journal. She admonished herself to read and write as well as pay bills, making lists as she wrote, and "in particular: write Marriage book."[28] Seven days later, she "began day with hope & joy. . . . By the time I was getting dressed, my mood had suddenly turned to sorrow—I think because of the recognition of how little I actually can do. I move so slowly. Everything requires more energy and I am so slow to recognize my own limitations. There are too many thoughts to put down." She read Father Jerzy Domanski's *The Life of the World,* a biography of St. Maximillian. A passage in which Maximillian remarked on God's goodness and his own ingratitude led Betsey to consider celibacy:

> Somehow this meditation led me to think about giving up sex. I have lived w/o it for years. Is that a gift to God? It does not seem so hard, but would have been when I was younger—or would the loss [?] have been the loss of love? My Epiphany: to want that love from God—to be able to feel it from Him—for Him—is the great transference—the necessary core of great faith.[29]

Transference in psychotherapy, where Betsey undoubtedly learned the term, has a number of meanings, many pointing back to childhood, none of them auguring well for Betsey's epiphany. She thought she was using the term joyfully, but I would argue that it was complex, well beyond our ability to recover.

Within a few lines, Betsey returned to her preoccupation with priorities and work: "I will never make really good decisions about the use of my time until I recognize—and accept—my limitations, eliminate the distractions, and get a firm grip on priorities."[30] She was battling lost mobility and driven by her fierce need to work, to defeat illness by acting like a well person. Over a year later, when she again wrote in the journal, she was saying much the same: "For Lent: order priorities and most important, write *Marriage;* figure out how much time I really need to do things and to get to appointments—and then *allow for it.* Gene is right on this one; decide what can go and then *let it go.*"[31]

Betsey wrote only a few more lines in the journal in 2005, and began 2006 grimly in March:

> Ash Wednesday. Hard day for Gene—Hahn review in TNR and Leon's letter. He feels impotent, vulnerable, without resources. I took him to Nino's for dinner on the assumption that God will understand. I plan to try to write something—no matter how little—each day.
>
> Terrible pain in left leg. I am praying it is not another pinched nerve.[32]

The next day she was still in pain, and the pain took its toll. She and Gene "snipped and snapped at each other," and by the end of the day she was dozing in a chair, "too tired to brush my teeth."[33] Three days later it was worse: "Two days without writing a word—and with little penance or spiritual reading. I have had a developing pinched nerve in my left 'good' leg and have done my best to deny or stare it down. I had finally—after a year—been feeling so good and suddenly this increasing pain. But today—even yesterday—it was, in spurts, so bad I could hardly walk."[34]

Betsey followed her words about pain with a list of work that she "must" do the next day, and then, having returned from Mass, noted "a wonderful homily tonight. Already it is evaporating but the point was: Jesus weeps for us."[35] And that was all she wrote in this last journal, although she kept daybooks throughout 2006, with lists of tasks, telephone numbers, prescription drugs, and other details of daily life. The words "must" and "should" figured in her notations about reading or writing she must do, and she often insisted to herself that she must write the book on marriage that she never finished. She was, in the last few entries, writing as she had in her earlier journals from 1966 or 1972, for herself rather than Jesus. She had clearly addressed earlier entries to a divine consciousness, but by 2005 this was less evident. She was just jotting notes—self-reminders. She had written what she most had needed to write; it was *The Mind of the Master Class.*

The Mind of the Master Class

The first volume of the trilogy of the same name—*The Mind of the Master Class: History and Faith in the Southern Slaveholders' Worldview*—emerged from the depths like a whale breaking the surface of the water. The book elicited many serious, probing reviews. Some glowed, some quarreled, others sought evidence of the Genovese and Fox-Genovese turn to the right and found it. Reviewers mourned the absence of historical materialism and the dominance of what they read as traditional intellectual history. Others found the book rife with dialectical conflict between northern bourgeois liberalism and southern corporate conservatism. Almost all commented on the sheer density of quotation; for some, it overwhelmed the argument. Mark Smith called it "a massive, elegant essay—an effort to persuade." Virtually all reviewers understood that it was encyclopedic and based on Genovese's and Fox-Genovese's previous work, so requiring serious attention.[36]

Betsey and Gene were not only revisiting, one last time, all the manuscript collections they had used previously, the familiar voices of elite southern society. In the interval since publication of *Roll, Jordan, Roll* and *Within the Plantation Household,* Fox-Genovese and Genovese had read what their subjects had read. As a result, they knew how elite southerners had furnished their minds and with what. In particular, they considered the master class's changing understanding and uses of history, what planter families heard from the pulpit and considered during religious reflection and self-examination, how slave owners came to justify the peculiar institution to themselves and others, and finally how planters deceived themselves into thinking slaves regarded themselves as loyal members of the masters' families. Together, the three volumes of the series explained the nature and failure of southern hegemony.

Enrico Dal Lago began his review of the first volume as if it were Genovese's book, much as other reviewers had read *Fruits of Merchant Capital* as Genovese's work. Dal Lago was wrong. While Genovese drafted much of it, the work of shaping, editing, and giving direction was Fox-Genovese's. Betsey had served her southern apprenticeship with Gene and now, as he grew old, she took over. That, I suspect, is what she meant when she wrote that "I feel part of this book in a way I have not in years." Dal Lago attributed the "traditional intellectual history" that he found in the book to Genovese more than Fox-Genovese, pointing out that the hegemony of the master class no longer took material form, as it had in Genovese's earlier work. He cited Steven Hahn, who had argued that hegemony, which had been real in Genovese's earlier work, now seemed disembodied.[37]

Reviewers recognized that this was a major work, and the capstone of two remarkable scholarly lives; they measured it against the earlier work because that was its place. The dense arrays of quotations made for difficult reading, and that was more Betsey than Gene, more

Within the Plantation Household than *Roll, Jordan, Roll.* They had provoked each other while drafting the manuscript, each finding passages the other had missed, piling on more evidence. Their defense of southern theologians' adherence to literal readings of the Bible as preferable to abolitionists' more subtle arguments of conscience tried one reviewer's patience. Mitchell Snay thought their current religious predilections led them to take sides, and others joined him, uncomfortable with seeing abolitionists mocked. No one raised the subtext: abolitionists—along with nineteenth-century capitalists, free-thinkers, and feminists—bore the brunt of Fox Genovese and Genovese's far more recent dislike of East Coast radicals.[38]

And that raises the important point that many reviewers missed, even as they, like Miller, cited the "prodigious scholarship."[39] Southerners marshaled their thoughts, writing, and often substantial educations to mount a difficult, progressive, rear-guard battle against the worst corrosive effects of liberal individualism and capitalism. Mark Smith did his best to draw attention to how planters' fears of what nineteenth-century modernity would bring drove the arguments that Fox-Genovese and Genovese sought.

Most of the reviewers mentioned that the book had been two decades in the writing, but it began much earlier. In 1969 Genovese's *The World the Slaveholders Made* contained a discussion of the social thought of George Fitzhugh, and that was where, with a quotation from Gramsci, Genovese began *The Mind of the Master Class.* For Betsey and Gene the turning of the project into a collaborative one began in 1974, at the *Time on the Cross* conference, when Betsey wrote about Poor Richard and made clear her intention to work on Gene's turf as his equal. By 1980 she had begun working on material for *Within the Plantation Household,* largely having finished with the French Atlantic world she brought to *Fruits of Merchant Capital.* By 2005 she dominated what they wrote: intellectual history, with historical materialism dismissed to the background of their earlier work. The great curiosity of the long first volume on history and faith was, as David Moltke-Hansen has pointed out, the importance of religion. That was Genovese's territory and had been since *Roll, Jordan, Roll*—not Betsey's. She had not had a word to say about religion in *Within the Plantation Household.*[40]

Betsey edited and restructured the first two volumes of *The Mind of the Master Class* trilogy, especially the first, the 792-page *The Mind of the Master Class: History and Faith in the Southern Slaveholders' Worldview.* Genovese probably wrote much of the early drafts, but as he aged, he had less grasp of overall structure and style. Betsey's style—those telling phrases—and remnants of the manuscript that survived on her last computer, tagged as EDG or EFG, offer clues. Even as illnesses slowed her, she forged ahead, shaping and ordering more than Gene. The phrase "Exactly so," which appears on page 381, is unmistakably Betsey's voice, precisely positioned in a paragraph where it acts as an ironic fulcrum, balancing what slaveholders thought they had said with what Betsey heard them saying.

The presence of Betsey's voice was less important than her control of the argument. Their original intent—to investigate the psychological, not intellectual, mind of the master class—slipped away, and the Janus face became a single-minded defense of slavery. Genovese's voice and his finer psychological understanding of the darkness of human nature would return in the final volume, which he completed after Betsey's death: *Fatal Self-Deception.*[41] In that volume he pulled the rug out from under the educated southerners working out their marvelous, intelligent, complex, anticapitalist discourse in defense of their society. With southerners mired in self-deception, the intellectual facade was now just that, and vulnerable to the kind of psychological insight that Genovese had once hoped to apply. Even more importantly, he returned agency and the ability to deceive to slaves. The dialectic of those last three volumes was as much between Betsey and Gene as between masters and slaves, capitalism and corporatism.

Elizabeth Fox-Genovese insisted until very near the end of her life that she never abandoned her Marxism, and that may be true. She certainly abandoned feminism as an open discussion among women in community, and she abandoned it for a closed, corporate, prescriptive form advocating traditional roles. This coincides with her work on *The Mind of the Master Class,* where she returned to a familiar male intellectual world. That antebellum southern intellectual world was much like the Physiocrats' universe, and in her everyday life she replicated it by withdrawing, in stages, from women's studies, by defending the all-male world of cadets at the Virginia Military Institute, Cardinal Bernard Law, and Supreme Court Justice Clarence Thomas (a birthright Catholic), among others. Nonetheless, it was a tactical withdrawal to a new position, with subtle hints of Marxism—perhaps more accurately moral economy—thrown in. Opposition to abortion became the key to her new antifeminism. Fox-Genovese argued that abortion did not ameliorate problems of poverty, low income, bad housing, or poor schools. Hers was a variant on the old working-class men's argument over birth control: don't tell us not to have children; pay us enough to support them.

In the midst of Fox-Genovese's new commitment to Catholicism and family, the familiar world of antebellum southern writers of various sorts was a relief, and a return to work she had done before she had tangled with feminism and lost. And despite all the controversies the series documented, *The Mind of the Master Class* volumes came from some quieter part of Betsey's—and Gene's—minds. Those historic struggles were knowable and manageable in a way controversies of the century dawning were not. Both Fox-Genovese and Genovese found it difficult to live into the new century. Genovese spent his last years, between stints at his desk and watching baseball or staunching frequent nose bleeds, stirring himself up while watching Fox News.

Fox-Genovese had been shaped by a world at war. Her father itched to serve in World War II but could not, limited as he was by his childhood illness; his father had spent years in a reserve unit after World War I. Betsey's godfather Kim Roosevelt Jr. was a career intelligence officer and the grandson of rough rider Theodore Roosevelt. Kim's father, Kermit Sr., served in both world wars, committing suicide during the second, when Betsey was two. His brother Quentin was a World War I air ace, shot down in 1918 at the age of twenty. If he had not been a communist, Gene might have seen service in the Korean War, fought when he was in his early twenties and Betsey was becoming a teenager. Those wars that seem distant to us were very close at hand to Fox-Genovese's and Genovese's generation: people born between the wars.

Out of that chaos, Betsey found solace in big systems—biology and math early on, Marx and Freud next, then the Catholic Church.

Catholicism offered forgiveness, replaced Freudian definitions of human nature, and yet provided structure, rules, and rituals to rival Freud and provide an alternative form of self-discipline to anorexia. In her mind, the systematic, scientific Marxism that had drawn her to economic and intellectual history, and allowed her to identify the plantation household as the center of a wheel from which and to which all spokes led, complemented Catholicism, rather than opposing it: moral economy pervaded her work.

By the summer of 2005 Betsey was in uncharted water. Her will to remain in control was tremendous, but driving was increasingly difficult, falling asleep in class a problem, and the taking of numerous drugs for pain and multiple sclerosis produced complications. Pain was almost constant, and the possibility of finishing a book on marriage based on her lectures for Princeton's James Madison Program in American Ideals and Institutions was evaporating. Betsey would not admit any of this, but her personal assistants, Laura Crawley and subsequently Tina Trent, knew. Crawley had also been managing editor of the *Journal* since 1998 and had an acute sense of how little Betsey was able to do by 2005 and how angry she could get at any admission of illness. Betsey was not mobile and not well. She remained determined, however, to shape her public self.

The debilitating problems that often made it impossible for Betsey to fulfill speaking engagements also progressively undercut her ability to edit the *Journal.* Crawley did much of the work for the last few issues, and I flew to Atlanta several times to help, but the work of writing introductions, which Betsey insisted on doing herself, was more and more difficult for her. When the *Journal* was withdrawn from her control she was furious, probably all the more because it revealed the seriousness of her illnesses.

On 5 June 2005, Betsey noted in her daybook, among phone numbers and errands to be done: "Called Sheila [O'Connor-Ambrose]—depressing[.] She says just let go—your friends won't need any explanation, your enemies won't believe it. She may be right—probably is—but I feel so let down by her."[42] Betsey was coping with the loss of her editorship and doing so by calling O'Connor-Ambrose and Crawley, seeking confirmation of her outrage, as well as her ability to continue, as if still well. She found O'Connor-Ambrose's advice depressing because it failed to confirm her preferred image of herself.

The same daybook, however, shows that Betsey was busy ordering cosmetics, presents for the children of friends and relatives, computer software and hardware. She also continued going out to dinner. In some senses, business continued as usual in her house while she and Gene talked about planters' fatal self-deception. On June 25 she began an entry with "order, prayer, peace—Please."[43] Two weeks later, she wrote, "Mass—only a little late but still bad, especially as I was up in plenty of time (6:00) and was trying to plan—but missed by 5 minutes."[44] There are several daybooks like this, from 2005 and 2006, filled with transactions, reminders for birthday gifts, meetings, material to be faxed, and occasional admissions of weakness. In the next daybook, her September 3 entry was the single word "pain," and on the 4th she wrote, "slept all day."[45]

The daybooks suggest that Betsey struggled to keep up with the cascading trivia as well as the important work of life, and that on some days she accomplished more than many of us who are well. She still handled the finances, established lists for the part-time housekeeper, oversaw care of the two dogs and various cats, and by the end of the summer was getting ready to begin fall classes. In August she had sketched out what was probably a common diagram used with multiple sclerosis patients, a triangle with corners labeled fatigue, cognition, and depression. Beneath it is a list: "Core, Sleep cycle, Nutrition, Rest, and Cognitive capacity."[46]

The measure of Betsey's illness was her writing, and she wrote little after 2004. Introductions to issues of the *Journal* stretched into 2005, but the last was a meager four pages; revisions and proofreading for *The Mind of the Master Class* spilled into 2004, and three articles—"Feminism and the Unraveling of the Social Bond" in *Voices,* another in *Touchstone,* and one in *Common Knowledge*—appeared in mid- to late 2004.[47] She met with her classes but had Laura Crawley or, later, Tina Trent sit with her in class because she fell asleep from painkilling drugs. She continued to invite a steady stream of guests to Gene's and her house.

Betsey and Gene moved in together as scholars in early 2006, only when Betsey became too ill—crippled—to go up and down stairs easily. Gene had his computer moved up from his basement lair, and she had hers moved down from her second-floor office. Years before, in 1959 as Betsey turned eighteen, her grandfather Philip Fox had died after a long struggle with what he had years earlier called an arthritic back. A friend wrote to Agnes Fox after missing the funeral service, describing "how I missed seeing him, these past months, smiling out of the car at Bigg's and parked along the street while you did the legwork in the shops. But he *was* tired, and to be helpless is no life for such a man. It must be a tragic [*sic*] for anyone!"[48]

Betsey Fox-Genovese did not go gently. By the fall of 2006 she was very fragile, and the lengthy spinal surgery she underwent promised little. Like her grandfather Philip, she was tired. She had been powerful and fierce and, although it was well hidden, afraid. A student of hers from the Rochester years remarked that "her defenses remained . . . unconquered by Freud, Marx, or Christ, and she adopted them all in an attempt to find an external reality that would provide her with the . . . safety she craved at the same time that her intellectual life suggested something else." Pondering Betsey's attraction to powerful paradigms, the former student continued, "They were not safe. They always introduced polemic."[49] Betsey had thrived on dynamic intellectual conflict, ambivalence, and the creation and re-creation of herself for years, and she died clinging to intellect above all. It was that remark on defenses, coupled with Betsey's constant re-creation of herself as an intellectual, that prompted me to think of her re-creation of Sarah Gayle throughout *Within the Plantation Household,* compelling, beautiful, and, I suspect, willfully inaccurate.

In her last days in the Emory hospital, Betsey spent hours with her assistant and friend Tina Trent:

> What was extraordinary was how she began drilling me on Edna St. Vincent Millay sonnets. She asked me to bring a book and test her memory of them. That was all through the last few visits. She recited them to me, and they were always right, and then she'd know she was OK. When the aphasia hit her in the last hours of consciousness,

> she kept reciting those poems to me, only she lapsed into French. Some lapse: her great mind was literally finding a way around the damage the infection was causing. I was very lucky to witness that, and I felt as if this was a culmination of her entire life, reciting those beautiful sonnets.[50]

Millay was New York, Greenwich Village, Vassar College—Betsey's mother's world, just a decade or so older than Betty Fox. Millay was many things Betsey was not—builder of an open, loosely structured marriage; bisexual; a dazzling and self-assured poet; a prodigy raised by a divorced and wildly unconventional mother. Cora, Millay's mother, once remarked that "she had been a slut herself so why shouldn't her girls be?"[51]

Why Millay? Those sonnets were undoubtedly part of Betty's gift to Betsey, that familiarity with literature and with women's writing in particular. They, and Millay herself, had been wildly popular during Betty's youth, when Millay had been the figure of Greenwich Village New Womanhood: blatantly sexual, a seducer who moved on heartlessly, yet not a modernist writer, a Romantic:

> Oh, think not I am faithful to a vow!
> Faithless am I save to love's self alone.
> Were you not lovely I would leave you now:
> After the feet of beauty fly my own.[52]

The content of the sonnets was pure Betty in 1928, not the Betsey Fox-Genovese of 2006, committed to defending marriage and the traditional family. "Oh, think not I am faithful to a vow!" mocks marriage, and the incongruence of Millay's life and writing with Betsey's—Millay was seducing the young women of her dorm at Vassar and flirting with older men—forces us to look for other connections, connections of form and connections to Betty.

The sonnet form would have appealed to Betsey, who appreciated form, structure, and precision, much as it served to contain within tradition Millay's passions. Millay was, after all, precisely the wild woman that her mother, tamed in her own life, might have been, and

Fox-Genovese stood in a similar relation to Betty, also thwarted, who taught Betsey about women's writing while shelving her own career as a diplomatic historian. Millay, beyond that precise structure and beyond her interest in French—she translated Baudelaire—rose to something like glory in the interwar years by embodying the New Woman unleashed. Inconstant, unrepentant, fearless, drinking too much, smoking, writing good poetry and bad, Millay was profoundly mobile, constantly moving, as if securing freedom could be done no other way. Millay's affairs, followed or contained in poetry, were analogous to Fox-Genovese's movement through academic fields, jobs, and groups of colleagues—both left before the love or the work could sour.

The question for Fox-Genovese is why Millay? She impressed Betty's generation, not Betsey's, and it must have been from Betty that Betsey learned and memorized those sonnets. Perhaps reciting them was a necessary homecoming, like the daughter's return in Virginia Woolf's *To the Lighthouse.* Betsey Fox-Genovese died, exhausted and fragile, on 2 January 2007.

There was one last piece of scholarly writing on Betsey's computer, "In Retrospect: Writing the Mind of the Master Class," dated September 2006. Only three sentences and a fragment of the fourth exist, but the first line especially is so familiarly Betsey's voice, daring us one more time to enter into her controversy:

> Nothing about Eugene Genovese['s] and my recent book, *The Mind of the Master Class: History and Faith in Southern Slaveholders' World View,* conforms to prevailing academic expectations and taste. Slaveholders—especially if white and Western—command little sympathy and less respect. The very sophisticated may know that most peoples throughout most of history, including many Ancient and many African peoples, held slaves and that, contrary to popular prejudice did not invariably treat them as cherished members of the family. And if white Western slaveholders occasionally received some attention,[53]

She never finished the essay, which she stored on her computer under the name "Newsletter2006.doc," but she was preparing to defend the book and the men in it—and place herself on the margins yet again—just before her surgery. The slaveholders—men and women—have not disappeared, either as egregious, profit-minded bullies or as well-educated defenders of their social system. Betsey need not have feared for them, so much as for her persistent sympathy with downtrodden men—her father must have made himself her first example.

Five months before writing this, she had responded sternly to a fundraising request from Bryn Mawr College. Citing her experience as an expert witness for the Virginia Military Institute and The Citadel—military schools—in the mid-1990s, arguing against women's demands for admission there, she lectured the Office of Annual Giving on the merits of single-sex education, ending, "I still cherish the memory of the Bryn Mawr I knew. Sadly I cannot support the policies with which it now allies itself."[54] She wished for a world that was fixed and comprehensible, where single-sex education was available if not ubiquitous; where "woman in soul and body," as St. Teresa Benedicta had written, "is formed for a particular purpose"; and where no one defied nature, but she did not live in that world. She was tired; she had been at her best when she had embraced, as an old student of hers said, ambiguity and ambivalence and the tensions of W. E. B. Du Bois's "double consciousness."[55] She had been edgy and unsettled, making and remaking herself for many years, and that, in concert with anorexia, multiple sclerosis, and spinal weakness, wore her out.

Reaction to her death came through media and in private correspondence. Genovese saved a good many cards and letters of condolence, often containing announcements of Masses that would be said for her. Many were from deeply religious people, the acquaintances of her later years, but many of the first to arrive were from old acquaintances, leftists and liberals. They had not forgotten her. Newspapers highlighted her turn to the right, oddly offset by references to her books, her collaborations with Genovese, including *Marxist Perspectives.* As conservatives recalled her, she emerged as courageous and truthful for speaking out against abortion. Yet her connections to the truth about her life—and other lives—were always tenuous. Her statue of herself was Fido, a good scout, truthful, brave, cheerful, and hard-working. Lurking beneath the brave face of Fido was her persistent critique of individualism, a striking survival and sublimation of her self-destructive anorexic starvation. She fought fiercely to live and to die, and her commitments to the communal, the corporate, and the critique of individualism were shaped by that fight.

Epilogue

A FEMINIST MANQUÉ

KNOWN FOR at least a third of her life as a leftist and feminist, Elizabeth Fox-Genovese also proved herself always fierce and loyal to an old order that put her at odds with feminism. Psychoanalysis taught her the importance of those "unspeakable things unspoken," which, when named consciousness-raising, had been so important to second-wave feminism in the 1970s.[1] Contradictions never fazed her, and as analysand, historian, and literary critic she was drawn to the process of telling stories, not so much hers, often others'. In 1993, as she worked on *Ghosts and Memories*, a book she never finished, she noted this passage from Tina McElroy Ansa:

> Lena wanted to tell Rachel, "I'm just a little girl. I don't want to hear all of this. I don't want to know all this. Please don't tell me anymore."
>
> Rachel: "Child, she said softly. Do you know how long I been waiting for somebody like you to come along so I can tell them all of this, so I can share some of this. You t'ink I'm not gonna tell you now I got you here on my beach?"[2]

Betsey could hear others tell their stories but could not listen to her own. Betsey, who wrote so much, spoke so often, and created her archive, was drawn to the line between silence and speech. She had first discovered this space in psychoanalysis and again when Toni Morrison's novel *Beloved* appeared. The story of a slave mother who protects her daughter from the ravages of slavery by killing her held Betsey's attention, briefly. It was not the silence she craved, it was knowing why one could not speak: Freud's repression, Gramsci's cultural hegemony, and the sociolinguistics of the Bakhtinian circle made sense to her—until they no longer proved adequate. By the 1990s she sought out a new community and a new discipline, conservative yet feminist. She wanted to keep much of what she had and add to it a spiritual life inside the university, not outside.

As she developed a conservative feminist ideology, Betsey accepted a principle she had previously derided—the personal is political—by using interviews and conversations throughout *Feminism Is Not the Story of My Life*. But her life was not there, or barely. For life-writing, the hands-down winner for Betsey were the hundreds of pages she wrote for her psychoanalysts: dreams, reflections, responses to the ebb and flow of emotion in daily life. Those journals, from the 1960s and 1970s, went, probably unread, to the Southern History Collection at the Wilson Library of the University of North Carolina at Chapel Hill well before her death.

She created her archive deliberately. Fox-Genovese began discussing depositing her own, her parents', her grandparents', and extended family papers in late 1991 and 1992. Those papers were the statue of herself that she intended us to have, and perhaps she modeled it on the family papers she had spent so much of her life reading. She left, however, far more than she had time to edit—ultimately tens of thousands of pages, including hundreds of pages of journals; daybooks full of diurnal notes, lists, and phone numbers; and disks of emails sent and received. She was determined that the totality of her time not be lost but reckoned with.

And people remembered. Her funeral drew a good many; she had died during the annual meeting of the American Historical Association in Atlanta that year. A violent storm with hurricane-force winds drove through the neighborhood just as Ave Maria started on the church speakers, and thunder, lightning, and a few falling trees punctuated the service. At least one old friend, banished by Betsey a couple of years before, crept into the back of the nave. Condolences poured in. Genovese sent most of them to Betsey's archive, although he told me that those coming from people he considered enemies he threw out. It is good to remember that in any archive there are silences.

Genovese's book *Miss Betsey: A Memoir of Marriage* was his attempt both to shape and control how Fox-Genovese was remembered, as well as to deal with his grief. It may well have helped him, but it does little, except by telling us about Genovese, to help us understand his complex wife. His carefully polished anecdotes about Betsey and her extraordinary abilities, many of which he had told for years at dinners, are really about himself and his experiences. And because he destroyed almost all of his private papers, much of what we will know about Gene is in this slender book about remembering his wife. I could not, in the years he lived on after her, usefully interview him—he just cried, in the kitchen, in the living room, in restaurants.

When I first met Fox-Genovese in 1980, she was already a feminist, and an important one. It was as if I had been given one of the Furies as a graduate mentor. I was, and remain, astonished by her brilliance, bemused by her fits of blindness, and terrified of her. Others remembered her differently. Many were struck by her kindness, and it became a motif among remembrances: Robert L. Paquette, Bertram Wyatt-Brown, Sheila O'Connor-Ambrose, Douglas Ambrose, Lorraine V. Murray, and Mary Odem recall just that.[3] However, the recollection does not address her feminism, her Marxism, or her conservatism, and most of all, where she stood at the end of her life.

After her death, Elizabeth Fox-Genovese was mourned, celebrated, reviled, ignored, and—published. Eight volumes of which she was author or coauthor appeared posthumously. Five of those volumes were collections of articles and essays, most of them fugitive, some obscure. Two were the concluding volumes of *The Mind of the Master Class* trilogy, and the last was a collection of lectures toward her long-promised book on marriage, edited for publication by Sheila O'Connor-Ambrose. Those volumes figure as one more statue filling the spot she occupied but without telling us what we want to know about her feminism, her Marxism, or her conservatism.

David Moltke-Hansen has consistently remarked on the enormous range and overwhelming quantity of her work while pressing the importance of her abiding insistence, from left and right, on a critique of individualism. He calculated that, over the course of her professional life, she wrote on average some six thousand words a month for eventual publication; she spoke, she traveled, and she was visible, more so in later life when her turn to traditional conservatism was easily misunderstood. She was, he noted, a very public intellectual, "criticized—or praised— . . . for having changed foci and positions."[4]

Unfamiliarity with her huge body of work encouraged responses based on her most public stances. Yet, most responders did not grasp the range and complexity of her thought. One aspect of her conservatism, her stand against the postmodern insistence on history as "just another form of storytelling, equivalent to fiction," has come back to haunt us in our fact-free, truth-free, belief-engorged culture. Moltke-Hansen was particularly well-placed, as general editor of five volumes of her collected fugitive essays, to understand the range and pattern of her work.[5]

Evelyn Brooks Higginbotham, a Genovese student at Rochester and a distinguished historian who had known Fox-Genovese since 1975, recalled Betsey's shifts and changes, coming to much the same point: "Pondering the diversity of Betsey's writings, I cannot help but acknowledge that she remained steadfast to an understanding of the implications and meaning of individualism similar to Macpherson's, as well as to arguments like his about the belief that individual rights derive from society instead of from innate nature. She made points along these lines in a range of contexts—physiocracy, the slaveholding South, and feminism."[6] Higginbotham recognized Betsey's forest, just as she knew all the trees; she saw the impact of C. B. Macpherson and knew that meant Betsey would never be a neoconservative.

Laura F. Edwards remembered, not Betsey but buying *Within the Plantation Household* when it was new and she was a struggling graduate student:

> At a particularly difficult moment, I ordered *Within the Plantation Household* through a local bookstore. Having just realized the importance of women and gender to my dissertation, I had been searching for new scholarship on the topic in Southern history, regardless of time period. Fox-Genovese's book appeared as a welcome and promising find. It was also a purchase that required a substantial waiting period and considerable thought on my part, for it came at a time when my budget did not allow for anything beyond the basics.[7]

What followed was a trenchant exposition of how Betsey's book was read by one graduate student in 1988, and how it fit with and altered existing scholarship. Edwards saw Fox-Genovese "remaining true to her Marxist intellectual roots," subordinating "women, race, and gender within an analytical framework rooted in the solid base of class relations." Underling all the connections, she included several pages of bibliography, pointing to previous and subsequent work in southern women's history. It is worth comparing Edwards's comments to those on a blog written in 2008 by a graduate student in history, for the sake of a different generation's take on the book when it was twenty years old.[8]

Bertram Wyatt-Brown remembered Betsey's kindnesses, calling her a "most generous scholar." She had late in life agreed to go to Gene's and her sub-basement storage area to retrieve some information for him, and he recognized after her death that it had been her declining mobility that had slowed the process. His embarrassment at this unintentional imposition recalled, he proceeded to give a respectful but critical reading of *Within the Plantation Household.* In anecdotes drawn from his and Betsey's work, he made clear that he took her work seriously—and measured it against his own.[9]

In a much more personal vein, and perhaps more consistent with her later years, Mark Bauerlein, a conservative colleague at Emory, has described her as a victim of liberal prejudice, a lightning rod for overreaction against, among other things, an attempted revival of a great books program. He also noted her "elegance and grace," her "composure," and her ability to intimidate. The last had always been true, and she intimidated more men than women over the years, right and left. Bauerlein, who would have seen this dynamic at work at the end of the twentieth century and a bit beyond, had no way of knowing that the whispering and fear had gone on for decades. His observations are consistent with those of a graduate student at Emory, Andrew Ladd, who reflected on "My Women's Studies Seminar."[10]

Thomas L. Pangle, in his foreword to *Intersections,* the third volume of Fox-Genovese's *Selected Writings,* described essays written between 1973 and 1999 thus: "The chief theoretical basis for the essays in this volume is an identifiably American Marxism, modified by, and modifying, late-twentieth-century American feminism. From Marxist theory comes, first and foremost, Elizabeth Fox-Genovese's distinguishing insistence on the political structure of all history."[11] Consider that this is both accurate and partial. The last three essays collected from the late 1990s, on multiculturalism, Dick Francis's mysteries, and comparative literature, fulfil Pangle's premise. If one were to listen, however, to her 1996 lecture at the Georgia Public Policy Institute or to her 1994 appearance on *Firing Line,* it would become clear that she was also a profound cultural conservative. That fact, of course, does not necessarily negate Pangle's judgment that "the political structure of all history" preoccupied Fox-Genovese always.[12] Structure was essential to her, but only certain structures made sense, securely fastening all the elements of a workable society.

A powerful examination of Betsey's evolving feminisms came from Peter N. Stearns, whose foreword to *Women Past and Present,* the first volume of Fox-Genovese's *Selected Writings,* set out what he considered her contributions to women's history. Fox-Genovese, he pointed out, bucked mainstream opinion:

> This collection is, above all, an invitation to understand the complexities of women's issues and common feminist political assumptions in modern society and, particularly, the United States. The volume captures deep and fairly consistent concerns about excessive individualism and a commitment to work for real improvements in women's lives, along with a desire to use both history and a sense of contemporary social issues to suggest alternatives to conventional priorities. The essays reveal deep and wide reading, . . . and an eager quest for clarity and common sense in the obviously contested arena of gender.[13]

What Pangle called structure, Stearns called commonsense, much as the eighteenth-century Scots thinkers whom Betsey knew so well would have put it. Even better, Stearns noticed Betsey's need to refute conventional priorities, and although he was a critic, certainly, of her later work, he could still recommend what she attempted that was new:

> In watching Betsey pass to the offensive against mainstream feminism, it might be too easy to pass over her effort to provide constructive

> alternatives. Here, ultimately, her essay "The Legal Status of Families as Institutions" may particularly reward attention. Betsey posited in this article the need for new options, as against feminism and conservatism alike, in calling for a new concept of family as a corporate entity, not an individual contract but also not an institution dependent on the subordination of women.[14]

Illness and her commitment to finishing *The Mind of the Master Class* prevented her from developing her ideas further.

Fox-Genovese's "constructive alternative," as Amy R. Baehr, editor of *Varieties of Feminist Liberalism* (2004), pointed out, was to attempt to create a conservative feminism, a project that Baehr examined in detail. Differentiating conservative from libertarian, and traditionally conservative from religiously conservative, she identified Betsey's consistent interest in the moral economy, coupled with the material basis of life. This combination drove Fox-Genovese's insistence on women's need to live within traditional marriage as the best chance of material security. Baehr offered philosophical clarity and solid insight into Fox-Genovese's late feminist position, although she concluded that it was not a conservative feminism but something else.

Had Baehr known more of Fox-Genovese as a historian, she could have seen that Betsey was attempting, as the Physiocrats had done, to square a circle—to do the impossible, to make a free market in grain fit into an absolute monarchy without bursting the seams. It was, for that matter, a project much like that of southern planters on the eve of the Civil War, defending slavery as the most secure arrangement for slaves, within the extended family white and Black. And Baehr, rather strikingly, omitted any reference to Fox-Genovese's religious commitment, even misinterpreting her late position on abortion as the same as her earlier guarded tolerance for first-trimester abortion.[15]

One of the most public and also significant markers of who Betsey was, and how she was seen, was her obituary in the *New York Times*, by Margalit Fox. It was read by far more people than any other brief summary of her life. Genovese considered it inadequate and uncomprehending, as well as dismissive. Yet, it was a good summary, reiterating, with all the right quotes, the obvious aspects of Betsey's often very public life. For a number of Fox-Genovese's friends, it was the first intimation they had of her death, and it was dignified, unflinching, and professional. I have thought for many years that the best sentence was simplest but most suggestive: "She was 65 and had lived in Atlanta for many years." It was the sentence that could begin the novel no one has written about her.[16]

She lived on as an author. Reviews of her posthumous books—the last two volumes of The Mind of the Master Class trilogy, the five volumes of her selected writings, her book on marriage, and Genovese's book on their marriage—came from scholarly, conservative, and religious communities. Slavery in White and Black, less widely reviewed than the first volume of the trilogy, drew serious attention and debate, with Christopher Phillips asserting that Genovese and Fox-Genovese were "arguably the most influential historians of the antebellum South."[17] They had insisted that the idea of "slavery in the abstract," suitable for all laborers, was widespread in the South on the eve of the war and generated serious debate. Fatal Self-Deception, the last volume, was reviewed still less, and with little understanding of what Genovese had done. Staughton Lynd, a contemporary of Genovese's, a socialist, and in the 1960s an activist, produced an oddly personal essay in which he came to terms with Genovese, not this book.[18] It was, perhaps unintentionally, the right thing to do. It was Genovese's book, Genovese's paternalism, and Genovese's choice to return to the original project of the 1980s, the psychology rather than the ideology of the master class. By pointing out that the planter elite misjudged their slaves, the people living and working right in front of them, fatally self-deceiving themselves, Genovese pulled the rug out from under planters' great artifice, their generations-long legal, religious, and historical defense of the rightness of slavery. Self-deception, yes, but Gene knew full well that willful blindness at home—and across networks of slave-owning homes—did not augur well for their insight. Both Betsey and Gene had planned the three volumes for some time, but Betsey would have leaned toward admiration for their construction of their worldviews, while Gene celebrated the inscrutable stupidity of their self-deception. He did so with great subtlety, leaving us to grasp how that conclusion must alter, and it must, our reading of the first two volumes.

Fox-Genovese's selected fugitive writings, the less accessible but more important of her many essays, appeared in 2011 and 2012. One scholar, John David Smith, reviewed the whole five volumes, commenting, "Critics who ignore the ironies and discontinuities in [Fox-Genovese's] thought, who overvalue her provocation and undervalue her importance as an insightful critical thinker do so at their own loss." Her essays were her favorite form, by no means a secondary literature to her books, and a much closer-to-the-ground measure of her changing thought.[19]

The most compelling and intentional monument to Betsey, however, was Gene's memoir, *Miss Betsey.* Partly a compilation of his favorite cocktail-hour stories about Betsey, friends and relatives had heard most of these recollections before and seen Betsey's alternately indulgent and wry smile. Gene had polished these episodes by repeated telling, but he was not simply memorializing them. A good Sicilian, he had a purpose, a political battle to wage: how Betsey was remembered mattered, and not just to him.

Gene questioned nothing about the received version of her life as she had presented it to him or had allowed him to see it, but he tailored it carefully. He allowed Betsey to take full responsibility for her anorexia and never questioned her northeastern WASP manner, camouflaged as it was under a French veneer. He insisted that they had taught happily together at Rochester and wrote together easily. The reality, however, is that Betsey left Rochester in part to avoid teaching with him, she dominated in pages and in final editing of *Fruits of Merchant Capital*—Gene was ill at the time—and she chose to finish the draft of *The Mind of the Master Class* when Gene was getting old and less able to frame, shape, and direct the massive project. She led much of their life together by making her intellectual and scholarly pursuits at least in part complementary to his. In turn, Genovese, who acknowledged in the memoir that his third marriage would be his last, made the marriage work, at some cost to his intellectual arc.

In contrast, Betsey's book on marriage was impersonal, structural, all about social stability, authority, and safety. Disregarding a long history of women's demands for protection from husbands, beginning with Abigail Adams's famous reuse of Daniel Defoe's line, "Remember, all men would be tyrants if they could" and ending with legalized divorce, Betsey ignored complaints of abuse and profligacy, preferring Christopher Lasch's phrase describing home and family as a "haven in a heartless world."[20] The haven she advocated for women was marriage, and in doing that, she accepted John Locke's argument that the foundation of modern society, of individual rights, was property—and women are best served by marrying it, not owning it. That vision underpinned her book on southern women, *Within the Plantation Household,* where planter-class women embraced subordination in return for ostensibly very comfortable lives. Writing that book led her to consider marriage in the present as a necessary means of bringing order and stability to lives run amuck in exaggerated individualism. And yet, as she well knew, she was returning women to a supporting role—emotionally, not financially—in Locke's structure, where property—including women—supported individualism. Perhaps it was this unacknowledged dilemma that kept her from finishing the book herself.

Regardless, the marriage book related materialism, politics, and moral economy once more. Power inequalities and centers continued to define gender roles in ways contemporary feminists found abhorrent. Fox-Genovese never got past that dilemma, try as she might. History was stacked—and not in women's favor. She nevertheless tried to prove otherwise in her own life. The testimony of that life remains full of irony and conflict, as well as accomplishment and self-destructiveness. Betsey's wide-ranging scholarly work aided and abetted her shifting sense of who she was becoming in her continuing struggle to emerge and claim independence while fighting against liberal individualism at every turn.

Her archive provides the documentation, the endnotes to that life. Even shorn of the significance of her work, her life would still stand as a rich example of a post–World War II, Western, privileged, psychologically fraught woman's striving to escape herself and find herself, escape the paternalisms of her education and culture while reclaiming them.

As for her work, which is likely to join her in the dustbins and footnotes where old scholars go—all the more quickly because she took extreme positions—it deserves better. Discrete pieces are worth reading for multiple reasons. Some show compelling insight, others forceful argument, still others remarkable erudition and command. Often her interventions in theoretical arguments across numerous cultural study and historical fields were trenchant and tough-minded. In addition, what she wrote about lives lived through words, fiction, or autobiography she often produced in a white heat of private necessity, not to serve others but to make small advances into her own unspoken self. In that urgency, occasional but persistent, she remained a feminist, committed to what she needed to confront.

NOTES

Prologue

1. David Moltke-Hansen, "Introduction: Elizabeth Fox-Genovese as Essayist," in *History and Women, Culture and Faith: Selected Writings of Elizabeth Fox-Genovese,* vol. 3, *Intersections: History, Culture, Ideology,* ed. David Moltke-Hansen (Columbia: University of South Carolina Press, 2011), xx.
2. Elizabeth Fox-Genovese (hereafter EFG), 20 February 1972, "1972 Journal/Diary," Elizabeth Fox-Genovese Papers #4851 (hereafter EFG Papers #4851), Southern Historical Collection, Wilson Library, University of North Carolina at Chapel Hill (hereafter SHC).
3. George Packer, "Turned Around: Why Do Leftists Move to the Right?" *New Yorker,* 22 February 2016, https://www.newyorker.com/magazine/2016/02/22/why-leftists-go-right. For the term "culture wars," see James Davison Hunter, *Culture Wars: The Struggle to Define America* (New York: Basic Books, 1991). The term is not new; see Leo Ribuffo, a Genovese student, and others arguing the specificity or generality of culture wars and cultural flux in Andrew Hartman, "Are the Culture Wars History? Part IV," Society for U.S. Intellectual History Blog, 17 January 2016, and Leo Ribuffo, "Are the Culture Wars History, Part V," Society for U.S. Intellectual History Blog, 18 January 2016, http://s-usih.org. Precise understanding of left and right, with variations, is necessary; Fox-Genovese did not confuse liberal with left or traditional conservative with neoconservative. For Henry Cockburn, see Karl Miller, *Cockburn's Millennium* (Cambridge, MA: Harvard University Press, 1976), from a series edited by Betsey's Harvard professor John Clive.
4. C. B. Macpherson, *The Political Theory of Possessive Individualism: From Hobbes to Locke* (Oxford: Clarendon Press, 1962).
5. EFG, 7 September 1986, "1982–1986 Journal," 5–6, previously the property of Eugene D. Genovese, in transit to EFG Papers #4851, SHC. Becky is her sister, Rebecca MacMillan Fox.
6. EFG, 6 July 1972, 10:30 a.m., "1972 Journal/Diary."
7. EFG, 4 August 1972, 5:30 [?], "1972 Journal/Diary."

8. Kibibi Mack-Shelton and Christina Bieber Lake assembled relevant articles into a semblance of what Fox-Genovese might have intended: *History and Women, Culture and Faith: Selected Writings of Elizabeth Fox-Genovese*, vol. 2, *Ghosts and Memories: White and Black Southern Women's Lives and Writings*, ed. Kibibi Mack-Shelton and Christina Bieber Lake (Columbia: University of South Carolina Press, 2011).
9. Elizabeth Fox-Genovese, "Psychohistory versus Psychodeterminism: The Case of Rogin's Jackson," *Reviews in American History* 3, no. 4 (December 1975): 407–18; Michael Paul Rogin, *Fathers and Children: Andrew Jackson and the Subjugation of the American Indian* (New York: Knopf, 1975).
10. David Moltke-Hansen, "From Edinburgh to Rome," *Journal of the Historical Society* 13, no. 2 (June 2013): 163–75.
11. EFG, 29 April 1972, "1972 Journal/Diary."

1. The Family as Matrix

1. Clara McRae to Agnes Whiting Fox (hereafter AWF), 20 March 1935, Fox and Simon Family Papers #5363 (hereafter F-S #5363), SHC.
2. Much of this information emerges in AWF's letters; some specific material is from "Board Names Playfield for Mrs. Philip Fox," *Springfield [Mass.] Union*, 17 December 1959, 48; reference courtesy of Margaret Humbertson, head of library and archives, Lyman and Merrie Wood Museum of Springfield History, Springfield, Mass., personal correspondence with author, 3 February 2012.
3. Robert E. Simon (hereafter RES Sr.) to Elizabeth Simon Fox (hereafter ESF), 17 November 1934, F-S #5363.
4. Edward, Agnes, and Philip all made the trip to Baltimore; Philip then returned to Springfield, Massachusetts, by train. I am indebted to David Moltke-Hansen for much of the sense we have made of the car.
5. AWF to Philip Fox (hereafter PF), 4 March 1929, F-S #5363. When Edward reported the accident to his father, he admitted he had been driving; see Edward Whiting Fox (hereafter EWF) to PF, [?] March 1929, F-S #5363.
6. AWF to PF, 5 March 1929, F-S #5363. On wealthy homes, see AWF to PF, 22 March 1929, F-S #5363.
7. AWF to PF, 11 March 1929, F-S #5363.
8. EWF to PF, 4 April 1929, F-S #5363.
9. EWF to PF, 4 March 1929, F-S #5363.

10. On Edward and the car, see EWF to PF, n.d., a series of letters addressed "Here Friday," "In our Villa-by-the-sea 6 PM," "Thursday 7AM," "Sunday 6 PM," and "The Villa-by-the-sea Sunday night," all F-S #5363.
11. AWF to PF, 10 March 1929, F-S #5363.
12. AWF to PF, 4 April 1929; EWF to PF, 27 March 1929, F-S #5363.
13. AWF to PF, 29 March 1929, F-S #5363.
14. AWF to PF, 6 April 1929, F-S #5363.
15. AWF to PF, 5 April 1929; PF to AWF, 4 March 1929, F-S #5363.
16. EWF to PF, 4 April 1929, F-S #5363.
17. AWF to PF, 15 March 1929, F-S #5363.
18. EWF to PF, 5 March 1929, enclosed in AWF to PF, 5 March 1929, F-S #5363.
19. AWF to PF, 9 April 1929, F-S #5363.
20. AWF to PF, 5 March, 11 April 1929; EWF to PF, [?] March 1929, F-S #5363.
21. EWF to PF, n.d., addressed "Villa-by-the-sea Tuesday noon," F-S #5363.
22. PF to AWF, 8 March 1929; AWF to PF, 4, 10, 11 April 1929, F-S #5363.
23. Edward Fox listed himself as born in Seattle. The U.S. Census for 1920 lists his birthplace as Spokane, Washington. U.S. Census, 1920, roll T625, p. 4B, Enumeration District 10.
24. Loring T. Swaim, obituary, *Journal of Bone and Joint Surgery* 46-A, no. 6 (September 1964): 1359–60. For Edward's rheumatism, see L. T. Swaim to PF, 25 June 1935, F-S #5363.
25. L. T. Swaim to PF, 16 March 1931, F-S #5363.
26. Clara McRae to AWF, 20 March 1935, F-S #5363.
27. EWF to AWF, 15, 16 July 1932, F-S #5363.
28. EWF to AWF, 16 May 1935, F-S #5363.
29. Rita Padnick, "Faculty Profile . . . Prof. Edward W. Fox: Scholar and Traveler," *Cornell Daily Sun,* May 23, 1961, 7.
30. EWF to AWF, 16 May 1935; ESF to parents, n.d. [summer] 1935; ESF to RES Sr. and Elsa Weil Simon (hereafter EWS), on Fox head stationery beginning "We finally have got some definite news"; Robert Simon (ESF's brother) to ESF, 24 February 1935; ESF to AWF and PF, 30 July 1935; AWF and PF to Dr. Swaim, n.d. (draft), filed next to L. T. Swaim to AWF and PF, 25 June 1935, F-S #5363; "Wedding: Elizabeth Mary Simon to Edward Whiting Fox," *New York Times,* 15 June 1935, www.nytimes.com.
31. EWF to AWF, 8 February 1936; EWF to AWF, 13 November 1936, F-S #5363.
32. EWS to ESF, 18 October 1938 [?]; ESF to EWS, 3 October 1939, F-S #5363.
33. ESF to AWF, 30 October 1935, F-S #5363.

34. EWF to PF, 13 November 1936; EWF to AWF, 14 December 1936, F-S #5363.
35. EWF to PF, 13 November 1936; AWF to PF, 6 May 1937; EWF to AWF, 9 February 1937, F-S #5363.
36. AWF to PF, 6 May 1937; EWF to AWF, 9 February 1937, F-S #5363.
37. EWF to PF, [January?] 1937, F-S #5363.
38. See *The Annual Reports of Radcliffe College, 1931–3* (Cambridge, MA: Radcliffe College, February1933), available online at Harvard-Radcliffe Online Historical Reference Shelf, http://pds.lib.harvard.edu/pds/view/2581070?n=1339&s=4&printThumbnails=no.
39. EWF to AWF, 9 February 1937, F-S #5363.
40. EWF to AWF, 1 April 1937, F-S #5363.
41. "Mr. Reavey" to PF and AWF, 14 July 1932, F-S #5363.
42. PF, three undated lined notebook pages, intended as a reply to "Mr. Reavey" to PF and AWF, 14 July 1932, F-S #5363.
43. On poverty, see "Mr. Reavey" to PF and AWF, 14 July 1932; "Marguerite and Ralph" to AWF and PF, 17 April 1934, 12 March 1936; "Edna" to AWF, 24 June 1935; "Eunice R." to AWF, 24 June 1935, F-S #5363.
44. For the car, see Clara McRae to AWF, 20 March 1935, pp. 2–3, F-S #5363, in which McRae commiserates over an accident that caused Philip's hair to turn white.
45. On boarders, see Clara McRae to AWF, 20 March 1935, F-S #5363, congratulating Agnes on having "no roomers or boarders" that year.
46. F. [relative in Melbourne, FL] to AWF, [?] April 1932; AWF to PF, 16 July 1935, F-S #5363.
47. AWF to PF, 11 April 1929, F-S #5363.
48. Carl Thomas to AWF, 26 December 1936, F-S #5363. Emma Brigham ran for office in Springfield, Massachusetts, shortly after ratification of the Nineteenth Amendment and held city and state positions in the 1920s and 1930s.
49. Grace Tyler to AWF, 3 June 1939, F-S #5363.
50. For Radcliffe, or the Harvard Annex as it was first known, see "Radcliffe Enters Historic Merger with Harvard," *Harvard Crimson*, April 21, 1999, http://www.thecrimson.com/article/1999/4/21/radcliffe-enters-historic-merger-with-harvard/.
51. Robert Simon Jr., Betty's brother, sold Carnegie Hall in 1960 and built Reston, Virginia, an internationally praised attempt to build housing at mixed income levels, with lakes, canals, stores, offices, and manufacturing in neighborhoods designed to be beautiful. The project marked Simon as

much more than an ordinary real estate entrepreneur. Betsey would grow up knowing him as Uncle Bob, and even though her mother treated him with suspicion, his later project connected all the Simons to Robert Sr., a determined humanist and reformer. For online archives of Robert E. Simon Jr.'s papers from Carnegie Hall and Reston, see Robert E. Simon Jr. Collection of Carnegie Hall, Carnegie Hall Archives, New York, https://carnegiehall.github.io/archives-findingaids/namedcolls-fa/robertSimon.html, and on Reston, Robert E. Simon Jr. Papers, CO162, George Mason University Special Collections, Washington, DC, http://sca.gmu.edu/finding_aids/simon.html.

52. RES Sr. to ESF, 29 February 1935, F-S #5363.
53. Robert E. Simon Jr., conversation with author, March 2012.
54. RES Sr. to ESF, 22 January 1935, F-S #5363. See, for example, the naming of PS 165, New York City, for Robert E. Simon Sr. *New York Times,* 8 September 1935, also contains additional information on his civic interests and real estate holdings, including the Mercer Realty Corporation; Carnegie Hall, Inc.; the Real Estate Securities Exchange, and others. ESF compiled a fifty-three-page notebook of clippings and memorial pamphlets pertaining to her father's death; see F-S #5363.
55. Robert E. Simon Jr., conversation with author, July 2011.
56. RES Sr. to ESF, 23 January 1933; 15 March 1935, F-S #5363.
57. Robert E. Simon Jr., conversation with author, March 2012; RES Sr. to ESF, 22 January 1935, F-S #5363.
58. RES Sr. to ESF, 22 January 1935, F-S #5363. Mary Hemingway was Elsa Simon's best friend.
59. Brooks Atkinson, "Christmas Eve in the Theatre—S. N. Behrman's 'Rain from Heaven,'" *New York Times,* December 25, 1934, www.snbehrman.com/productions/plays/reviews/RFH1_times.htm; Don Shirley, "Fascist Threat Informs 1934 'Rain From Heaven,'" *Los Angeles Times,* April 24 1987, http://articles.latimes.com/1987-04-24/entertainment/ca-597_1_fascist-threat.

    The play was published by Random House in 1934–35, and Behrman's "prefatory note" is by far its most political statement; he found all "mobs," whether fascist, communist, pogrom, or southern lynching, to be antithetical to civilization. For a reminder of the extent of public knowledge of the rampant anti-Semitism, see Joshua Bloch, "Nazi-Germany and the Jews: An Annotated Bibliography," *American Jewish Yearbook* 38 (September 17, 1936–September 5, 1937/5697): 135–74.

60. EWF to ESF, 4 November 1934, F-S #5363.
61. ESF to RES Sr., [June–November 1935?], addressed "8 Ellsworth Avenue," begins "Dad Darling"; RES Sr. to ESF, [June–November 1935?], addressed "404 Riverside Drive, Cathedral 8–9628," begins "Dearest Betty," F-S #5363.
62. ESF to EWS and RES Sr., [July 1928], addressed "On board the Cunard RMS Scythia," begins "I meant to write you," F-S #5363.
63. ESF to EWS and RES Sr., [July 1928], addressed "On board the Cunard RMS Scythia," begins "I meant to write you," F-S #5363.
64. ESF to EWS, [July 1928], begins "Dearest Mum, You sounded sorta lonesome," F-S #5363.
65. ESF to EWS, [July 1928], begins "Here we are at London," F-S #5363.
66. ESF to EWS and RES Sr., [July–August 1928], addressed "The Rose Hotel Canterbury," begins "I meant to write Sunday," F-S #5363.
67. RES Sr. to ESF, 9 August 1928, F-S #5363.
68. EWS to ESF, 2 May 1920, F-S #5363.
69. ESF to EWS and RES Sr., n.d., on calling card engraved "Elisabeth Mary Simon," F-S #5363.
70. ESF to EWS and RES Sr., n.d., begins "Dearest Mummie and Daddy," F-S #5363.
71. ESF to RES Sr., "F Monday" [n.d.], begins "Dearest Popsie, On Thursday," F-S #5363.
72. ESF, "Record for 1st Semester 1930–1931," F-S #5363.
73. RES Sr. to ESF, 19 February 1931, F-S #5363.
74. ESF to RES Sr. and EWS, 21 February 1931, F-S #5363.
75. RES Sr. to ESF, 11 April 1931, F-S #5363.
76. RES Sr. to ESF, 9 March 1931, F-S #5363.
77. ESF to RES Sr. and EWS, [winter 1931], begins "Please don't mention honors again"; ESF to RES Sr. and EWS, [winter 1931], begins "I know I'm a wretch," F-S #5363.
78. ESF to RES Sr. and EWS, [1932], headed "Everett House," begins "I've been working like blazes," F-S #5363.
79. ESF to RES Sr. and EWS, [1932], headed "Everett House," begins "I've been working like blazes"; ESF to RES Sr. and EWS, [spring 1932], headed "Everett House," begins "check torn up"; ESF to unknown, [1932], headed "Everett House," begins "number of other things"; RES Sr. to ESF, 16 October 1932; Waldo Walker to ESF, 17 May 1933, F-S #5363.
80. ESF to RES Sr. and EWS, [spring 1932], headed "Everett House," begins "check torn up"; ESF to unknown, [1932], headed "Everett House," begins "number of other things," F-S #5363.

81. Perhaps the *Literary Digest*, where her name appears in vol. 113, published in 1932.
82. ESF to RES Sr. and EWS, [spring 1932], headed "Everett House," begins "check torn up"; ESF to unknown, [1932], headed "Everett House," begins "number of other things"; RES Sr. to ESF, 16 October 1932; Waldo Walker to ESF, 17 May 1933, F-S #5363.
83. RES Sr. to ESF, 19 November 193[3], F-S #5363.
84. ESF to RES Sr. and EWS, 16 December 1932; RES Sr. to ESF, 12 November 1933, F-S #5363.
85. RES Sr. to ESF, 15 March 1934; RES Sr. to ESF, 17 November 1934, F-S #5363.
86. For Walter L. Langer, see Richard Pearson, "Walter L. Langer, Harvard Professor, Ex-CIA Aide, Dies," *Washington Post*, 28 December 1977, https://www.washingtonpost.com/archive/local/1977/12/28/wl-langer-harvard-professor-ex-cia-aide-dies/75064b0a-ecf0-4472-b1c8-894196e2d44b/?utm_term=.154072549b28.
87. RES Sr. to ESF, 19 February 1931; ESF and EWF to EWS, [1936], begins "I had planned to work today," F-S #5363.
88. EWF to ESF, [5 November 1940], [ca. 4 November 1940], F-S #5363.
89. Rebecca MacMillan Fox, personal correspondence with author, 11 January 2012; the word "revelation" is hers.
90. ESF to EWS, postcard, 16 April 1941, F-S #5363.
91. ESF to AWF, [May 1941], F-S #5363.
92. AWF to PF, 4 February 1943, F-S #5363.
93. EWS to ESF, 15 May [1944]; ESF to EWS, n.d. [1941], begins "Dear Mummy, I've tried for several days," F-S #5363.

2. Fitting the Child to the Childhood

1. ESF to EWS, [1942], addressed "19A Frances Avenue, Cambridge," begins "you that, having observed," F-S #5363.
2. The name was Carl Jung's, not Freud's, although both discussed it.
3. EWS to ESF, 2 May 1920; 30 March 1936; 18 October [1938]; ESF to EWS, [late 1938]; RES Sr. to ESF, 17 November 1934; ESF to RES Sr., 2 December 1929, F-S #5363. Drawn as the Great Depression hit, a check Betty sent to her father on 2 December 1929 was a response to her father's admission that he needed money. He never cashed it. For Betty's defending her father, see ESF to EWS and RES Sr., [1931/32], addressed "Everett House," begins "This week has been work," F-S #5363. Betty's sisters, Carol and

Helen, were closer to their mother than Betty. Robert E. Simon Jr., conversation with author, March 2012.

4. ESF to EWS, 12 June [1948/49], addressed "E. W. Fox, Warren Road, Ithaca New York," begins "Your letter came a minute ago," F-S #5363.
5. Edward W. Fox, report in *Harvard Class of 1935: Twenty-Fifth Anniversary Report* (Cambridge, MA: Printed for the Class, 1960), 452–54; "Edward W. Fox, Curriculum Vitae," 1977, in transit to EFG #4851; Padnick, "Faculty Profile," 7. See also Rebecca MacMillan Fox, conversation and personal correspondence with author, 13 November 2008–26 February 2020; Edward Whiting Fox Jr. (hereafter EWF Jr.), "Notes on BA," in transit to EFG #4851; EWF Jr., personal correspondence with author, 9 February, 3 April 2017.
6. Eugene D. Genovese did not agree, insisting his wife was simply middle class, but he may have missed qualities of dress, demeanor, and language.
7. EWF to EWS, 29 August 1948; EWF to EFG, postcard, 19 July 1948, F-S #5363. On the Marie government, see Lansing Warren, "Government Falls in France on Issue of Economic Plans," *New York Times,* 28 August 1948, https://www.nytimes.com/1948/08/28/archives/government-falls-in-france-on-issue-of-economic-plans-reynauds.html.
8. EWS to ESF, 30 August 1948, F-S #5363.
9. ESF to EWF, 3 November 1940, F-S #5363.
10. EWF to ESF, postcard, 7 November 1940; EWF to ESF, 6, 7 November 1940, F-S #5363.
11. ESF to EWF, 13 January 1944, 1st letter, F-S #5363.
12. ESF to EWF, 13 January 1944, 2nd letter, F-S #5363.
13. EWF to EWS, 19 September 1944, F-S #5363.
14. ESF to EWF, 10 November 1940, F-S #5363.
15. ESF to EWS, [1945], headed "3314 Newark Street N.W.," begins "Dearest Mummy, I suppose I was inconsiderate," F-S #5363.
16. ESF to EWS, [1945], headed "3314 Newark Street N.W.," begins "Dearest Mummy, I suppose I was inconsiderate," F-S #5363.
17. Elizabeth Fox-Genovese, *Within the Plantation Household: Black and White Women of the Old South* (Chapel Hill: University of North Carolina Press, 1988), 111.
18. Philip Fox's sisters owned a cottage in Cohasset, Massachusetts, and EFG may also have visited there.
19. For Samuel Whiting in the Massachusetts Bay Colony, see William Whiting, *Memoir of Reverend Samuel Whiting, D.D., and His wife Elizabeth*

St. John with Reference to Some of Their English Ancestors and American Descendants (Boston: Rand, Avery, 1873).

20. EFG to Ann Wahlenmeier, 28 September 1992, folder EFG: Stuff, in transit to EFG #4851.
21. Eugene D. Genovese, conversation with author, March 2009.
22. EFG to Ann Wahlenmeier, 28 September 1992, folder EFG: Stuff, in transit to EFG #4851.
23. ESF, travel notebook 1952, 3, F-S #5363.
24. ESF, travel notebook 1952, 4.
25. ESF, travel notebook 1952, 4–24.
26. ESF, travel notebook 1952, 3–24.
27. ESF to EFG, 12 August 1952, F-S #5363. It is not clear when the children joined their parents but it may have been related to Edward's continuing if episodic work with the CIA.
28. ESF to EFG, 23 January 1952, F-S #5363.
29. Fox, report in *Harvard Class of 1935*, 454.
30. EWF to "Paul," 22 March 1956, in transit to EFG #4851.
31. David Riesman to EWF, 11 July 1953; EWF to Riesman, 17 July 1953, in transit to EFG #4851.
32. North Country School, http://www.nct.org/page.cfm?p=544.
33. The reports sent to parents included a full-page letter from the director and a two-page, single-spaced report including comments from all faculty, sent twice a year. See reports, folder North Country School, in transit to EFG #4851.
34. Walter Clark to EWF and ESF, 25 September 1953; EWF to Walter Clark, 2 October 1953, folder North Country School, in transit to EFG #4851.
35. Leo and Walter Clark to EFG, 5 September 1953, folder North Country School, in transit to EFG #4851.
36. Walter Clark to EWF and ESF, 25 September 1953; EWF to Walter Clark, 2 October 1953; Leo and Walter Clark to EFG, 5 September 1953, folder North Country School, in transit to EFG #4851.
37. Walter Clark to EWF and ESF, 22 January 1954; "Midyear Report, January 1954, Betsy [*sic*] Fox," folder North Country School, in transit to EFG #4851.
38. EFG to Ann Wahlenmeier, 28 September 1992, folder EFG: Stuff, in transit to EFG #4851.
39. Walter Clark to EWF and ESF, 22 January 1954; "Midyear Report, January 1954, Betsy Fox," folder North Country School, in transit to EFG #4851.

40. Walter Clark to EWF and ESF, 22 January 1954; "Midyear Report, January 1954, Betsy Fox," folder North Country School, in transit to EFG #4851 SHC.
41. "Midyear Report, January 1954, Betsy Fox," folder North Country School, in transit to EFG #4851. For ESF's introducing EFG to literature, see EFG to Ann Wahlenmeier, 28 September 1992, folder EFG: Stuff, in transit to EFG #4851.
42. Walter Clark to EWF and ESF, 14 May 1954; "Report for Last Half Year, May 1954, Betsey Fox," folder North Country School, in transit to EFG #4851.
43. Walter Clark to EWF and ESF, 14 May 1954; "Report for Last Half Year, May 1954, Betsey Fox," folder North Country School, in transit to EFG #4851.
44. Walter Clark to EWF and ESF, 13 January 1955, folder North Country School, in transit to EFG #4851.
45. Walter Clark to EWF and ESF, 10 May 1955, folder North Country School, in transit to EFG #4851.
46. "Year-End Report, May 1955, Elizabeth Fox," folder North Country School, in transit to EFG #4851.
47. EFG to Ann Wahlenmeier, 28 September 1992, folder EFG: Stuff, in transit to EFG #4851.
48. Mrs. George J. Nelson to EWF, 6 April 1955, folder Schools 1955–6; A. Beauverd to EWF, 7 September 1955, folder B.A.F. College Cevenol, in transit to EFG #4851.
49. Statement of account, Carrefour Librairie, 24 October 1955; school reports, 23 March, 18 May 1956, Collège Cévenol, folder B.A.F. College Cevenol, in transit to EFG #4851.
50. EFG to EWF, n.d. 1955–56; EWF Jr. to EWF, n.d. 1955–56, folder B.A.F. College Cevenol, in transit to EFG #4851. For the lack of heat, see EWF Jr., "Notes on BA."
51. EFG to EWF, n.d. 1955–56; EWF Jr. to EWF, June [?] 1956, folder B.A.F. College Cevenol, in transit to EFG #4851.
52. EWF to EWF Jr., undated slip of paper with accounts, folder B.A.F. College Cevenol, in transit to EFG #4851.
53. Sainte Marie des Invalides, "Compte de R. Fox," paid in June, April, and n.d., folder B.A.F. College Cevenol, in transit to EFG #4851.
54. EFG to ESF, 20 August, 6, 8, 12, 13, 16 October 1955, F-S #5363.
55. EFG to ESF, 19, 22, 25 October, 2, 10/11?, 25 November 1955; 28, n.d. February, 15 March 1956, F-S #5363.

56. EFG to ESF, n.d. [1957], begins "I am enclosing"; EFG to ESF, n.d. [1957], begins "I am writing this between classes"; both on lined notebook paper, folder EF-G Correspondence—Early Days, in transit to EFG #4851.
57. Elizabeth B. Hall to EWF, 26 September 1957, folder Concord Academy: Betsey Fox, in transit to EFG #4851.
58. EWF to Elizabeth B. Hall, 1 October 1957, folder EF-G Correspondence—Early Days, in transit to EFG #4851.
59. EFG to EWF, [summer 1957], addressed "Uncle Rover," folder EF-G Correspondence—Early Days, in transit to EFG #4851.
60. EFG to EWF, 10 September [1957], folder EF-G Correspondence—Early Days, in transit to EFG #4851.
61. EFG to EWF, [summer 1957], addressed "Uncle Rover," folder EF-G Correspondence—Early Days, in transit to EFG #4851.
62. EFG to EWF, 10 September [1957], folder EF-G Correspondence—Early Days, in transit to EFG #4851.
63. EFG to Ann Wahlenmeier, 28 September 1992, folder EFG: Stuff, in transit to EFG #4851.
64. Concord Academy "Report of Elizabeth Fox 1956–57 Class III," folder B.A.F.—Concord Academy, in transit to EFG #4851.
65. Advisor's comments, Concord Academy "Report of Elizabeth Fox 1957–58 Class I," folder B.A.F.—Concord Academy, in transit to EFG #4851.
66. "Miss Morse," Biology, in Concord Academy "Report of Elizabeth Fox 1957–58 Class I," folder B.A.F.—Concord Academy, in transit to EFG #4851.
67. EWF to Frederick R. Avis, April 1958; Concord Academy "Report of Elizabeth Fox 1957–58 Class I," folder B.A.F.—Concord Academy, in transit to EFG #4851.
68. EFG to ESF, fall 1957, begins "Dear Mummy," folder EFG Correspondence—Early Days, in transit to EFG #4851.
69. EFG to EWF, February 1957, folder EFG Correspondence—Early Days, in transit to EFG #4851.
70. Concord Academy "Report of Elizabeth Fox 1957–58 Class I," folder B.A.F.—Concord Academy, in transit to EFG #4851.
71. EFG to Ann Wahlenmeier, 28 September 1992, folder EFG: Stuff, in transit to EFG #4851.
72. EFG to EWF, 17 October 1960, folder EFG Correspondence—Early Days, in transit to EFG #4851.
73. PF and AWF, 1958 Christmas letter, F-S #5363. Philip Fox would die within months.

74. Bundle of receipts, 1958–60 [?], folder EF-G Correspondence—Early Days, in transit to EFG #4851.
75. Elizabeth B. Hall to EWF, 5 April 1957, folder B.A.F.—Concord Academy, in transit to EFG #4851.
76. EFG to EWF, 17 October 1960, folder EFG Correspondence—Early Days, in transit to EFG #4851.
77. EFG to EWF, 17 October 1960, folder EFG Correspondence—Early Days, in transit to EFG #4851.
78. EFG to EWF, n.d. [1960–61], headed "Bryn Mawr," onion skin paper; EFG to EWF, n.d. [1960–61], headed "Bryn Mawr," wide-ruled paper, folder EFG Correspondence—Early Days, in transit to EFG #4851.
79. EFG to EWF, n.d. [1960–61], headed "Bryn Mawr," wide-ruled paper, folder EFG Correspondence—Early Days, in transit to EFG #4851 SHC.
80. EFG, 7 December 1961, Paris Journal, 1961–62 [apparently loose pages appended to EFG, 1966 Journal], EFG #4851.
81. EFG, 23 January 1962, Paris Journal, 1961–62.
82. EFG, 23 January 1962, Paris Journal, 1961–62.
83. EFG, 24 January 1962, Paris Journal, 1961–62.
84. EFG, 25 January 1962, Paris Journal, 1961–62.
85. EFG, 25 January 1962, Paris Journal, 1961–62.
86. EFG, 26 January 1962, Paris Journal, 1961–62.
87. EFG, 12 February 1962, Paris Journal, 1961–62.
88. EFG, 15 February 1962, Paris Journal, 1961–62.
89. EFG, 15 February 1962, Paris Journal, 1961–62.
90. EFG to EWF, 31 August 1962, postcard, folder EFG Correspondence—Early Days, in transit to EFG #4851.
91. P. M. [?] Brunetti to EWF, 9 August 1962, folder EFG Correspondence—Early Days, in transit to EFG #4851.
92. For her interest in German, see EFG to EWF, 17 February 1963, folder EFG Correspondence—Early Days, in transit to EFG #4851.
93. EFG to EWF, 17 October 1962, folder EFG Correspondence—Early Days, in transit to EFG #4851.
94. EFG to EWF, 19 October 1962, folder EFG Correspondence—Early Days, in transit to EFG #4851.
95. EFG to EWF, 17 February 1963, folder EFG Correspondence—Early Days, in transit to EFG #4851.
96. ESF to EWS, [1942], addressed "19A Frances Avenue, Cambridge," begins "you that, having observed," F-S #5363; Elizabeth Ann Fox, "Snow Flakes,"

in *Short Poems* (Lake Placid, NY: North Country School, 1954 [or 1955]), clearly a school project, this survives in folder North Country School, in transit to EFG #4851.

3. From Fido to Fox-Genovese

1. Bianca Simon to ESF, March 13, 1932, F-S #5363; translated by David Veeder.
2. EWF to ESF, n.d. 1966; *Springfield Republican*, 1935, clipping of wedding photo, F-S #5363.
3. See Susan E. Maycock and Charles M. Sullivan, *Building Old Cambridge* (Cambridge, MA: MIT Press, 2016).
4. EFG to Ann Wahlenmeier, 28 September 1992, folder EFG: Stuff, in transit to EFG #4851.
5. Rebecca MacMillan Fox, personal correspondence with author, April 2013. Although a feature of cosmopolitan dining, French cooking was new in most homes in the United States; Julia Child's first cookbook appeared in 1961.
6. EWF to ESF, n.d. 1966, F-S #5363.
7. Eugene D. Genovese, *Miss Betsey: A Memoir of Marriage* (Wilmington, DE: ISI Books, 2009), 91.
8. EFG to EWF, 30 November 1965, F-S #5363.
9. Genovese, *Miss Betsey*, 91.
10. EFG to EWF, 13 December 1965, F-S #5363. Kitten remains unidentified.
11. EFG, 1966 Journal, 25.
12. Richard Galdston, "Observations on Children Who Have Been Physically Abused and Their Parents," *American Journal of Psychiatry* 122 (1965): 440–43; Galdston, "Dysfunctions of Parenting: The Battered Child, the Neglected Child, the Exploited Child," in *Modern Perspectives in International Child Psychiatry*, ed. John G. Howells (New York: Brunner Mazel, 1971), 571–84.
13. EFG, 1966 Journal, 3.
14. EFG, 1966 Journal, 4–5.
15. P.M. [?] Brunetti to EWF, 9 August 1962, folder EFG Correspondence—Early Days, in transit to EFG #4851.
16. EFG, 1966 Journal, 5–7.
17. EFG, 1966 Journal, 8.
18. "Year-End Report, May 1955, Elizabeth Fox," folder North Country School, in transit to EFG #4851.

19. EFG, 1966 Journal, 9.
20. Elizabeth Fox-Genovese, ed., *The Autobiography of Du Pont de Nemours* (Wilmington, DE: Scholarly Resources, 1984), 38.
21. EFG, Curriculum Vitae, 2005, EFG #4851.
22. EFG, 1966 Journal, 30–31.
23. EFG, 1966 Journal, 31.
24. EFG, 1966 Journal, 32.
25. EFG, 1966 Journal, 33–34.
26. EFG, 1966 Journal, 33, 34.
27. EFG, 1966 Journal, 35.
28. EFG, 1966 Journal, 36.
29. EFG, 1966 Journal, 36–37, 38.
30. Hilde Bruch, *The Golden Cage: The Enigma of Anorexia Nervosa* (1978; reprint Cambridge, MA: Harvard University Press, 2001).
31. EFG, 1966 Journal, 39.
32. EFG, 1966 Journal, 39–40.
33. Marya Hornbacher, *Wasted: A Memoir of Anorexia and Bulimia* (New York: HarperCollins, 1998).
34. Helene E. Roberts, "The Exquisite Slave: The Role of Clothing in the Making of the Victorian Woman," *Signs* 2 (Spring 1977): 556–69; David Kunzle, "Dress Reform as Antifeminism: A Response to Helene E. Roberts's 'The Exquisite Slave,'" *Signs* (Winter 1977): 570–79; Helene E. Roberts, "Reply to David Kunzle's 'Dress Reform as Antifeminism': A Response to Helen E. Roberts's The Exquisite Slave," *Signs* (Winter 1977): 518–19.
35. EFG, 1966 Journal, 41, 42–43.
36. EFG, 1966 Journal, 43–44.
37. EFG, 1966 Journal, 43–44.
38. EFG, 1966 Journal, 45–46.
39. Virginia Woolf, *A Room of One's Own* (New York: Harcourt Brace, 1989), 4.
40. EFG, 1966 Journal, 41.
41. Catherine Steiner-Adair, foreword, in Bruch, *Golden Cage*, ix.
42. Monroe Engel, *The Maturity of Dickens* (Cambridge, MA: Harvard University Press, 1959), 136.
43. EFG, 1966 Journal, 60–61.
44. Anonymous, "John Clive," *Harvard Crimson*, 22 January 1990, http://www.thecrimson.com/article/1990/1/22/john-clive-pmost-students-thought-that/; Glenn Fowler, "John L. Clive, Harvard Historian and Acclaimed

Biographer, 65," *New York Times*, 10 January 1990, http://www.nytimes.com/1990/01/10/obituaries/john-l-clive-harvard-historian-and-an-acclaimed-biographer-65.html.

45. EFG, 1966 Journal, 33–34, 44–45.
46. EFG, 1966 Journal, 16, 48.
47. EFG, 1966 Journal, 48–50.
48. EFG, 1966 Journal, 52, 62.
49. EFG, 1966 Journal, 62–63. Frank Manuel was possibly her godfather, along with Kim Roosevelt; Fritzie P. and Frank Manuel were her choice of godparents.
50. EFG, 1966 Journal, 63–64.
51. EFG, 1966 Journal, 57–58.
52. EFG, 1966 Journal, 72–75.
53. EFG, 1966 Journal, 78, 80.
54. EWF to ESF, 25 April 1966, F-S #5363.
55. EWF to ESF, 20 April 1966, F-S #5363.
56. EWF to ESF, 6 April 1966, F-S #5363.
57. EWF to ESF, 18 April 1966, F-S #5363.
58. EWF to ESF, 7 April 1966, F-S #5363.
59. EWF to ESF, 27 March 1966, F-S #5363.
60. EWF to ESF, 27 March 1966, F-S #5363.
61. EWF to ESF, 6 April 1966, F-S #5363.
62. EWF to ESF, 9 March 1966, F-S #5363.
63. EWF to ESF, 28 March 1966, F-S #5363.
64. EWF to ESF, 6, 7, 11 April, 2, 4, 6 May 1966, F-S #5363.
65. EWF to ESF, 4 May 1966, F-S #5363.
66. EWF to ESF, 11 May 1966, F-S #5363.
67. EWF to ESF, 4 May 1966, F-S #5363.
68. EFG, 1966 Journal, 100, 103–4.
69. EFG, 1966 Journal, 106.
70. Bruch, *Golden Cage*, 10.
71. EFG, 1966 Journal, 111–12.
72. EFG, 1966 Journal, 113, 114, 115.
73. EFG, 1966 Journal, 117–19, 120.
74. EFG, 1966 Journal, 121–22.
75. EFG, 1966 Journal, 123–24.
76. EFG, 1966 Journal, 125. See also Bruch, *Golden Cage*, 11.
77. EFG, 1966 Journal, 128, 129.

78. EFG, 1966 Journal, 129–30.
79. EFG, 1966 Journal, 131, 132–33.
80. EFG, 1966 Journal, 137–39, 129.
81. EFG, 1966 Journal, 145.
82. EFG, 1966 Journal, 149.
83. EFG, 1966 Journal, 150–51.
84. EFG, 1966 Journal, 151.
85. For the Columbia protests, see Paul Cronin, ed., *A Time to Stir: Columbia '68* (New York: Columbia University Press, 2018), and a review at "Columbia 68," The Sticking Place, http://www.columbia1968.com/history/.
86. For a quick review, see Peter Steinfels's later analytic article at "Paris, May 1968: The Revolution That Never Was," *New York Times,* 11 May 2008, http://www.nytimes.com/2008/05/11/world/europe/11iht-paris.4.12777919.html?_r=0.
87. EFG, 1966 Journal, 149–50.
88. EFG, 1966 Journal, 152–53.
89. EFG, 1966 Journal, 154, 155.
90. Genovese, *Miss Betsey,* 6–7.
91. EFG, 1966 Journal, 155–56, 157.
92. EFG, 1966 Journal, 158.
93. EFG, 1966 Journal, 159.
94. EFG, 1966 Journal, 159–60. Aisner may have been Dr. Mark Aisner, associated with Tufts School of Medicine and later practicing at Newton-Wellesley Hospital.
95. Genovese, *Miss Betsey,* 23.
96. Elizabeth Fox-Genovese, "Feminism and the Unraveling of the Social Bond," *Voices: Women for Faith and Family* 19, no. 3 (2004), https://www.catholiceducation.org/en/controversy/feminism/feminism-and-the-unraveling-of-the-social-bond.html.
97. Genovese, *Miss Betsey,* 23.
98. Genovese, *Miss Betsey,* 12–14.
99. EFG, steno notebook page, 14 November, early journals, EFG #4851.

4. The Quiet Voice

1. Vera Brittain, *Testament of Youth* (Harmondsworth, U.K.: Penguin, 1989), 82–83.

2. EFG, 1966 Journal, 137–38.
3. Stephanie McCurry quoted in Danielle Balderas, "Making Trouble in Women's Studies: Elizabeth Fox-Genovese and the Culture Wars" (M.A. thesis, University of North Carolina at Chapel Hill, 2016), 32–33.
4. Genovese, *Miss Betsey,* 50–51.
5. Genovese, *Miss Betsey,* 8.
6. Steven Schuker, personal correspondence with author, July 2013.
7. Genovese, *Miss Betsey,* 8.
8. Frank E. and Fritzie Prigohzy Manuel were intellectual historians, friends of EFG's parents, and he may have been a godparent to her, as Kim Roosevelt was. The Manuels also collaborated on work, notably *Utopian Thought in the Western World* (1979). Betsey may not have had a godmother, but the Manuels were the godparents she chose.
9. EWF to Adlai Stevenson, n.d., draft, folder EFG Correspondence—Early Days, in transit to EFG Papers #4851.
10. Rebecca MacMillan Fox, conversation with author, March 2017.
11. EFG to Matthew Hodgson, 22 June 1992, folder EFG: Stuff, in transit to EFG Papers #4851.
12. EFG to Matthew Hodgson, 22 June 1992, folder EFG: Stuff, in transit to EFG Papers #4851.
13. Genovese, *Miss Betsey,* 17–18.
14. Kreiser remembered negotiating teaching different areas of French history with EFG before 1973; Kreiser, conversation with author, 23 February 2015; Richard Kaeuper, personal correspondence with author, 27 March 2015; Melissa S. Mead, John M. and Barbara Keil University Archivist and Rochester Collections Librarian, University of Rochester, personal correspondence with author, 10 June 2019, using synopses and redacted material from the archives.
15. EFG to Ann Wahlenmeier, 28 September 1992, folder EFG: Stuff, in transit to EFG Papers #4851.
16. Paula Gordon, "Beauty in My Friend's Death," Huffington Post, January 4, 2007, http://www.huffingtonpost.com/paula-gordon/beauty-in-my-friends-deat_b_37803.html.
17. Robert Kreiser, personal correspondence with author, 14 October 2019.
18. Edward Whiting Fox, *History in Geographic Perspective: The Other France* (New York: Norton, 1971). After editing two historical atlases for Oxford University Press, Fox authored his first book. Directed to a broad audience, there were no notes or bibliography, but the style, synthetic and

broad like Eric Hobsbawm, if without his strengths and clarity, probably influenced, and was influenced by, Fox-Genovese.

19. Fox, *The Other France*, 17–18.
20. EFG, 1973 Journal, 5. The title "1973 Journal" is misleading; it runs from January to August 1972 and is in a folder with some loose pages from 1973.
21. EFG, 1973 Journal, 5.
22. Marsha Mills, archival specialist, Hagley Museum and Library, personal correspondence with author, 11 April 2014. Fox-Genovese stayed from August 1972 until November, reapplied in the spring, but did not return immediately.
23. EFG to Ann Wahlenmeier, 28 September 1992, EFG Papers #4851.
24. Melissa S. Mead, personal correspondence with author, 10 June 2019.
25. For reader's reports, see the anonymous, undated letter, undoubtedly the one from the Harvard reviewer, which begins "This is an extremely interesting essay," and a later one from Yale, dated 27 March 1973, which begins "Report on Elizabeth F. Genovese," EFG Papers #4851.
26. Elizabeth Fox-Genovese, "The Legacy of Past Structure: Trade between Bordeaux and the United States, 1784–89," in Elizabeth Fox-Genovese and Eugene D. Genovese, *Fruits of Merchant Capital: Slavery and Bourgeois Property in the Rise and Expansion of Capitalism* (Oxford: Oxford University Press, 1983), 76–89; "Helene" to EFG, 10 December 1972; EFG to J. H. Plumb, 11 October 1972; H. J. Hanham to EFG, 26 September 1972; Steve Schuker to EFG, 29 October 1972; EFG to Ann Wahlenmeier, 28 September 1992, EFG Papers #4851. We know the title from Harvard University Press's rejection letter; see H. J. Hanham to EFG, 26 September 1972, EFG Papers #4851.
27. On suspecting that she was unable to bear children, see EFG, 1966 Journal, 159–60; Genovese, *Miss Betsey*, 24–25; EFG, 1966 Journal, 159–60; and EFG, 27 March 1972, 1973 Journal.
28. EFG, 19 January 1972, 1973 Journal.
29. Pencil sketches of Vas Dias survive online at University of Victoria Art Collections, http://collection.legacy.uvic.ca/index.php?id=7207&artifact_action=info.
30. EFG, 19 January 1972, 1973 Journal.
31. EFG, 20 February 1972, 1973 Journal.
32. EFG, 14 June 1972, 1973 Journal. When the journal entries are addressed to anyone, as here, I have assumed that it was to her therapist.
33. EFG, 3 July 1972, 1973 Journal. On EWF as a CIA officer, see EWF Jr., "Notes on BA."

34. EFG, 25 July 1972, 1973 Journal.
35. EFG, 25, 28 July 1972, 1973 Journal.
36. EFG, 12 March 1972, 1973 Journal.
37. EFG, 4 August 1972, 1973 Journal.
38. On the job offer debate within the history department, I am indebted to Melissa S. Mead, personal correspondence with author, 10 June 2019.
39. Genovese, *Miss Betsey*, 42–43; "Helene" to EFG, December 1972; Albert Soboul to EFG, 30 June [?] 1972; EFG to J. H. Plumb, 11 October 1972; Plumb to EFG, 9 November 1972; Steve Schuker to EFG, 17, 29 October, 9 December 1972; Edward Tripp to EFG, 7 December 1972, EFG Papers #4851.
40. Nancy Wilson to EFG, 11 February 1973, EFG Papers #4851.
41. Karl H. Niebyl to EFG, 22 September, 14 December 1972, EFG Papers #4851. The review appeared in the February 1973 issue of the *Journal of European Economic History.*
42. EFG, 27 March 1972, 1973 Journal.
43. David Moltke-Hansen discusses "Elizabeth Fox-Genovese as Essayist" in Moltke-Hansen, "Introduction," xix–xxxiv.
44. Edward P. Thompson, "The Moral Economy of the English Crowd in the Eighteenth Century," *Past & Present* 50 (February 1971): 76–136; A. W. Coats, "Contrary Moralities: Plebs, Paternalists and Political Economists," *Past & Present* 54 (February 1972): 130–33; Elizabeth Fox-Genovese, "The Many Faces of Moral Economy: A Contribution to a Debate," *Past & Present* 58 (February 1973): 161–68.
45. Fox-Genovese, "The Many Faces of Moral Economy," 168.
46. Nancy Wilson to EFG, "Sunday" [March?] 1973, EFG Papers #4851.
47. Nancy Wilson to EFG, 11 February 1973, EFG Papers #4851.
48. Mary Young, University of Rochester, personal correspondence with author, 26 September 2013. Fox-Genovese participated in a committee, "wrote up the final proposal," and taught and advised in women's history from 1973 on.
49. EFG, 20 November 1974, 1974 Journal, EFG Papers #4851.
50. EFG, 1974 Journal, 1–3, 4–13, are from 1976–77 and are directed to women's writing.
51. EFG, "For Juliet," currently filed with EFG, 1966 Journal; the probable date from internal evidence in the 1974 Journal is October 1974.
52. The words "fragility and longing" are those of another student of Fox-Genovese, Maggi Shade, personal correspondence with author, 10 July 2013.
53. Louis A. Ferleger, personal correspondence with author, 12 May 2014.

54. First published in the *Review of Radical Political Economy* in 1975, a longer version appeared in Fox-Genovese and Genovese, *Fruits of Merchant Capital.*
55. Fox-Genovese, "Psychohistory versus Psychodeterminism."
56. Louis A. Ferleger, personal correspondence with author, 12 May 2014.
57. EFG, 20 November 1974, 1974 Journal.
58. For the review of Quentin Bell's biography that Fox-Genovese would have read, see Jane Marcus, "Tintinnabulations," *Marxist Perspectives* 2, no. 1 (Spring 1979): 144–67.
59. Linda K. Kerber, *Toward an Intellectual History of Women* (Chapel Hill: University of North Carolina Press, 1997), 8.
60. Elizabeth Fox-Genovese, *The Origins of Physiocracy: Economic Revolution and Social Order in Eighteenth-Century France* (Ithaca, NY: Cornell University Press, 1976), 34.
61. Fox-Genovese, *The Origins of Physiocracy,* 167.
62. Fox-Genovese, *The Origins of Physiocracy,* 171.
63. Elizabeth Fox-Genovese, "Poor Richard at Work in the Cotton Fields: The Psychological and Ideological Presuppositions of *Time on the Cross,*" *Review of Radical Political Economy* 7, no. 3 (October 1975): 67–83; with Eugene D. Genovese, "The Debate over *Time on the Cross,*" in Fox-Genovese and Genovese, *Fruits of Merchant Capital,* 136–71.
64. "Miss Morse," Biology, in Concord Academy "Report of Elizabeth Fox 1957–58 Class I," folder B.A.F.—Concord Academy, in transit to EFG Papers #4851.
65. Elizabeth Fox-Genovese, introduction, in Fox-Genovese, ed., *Autobiography,* 1–74.
66. Miller, *Cockburn's Millennium.*
67. Moltke-Hansen, "Introduction," xix–xxxiv.
68. EFG, "Freud and Womankind," 6, unpublished, in transit to EFG Papers #4851.
69. EFG, "Freud and Womankind," 7; Woolf, *A Room of One's Own,* 32–35.
70. Jerah Johnson, "The Origins of Physiocracy," *Canadian Journal of History* 12, no. 2 (December 1977): 261–63; Jacques Fomerand, "The Origins of Physiocracy," *Library Journal* 101, no. 14 (August 1976): 1631; Nelly S. Hoyt, "The Origins of Physiocracy," *American Historical Review* 82, no. 2 (April 1977): 367–68.
71. EFG, small notebooks, 26 May 1976, in EFG, 1966 Journal. Her book was released in June 1976; Michael A. Morris, Cornell University Press, personal correspondence with author, 19 November 2012.

72. I am indebted for much of this insight to David Moltke-Hansen, personal correspondence with author, 5 March, 4 September 2013; Rebecca MacMillan Fox, personal correspondence with author, 29 March, 1 April 2013.
73. EFG, 26 August 1976, 1974 Journal.
74. On late calls, see Richard Kaeuper, personal correspondence with author, 27 March 2015.
75. Fox-Genovese, "Psychohistory versus Psychodeterminism"; EFG, "Freud and Womankind."
76. EFG, conversation with author, ca. 1980–81.
77. Eugene D. Genovese, *Roll, Jordan, Roll: The World the Slaves Made* (New York: Pantheon, 1974), 3, 4.
78. I have paraphrased a random online definition from Dictionary.com, http://dictionary.reference.com/browse/paternalism.
79. William Kauffman Scarborough, *Masters of the Big House: Elite Slaveholders of the Mid-Nineteenth-Century South* (Baton Rouge, LA: LSU Press, 2003), 206, quoted in J. William Harris, "Eugene Genovese's Old South," *Journal of Southern History* 80, no. 2 (May 2014): 327–72, 344–45 (quotation).
80. "St. Gronlesex: Paternalism" was neither Marxian nor Gramscian—it was a pun in a language created by Genovese to express his disgust with the Metropolitan Museum of Art's director in charge of an exhibit dealing with Harlem that Genovese found appalling. Genovese invented it and probably meant it to translate, for his private amusement, as "ultimate sex paternalism." It expressed Genovese's wish to say that Harlem had been, in common parlance, "screwed" by a museum director. See "Black Culture and St. Gronlesex Paternalism," *Artforum*, February 1969, 34–37, cited without an author by Louis A. Ferleger and Robert L. Paquette, eds., in *Slavery, Secession, and Southern History* (Charlottesville: University Press of Virginia, 2000), 213.
81. Eugene D. Genovese, "The Legacy of Slavery and the Roots of Black Nationalism," in Eugene D. Genovese, *In Red and Black: Marxian Explorations in Southern and Afro-American History* (New York: Pantheon, 1969), 129–57, 134 (quotation).
82. Eugene D. Genovese, "Race and Class in Southern History: An Appraisal of the Work of Ulrich Bonnell Phillips," *Agricultural History* 41, no. 4 (October 1967): 354, 357.
83. That foreword was reprinted in Genovese, *In Red and Black*, 269; see also p. 270, on Kenneth Stampp's interest in undercutting Phillips's benign view of masters with one much more harsh.

84. Her dissertation was published in 1976 as *The Origins of Physiocracy.* It had been preceded by "The Many Faces of Moral Economy" (1973); "Poor Richard at Work in the Cotton Fields" (1975); two book reviews; and, with Eugene D. Genovese, "The Political Crisis of Social History: A Marxian Perspective," *Journal of Social History* 10, no. 2 (Winter 1976): 205–20. See also David Moltke-Hansen, "The Turn to the South: Elizabeth Fox-Genovese's Southern Studies," *Mississippi Quarterly* 65, no. 4 (2012): 557–76.

5. Woman of Letters

1. "The West Curve of Park Crescent, London," Wikipedia, http://en.wikipedia.org.
2. EFG, 26 August 1976, 1974 Journal.
3. Paula R. Backscheider, personal communication with author, 29 August 2018. Backscheider was interested in both Bakhtin and Gramsci and recalled discussing both with Eugene Genovese often. See Moltke-Hansen, "From Edinburgh to Rome," 167–69.
4. EFG, 26 August 1976, 1974 Journal.
5. EFG, 26 August 1976, 1974 Journal.
6. EFG, 26 August 1976, 1974 Journal.
7. EFG, 26 August 1976, 1974 Journal.
8. EFG, 12 January 1977, 1974 Journal.
9. EFG, 1966 Journal, 72–75.
10. EFG, 12 January 1977, 1974 Journal.
11. See EFG, Curriculum Vitae (dated by contents 1992), EFG Papers #4851.
12. EFG, 12 January 1977, 1974 Journal.
13. EFG, 12 January 1977, 1974 Journal.
14. The BMI, or body mass index, currently in use may be out of date but suggests 130 pounds as a minimal weight for a woman 5′9″.
15. EFG, 12 January 1977, 1974 Journal.
16. EFG, 12 January 1977, 1974 Journal.
17. Mary Young to EFG, 19 April 1977; "Helene" to EFG, 5 November 1976, folder EFG-EDG 72–88 Correspondence, EFG Papers #4851. Joanne Halford found no record of Fox-Genovese at the Institute of Psychoanalysis, London, nor did Angela Haselton at the Tavistock; Halford, personal communication with author, 27 September 2013; Haselton, personal communication with author, 30 September 2013.

18. "Helene" to EFG, 5 November 1976, folder EFG-EDG 72–88 Correspondence, EFG Papers #4851; EFG, 12 January 1977, 1974 Journal.
19. Elizabeth Fox-Genovese, "The Ambiguities of Female Identity: A Reading of the Novels of Margaret Drabble," *Partisan Review* 46, no. 2 (1979): 234–48, 237, 236, 241 (quotations).
20. Fox-Genovese, "The Ambiguities of Female Identity," 248.
21. Fox-Genovese, "The Ambiguities of Female Identity," 248.
22. EFG, 20 November 1974, 1974 Journal.
23. EFG, small notebooks, 8 February 1976, in EFG, 1966 Journal.
24. Barbara Jeanne Fields, "Eugene D. Genovese"; Peter Coclanis, "White Heat: Eugene D. Genovese and the Challenge of and to Southern History"; and Mark Smith, "On Gene on Eric: Genovese, Hobsbawm, and the Trans-Atlantic Left," among others, in "Eugene Dominick Genovese: A Forum," *Georgia Historical Quarterly* 98, no. 4 (Winter 2014): 341–86.
25. Genovese, *Miss Betsey,* 45–48. The description suggests the degree to which he was in awe of his wife.
26. EFG, 12 January 1977, 1974 Journal.
27. Very little is in print about this; the work of Sheila Rowbotham and Juliet Mitchell; or Eve Setch, "The Face of Metropolitan Feminism: The London Women's Liberation Workshop, 1969–79," *Twentieth Century British History* 13, no. 2 (2002): 171–90. The best sources may be *Spare Rib,* published from 1972 to 1993; Feminist Archive North, Special Collections, Brotherton Library, University of Leeds, Leeds, U.K., www.feministarchivenorth.org.uk; and Sandra Allen, Lee Sanders, and Jan Wallis, eds., *Conditions of Illusion: Papers from the Women's Movement* (Leeds, U.K.: Feminist Books, 1974).
28. EFG, 12 January 1977, 1974 Journal.
29. Elbert recommended reaching them through the Women's Research and Resource Centre on Gower Street, London. See Sarah Elbert to EFG, 2 September 1976, folder EFG-EDG 1972–1988 Correspondence, EFG Papers #4851.
30. Fox-Genovese, "The Ambiguities of Female Identity"; Elizabeth Fox-Genovese, "Yves Saint Laurent's Peasant Revolution," *Marxist Perspectives* 1, no. 1 (Summer 1978): 58–92.
31. EFG to Ann Wahlenmeier, 28 September 1992, folder EFG: Stuff, in transit to EFG Papers #4851. She contributed to work being done by several women at Rochester.
32. Paula R. Backscheider, personal communication with author, August, October 2018. Both she and Mary Young taught at the University of Rochester

in the 1970s and confirmed Fox-Genovese's peripheral participation in women's studies.

33. Paula R. Backscheider, personal communication with author, 24 September 2019.
34. EFG to Ann Wahlenmeier, 28 September 1992, folder EFG: Stuff, in transit to EFG Papers #4851; EFG, 12 January 1977, 1974 Journal.
35. ["Andy"?] to EFG, 6 April 1977, folder EFG-EDG 1972–1988 Correspondence, EFG Papers #4851.
36. Anna Coote and Beatrix Campbell, *Sweet Freedom: The Struggle for Women's Liberation* (London: Blackwell, 1987).
37. Fox-Genovese participated in a committee, "wrote up the final proposal," and taught and advised in women's history from 1973 on. Mary Young, personal communication with author, September–October 2012, September 2013.
38. *Marxist Perspectives*, 1, no. 1 (Spring 1978), front matter, https://www.dissentmagazine.org/blog/marxist-perspectives-revived.
39. Genovese, *Miss Betsey*, 63.
40. Sarah Elbert to EFG, 2 September 1976, folder EFG-EDG 1972–1988 Correspondence, EFG Papers #4851.
41. Sarah Elbert to EFG, 2 September 1976, folder EFG-EDG 1972–1988 Correspondence, EFG Papers #4851.
42. Sarah Elbert to EFG, n.d. [1977], begins "I certainly sympathize," folder EFG-EDG 1972–1988 Correspondence, EFG Papers #4851.
43. Sarah Elbert to EFG, n.d. [1977], begins "I certainly sympathize," folder EFG-EDG 1972–1988 Correspondence, EFG Papers #4851. When the Saint Laurent essay was published in *Marxist Perspectives,* there were illustrations and a bibliography but no footnotes.
44. Sarah Elbert to EFG, n.d. [1976–77], begins "Your St. Laurent piece," folder EFG-EDG 1972–1988 Correspondence, EFG Papers #4851.
45. Sarah Elbert to EFG, n.d. [1976–77], begins "Your St. Laurent piece," folder EFG-EDG 1972–1988 Correspondence, EFG Papers #4851.
46. Sarah Elbert to EFG, n.d. [1976–77], begins "Your St. Laurent piece," folder EFG-EDG 1972–1988 Correspondence, EFG Papers #4851.
47. On the Bordeaux study, see Mary Young to EFG, 19 April 1977, folder EFG-EDG 1972–1988 Correspondence, EFG Papers #4851.
48. Mary Young to EFG, 13 October 1976; unknown to EFG, 19 April 1977; Jacques Marchand to EFG, 27 January 1977; "Helene" to EFG, 5 November 1976, folder EFG-EDG 1972–1988 Correspondence, EFG Papers #4851.

49. Joanne Halford, archivist, Institute of Psychoanalysis, personal communication with author, 27 September 2013. See also correspondence throughout the file, notably "Helene," Anne Kallenberg, and "L" to EFG, 5 September 1975, folder EFG-EDG 1972–1988 Correspondence, EFG Papers #4851.
50. Deborah Hertz, personal communication with author, 21 October 2013.
51. Leo P. Ribuffo, "Eugene D. Genovese: Recollections of a Former Student," Society for U.S. Intellectual History Blog, October 3, 2012, https://s-usih.org/2012/10/eugene-d-genovese-recollections-of/.
52. Elizabeth Fox-Genovese, "Tuchman and History," *New York Review of Books,* December 7, 1978, www.nybooks.com/articles/archives/1978/dec/07/tuchman-and-history/?pagination=false&printpage=true. Tuchman was her cousin. Stone's response appeared immediately below.
53. EFG, 1966 Journal, 157.
54. Genovese, *Miss Betsey,* 8.
55. Elizabeth Fox-Genovese, "Kate Chopin's Awakening," in Mack-Shelton and Lake, *Selected Writings,* vol. 2, *Ghosts and Memories,* 125.

6. Returning to Ithaca

1. Carl E. Prince to EFG, 12 November 1979, in folder EFG: STUFF in transit to EFG Papers #4851.
2. EFG, 4 August 1972, 1973 Journal.
3. Elizabeth Fox-Genovese, "The Personal Is Not Political Enough," *Marxist Perspectives* 1, no. 3 (Fall 1979): 94–113.
4. The grant from the Organization of American Historians and the Department of Education ran over two academic years, as a Fund for the Improvement of Postsecondary Education (FIPSE) grant, no. P116B790046. See also EFG to Carl Prince, 25 October 1979, in transit to EFG Papers #4851.
5. Organization of American Historians–Fund for the Improvement of Postsecondary Education material is extensive. According to a curriculum vitae, EFG undertook the following: *Restoring Women to History* (Organization of American Historians, 1984–86), as general editor of all four volumes, author of one, and coauthor of the other three. They typified the position of women's history: each was a low-cost, copied, stapled, roughly one-hundred-page compendium of sources and possible methods for integrating material on women into Western Civilization and U.S. survey courses. EFG, Curriculum Vitae, 2005, EFG Papers #4851.

6. On Genovese's rides, see Eugene D. Genovese (hereafter EDG) to EFG, 14 May 1982, EFG Papers #4851.
7. On her early driving lessons, see EWF Jr., "Notes on BA."
8. Thomas W. Africa, professor emeritus, Binghamton University, personal communication with author, 2014.
9. EFG, 4 July 1982, "1982–1986 Journal," 1.
10. Fox-Genovese, "The Personal Is Not Political Enough," 60, 54.
11. Robin Morgan, ed., *Sisterhood Is Powerful* (New York: Random House, 1970).
12. Fox-Genovese, "The Many Faces of Moral Economy," 168.
13. For socialist women in brief, see Marilyn J. Boxer and Jean Quataert, eds., *Socialist Women: European Socialist Feminism in the Nineteenth and Early Twentieth Centuries* (New York: Elsevier North, 1978).
14. On Frank and Fritzie Manuel, see Carole S. Kessner, *Marie Syrkin: Values beyond the Self* (New York: Brandeis University Press, 2008), 397–98.
15. Eva Hoffman, "Marxist Journal Ceases after 101 Issues; Disputes on Staff Are Hinted," *New York Times*, 1 February 1981, http://www.nytimes.com/1981/02/01/us/marxist-journal-ceases-after-101-issues-disputes-on-staff-are-hinted.html.
16. Louis A. Ferleger, personal communication with author, 14 January 2015.
17. This and subsequent views of the dissolution of the journal come from Louis A. Ferleger, at the time and long after a close friend of Fox-Genovese and her associate at *Marxist Perspectives*. Ferleger, personal communication with author, April–June 2014, January 2015.
18. For distrust of the new direction, see Genovese and Fox-Genovese, "The Political Crisis of Social History." Much of this paragraph is paraphrased from Louis A. Ferleger, personal communication with author, 12 January 2015, because there is no more accurate way to render his description without quoting directly from emails not intended for publication.
19. Hoffman, "Marxist Journal Ceases after 101 Issues."
20. Louis A. Ferleger, personal communication with author, 14 April 2014.
21. Genovese, *Roll, Jordan, Roll*, 7–24.
22. I am indebted to Douglas Ambrose, Louis A. Ferleger, Tracy Mitrano, and Robert Paquette for time spent sorting out events in 1981, as well as other years. Their recollections have been invaluable, but the conclusions expressed here are my own.
23. Genovese, *Miss Betsey*, 45–48.
24. Samia I. Spencer, ed., *French Women in the Enlightenment* (Bloomington: Indiana University Press, 1984).

25. EDG to EFG, 3 May 1982, EFG Papers #4851.
26. EDG to EFG, 29 April 1982, EFG Papers #4851.
27. EDG to EFG, 6 May 1982, EFG Papers #4851.
28. EDG to EFG, 29 April 1982, EFG Papers #4851.
29. Fox-Genovese, "Poor Richard at Work in the Cotton Fields" (1975); this early version was expanded for "Poor Richard at Work in the Cotton Fields," in Fox-Genovese and Genovese, *Fruits of Merchant Capital,* 90–135.
30. Lawrence T. McDonnell, "The Janus Face of *Fruits of Merchant Capital,*" *Labour/Le Travail* 15 (Spring 1985): 186.
31. See Fox-Genovese, "Poor Richard at Work in the Cotton Fields" (1983), 122, which follows the phrase quoted by McDonnell above.
32. I am indebted to Nancy Wilson, with whom Betsey stayed in New York every month while in therapy there, for remembering Nini Vas Dias's name.
33. Fox-Genovese, "Psychohistory versus Psychodeterminism."
34. We know the original title of their project used the word "psychology," not "mind," from the recording of their 1984–85 interview at the National Humanities Center, which aired on the radio show *Soundings,* https://blogs.lib.unc.edu/soundings/1985/10/27/the-mind-of-the-master-class/.
35. Moltke-Hansen, "Introduction," xix–xxxiv; Deborah A. Symonds, "Gene and Betsey," in "Eugene D. Genovese: A Forum," *Georgia Historical Quarterly* 98, no. 4 (Winter 2014): 365–75.
36. Moltke-Hansen, "Introduction," xix–xxxiv.
37. David Brion Davis, "Roll Jordan Roll," *New York Times Book Review,* September 29, 1974, 457.
38. For reviews, see Richard King, "Fruits of Merchant Capital," *Journal of Southern History* 50, no. 1 (February 1984): 101–2; Gavin Wright, "Fruits of Merchant Capital," *Journal of Economic History* 44, no. 2 (June 1984): 631–32; Robert Detweiler, "Fruits of Merchant Capital," *History Teacher* 19, no. 1 (November 1985): 185–86; McDonnell, "The Janus Face of *Fruits of Merchant Capital,*" 185–90; Edward L. Ayers, "Fruits of Merchant Capital," *Virginia Magazine of History and Biography* 92, no. 1 (January 1984): 114–15; James A. Rawley, "Fruits of Merchant Capital," *Political Science Quarterly* 98, no. 4 (Winter 1983–84): 736–37; Peter Kolchin, "From Rebellion to Revolution" and "Fruits of Merchant Capital," *Journal of American History* 70, no. 4 (March 1984): 863–65; Pat Hudson, "Fruits of Merchant Capital," *Social History* 10, no. 2 (May 1985): 237–40; and Victor B. Howard, "Fruits

of Merchant Capital," *Journal of Social History* 18, no. 3 (Spring, 1985): 494–96.

39. EFG to Judith A. Miller, 29 January 1995, EFG Papers #4851.
40. Fox-Genovese, ed., *Autobiography,* 45.
41. Fox-Genovese, ed., *Autobiography,* xiv; Peter Wilson, personal communication with author, 9 August 2014. Wilson stressed Betsey's interest in Freud.
42. Fox-Genovese, ed., *Autobiography,* xvii.
43. Elizabeth Fox-Genovese, "Strategies and Forms of Resistance: Focus on Slave Women," in *In Resistance: Studies in African, Caribbean, and Afro-American History,* ed. Gary Y. Okohiro (Amherst: University of Massachusetts Press, 1986), 143–65.
44. See Eugene Genovese and Elizabeth Fox-Genovese, The Mind of the Master Class, *Soundings* Project Blog, 27 October 1985 recording, https://blogs.lib.unc.edu/soundings/1985/10/27/the-mind-of-the-master-class/.
45. Elizabeth Fox-Genovese, "The Great Tradition and Its Orphans; or, Why the Defense of the Traditional Curriculum Requires the Restoration of Those It Has Excluded," in Moltke-Hansen, ed., *Selected Writings,* vol. 3, *Intersections,* 156–72; Fox-Genovese, "The Claims of a Common Culture: Gender, Race, Class, and the Canon," *Salmagundi* 72 (Fall 1986): 131–43.
46. EFG to William J. Bennett, 22 March 1985, EFG Papers #4851. See also William J. Bennett, *To Reclaim a Legacy: A Report on the Humanities in Higher Education* (Ann Arbor: University of Michigan Library, 1984), http://eric.ed.gov/?id=ED247880. Jacob Neusner is a conservative and rabbinic scholar who seems unlikely to have advocated opening the canon to new work unless it were Jewish.
47. EFG to Nancy Wilson, 5 January 1985, property of Nancy Wilson, used with permission.
48. Fox-Genovese's connection to the Manuels appeared to me in reviewing some of Frank Manuel's notes on Hobbes from his papers archived at Brandeis University's Robert D. Farber University Archives and Special Collections, retrieved for me by Chloe Morse-Harding, personal communication with author, 9 June 2015. What they reveal is a reading list on Hobbes that could have been Fox-Genovese's, indicating the preoccupation of scholars in the 1960s and 1970s with Hobbes, Locke, Filmer, and patriarchy. See Lorenne M. G. Clark, "Women and John Locke; or, Who Owns the Apples in the Garden of Eden?" *Canadian Journal of Philosophy* 7, no. 4 (December 1977): 699–724, published the same year

Fox-Genovese published "Property and Patriarchy in Bourgeois Political Theory."

49. Stephen A. Schuker, personal communication with author, 14 August 2014.
50. EFG, 12 January 1977, 1974 Journal.
51. EFG to Nancy Wilson, 5 January 1985, property of Nancy Wilson.
52. EFG to Nancy Wilson, 5 January 1985, property of Nancy Wilson.
53. EFG to Nancy Wilson, 5 January 1985, property of Nancy Wilson.
54. EFG, 1966 Journal, 33–34.
55. EFG to Nancy Wilson, 5 January 1985, property of Nancy Wilson.
56. Okohiro, ed., *In Resistance.*

7. Leaving Home

1. Previous department chair, Binghamton University, personal communication with author, October 2018. See also Balderas, "Making Trouble in Women's Studies," 26–28.
2. On Emory's refusal, see Louis A. Ferleger, personal communication with author, 20 October 2015. For his appointment within the consortium, see Charles B. Bedford to EDG, 27 November 1989, EFG Papers #4851.
3. EFG, 7 September 1986, "1982–1986 Journal," 4.
4. EFG to David Minter, 28 April 1986, EFG Papers #4851.
5. George P. Cuttino, "Secret Committee Promotes Shibboleth," *Emory Wheel,* 1 November 1985, 7, reprinted in Mary E. Odem and Candace Coffman, "Feminist Activism and the Origins of Women's Studies at Emory," in *Where Courageous Inquiry Leads: The Emerging Life of Emory University,* ed. Gary Hauk and Sally Wolff King (Atlanta: Emory University, 2010), 227–28.
6. On George P. Cuttino, see "Memoirs of the Fellows and Corresponding Fellows of the Medieval Academy of America," *Speculum* 67, no. 3 (July 1992): 790–97.
7. Cuttino, "Secret Committee Promotes Shibboleth," 7.
8. Odem and Coffman, "Feminist Activism and the Origins of Women's Studies at Emory," 227–28.
9. Odem and Coffman, "Feminist Activism and the Origins of Women's Studies at Emory," 227.
10. Office of the Dean of Emory College and Vice President for Arts and Sciences to EFG, 9 June 1986, EFG Papers #4851.

11. For Fox-Genovese's requests, see EFG to David Minter, 28 April 1986, EFG Papers #4851. For a record of the Woodruff contributions to Emory University, see Katheryn Hayes Tucker, "The Gift That Keeps on Giving," Georgia Trend, 1 March 2007, http://www.georgiatrend.com/March-2007/The-Gift-That-Keeps-On-Giving/.
12. Martine W. Brownley, personal communication with author, 30 March 2015.
13. See "Pioneering Women's History Summer Institute," Jewish Women's Archive, 18 July 1979, http://jwa.org/thisweek/jul/18/1979/gerda-lerner.
14. Elizabeth Fox-Genovese, untitled typescript in the author's possession, in transit to EFG Papers #4851; identifiable by internal evidence as an early version of the more polished essay "Placing Women's History in History," *New Left Review* 155 (May–June 1982): 5–29.
15. Robert Kreiser, personal communication with author, 25 March 2015. He remembers that Fox-Genovese started teaching in Rochester not long after they both arrived in 1969, when he began; he also taught early modern France and was anxious about possible competition with her for tenure.
16. EFG, 7 September 1986, "1982–1986 Journal," 3.
17. Elizabeth Fox-Genovese, "Women and the Enlightenment," in *Becoming Visible: Women in European History,* 2nd edition, ed. Renate Bridenthal, Claudia Koonz, and Susan Stuard (Boston: Houghton, Mifflin, 1987), 256.
18. Elizabeth Fox-Genovese, "For Feminist Interpretation," *Union Seminary Quarterly Review* 35, nos. 1–2 (Fall–Winter 1979–80): 5–14, 5 (quotation).
19. "50 Years of Women at Emory College," *Emory Magazine,* Spring 2004, http://www.emory.edu/EMORY_MAGAZINE/spring2004/precis_women.html.
20. Something of the plan laid out for an incoming director is visible in Odem and Coffman, "Feminist Activism and the Origins of Women's Studies at Emory," 227.
21. Cory Dean, "Strong Marriages, Wishful Thinking?" *New York Times Book Review,* 8 January 1989, 26.
22. EFG to Ann Wahlenmeier, 28 September 1992, folder EFG: Stuff, in transit to EFG Papers #4851.
23. Her essay on slave women's resistance, "Strategies and Forms of Resistance," was held up in press for several years so its publication in Okohiro, ed., *In Resistance,* distorts its date of composition. See also readers' reports and letter from Gary Y. Okohiro to EFG, 5 February 1985, EFG Papers #4851; he complains about "the very extended review process."

24. EFG to Ann Wahlenmeier, 28 September 1992, EFG Papers #4851.
25. See Barbara Jeanne Fields, "Eugene D. Genovese," and Mark Smith, "On Gene on Eric: Genovese, Hobsbawm, and the Trans-Atlantic Left," in "Eugene Dominick Genovese: A Forum," *Georgia Historical Quarterly* 93, no. 4 (Winter 2014): 341–86.
26. Fox-Genovese and Genovese, *Fruits of Merchant Capital,* 16.
27. Cited in Fox-Genovese, "The Many Faces of Moral Economy"; Eric Kerridge, *The Agricultural Revolution* (London: George Allen and Unwin, 1969); Joan Thirsk, ed., *The Agrarian History of England and Wales,* vol. 4, *1500–1640* (Cambridge: Cambridge University Press, 1967); E. L. Jones, *Agriculture and Economic Growth in England, 1650–1815* (London: Methuen, 1967). Her favorite Scots were Henry Home (Lord Kames) and Adam Smith.
28. Anand Chitnis, *The Scottish Enlightenment: A Social History* (London: Croom Helm, 1976). This information was found with the help of Atlanta Vintage Books, who handled many of the books from the Genovese estate.
29. Elizabeth Fox-Genovese, "Antebellum Southern Households: A New Perspective on a Familiar Question," Ferdinand Braudel Center *Review* 7, no. 2 (Fall 1983): 215–53, 218 (quotation).
30. Fox-Genovese, "Antebellum Southern Households," 248, 249.
31. Bertram Wyatt-Brown, "Matrons and Mammies," *Reviews in American History* 17, no. 2 (1989): 219–24.
32. Laura F. Edwards, "At the Threshold of the Plantation Household: Elizabeth Fox-Genovese and Southern Women's History," *Mississippi Quarterly* 65, no. 4 (Fall 2012): 577–90, 577–78 (quotation).
33. Fox-Genovese, *Within the Plantation Household,* 30, 57.
34. Elizabeth Fox-Genovese, "Household Structures and the World Economy," prepared with members of the Household Research Working Group, Fernand Braudel Center for the Study of Economies, Historical Systems, and Civilizations, Binghamton University, for the Colloquium on Households and the World-Economy, University of Bielefeld, May 20–22, May 1982; Fox-Genovese, "The Ideological Bases of Domestic Economy: The Representation of Women and the Family in the Age of Expansion," in Fox-Genovese and Genovese, *Fruits of Merchant Capital,* 299–336; Fox-Genovese, "Antebellum Southern Households."
35. See Walter LaFeber, L. Pearce Williams, and Richard Rosecrance, "Edward Whiting Fox," Cornell University, eCommons, http://ecommons.library.cornell.edu/handle/1813/17813, for a quick review of his ideas.

Fox-Genovese acknowledged him in *Within the Plantation Household,* 71n60.

36. Christine Stansell, "Explosive Intimacy," *Nation,* 27 March 1989, 417.
37. Fox-Genovese, *Within the Plantation Household,* 57.
38. While she acknowledged plantation mistresses' furious tempers with slaves, she did not wish to see what Stephanie E. Jones-Rogers described in *They Were Her Property: White Women as Slave Owners in the American South* (New Haven, CT: Yale University Press, 2019).
39. EFG to Senator Sam Nunn, 18 May 1989, EFG Papers #4851.
40. Fox-Genovese, *Within the Plantation Household,* 197.
41. Stansell, "Explosive Intimacy," 422.
42. I am indebted to Joan E. Cashin for her comments on Sarah Gayle and on Sarah Woolfolk Wiggins's work on her journal. Cashin, personal communication with author, 2015.
43. Betsey learned of Bakhtin from Paula R. Backscheider at the University of Rochester, or more accurately from Backscheider's graduate students, and from Genovese, who was more familiar with Backscheider. Backscheider, personal communication with author, 25 October 2013, 29 August 2018. As David Moltke-Hansen has observed, Genovese insisted in conversations after Betsey's death that Bakhtin became more crucial to her thinking than Gramsci, who continued to matter more to him. See also Moltke-Hansen, "From Edinburgh to Rome," 163–75, esp. 167–68.
44. See especially Stansell, "Explosive Intimacy," 417–22, and Suzanne Lebsock, "Complicity and Contention: Women in the Plantation South," *Georgia Historical Quarterly* 74, no. 1 (1990): 59–83. See also Nancy L. Grant, review of *Within the Plantation Household, Journal of Interdisciplinary History* 21, no. 2 (1990): 343–45; Dorothy Sterling, review of *Within the Plantation Household, Journal of Southern History* 56, no. 3 (1990): 527–28; Jacqueline Jones, "One Big Happy Family?" *Women's Review of Books* 6, no. 5 (1989): 4–6; Jan Lewis, review of *Within the Plantation Household, Journal of Social History* 23, no. 2 (1989): 402–5; Wyatt-Brown, "Matrons and Mammies"; Marion Rust, "Invisible Woman: Female Slavery in the New World," *NWIG: New West Indian Guide/Nieuwe West-Indische Gids* 66, nos. 1–2 (1992): 83–88; Wilson J. Moses, review of *Within the Plantation Household, Journal of American Ethnic History* 10, no. 4 (1991): 122–24; Steven M. Stowe, review of *Within the Plantation Household, American Historical Review* 95, no. 3 (1990): 906–7; Nancy A. Hewitt, review of *Within the Plantation Household, Florida Historical Quarterly* 68,

no. 2 (1989): 227–29; Catherine Clinton and Ronald G. Walters, review of *Within the Plantation Household*, *Journal of American History* 76, no. 3 (1989): 895–96; Farah Jasmine Griffin, "'Sister, Sister?': Recent Writings on Black and White Southern Women," *NWSA Journal* 3, no. 1 (1991): 98–109; Sarah Woolfolk Wiggins, review of *Within the Plantation Household*, *Register of the Kentucky Historical Society* 88, no. 1 (1990): 93–94; Margaret M. Caffrey, review of *Within the Plantation Household*, *Tennessee Historical Quarterly* 48, no. 4 (1989): 246–47; Kathleen C. Berkeley, review of *Within the Plantation Household*, *North Carolina Historical Review* 66, no. 3 (1989): 361–62; John White, review of *Within the Plantation Household*, *Journal of American Studies* 24, no. 2 (1990): 284–85; Paul A. Gilje, review of *Within the Plantation Household*, *Journal of the Early Republic* 10, no. 1 (1990): 107–8.

45. Fox-Genovese, *Within the Plantation Household*, 28, xv.
46. Sarah Woolfolk Wiggins and Ruth Smith Truss, eds., *The Journal of Sarah Haynsworth Gayle, 1827–1835* (Tuscaloosa: University of Alabama Press, 2013); for opium use, see p. xxv; for restoration, defacement, and the inaccuracies of transcriptions, see the short important essay "Editorial Policy," xi–xvi.
47. Wiggins, review of *Within the Plantation Household*.
48. Fox-Genovese, *Within the Plantation Household*, 15.
49. Fox-Genovese, *Within the Plantation Household*, 22.
50. EFG, 26 August 1976, 1974 Journal.
51. Stansell, "Explosive Intimacy," 417.
52. Stansell, "Explosive Intimacy," 420.
53. Caroline Eliza Burgwin Clitherall, Journal no. 5, Caroline Eliza Burgwin Clitherall Diaries #158, SHC.
54. I am indebted to Joan E. Cashin for her comments on Brevard's life. Cashin, personal communication with author, 2019.
55. Lebsock, "Complicity and Contention," 59, 61.
56. Lebsock, "Complicity and Contention," 59–60; Stansell, "Explosive Intimacy," 417.
57. Bruce Clayton, "Women of the House Were Racists, Too," *Raleigh [NC] News and Observer*, February 12, 1989, 4D.
58. Wyatt-Brown, "Matrons and Mammies," 219; Moses, review of *Within the Plantation Household*, 122; Caffrey, review of *Within the Plantation Household*, 24; Clinton and Walters, review of *Within the Plantation Household*,

895; Grant, review of *Within the Plantation Household,* 345; Lewis, review of *Within the Plantation Household,* 404.

59. See Sterling, review of *Within the Plantation Household,* on the Grimkés. On absent African Americans, see Sterling, review of *Within the Plantation Household;* David Weiman, review of *Within the Plantation Household, Journal of Economic History* 50, no. 3 (1990): 759–61; Griffin, "'Sister, Sister?'"; Gilje, review of *Within the Plantation Household;* and Stansell, "Explosive Intimacy." On sexuality, see Stowe, review of *Within the Plantation Household,* and Clinton and Walters, review of *Within the Plantation Household.*
60. Fox-Genovese, *Within the Plantation Household,* 333.
61. EFG to Michael O'Brien, 11 January 1994, courtesy of Michael O'Brien, used with his permission.
62. Both essays and relevant others can be found in Mack-Shelton and Lake, *Selected Writings,* vol. 2, *Ghosts and Memories.*
63. Author's recollection, Binghamton University, ca. 1982; Ann Short Chirhart, personal communication with author, 20 July 2015.
64. EFG to Bernard Cardinal Law, 4 May 2002, EFG Papers #4851. On Bernard Cardinal Law, see Michael Rezendes, "Church Allowed Abuse by Priest for Years," *Boston Globe,* 6 January 2002, https://www.bostonglobe.com/news/special-reports/2002/01/06/church-allowed-abuse-priest-for-years/cSHfGkTIrAT25qKGvBuDNM/story.html.
65. Fox-Genovese made no secret of her, and Genovese's, dislike and distrust of Anita Hill; I heard her often at the time of the hearings, as did David Moltke-Hansen. Moltke-Hansen, conversation with author, 24 June 2019; Ann Short Chirhart, personal communication with author, 20, 21 June 2019.
66. Wyatt-Brown, "Matrons and Mammies," 222.
67. EFG, 4 July 1982, "1982–1986 Journal."
68. EFG to Michael O'Brien, 30 August 1988, courtesy of Michael O'Brien.
69. Ronald Radosh, "A Historian Taught by History," *Weekly Standard,* 15 October 2012, https://www.hudson.org/research/9304-a-historian-taught-by-history.
70. Christopher Hitchens, "Radical Pique," *Vanity Fair,* February 1994, 32–35.
71. Robert J. Scholnick to EFG, 7 January 1988; George J. Graham Jr. to EFG, 5 December 1988, EFG Papers #4851. See also Robert J. Scholnick, personal communication with author, 1 October 2018, and Chandos Brown,

personal communication with author, 2 October 2018, on Genovese at William and Mary.

72. EFG to Michael O'Brien, 30 August 1988, courtesy of Michael O'Brien.
73. EFG to Nancy Wilson, 5 January 1985, property of Nancy Wilson.
74. EFG to Jeannette Hopkins, 2 May 1988, EFG #4851.
75. Nine of the thirteen essays she first selected were reprinted, after her death, in an edition of her fugitive work by scholars who agreed unknowingly with her 1988 choices. EFG to Jeannette Hopkins, 2 May 1988, EFG Papers #4851; Suzanna Tamminen, personal communication with author, 28 August 2015.
76. EFG, "Professional Activities 1991," covering the academic year from fall 1991 through spring 1992, in transit to EFG Papers #4851.
77. Fox-Genovese, "The Personal Is Not Political Enough."
78. Elizabeth Fox-Genovese, "Beyond Sisterhood," in *Feminism without Illusions* (Chapel Hill: University of North Carolina Press, 1991), 11.
79. Fox-Genovese, "The Personal Is Not Political Enough."
80. Fox-Genovese, "Beyond Sisterhood," 32; for the penultimate line of the early version, see Fox-Genovese, "For Feminist Interpretation," 14.
81. Fox-Genovese, "The Ambiguities of Female Identity," 234–48.
82. Fox-Genovese, "For Feminist Interpretation," 5.
83. Fox-Genovese, "For Feminist Interpretation," 9.
84. Louise A. Tilly, review of *Feminism without Illusions, American Historical Review* 97, no. 4 (October 1992): 1175–76.
85. Ellen DuBois, "Illusions without Feminism," *Nation,* January 20, 1992, 57.
86. Elizabeth Fox-Genovese, "Toward a Feminist Critique of Individualism," in *Feminism without Illusions,* 226.
87. Fox-Genovese, "For Feminist Interpretation," 6.
88. For a clear dissection of the Western roots of various kinds of feminism, see R. M. Janes, "On the Reception of Mary Wollstonecraft's *A Vindication of the Rights of Woman,*" *Journal of the History of Ideas* 39, no. 2 (April–June 1978): 293–302.
89. Jennifer Hyman, "On Second Thought: Historian Asks Defenders of Abortion to Reconsider," *Democrat and Chronicle* (Rochester, NY), 1991, 1C, 3C, undated copy.
90. Nancy Gabin, *Feminism in the Labor Movement: Women and the United Auto Workers, 1935–1975* (Ithaca, NY: Cornell University Press, 1990). For a current survey of what has been done, and a bibliography giving the dimensions of the literature on this, see Nancy MacLean, *Freedom Is*

Not Enough: The Opening of the American Workplace (Cambridge, MA: Harvard University Press for the Russell Sage Foundation, 2006). On the origins of second-wave feminism in the labor movement, see Daniel Horowitz, "Betty Friedan and the Origins of Feminism in Cold War America," *American Quarterly* 48 (1998): 1–42.

91. DuBois, "Illusions without Feminism," 57.
92. The phrase is David Moltke-Hansen's.
93. DuBois, "Illusions without Feminism," 57; Tilly, review of *Feminism without Illusions.*
94. Hyman, "On Second Thought," 3C.
95. Hyman, "On Second Thought," 3C.
96. Phillip Blond, *Red Tory: How the Left and Right Have Broken Britain and How We Can Fix it* (London: Faber and Faber, 2010).
97. Andrew Ladd, "My Women's Studies Seminar," First Things, 25 February 2015, http://www.firstthings.com/web-exclusives/2015/02/my-womens-studies-seminar.
98. Martine W. Brownley, personal communication with author, 2 October 2016. See also Ann Short Chirhart, personal communication with author, 20, 21 June 2019.
99. EFG to George H. Jones and David F. Bright, 10 January 1992, EFG Papers #4851.
100. See the interview with Stephanie McCurry in Balderas, "Making Trouble in Women's Studies," 26–28.
101. Beverly Shepard, "Emory Scholar Target of Bias Suit," *Atlanta Journal/ Atlanta Constitution,* 19 February 1993, E1–7. See also articles from the *Chronicle of Higher Education* and the *Wall Street Journal,* among many others, and "Alas, Poor Emory," by the presumably pseudonymous Ambrose Hofstader Bierce III, author of *The Broad-Gauge Gossip,* 26 August 2008, http://historianbroadgauge.blogspot.com/2008/08/alas-poor-emory.html.
102. David F. Bright and George H. Jones to EFG, 3, 16 January 1992, EFG Papers #4851.
103. See Balderas, "Making Trouble in Women's Studies," 26–28.
104. EFG to George H. Jones and David F. Bright, 10 January 1992, EFG Papers #4851.
105. EFG to George H. Jones and David F. Bright, 10 January 1992, EFG Papers #4851.

106. Eugene D. Genovese, "Dellachiesa among the Professors," unpublished ms., Louis A. Ferleger Papers, Mugar Library, Boston University. Genovese destroyed his copies but forgot this one.
107. On Fox-Genovese's entry into teaching at Rochester, Melissa S. Mead, personal communication with author, 10 June 2019.
108. David Moltke-Hansen, telephone interview, 24 June 2019.
109. Ann Short Chirhart, personal communication with author, 20 June 2019.
110. Ann Short Chirhart, personal communication with author, 21 June 2019.
111. David F. Bright and George H. Jones to EFG, 3 January 1992, EFG Papers #4851.
112. Odem and Coffman, "Feminist Activism and the Origins of Women's Studies at Emory," 229.
113. For Navarro, see Courtney Leatherman, "Sex-Bias Suit Rocks Emory," *Chronicle of Higher Education,* 3 March 1993, https://www.chronicle.com/article/Sex-Bias-Suit-Rocks-Emory/72150.
114. See "Field Notes: Personal Politics," *Lingua Franca,* June–July 1992, 8–10.
115. Martine W. Brownley, personal communication with author, 2 October 2016.
116. The words were Fox-Genovese's; see "Field Notes: Personal Politics," 10. A few depositions survive in EFG Papers #4851.

8. Retreating and Regrouping

1. Sarah E. Gardner, personal communication with author, 3 April 2015.
2. For Eugene Genovese's attribution of the onset of MS to 1992, see Margalit Fox, "Elizabeth Fox-Genovese, Historian, Is Dead at 65," *New York Times,* January 7, 2007, http://www.nytimes.com/2007/01/07/arts/07fox-genovese.html?_r=0.
3. Louis A. Ferleger, conversation with author, 30 October 2017.
4. See "Historians Cast a Wider Net," *Chronicle of Higher Education* 45, no. 40 (11 June 1999): 1, A16.
5. Fox-Genovese, "Psychohistory versus Psychodeterminism."
6. See "Witness List for Pre-Trial Order, Fox-Genovese (Alphabetized)" and "St. Paul/Fox-Genovese, Doc. No. 44550, List of Depositions Obtained as of 1/24/96," EFG Papers #4851.
7. EFG to Halsey Knapp, 26 July 1993, EFG Papers #4851.
8. See David Brion Davis to "Chair, 'Window of Opportunity' Search, Vanderbilt University," 22 December 1993, EFG Papers #4851.

9. George J. Graham Jr. to EFG, 5 December 1988, EFG Papers #4581, urging her to apply at Vanderbilt University; Graham was the chair of the political science department.
10. Eugene D. Genovese, in several of many conversations with author, March 2011. He said the advance was $250,000.
11. EFG, "Activities 92–93," EFG Papers #4851.
12. "Field Notes: Personal Politics," 8–10.
13. Christopher Hitchens, "Radical Pique," *Vanity Fair,* February 1994, 32–35, 34 (quotation).
14. Michael Skube, "1960s' Left Is Being Eaten by Its Young," *Atlanta Journal/Atlanta Constitution,* 16 January 1994, N8.
15. Nancy Barr to EFG, 4 September 1994, EFG Papers #4851.
16. Deborah A. Symonds, introduction, in *History and Women, Culture and Faith: Selected Writings of Elizabeth Fox-Genovese,* vol. 1, *Women Past and Present,* ed. David Moltke-Hansen (Columbia: University of South Carolina Press, 2011), xxxii–xxxiii.
17. Maggi Shade, personal communication with author, 30 March 2011.
18. Elizabeth Fox-Genovese, "Difference, Diversity, and Divisions in the Women's Movement," in *Color, Class and Country: Experiences of Gender,* ed. Gay Young and Bette J. Dickerson (London: Zed, 1994), 239.
19. Elizabeth Fox-Genovese, "Unspeakable Things Unspoken: Ghosts and Memories in the Narratives of African-American Women," 1992 Elsa Goveia Memorial Lecture, Department of History, University of the West Indies, Mona, Jamaica.
20. Elizabeth Fox-Genovese, "Unspeakable Things Unspoken: Ghosts and Memories in the Narratives of African-American Women," in Mack-Shelton and Lake, eds., *Ghosts and Memories,* 174.
21. Ann Short Chirhart, personal communication with author, 20 July 2015. See also Chirhart, *Torches of Light: Georgia Teachers and the Coming of the Modern South* (Augusta: University of Georgia Press, 2005).
22. EFG to Lou Ferleger, 27 January 1996, EFG Papers #4851.
23. EFG to Randall Packard, 20 January 1996, EFG Papers #4851.
24. EFG to EWF Jr., 1 October 1995, EFG Papers #4851.
25. EFG to EWF Jr., 19 January 1996, EFG Papers #4851.
26. EFG to James Van Melton, 22 January 1996, EFG Papers #4851.
27. EFG to Louis Ferleger, 27 January 1996, EFG Papers #4851.

28. Elizabeth Fox-Genovese, "Feminism Is Not the Story of My Life," *Washington Journal,* 25 January 1996, http://www.c-span.org/video/?69549-1/book-discussion-feminism-story-life.
29. EFG to J. P. Maddex, 18 March 1996, EFG Papers #4851.
30. Hal Smith, "Marxist Challenges Liberation Theologists," *SUNY-B Insider,* April 5, 1984.
31. EFG to EWF Jr., 19 March 1996, EFG Papers #4851.
32. EFG to Lisa Greenwald, 21 March 1996, EFG Papers #4851.
33. Mary Gordon, "What Makes a Woman a Woman," *New York Times,* 14 January 1996, sec. 7, p. 9.
34. Elizabeth Fox-Genovese, *Feminism Is Not the Story of My Life* (New York: Doubleday, 1996), 84–87; Gordon, "What Makes a Woman a Woman." I knew and have spoken with the woman who became readily identifiable. There were positive reviews as well; see David Gordon, "In Defense of Women," *Mises Review* 3, no. 1 (1 April 1997), https://mises.org/es/library/feminism-not-story-my-life-how-todays-feminist-elite-has-lost-touch-real-concerns-women; Mary Ann Glendon, "Rescuing Feminism from the Feminists," *First Things,* March 1996, https://www.firstthings.com/article/1996/03/001-rescuing-feminism-from-the-feminists; and one curiously mixed and interesting review from Elizabeth Kristol, review of *Feminism Is Not the Story of My Life, Commentary,* 1 April 1996, 59–60.
35. Ann Short Chirhart, personal communication with author, 9 November 2015.
36. See Ann Short Chirhart, personal communication with author, 9 November 2015, and two others who will remain nameless.
37. Walter Goodman, "Television Review: A Movement Disastrous or Just Annoying," *New York Times,* 22 December 1994, http://www.nytimes.com/1994/12/22/arts/television-review-a-movement-disastrous-or-just-annoying.html.
38. EFG, untitled paper beginning "During the past few weeks," in transit to EFG Papers #4851. This is an early version of the epilogue to *Feminism without Illusions.*
39. Fox-Genovese, *Feminism Is Not,* 255.
40. For a review of the four books following, see Elizabeth Kamarck Minnich, "Feminist Attacks on Feminisms: Patriarchy's Prodigal Daughters," *Feminist Studies* 24, no. 1 (Spring 1998): 159–75.
41. Edith Stein, "Ethos of Woman's Professions," in Stein, *Essays on Woman,* trans. Freda Mary Olsen (Washington, DC: ICS, 1996), 49.

42. Teresa of Avila, *The Life of St. Teresa of Avila by Herself,* trans. by David Lewis (N.p.: Digireads.com, 2009), 52.
43. Eugene D. Genovese and Leonard Hochberg, eds., *Geographic Perspectives in History* (New York: Basil Blackwell, 1989). EWF, "The Faculty's Responsibility for the Freedom of the University," digital typescript, n.d., in transit to EFG Papers #4851.
44. David Burner to EFG, 15 January 1995 [possibly misdated], 11 February, 30 December 1996, EFG Papers #4851.
45. David Burner to EFG, 11 February 1996, EFG Papers #4851.
46. Eugene D. Genovese to Friends, 15 November 1990, St. George Tucker Society Papers #4711, SHC.
47. Eugene D. Genovese to Fellows, 21 February 1991, St. George Tucker Society Papers #4711, SHC.

9. Right with God

1. Elizabeth Fox-Genovese, "Proslavery: The Unremarkable Life and Violent Death of an Idea," lecture at the University of St. Thomas, Houston, Texas, March 1999.
2. Several of her curricula vitae survive in her papers, both among those on deposit and those in transit to EFG Papers #4851. The two I have used here can be dated to 1999 and 2005.
3. Steven Hahn, "From Radical to Right-Wing: The Legacy of Eugene Genovese," *New Republic,* 1 October 2012, https://newrepublic.com/article/108044/radical-right-wing-the-legacy-eugene-genovese.
4. Elizabeth Fox-Genovese, "Editor's Introduction: Of Personalities and Revolutions, and by Way of Farewell," *Journal of the Historical Society* 5, no. 2 (Spring 2005): viii.
5. Letters courtesy of Louis A. Ferleger: EFG to Franklin Knight, 18 May 2005; Eugene D. Genovese to Franklin W. Knight, 18 May 2005, both in transit to EFG Papers #4851.
6. EDG to Franklin W. Knight, 25 October 2005. EDG sent copies of the letter to "interested parties" in The Historical Society. A copy will be sent to the EFG Papers #4851.
7. From conversations with Laura Crawley and Louis A. Ferleger, as this chapter was written, and with letters supplied by the latter, which are in transit to EFG Papers #4851.
8. Laura Crawley, conversation with author, 13 February 2016.

9. Elizabeth Fox-Genovese, "A Conversion Story," *First Things*, April 2000, http://www.firstthings.com/article/2000/04/a-conversion-story.
10. Elizabeth Fox-Genovese, "Caught in the Web of Grace," Voices: online, Eastertide 2007, http://archive.wf-f.org/07-1-ElizabethFoxGenovese.html.
11. EFG, 24 October 2002, Murray Hill, 2002–3 Journal, in transit to EFG Papers #4851.
12. EFG, 25 October 2002, Murray Hill, 2002–3 Journal.
13. EFG, 25 October 2002, Preparation for Confession, Murray Hill, 2002–3 Journal.
14. EFG, 26 October 2002, Meditation 7, Murray Hill, 2002–3 Journal.
15. EFG, 10 November 2002, Confession, 2002–3 Journal.
16. EFG, 10 November 2002, Confession, 2002–3 Journal.
17. EFG, 7 [?] February 2003, Adoration, 2003–6 Journal, in transit to EFG Papers #4851.
18. EFG, 25 October 2002, notecard at back, 2002–3 Journal. The word "not" was rendered as the mathematical symbol for "does not equal."
19. EFG, 7 [?] February 2003, Adoration, 2003–6 Journal.
20. EFG, 6 April 2003, Adoration, 2003–6 Journal.
21. EFG, 6 April 2003, Adoration, 2003–6 Journal.
22. EFG, 5 August 2003, 2003–6 Journal.
23. EFG, 17 August 2003, 2003–6 Journal.
24. A number of floppy and zip disks, storing material from the *Journal of the Historical Society*, drafts of *The Mind of the Master Class*, and email correspondence from 1999, remained in the house at the time of Eugene D. Genovese's death; they are now in transit to EFG Papers #4851.
25. EFG, 22 August 2003 Adoration, 2003–6 Journal.
26. EFG, 21 [?] September 2003 Adoration, 2003–6 Journal.
27. EFG, 28 December 2003, 2003–6 Journal.
28. EFG, 2 January 2004, 2003–6 Journal.
29. EFG, 9 January Adoration, 2004, 2003–6 Journal.
30. EFG, 9 January Adoration, 2004, 2003–6 Journal.
31. EFG, 6 February 2005, 2003–6 Journal.
32. EFG, 1 March 2006, 2003–6 Journal.
33. EFG, 2 March 2006, 2003–6 Journal.
34. EFG, 5 March 2006, 2003–6 Journal.
35. EFG, 5 March 2006, 2003–6 Journal.
36. For reviews, see Moltke-Hansen, "The Turn to the South," 557–76; Robert Gudmestad, review of *Mind of the Master Class*, *Tennessee Historical*

Quarterly 65, no. 3 (2006): 278–79; Mitchell Snay, review of *Mind of the Master Class, Journal of Southern History* 73, no. 2 (2007): 444–47; Enrico Dal Lago, "'Hegemony' by Another Name," *Reviews in American History* 34, no. 3 (2006): 332–41; John Patrick Daly, review of *Mind of the Master Class, Journal of American History* 93, no. 4 (2007): 1226–27; Michael E. Woods, review of *Mind of the Master Class, Journal of Social History* 43, no. 4 (2010): 1105–7; Keith Harper, review of *Mind of the Master Class, North Carolina Historical Review* 83, no. 2 (2006): 274–75; Mark M. Smith et al. review of *Mind of the Master Class, American Historical Review* 111, no. 3 (2006): 834–35; John Patrick Daly, review of *Mind of the Master Class, Register of the Kentucky Historical Society* 104, nos. 3–4 (2006): 712–14; Randall M. Miller, review of *Mind of the Master Class, Catholic Historical Review* 93, no. 4 (2007): 994–96; Michal Jan Rozbicki, review of *Mind of the Master Class, Virginia Magazine of History and Biography* 114, no. 4 (2006): 498–99; and Steven Hahn, "Divine Rights," *New Republic,* 5 February 2006, https://newrepublic.com/article/104864/divine-rights.

37. Dal Lago, "'Hegemony' by Another Name."
38. Snay, review of *Mind of the Master Class.*
39. Miller, review of *Mind of the Master Class.*
40. Moltke-Hansen, "The Turn to the South," 557–76.
41. I am indebted to David Moltke-Hansen for discussion and argument on the nature and persistence of Fox-Genovese's continuing Marxism, and her presence and absence in the trilogy.
42. EFG, 6 June 2005, Summer 2005 Daybook, in transit to EFG Papers #4851.
43. EFG, 25 June 2005, Summer 2005 Daybook.
44. EFG, 8 July 2005, Summer 2005 Daybook.
45. EFG, 3–4 September 2005, August–November 2005 Daybook, in transit to EFG Papers #4851.
46. EFG, 3 August 2005, Summer 2005 Daybook.
47. Fox-Genovese, "Feminism and the Unraveling of the Social Bond"; Elizabeth Fox-Genovese, "Liberte! Egalite! Academie!" *Touchstone,* December 2004, https://www.touchstonemag.com/archives/article.php?id=17-10-015-v; Elizabeth Fox-Genovese, "Why Must Religious Tradition Be Reconciled with Feminism, Restorative, Radical, or Otherwise? Thoughts on Tova Hartman-Halbertal's Essay," *Common Knowledge* 11, no. 1 (2005): 105–10.
48. "Adaline P." to AWF, 24 May 1959, F-S #5363.
49. Tracy Mitrano, personal communication with author, 9 February 2016.

50. Tina Trent, personal communication with author, 2 February 2016.
51. Judith Thurman, "Siren Songs," *New Yorker,* August 26, 2001, https://www.newyorker.com/magazine/2001/09/03/siren-songs/amp.
52. Edna St. Vincent Millay, "Oh, Think Not I Am Faithful to a Vow," in *Four Sonnets,* Poetry Foundation, https://www.poetryfoundation.org/poems/44722/four-sonnets-1922.
53. EFG, September 2006, from the hard drive of her last computer, duplicated to an external hard drive, in transit to EFG Papers #4851.
54. EFG to Bryn Mawr College Annual Giving Office, 17 May [?] 2006, in transit to EFG Papers #4851.
55. The words "ambiguity" and "ambivalence" are from Tracy Mitrano, personal communication with author, 9 February 2016.

Epilogue

1. Toni Morrison, "'Unspeakable Things Unspoken': The Afro-American Presence in American Literature," Tanner Lecture on Human Values, University of Michigan, 7 October 1988, https://tannerlectures.utah.edu/_documents/a-to-z/m/morrison90.pdf.
2. From Tina McElroy Ansa, *Baby of the Family* (New York: Harcourt Brace, 1989), 163–64, labeled by Fox-Genovese, "Elizabeth Fox-Genovese July 11, 1993 Notes for Ghosts and Memories EFG," in transit to EFG #4851. She did not quote exactly, eliding a sentence before adding "Rachel:" to remind herself of the speaker, and missing the k in "t'ink."
3. These and other reminiscences can be found in part 2, "Remembrances of Elizabeth Fox-Genovese," in *History and Women, Culture and Faith: Selected Writings of Elizabeth Fox-Genovese,* vol. 5, *Unbought Grace,* ed. Rebecca Fox and Robert L. Paquette (Columbia: University of South Carolina Press, 2012), 249–97.
4. Moltke-Hansen, "Introduction," xix–xxxiv.
5. Moltke-Hansen, "The Turn to the South," 557–76. See also Moltke-Hansen, "Introduction," xix–xxxiv, and Moltke-Hansen, "From Edinburgh to Rome," 163–75.
6. Evelyn Brooks Higginbotham, "Elizabeth Fox-Genovese: First and Lasting Impressions," *Common Knowledge* 14 (Winter 2008): 1–9.
7. Edwards, "At the Threshold of the Plantation Household," 577.
8. Edwards, "At the Threshold of the Plantation Household." For the blog, see "Vast Public Indifference: Within the Plantation Household," Vast Public

Indifference, October 2008, http://www.vastpublicindifference.com/2008/10/within-plantation-household.html.

9. Bertram Wyatt-Brown, "The Plantation Household Revisited: Elizabeth Fox-Genovese's Contribution to Southern History," *Mississippi Quarterly* 65, no. 4 (Fall 2012): 591–612.

10. Mark Bauerlein, "The Best Colleague," in Fox and Paquette, eds., *Selected Writings,* vol. 5, *Unbought Grace,* 269–75; Ladd, "My Women's Studies Seminar."

11. Thomas L. Pangle, "Foreword: Marxist Social and Political Theory, Americanized," in Moltke-Hansen, ed., *Selected Writings,* vol. 3, *Intersections,* ix–xviii.

12. Elizabeth Fox-Genovese, "It Takes a Family to Raise a Child," Georgia Public Policy Foundation, recorded 24 April 1996, https://www.youtube.com/watch?v=RevLAUMRxWY; "A Firing Line Debate: Resolved: That the Women's Movement Has Been Disastrous," *William F. Buckley Jr.'s Firing Line,* recorded 7 December 1994, https://www.youtube.com/watch?v=ANCeBwO7FMs.

13. Peter N. Stearns, "Foreword: Contributions to Women's History," in Moltke-Hansen, ed., *Selected Writings,* vol. 1, *Women Past and Present,* ix–xx.

14. Stearns, "Foreword," xviii.

15. Amy R. Baehr, "Conservatism, Feminism, and Elizabeth Fox-Genovese," *Hypatia* 24, no. 2 (Spring 2009): 101–24.

16. Fox, "Elizabeth Fox-Genovese, Historian, Is Dead at 65."

17. Christopher Phillips, review of *Slavery in White and Black, Journal of American History* 96, no. 4 (2010): 1183; Daniel Kilbride, review of *Slavery in White and Black, American Historical Review* 114, no. 5 (2009): 1455–56; Michael E. Woods, review of *Slavery in White and Black, Journal of Social History* 43, no. 4 (2010): 1105–7; Peter S. Carmichael, review of *Slavery in White and Black, Virginia Magazine of History and Biography* 118, no. 1 (2010): 80–82; Paul D. Escott, review of *Slavery in White and Black, Register of the Kentucky Historical Society* 107, no. 1 (2009): 107–9; Russell Menard, review of *Slavery in White and Black, Journal of American Ethnic History* 30, no. 2 (2011): 98–99.

18. Staughton Lynd, review of *Fatal Self-Deception, Journal of the Early Republic* 32, no. 4 (2012): 731–35; Richard Follett, review of *Fatal Self-Deception, Journal of American History* 99, no. 3 (2012): 907–8; Peter Kolchin, review of *Fatal Self-Deception, Civil War History* 59, no. 2 (2013): 242–43.

19. John David Smith, "History and Women, Culture and Faith: Selected Writings of Elizabeth Fox-Genovese," *Journal of Southern History* 80, no. 3 (August 2014): 773–76, 776 (quotation).
20. Elizabeth Fox-Genovese, *Marriage: The Dream That Refuses to Die,* ed. Sheila O'Connor-Ambrose (Wilmington, DE: ISI Books, 2008), 29.

INDEX

Note: The initials "EFG" denote Elizabeth Fox-Genovese.